CONFLICT: READINGS IN MANAGEMENT AND RESOLUTION

Conflict: Readings in Management and Resolution

Edited by John Burton and Frank Dukes
Center for Conflict Analysis and Resolution, George Mason University, Virginia, USA

MACMILLAN

First published 1990

Published by
THE MACMILLAN PRESS LTD
Houndmills, Basingstoke, Hampshire RG21 2XS
and London
Companies and representatives
throughout the world

Typeset by Wessex Typesetters
(A Division of The Eastern Press Ltd)
Frome, Somerset

Printed in the United States of America

British Library Cataloguing in Publication Data
Conflict: readings in management and resolution – (The
Conflict series: V.3).
1. Social conflict. Resolution
I. Burton, John W. (John Wear), *1915–*   II. Dukes, Frank
III. Series
303.6
ISBN 0–333–52149–8 (hardcover)
ISBN 0–333–52145–5 (paperback)

The Conflict Series

1. CONFLICT: RESOLUTION AND PROVENTION,* *by John Burton*

2. CONFLICT: HUMAN NEEDS THEORY, *edited by John Burton*

3. CONFLICT: READINGS IN MANAGEMENT AND RESOLUTION, *edited by John Burton and Frank Dukes*

4. CONFLICT: PRACTICES IN MANAGEMENT, SETTLEMENT AND RESOLUTION, *by John Burton and Frank Dukes*

*Provention
The term *prev*ention has the connotation of containment. The term *prov*ention has been introduced to signify taking steps to remove sources of conflict, and more positively to promote conditions in which collaborative and valued relationships control behaviors.

Foreword to the Series

Samuel W. Lewis
President, United States Institute of Peace

We seem to know much more about how wars and other violent international conflicts get started than we do about how to end them. Nor do we understand very well how to transform settlements that terminate immediate hostilities into enduring peaceful relationships through which nations can continue to work out their differences without violence. The lack of attention to these questions, at least with regard to relations among sovereign governments, is due in some degree to the way international relations as an academic subject has traditionally been studied. By and large, more academic theory and analysis have been devoted to patterns and causes in international behavior with an eye to perfecting explanatory theory than to effective, usable remedies to international conflicts. We have assumed the remedies would become plain once the correct theory was found.

That imbalance is now being corrected. Interest is now growing in the theory and practice of "conflict resolution," a new field concerned specifically with the nature of conflict as a generic human problem and with techniques or initiatives that might be applied productively in addressing conflicts. This new emphasis is reflected in the emergence of alternative dispute resolution methods in the law profession, of peace studies or conflict resolution programs in many of the nation's colleges and universities, of research journals devoted specifically to conflict and its resolution, and of community mediation or problem-solving strategies at the local level and "second-track diplomacy" at the international level.

Providing much of the conceptual foundation for an explicit focus on conflict itself has been a small but growing group of interdisciplinary scholars engaged in a search for formulas and processes that seem to work in ending conflicts among nations and groups. They are seeking to identify those institutional and societal structures that have the best chance of ensuring a lasting and just peace among conflicting interests. Unfortunately, the work of these scholars has not reached the widest circles of policy makers, professionals, students, and researchers who could benefit from the stimulating explorations of the conflict resolution school of thought.

The United States Institute of Peace wishes to commend the four book Conflict Series: an effort by one of the acknowledged founding fathers of the conflict resolution field to summarize the main insights of the field to date for a wider readership. In these books, John Burton, with the assistance of other major contributors, delineates the distinctive scope of the conflict resolution field, defines its key concepts, explains how the field emerged out of existing approaches to conflict and peace and how it differs from them, summarizes the field's leading substantive insights about conflict and its resolution, collects some of the best readings produced by the field, and probes where the field needs to go in the future to strengthen its theory and applicability to real problems. The series also surveys extant practical techniques for conflict management such as mediation, adjudication, ombudsmen, interactive management, and problem-solving work-shops and explores their utility for different types of conflict situations. Of course, the views expressed in these volumes are those of the authors alone and do not necessarily reflect views of the Institute of Peace.

Impressively, John Burton and Frank Dukes completed this broad examination of the conflict resolution field during Burton's year as a Distinguished Fellow of the United States Institute of Peace in 1988–89 while he was also a Distinguished Visiting Professor at the Center for Conflict Resolution at George Mason University in Virginia. No one in the world is better qualified to present the conflict resolution field's distinctive perspectives and unique contributions than is Burton, whom many in the field regard as its first leading explorer and one of its most ardent spokesmen before students, scholars, and governments since its beginnings in the later 1950s. In preparing this series, Burton has drawn on the wealth of his extensive academic training in economics and international relations and his 25 years of research and teaching at universities in three countries, as reflected in his previous ten books and numerous articles. He also has applied the lessons of his practical experience as diplomat for the Australian government and as a third party facilitator in efforts to end such conflict, as Lebanon, Cyprus, Northern Ireland, and Sri Lanka.

The United States Institute of Peace is a non-partisan, independent institution created and funded by the United States Congress to strengthen the nation's capacity to understand and deal more effec-tively with international conflict through peaceful means. It serves this purpose by supporting research and education projects that will expand and disseminate available knowledge about the nature of international conflict and the full range of ways it can be resolved within a framework that maximizes freedom and justice. Within this challenging mandate, one of our tasks is to identify serious, innovative, but less well known approaches that may bear further examination and to bring the insights from these approaches to wider circles so that fruitful dialogue among different perspectives is fostered.

John Burton's work complements another Institute project that is mapping all the major "roads to peace" – e.g., international law, diplomacy and negotiations, transnationalism, deterrence theory, non-violence traditions, and international organizations – that have been emphasized in the scholarly literature and world of practice as important methods and tools for achieving international peace. The conflict resolution method and outlook is one of the approaches the Institute wishes to see more widely understood so their respective strengths and limitations can be sorted out and constructive syntheses can be developed. In short, we seek to stimulate much faster dissemination of ideas and cross-fertilization than normally would occur across the barriers of different academic disciplines, professions, governmental spheres, and private organizations that are concerned in various ways with international conflict and its resolution, although they may not necessarily describe their concerns in exactly these terms.

By supporting John Burton's work, the United States Institute of Peace hopes that the perspectives, insights, and new directions for analysis of this relatively new field of conflict resolution will be brought before, and enrich the work of, a wider readership of international relations and conflict resolution students; practitioners in fields such as law, government, labor and industrial management, and social work; policy makers at all levels; as well as scholars concerned with conflict issues.

Washington, D. C.

Preface to the Series

It is not easy for those who are seeking new approaches to move from deterrence theories and practices of conflict *settlement* and *management* to conflict *resolution* theory and practice. The jump to prevention and the predictive capabilities that prevention requires, is even more challenging. These are different fields with different assumptions. While they exist concurrently they are in different conceptual worlds. Some practitioners and theorists seek more effective institutional and management constraints, power negotiating techniques and peace through technologies of mutual threat. There are consensus seekers who employ more sophisticated socialization processes largely within existing systems. Problem-solving advocates pursue more analysis of human behaviors and seek to deduce processes of conflict resolution and provention. There cannot be communication between different approaches, or with policy makers and the public generally, until there is a precisely defined language, appropriate concepts that enable a clear differentiation of the various approaches, and an adequate and agreed theory of human behaviors at all social levels. This is the purpose of these four books concerned with the study of Conflict.

There are four books in this Conflict Series. They are:

1. *Conflict: Resolution and Provention*. This book seeks to provide an historical and theoretical perspective, and a framework for consideration of theory and practice in conflict resolution and provention. It is in five parts: Part I defines the approach; Part II deals with the political context of conflict provention; Part III is concerned with the theory of decision making, and with conflict resolution processes; Part IV is concerned with the longer-term policy implications of provention; and Part V draws together some conclusions.

2. *Conflict: Human Needs Theory*. An adequate theory of behavior is required to provide a basis for the analysis and resolution of conflict, and particularly for prediction of conflict and a guide to conflict provention. "Needs theory" is put forward as this foundation. The chapters contributed in this book were written as a result of an international conference convened in July 1988 for that purpose.

3. *Conflict: Readings in Management and Resolution*. A new subject has origins in many fields, and this is an attempt to bring together some earlier contributions from a broad spectrum of discipli-

nes. A newly developing subject also has gaps requiring attention, and this book includes contributions requested to fill some of these gaps. It also contains an extensive annotated bibliography.

4. *Conflict: Practices in Management Settlement and Resolution*. It is useful to survey practices generally, even those that proceed from contradictory theories. This book is a general survey of management, settlement and conflict resolution practices.

Conflict, its resolution and provention, comprises an *a-disciplinary* study, that is, a synthesis that goes beyond separate disciplines, beyond interaction between separate disciplines, and beyond any synthesis of approaches from several disciplines. An a-disciplinary approach accepts no boundaries of knowledge. Consequently, it has as yet no shelf in any discipline-based library. These four books seek to make a start.

JOHN BURTON

CONFLICT: READINGS IN MANAGEMENT AND RESOLUTION

Acknowledgements

We wish to express our appreciation for the cooperation of authors and editors of journals in the preparation of this book of readings in conflict management and resolution. We particularly wish to thank those authors who contributed articles especially for this volume. The source of those articles that have previously been printed is acknowledged on the first page of each chapter.

Help was given in the selection of articles, and in the preparation of an annotated bibliography which is included in the volume, by graduate students in the Conflict Analysis and Resolution Program at George Mason University: Diane LeResche, Robert Reed, and Susan Shearouse. We wish to express our special thanks to Betty Nathan, who has been in effect a co-editor of this book, and indeed of this Conflict Series.

The editors and publishers acknowledge with thanks permission from the following to reproduce copyright material.

The Western Political Quarterly, for Chapter 1, from Q. Wright, "The Nature of Conflict" (1951).

Wheatsheaf, for Chapters 3 and 7, from E. Azar and J. Burton (eds), *International Conflict Resolution: Theory and Practice* (1986).

Lynne Reinner, for Chapter 8, adapted from R. A. Coate and J. A. Rosati (eds), *The Power of Human Needs in World Society* (1988).

Man, Environment, Space and Time, for chapter 9, from Anthony de Reuck, "A Theory of Conflict Resolution by Problem Solving" (1983).

Tantur/Jerusalem, for Chapter 10, from W. Klassen (ed.), *Dialogue Toward Inter-Faith Understanding* (1985).

Journal of College Science Teaching, for Chapter 14, from Mary E. Clark, "'What is Science *For*?': Reintroducing Philosophy Into the Undergraduate Classroom" (1988).

North American Conference on Peacemaking and Conflict Resolution (3 March 1989), for Chapter 16, from Christa Daryl Slaton and Theodore L. Becker, "A Tale of Two Movements: ADR and the Greens."

Journal of Conflict Resolution, for Chapter 2, from Kenneth E. Boulding, "Future Directions in Conflict and Peace Studies" (1978).

New York University Press, for Chapter 13, adapted from a chapter in Dennis J. Sandole and Ingrid Sandole-Staroste (eds), *Conflict Management and Problem Solving* (1987).

Contents

Notes on the Contributors		xix
Introduction		1

PART I   BEGINNINGS

1	The Nature of Conflict	15
	Quincy Wright	
2	Future Directions in Conflict and Peace Studies	35
	Kenneth E. Boulding	

PART II   CRISIS

3	The International Relations Discipline: Asset or Liability for Conflict Resolution?	51
	Michael Banks	
4	Paradigms in Conflict: the Strategist, the Conflict Researcher and the Peace Researcher	71
	A. J. R. Groom	

PART III   ANALYSIS

5	The Individual, the Group and War	101
	Bryant Wedge	
6	Legitimacy and Human Needs	117
	Paul Sites	
7	Protracted International Conflicts: Ten Propositions	145
	Edward E. Azar	
8	A Critical Assessment of the Power of Human Needs in World Society	156
	Jerel A. Rosati, David J. Carroll and Roger A. Coate	

PART IV APPLICATIONS

 9 A Theory of Conflict Resolution by Problem-solving   183
    Anthony de Reuck

10 Interactive Problem-solving: a Social-pyschological   199
    Approach to Conflict Resolution
    Herbert C. Kelman

11 Principles of Communication Between Adversaries in   216
    South Africa
    *Hendrik W. van der Merwe, Johann Maree, André
    Zaaiman, Cathy Philip and A. D. Muller*

12 Managing Complexity Through Small Group Dynamics   241
    John W. McDonald

13 The Emergence and Institutionalization of Third-party   256
    Roles in Conflict
    James H. Laue

PART V RESEARCH

14 "What is Science *For*?": Reintroducing Philosophy Into 275
    the Undergraduate Classroom
    Mary E. Clark

15 Action Research   288
    Frank Dukes

PART VI POLITICAL IMPLICATIONS

16 A Tale of Two Movements: ADR and the Greens   301
    Christa Daryl Slaton and Theodore L. Becker

17 Unanticipated Conflict and the Crisis of Social Theory 316
    Richard E. Rubenstein

18 Unfinished Business in Conflict Resolution   328
    John Burton

Annotated Bibliography   336

Name Index   352

Notes on the Contributors

Edward E. Azar came from Lebanon to Stanford to obtain his Ph.D. He created and is Director of the Center for International Development and Conflict Management at the University of Maryland, College Park. Among his interests is the role of development in the avoidance of conflicts with a special focus on the Middle East.

Michael Banks is a Reader in International Relations at the London School of Economics and a leading exponent of problem-solving approaches to international problems. A founding member of the Conflict Analysis Center, he has contributed to its publications and is the editor of *Conflict in World Society*. The article he contributed came from Azar and Burton's *International Conflict Resolution : Theory and Practice*.

Theodore L. Becker received his law degree from Rutgers, his Ph.D. from Northwestern and is presently Professor and Head of the Department of Political Science at Auburn University. The author of eight books on the legal system and American government, he was the Coordinator of the M.A. in Peacemaking and Conflict Resolution, Department of Political Science, University of Hawaii and a participating member of the Hawaii Greens. He is presently coordinating Green activities for the Transformational Politics Conference Group of the American Political Science Association and co-authoring *Transformational Mediation* with Christa Daryl Slaton.

Kenneth E. Boulding was educated at Oxford and the University of Chicago. He has been Director of Research of the Center for Research on Conflict Resolution at the University of Michigan and an instigator in the development and editor of the *Journal of Conflict Resolution*. He is Distinguished Professor of Economics, Emeritus at the University of Colorado at Boulder where he is Research Associate and Project Director at the Institute of Behavioral Science. His moral concerns as a Quaker have influenced his work as an economist on conflict and impending conflict. His works include *The Organizational Revolution*; *Economic Analysis*; *A Study in the Ethics of Economic Organization, Disarmament and the Economy*; *Conflict and Defense*; and *Human Betterment*.

John Burton received his Ph.D. at the London School of Economics and a D.Sc. from the University of London. He was a delegate to the United Nations Charter Conference in 1945 and the Paris Peace Conference in 1946. He was Permanent Head of the Department of External Affairs, Government of Australia 1947–51. His academic appointments have included University College London, where he founded the Centre for the Analysis of Conflict, the University of Kent at Canterbury, and the University of Maryland. He is currently associated with the Center for Conflict Analysis and Resolution at George Mason University, Virginia. In 1988–9 he was a Jennings Randolph Distinguished Fellow at the US Institute of Peace. His publications include *The Alternative* (1954); *Peace Theory* (1962); *International Relations: A General Theory* (1965); *Systems, States, Diplomacy and Rules* (1968); *Conflict and Communication* (1969); *World Society* (1972); *Deviance, Terrorism and War: The Solving of Unsolved Social and Political Problems* (1979); *Dear Survivors* (1982); *Global Conflict: The Domestic Sources of International Crisis* (1984); *Resolving Deep-Rooted Conflict: A Handbook* (1987).

David J. Carroll is a Ph.D. candidate in international studies at the University of South Carolina.

Mary E. Clark was born in California and received her undergraduate and masters degrees at the University of California, Berkeley where in 1960 she received her Ph.D. in zoology. She is a professor at San Diego State University, California where she teaches biology and has carried out research on the biochemical adaptations of organisms to condions of water stress, particularly high salinities. She has been dedicated to making the living world understandable to non-specialist students and wrote the first major textbook, *Contemporary Biology*, which incorporated not only "facts" but applications of those facts in everyday life. She has just published (St. Martin's Press, 1989) *Ariadne's Thread: The Search for New Modes of Thinking*, which addresses limits to growth, human nature, the development of the Western worldview, and effecting change.

Roger A. Coate is an Associate Professor in the Department of Government and International Studies at the University of South Carolina. He received his Ph.D in political science from Ohio University in 1977, having previously received his M.A. in International Relations from Johns Hopkins School of Advanced International Studies. He is a specialist in international organization, international relations theory, and the role of science and technology in world affairs. His most recent publications include: *The Challenge of Relevance: The United Nations in a Changing World Environment* with Donald Puchala (1989); *Unilateralism, Ideology, and United States Foreign Policy: The U.S. In and Out of UNESCO* (1988); and *The Power of Human Needs in World Society* with Jerel Rosati (1988).

Anthony de Reuck retired recently as Head of International Relations at the University of Surrey. As a physicist he worked at Imperial College, as an editor of *Nature* and on the International Relations staff of the Royal Society. He later edited 30 books including *Conflict in Society* (1966), *Caste and Race* (1967), and *Communication in Science* (1968) for the CIBA Foundation. He was a founding member of the Centre for the Analysis of Conflict at University College London from where he graduated in International Relations, and a founding member also of the Peace Research Association, Groningen.

Frank Dukes is a Ph.D. candidate in Conflict Resolution at the Center for Conflict Analysis and Resolution at George Mason University from which he received his M.S. in Conflict Management in 1988. He is an experienced mediator of community disputes.

A. J. R. Groom is Professor of International Relations at the University of Kent at Canterbury. A graduate of University College London, he completed his Ph.D. in International Relations in Switzerland and returned to University College where the Centre for the Analysis of Conflict was founded in 1965. On his appointment to Kent he took with him this Centre of which he then became Director. His most recent publication with William C. Olson is an intellectual history of International Relations theory entitled *International Relations: Then and Now*.

Herbert C. Kelman received his Ph.D. in psychology from Yale University in 1951. He was Professor of Psychology and a member of the Center for Research on Conflict Resolution at the University of Michigan from 1962 to 1969 and has been the Richard Clarke Cabot Professor of Social Ethics at Harvard University since 1968. He has been Chair of the Middle East Seminar at the Harvard Center for International Affairs since 1977 and has been appointed a Jennings

Randolph Distinguished Fellow of the US Institute of Peace of 1989–90. He has been on the editorial board of several professional journals and has contributed articles and chapters on attitude change and social influence, nationalism and political ideology, international relations, the Arab–Israeli conflict, conflict resolution, psychotherapy, and the ethics of social research. Publications include: *International Behavior: A Social Psychological Analysis; A Time to Speak: On Human Values and Social Research; Ethics of Social Intervention* (with G. Bermant and D. Warwick); and *Crimes of Obedience: Toward a Social Psychology of Authority and Responsibility* (with V. Lee Hamilton).

James H. Laue is Vernon M. and Minnie I. Lynch Professor of Conflict Resolution at George Mason University. Trained in Sociology at the University of Wisconsin-River Falls (B.S.) and Harvard (A.M. and Ph.D.), he has been involved in developing the field of community and racial conflict intervention in the United States since the 1960s. He was program development director for the Community Relations Service of the US Department of Justice, co-founder of the National Peace Academy Campaign and Vice-Chair of the US Peace Academy Commission, and the first president of the Conflict Clinic, Inc. He is the author of *Direct Action and Desegregation*, editor of special issues on community and policy mediation of *The Journal of Intergroup Relations* and *Mediation Quarterly*, and author of numerous chapters, articles in professional journals and training exercises.

John W. McDonald, a lawyer by training, was a US diplomat for forty years and is now President of the Iowa Peace Institute at Grinnell, Iowa. He was personally deeply involved in every one of the case studies discussed in his Chapter 12 except for WARC '79, where he only briefed the US Delegation and had his advice ignored. Fortunately, in that instance leadership from other sources emerged and successfully applied the small group approach.

Jerel A. Rosati is an Associate Professor of Political Science in the department of Government and International Studies at the University of South Carolina. His work focuses on the theory and practice of foreign policy, with an emphasis on political psychology and US foreign policy. During 1986–7 he was the chair of the International Studies Association's foreign policy analysis section. He is the author of *The Carter Administration's Quest of Global*

Community: Beliefs and their Impact on Behavior, and editor (with Roger A. Coate) of *The Power of Human Needs in World Society*.

Richard E. Rubenstein is Professor of Conflict Resolution and Public Affairs at George Mason University and a core faculty member and Director of the Center for Conflict Analysis and Resolution. He is the author of *Rebels in Eden: Mass Political Violence in the United States* (1970); *Left Turn: Origins of the Next American Revolution* (1973); and *Alchemists of Revolution: Terrorism in the Modern World* (1987). Rubenstein was educated at Harvard College, Oxford University and Harvard Law School. Before joining the faculty at George Mason University, he had been a practising attorney, Professor of Political Science at Roosevelt University in Chicago and Professor of Law at Antioch School of Law in Washington, D.C. He has been an advisory consultant to the National Commission on the Causes and Prevention of Violence and assistant director of the Adlai Stevenson Institute of International Affairs.

Paul Sites has served as Chair of the Department of Sociology and Anthropology and is now Emeritus Professor at Kent State University. He is the author of *Lee Harvey Oswald and the American Dream; Control: The Basis of Social Order; Control and Constraint* and many professional papers and articles. He has a special interest in seeing Human Needs Theory being accepted as part of social theory.

Christa Daryl Slaton, Ph.D. in political science, was the co-founder and co-ordinator of the first neighborhood justice center in Hawaii, the Community Mediation Service. She was also the co-designer and co-trainer of the Honolulu Neighborhood Mediation Network of the City and County of Honolulu. Ms Slaton subsequently became a co-organizer of the Hawaii Greens and is presently co-organizing the Auburn Greens in Auburn, Alabama. She is currently writing a book titled *Televote: Citizen Participation in the Quantum Age* and is co-authoring *Transformational Mediation* with Theodore L. Becker.

Henrik W. van der Merwe is Director of the Center for Intergroup Studies at the University of Cape Town in South Africa, and founder of the South African Association for Conflict Management. He is a graduate of the universities of Stellenbosch and California, and is the joint author and editor of several books including *White South African Elites*; and *Legal Ideology and Politics in South Africa*. His latest book is *Pursuing Justice and Peace in South Africa*. The main focus of his work has been on the promotion of communication between conflicting groups in South Africa.

Hendrik van der Merwe was assisted in writing this chapter by his colleagues, André Zaaiman, Cathy Philip and A. D. Muller. **Andre Zaaiman** and **Cathy Philip** were research assistants at the Centre for Intergroup Studies at the University of Cape Town; **A. D. Muller** holds joint appointments as senior Consultant to the Centre and Professor of Industrial Psychology at the University of the Western Cape; and **Johann Maree** is Head of the Department of Sociology at the University of Cape Town.

Bryant Wedge was a psychiatrist and an authority on the peaceful resolution of conflict, who played a major role in the establishment of the United States Institute of Peace. In 1979 he helped organize and became the director of the Center for Conflict Analysis and Resolution at George Mason University. He maintained a private practice in psychiatry and was an adviser to the Central Intelligence Agency and the Social Security Administration. He received his medical degree from the University of Michigan and taught at Yale Medical School from 1954 to 1960.

Quincy Wright was born in Massachusetts in 1890 and received his Ph.D. from the University of Illinois in 1915. He had been Professor of International Law and Political Science at the University of Chicago from 1923 to 1956 and Professor Emeritus from 1956 to 1970 when he died in Charlottesville, Virginia. In 1945 he was with the UNESCO, and also served as a technical adviser with the International Military Tribunal in Nuremburg. He is the author of *Control of American Foreign Relations*; *Mandate Under the League of Nations*; and *A Study of War*.

Introduction

The purpose of this collection of essays, along with the three other books in this Conflict Series, is to provide the student, the practitioner and the general reader with a start-up library on this new subject, conflict and its resolution. We have sought to cover the subject fully and have separated the contribution into six parts: Beginnings; Crisis; Analysis; Applications; Research; and Political Implications.

AN EMERGING SUBJECT

The subject is new. Despite the fact that the problem of conflict, especially with other tribes and nations, has always been a dominant concern of societies and civilizations, as a formal field of study it had its origins only in the 1950s, and then primarily in relation to international relations. Prior to that violence and conflicts within societies were widely accepted as a normal part of civilian life to be controlled by authorities at the relevant societal level – the family, industry, the community, the nation. Wars between nations were treated as a separate phenomenon, and widely tolerated as inevitable, giving rise to deterrent strategies. There were few studies of conflict as a generic phenomenon.

Perhaps a formal study of conflict, its nature and prevention, was stimulated by the growth of communication within societies and consequently an awareness of violence at all levels, and of living conditions associated with violence. Perhaps it was encouraged by significant post-Second World War challenges that affected the legitimization of authorities in all social relationships from the family through to international relations. Perhaps it was provoked by the invention of weapons of mass destruction, challenging the acceptance of conflict as inevitable. Perhaps the study of conflict was at last made intellectually possible by the breakdown of boundaries between separate disciplines. Whatever the final reasons, it is now coming to be recognized, at least in the world of scholarship if not in the practices of politics, that there is a generic phenomenon of conflict that is not uniquely national or international, and that there is a major problem area to be researched. We now have graduate courses in conflict management and resolution in many countries. Even more

1

important for the longer term, appropriate versions of problem-solving are being taught at primary and secondary levels.

THE NEED FOR A LIBRARY

But we do not yet have a "library" – that is, a recognized literature and category of references based on agreed definitions of the field. There is no section or shelf in libraries devoted to the study of conflict as there are for recognized disciplines. Relevant articles are scattered throughout many professional journals and usually not seen by those who identify with a particular discipline. Books touching on aspects of conflict are found in many separate disciplines.

Indeed, there may never be a "conflict resolution literature" in this traditional sense. Conflict relates to human relationships at all societal levels, and these are affected by the total environment, by future planning, by levels of education and human needs satisfactions. In addition, this new study and its application are greatly concerned with ways in which to think about complex issues. It is concerned not merely with conflict as a specific and overt happening, but with the underlying human and institutional problems that create it. Conflict resolution is, in short, concerned with almost all branches of knowledge.

Rarely has the relevance of the totality of knowledge to conflict studies been more clearly demonstrated than in Mary Clark's *Ariadne's Thread: A Search for New Modes of Thinking*.[1] It does not focus on conflict specifically, but on the wider issues that must be dealt with if conflict is to be resolved and prevented. It begins by asking: What are the limits of growth; can present trends continue? After answering "no," it asks: Is human nature concerned primarily with material growth and with its destructive consequences? In response to a further "no" answer it asks: Can there be change in policy directions in economic thinking, North–South rethinking, ethnic and social relations rethinking, political and military rethinking, which might make possible an escape from the destruction that looms ahead?

With this scope it is not so much a library or an agreed literature that we seek immediately, but a basis on which to determine relevance: What knowledge is to be selected, and what rejected, from that mass of information scattered in libraries?

By some means we must be able to select from the totality of knowledge without discarding that which might be valuable, and without so breaking up knowledge that we cannot deal adequately and realistically with generic problems of conflict, its management and resolution. Selection from available knowledge requires, therefore, a focus, a framework, and at the same time a means of questioning constantly that focus and that framework. The first is the subject knowledge field, and the second is the how-to-think field.

SOME PHILOSOPHICAL CONSIDERATIONS

Let us take first the second area: how to think and to be analytical. In *Conflict: Resolution and Provention*, there is a stress on the importance of language and clarification of concepts, and deductive thought processes. They were found to be important in facilitated conflict resolution processes no less than in thinking about conflict and its resolution. There is a healthy movement beginning to take place away from reliance on empirical evidence, away from the "specialist" and away from unique events, toward holistic analyses and explanations in which the particular case may be examined. This is a major influence in the field of conflict studies, making possible generic explanations of conflicts. Selection of relevant knowledge must take into account, therefore, the methodological approaches that are employed.

THE KNOWLEDGE FIELD

The knowledge field for the study of conflict and its resolution is the totality of decision making. Decision making is traditionally broken up into social levels and particular situations. But this is artificial and misleading. At family levels the quality of decision making is greatly affected by knowledge of human development and human relationships, and abilities to adjust to altering environmental circumstances. At public policy levels the wide scope of human knowledge, and abilities to predict, become relevant. Regardless of societal level we require some organized body of knowledge of human behaviors, relationships and responses to the environment that does not exclude anything that may be relevant.

In *Conflict: Resolution and Provention*, there is reference to a unifying theory of decision making that takes fully into account the human struggle for needs fulfillment. In *Conflict: Human Needs Theory*, the conceptual framework of needs theory is used to map the field of human relationships, both conflictual and cooperative. In *Conflict: Practices in Management, Settlement and Resolution*, we argue that courts and conflict resolution processes will become one when precedents and traditional norms give place to human needs fulfillment as the overriding norm, thus directing attention to the search for agreement on satisfiers in particular cases.

If the human needs approach can be validated, it will provide, subject always to some new discovery, a unifying theme or focus that makes order out of decision making complexities. Around it, knowledge can be selected and organized, thus providing us with a conflict resolution literature. (We have not selected articles relating to a unifying theory, for this topic has been covered in other books in this Conflict Series.)

THE CLASSICS

The problem of relevance, however, is not just one of scope. There is the problem of historical relevance. Past contributions did not use the same language and concepts. There was, for example, less precision and differentiation between disputes and conflicts, goals and satisfiers, and "blame" was usually placed on the person or group rather than the institutions and environmental conditions that provoked conflict (except, as we shall see later, in some exceptional cases). There was little conceptualization of conflict as a universal phenomenon with generic sources. Unless they are placed in their historical perspective the "classic" status of some past contributions can inhibit important qualitative developments in conceptual thinking.

Nor were past thinkers responding to a similar environment. It may have been reasonable at one point in history to assume that war was inevitable, but in the nuclear age such a complacent attitude is not reasonable. The assumptions on which the notion of war's inevitability was based have, therefore, to be reexamined. With these and other such changes in thinking, we have a special problem with thinkers who were caught up in the empirical frameworks of the time. Many of the "classics" of the past are not necessarily valuable in the present. They are there for reference as a resource when some profound rethinking of a problem is required. (They are in practice frequently interpreted and misused by scholars to legitimize their opinions.)

In a rapidly developing field there are major changes in perspectives and assumptions, and these lead us ultimately to discard much past and present thinking. There are reformulations that take change into account. This raises the difficult question: To what extent can we assume that scholars absorb the past and reflect it in their expositions, so that we do not have to go further back? How far back should we go in exploring past thinking?

Some thinking of the more recent past is valuable in giving a perspective, in showing trends, and in bringing to attention assumptions that are now more clearly questionable (Part I). Quincy Wright, a most distinguished scholar, wrote *The Nature of Conflict* (Chapter 1) in 1951. His first sentence is quite disturbing: "War is a species of conflict; consequently, by understanding conflict we may learn about the probable characteristics of war under different conditions and the methods most suitable for regulating, preventing, and winning wars." He was, nevertheless, at that early nuclear time, arguing against the consensus pre-nuclear view that lethal conflict was inevitable, thereby making strategic studies the main concentration. The intellectual and practical problems of the time do help to give a perspective to the history of thought in the field. In making selections it is necessary to see whether there are observations in such classics that have been missed, or have become significant as a result of subsequent developments.

SOME EXCEPTIONAL THINKERS

In the conceptual area it is impossible to detail historical trends in a time sequence because there are from time to time exceptional thinkers who detach themselves from their present and its empirical emphases.

In the 1920s, twenty years before Quincy Wright, Mary Follett wrote about the "new state." Her writings make many passages in book 1 of this Series seem like a plagiarism, though the author met her work only after writing his own.[2] There are such contributions that were ignored at the time because they did not reflect the contemporary consensus. Delving into these can be rewarding. It is part of a selection process to bring these to attention. It may be significant that Mary Follett's experiences as a woman gave her a perspective that was not conventional. It was a human, and not an institutional one. There are other examples relevant to our study, as for example, the writings of C. S. Peirce, to whom reference was made in *Conflict: Resolution and Provention*. These are among the real classics, even though not recognized as such at the time.

In 1964 Johan Galtung introduced the notion of "structural violence" in an article in his *Journal of Peace Research*. This was another early challenge to the traditional idea that the source of social problems was the behavior of the individual. The idea that structures could be violent in their effects on individuals was challenging – and not understood. It has taken some decades for this notion to be translated into the concept of human needs that must be satisfied by institutions and structures. There were intellectual reasons for the delay: tradition had focused attention on the individual as the problem. But there were political reasons also – this emphasis on structure as a source of deviant behaviors was often regarded as unacceptable subversion, all the more unacceptable and subversive because the thinking did not fall into any category of "ism" or ideology. Notions such as human needs become richer when their evolution is revealed. Perhaps they become even more relevant when the evolution of societies includes multi-ethnicity and high levels of alienation. We have not included an article by Galtung because his collected works are readily available in libraries and there is a major contribution by him in *Conflict: Human Needs Theory* (Chapter 15).

Kenneth Boulding was more concerned with the international and the emerging peace studies movement; but his perception was wider than peace research. *Future Directions in Conflict and Peace Studies* is the article which we have included (Chapter 2). The title suggests, as do his many other writings, an awareness that he was dealing with a problem of universal significance.

INTERNATIONAL STUDIES

The Folletts, Galtungs and Bouldings are exceptions: they conceptualize in ways that enable them to think about conflict as a generic phenomenon. The majority of thinkers have separated domestic conflict from international conflict. The domestic – the central authority model – was the model then thought to be the model for international relations. The League and the United Nations were based on it. Sigmund Freud wrote to Albert Einstein in 1932, and in his letter came to the conclusion that "Wars will only be prevented with certainty if mankind unites in setting up a central authority to which the right of giving judgement upon all conflicts of interest shall be handed over. There are clearly two separate requirements involved in this: the creation of a supreme authority and its endowment with the necessary power."[3]

We now find that the domestic model is the problem, and that the functional international model with no central authority or central power is the one that operates relatively smoothly in making functional transactions orderly!

This assumption that a central authority is the solution, making the domestic model the ideal, meant that the study of conflict management and resolution had its origins in the international – where the problem was thought to be. The bulk of the early literature on conflict is from an international perspective. In fact in making a selection for this book of readings it has been difficult to find articles of substance that were not primarily in the international field.

Few of these have a generic perspective. Many, however, because of their theoretical frameworks, have a wider implication, even though the authors were concentrating on the international. In 1986 Michael Banks in *The International Relations Discipline: Asset or Liability for Conflict Resolution?* (Chapter 3) reflected the sense of crisis many scholars had been experiencing for a decade or more – a sense that scholars and practitioners had taken a wrong turn that had led the international society toward confrontations and deterrence strategies quite unnecessarily, and to the exclusion of processes of resolving problems by processes that reveal differences in tactics and goals. We include this article in Part II, Crisis. In another article written in 1985 he had reviewed several books under the title "Where We Are Now,"[4] reflecting grave doubts about past trends in the field, and detecting some signs of change.

The conflict field generally became separated into different interest areas, some of which were more concerned with containing than with tackling the sources of conflict. As a consequence there are "strategists" and "peace researchers" (interested in arms control and such management issues), in addition to "conflict researchers" (interested in sources of conflict). John Groom has tried to define these different interests in *Paradigms in Conflict: the Strategist, the Conflict Researcher and the Peace Researcher* (Chapter 4). It will be seen that each of these separate interest areas have their domestic counterparts: authoritative controls, management and resolution.

In Part III, Analysis, we include contributions that reflected the more analytical framework that Michael Banks had welcomed. In *The Individual, the Group and War*, Bryant Wedge, a psychiatrist, looks back into thinking about the connection between individual and group behaviors, a topic which was a general concern at the time (Chapter 5). Then we have several articles on the human dimension, which is a central theme in *Conflict: Resolution and Provention* and in *Conflict: Human Needs Theory*. In the first Paul Sites discusses *Legitimacy and Human Needs* (Chapter 6). Edward Azar in *Protracted International Conflicts: Ten Propositions* (Chapter 7), is particularly concerned with identity groups, and their relations with central authorities. He thus throws light on ethnicity problems within nations. In their article, *A Critical Assessment of the Power of Human Needs in World Society* (Chapter 8), Jerel Rosati and his two co-authors provide a general thesis that has applications at both international and nation levels.

We turn in Part IV to Applications. Perhaps for a first time we have practice deduced from theory. Those who have contributions in Part IV are no less at ease in a theoretical framework. The first by Anthony de Reuck (a physicist initially), *A Theory of Conflict Resolution by Problem-solving* (Chapter 9), clearly demonstrates the connection between theory and practice.

As has been pointed out, the human dimension – and in particular human needs – has been important in the development of conflict resolution theory. Despite this the psychological and psychiatric literature is disappointing. The reason is that the traditional professions dealing with the person have tended to accept the norms of society and have assumed that the individual must adjust to them. Fault has tended to be located with the individual, not with society. Herbert Kelman, a social psychologist deeply involved in Middle East affairs, in *Interactive Problem-solving: A Social-psychological Approach to Conflict Resolution* (Chapter 10), is amongst the exceptions. He broke through the boundaries of his discipline and away from its traditional assumptions.

The next article, *Principles of Communication Between Adversaries in South Africa*, by Hendrik van der Merwe and his colleagues (Chapter 11), extracts insights on processes from theory and also from experience with a particular situation. This helps once again to bring together theory and practice.

There is one contribution in Part IV that is unusual. Conflict resolution practices tend to dwell on the need for interaction between parties: it is those concerned who must be involved in the decision making. In an interesting survey of international practices John McDonald argues in *Managing Complexity Through Small Group Dynamics* (Chapter 12) that an efficient way to tackle problems when there are many parties involved is to work with a small selection of those affected, referring back to the total group for ratification. This empirical experience provides an important input at a time at which there is in the conflict community an almost emotional value attached to direct "democratic" participation, requiring processes that are more like voting than an agreement based on an analysis of the problem. Chapter 13, *The Emergence and Institutionalization of Third-party Roles in Conflict*, is by James Laue, a sociologist with considerable experience as a practitioner. Laue traces the development of five intervention roles which appear in most conflicts: activist, advocate, mediator, researcher, and enforcer. He stresses the different bases and functions of these roles, and places the role of mediator or facilitator in context as only one of a range of approaches that third parties may take toward their work in disputes and conflicts.

This takes us into the area of Research – Part V. It will be clear that the analytical problem-solving approach to conflict resolution depends finally on questioning of assumptions and trying to evolve in a continuing way a greater realism. Philosophical aspects of the study of conflict and its resolution are the final basis. Mary Clark asks, *"What is Science* For?" (Chapter 14). She deplores the absence of teaching the philosophy of science as a part of disciplines. This article serves to introduce one by Frank Dukes, *Action Research* (Chapter 15), which shows how to bring together the philosophical, theoretical and applied aspects of the study.

In Part VI, Political Implications, we have three articles that look to the future. The first by Christa Slaton and Theodore Becker, *A Tale of Two Movements: ADR and the Greens* (Chapter 16), brings us into the contemporary world of politics. The Greens, being concerned with the environment, must look to the future, and cost the consequences of contemporary environmental abuse. This links them with "futurists". The same future costing of political and social problems links the Greens and futurists to conflict resolution in ways that cut through all party and ideological approaches to such problems. Richard Rubenstein then points to *Unanticipated Conflict and the Crisis of Social Theory* (Chapter 17), noting in particular the weakness of studies that fail to break through the boundaries of disciplines.

A SAMPLE ONLY

Generally speaking articles have been selected because of their conceptual richness and their consequent generic significance. They remain, however, no more than a sample, and a taste which hopefully will stimulate a desire for further researches in areas of particular interest. The selection has been made from hundreds of articles, and it has been difficult to know what to exclude.

There are important areas which we have not covered. Two in particular – problems of leadership, and the associated problems of representative government – have so far not been dealt with adequately by the conflict resolution literature.

Conflict resolution must move toward these and begin to question many widely held beliefs. Democracy, meaning majority government, is proving to be most undemocratic in multi-ethnic societies. But it is also proving to be corrupt when pressure groups exert a greater influence than does the electorate. Freedom of expression glosses over the tremendous influence of the media, which is not controlled by any democratic participation. The private enterprise system has consequences that create social problems which are conflict making, as Feagin[5] has pointed out. Behind these institutional problems there are leadership problems that will force some reconsideration of leadership qualifications and roles at some future time. There cannot be conflict resolution until there is prediction, forward planning and the avoidance of conditions that provoke conflict. But political leaders in representative systems are more interested in the present and the preservation of their roles. Communism is facing problems of representation and of incentive, and runs into trouble because of the means it employs in trying to avoid some of the problems that a free society faces. There are some fundamental dilemmas not yet addressed because of ideological environments that do not encourage such questioning. These issues are touched upon but not seriously tackled in many writings. Conflict resolution thinking will not be complete until these are developed. In a final essay (Chapter 18) John Burton tries to point to *Unfinished Business in Conflict Resolution*.

The main contributions to thought are probably in books. Articles can dwell only on some aspects of a subject. For this reason there is an annotated bibliography included at the end of the book. The selection, like the selection of articles, provides just a sample. An attempt has been made to include what appear at the time of writing to be the main publications that focus on conflict, its management and resolution.

NOTES AND REFERENCES

1. Mary Clark, *Ariadne's Thread: The Search for New Modes of Thinking* (New York: St. Martin's Press, 1989).
2. See Henry Metcalf and L. Urwick (eds), *Dynamic Administration: The Collected Papers of Mary Parker Follett* (New York: London: Harper Bros, 1940).
3. See Sigmund Freud, *Collected Papers*, vol. 5, James Strachey (ed.) (New York: Basic Books, 1959): 278.
4. Michael Banks, "Where We Are Now," *Review of International Studies*, 11 (1985): 215–330.
5. Joe R. Feagin, *Social Problems: A Critical Power-Conflict Perspective*, (New Jersey: Prentice-Hall, 1982).

I
Beginnings

Chapter 1   The Nature of Conflict   15
             Quincy Wright
Chapter 2   Future Directions in Conflict and Peace Studies   35
             Kenneth E. Boulding

1 The Nature of Conflict
Quincy Wright*

War is a species of conflict; consequently, by understanding conflict we may learn about the probable characteristics of war under different conditions and the methods most suitable for regulating, preventing, and winning wars.[1]

In the legal sense, war has been considered a situation during which two or more political groups are equally entitled to settle conflicts by armed force. Its essence is the legal equality of the parties and the obligations of impartial neutrality by outsiders. In this sense, the Kellogg Briand Pact and the United Nations Charter have eliminated war. Procedures have been established to determine who is the aggressor if hostilities occur, and all states have bound themselves not to be neutral but to assist the victim of aggression and to give no aid to the aggressor.[2]

In the sociological sense, which is the sense of ordinary usage, war refers to conflicts among political groups carried on by armed forces of considerable magnitude. The street fight of two small boys, the forensic contention in a law court, the military suppression of mob violence in the state, the collison of two automobiles, and the combat of two stags are not war; but they are conflict. Perhaps an analysis of the broader concept will help better to understand the lesser.[3]

CONFLICT AND INCONSISTENCY

Conflict is sometimes used to refer to inconsistencies in the motions, sentiments, purposes, or claims of entities, and sometimes to the process of resolving these inconsistencies. Thus, it is said that the values of the communist and democratic systems are in conflict: it may mean that it is impossible for a person rationally to believe in these two systems at the same time; or it may mean that some process of-propaganda, education, synthesis, or war is going on for reconciling them or for superseding one by the other. The two meanings are not necessarily identical, because inconsistent systems of thought and action may coexist in different places for long periods of time.

* From *The Western Political Quarterly*, IV(2) (June 1951).

However, as contacts increase and the world shrinks under the influence of new inventions, such inconsistencies tend to generate processes of reconciliation or supersession and thus to constitute conflict in the second sense of the term.

The word conflict is derived from the Latin word *confligere* meaning to strike together. Originally, it had a physical rather than moral connotation, though the English word has both. In the physical sense of two or more different things moving to occupy the same space at the same time, the logical inconsistency and the process of solution are identical. For example, the logical inconsistency of two billiard balls being in the same place at the same time is resolved by the conflict which results in their rolling to different positions.[4]

In an analysis of conflict, as used in the sociological sense and in accord with the the etymology of the word, it seems best to limit its meaning to situations where there is an actual or potential process for solving the inconsistency. Where there is no such process, conflict does not seem to be the proper word. If used to describe mere differences or inconsistencies in societies or value systems, it may induce the belief that peaceful coexistence is impossible. Where such differences have existed violent conflict has sometimes been precipitated when one was necessary. An example may, perhaps, illustrate this terminological distinction. Islam began a career of conquest in the seventh century with the thesis that it was the only true faith and was necessarily in conflict with all other religions. This was represented by the doctrine of the *Jihad*, or perpetual war of the "world of Islam" with the "world of war." According to Majid Khadduri,

> The world of war constituted all the states and communities outside the world of Islam. Its inhabitants were usually called infidels or, better termed, unbelievers. In theory the believers were always at war with the unbelievers.[5]

Belief in the *Jihad* induced continuous attacks by the Arabs upon the decadent Roman Empire and rising Christendom during the seventh and eighth centuries and resulted in extensive Moslem conquests in the Near East, North Africa, and Spain. Christendom, however, reacted militantly in the Crusades of the eleventh, twelfth, and thirteenth centuries turning on Islam with the doctrine of papal sovereignty of the world. The Ottoman Turks then took the leadership of Islam, and during the fifteenth, sixteenth, and seventeenth centuries were almost continuously at war with Christian Europe, conquering

Constantinople, the Balkans, and Hungary, as well as most of the Arab countries. Turkish power then waned, and eventually the Ottoman Empire broke up into national states, as did the Holy Roman Empire. Today Christian and Moslem states coexist and cooperate in the United Nations. Both the *Jihad* and the Crusades are things of the past. When, as a political measure, the Ottoman sultan, after entering World War I on the German side, proclaimed the *Jihad* on November 16, 1914, his action was repudiated by the Arab leader, Hussein Ibn Ali, of Mecca, who had entered the war on the Allied side.[6]

Similarly, the identification of religious differences with conflict led to a century and a half of war between Protestants and Catholics in the sixteenth and seventeenth centuries, ended by the Peace of Westphalia which recognized the sovereignty of territorial states and the authority of the temporal monarch to determine the religion of his people if he wished. Since then Protestant and Catholic states have found it possible to coexist peacefully.

These bits of history suggest the question whether the inconsistency of democracy and communism makes conflict between the Western and the Soviet states inescapable. May it not be possible for communist and democratic states to coexist, even in this technologically shrinking world, as do Moslem and Christian states, Protestant and Catholic states? The answer may depend on the policy pursued by the governments or other regulatory agencies, rather than on the ideologies themselves. In 1858 Lincoln thought that, "A house divided against itself cannot stand. A government cannot endure permanently half-slave and half-free." Three years later, however, in his first Inaugural, he asserted that he had "no purpose, directly or indirectly, to interfere with the institution of slavery in the States where it exists. In your hands, my dissatisfied fellow citizens, and not in mine," he said, "is the momentous issue of civil war. The government will not assail you. You can have no conflict without being yourself the aggressor." Coexistence in the Union of diverse institutions of North and South then seemed to him possible. The Civil War occurred, and eventually emancipation was proclaimed. Some historians, however, think that emancipation could have been achieved peacefully if war had been avoided for ten years longer. They are not certain that "the inevitable conflict" really was inevitable.[7]

Historically, radical differences of religion, ideology, or institutions have tended to induce conflict. They do not, however, necessarily do so, nor does conflict if it occurs necessarily eliminate the differences.

Consequently, it is unwise to identify inconsistencies of opinion with conflict. Coexistence of inconsistent opinions may, in fact, be an essential condition of human progress. It is through the contact and competition of differing opinions and methods, and the eventual synthesis of thesis and antithesis, that history is created.

CONFLICT AND TENSION

It depends on the policies of governments whether inconsistencies of social ideologies develop into conflicts, but these policies are likely to be influenced by the amount of social tension which the inconsistencies have generated. Social tension has been defined as the condition which arises from inconsistencies among initiatives in the structure of a society.[8] Ideologies accepted by different groups within a society may be inconsistent without creating tension; but if initiatives or actions are taken by individuals or groups in accord with those inconsistent ideologies, and if these actions lead to contact, tension arises. The degree of intensity of tension tends to increase with decreases in the social distance between the groups and with increases in the amount of energy behind them. If the groups with inconsistent ideologies are in close contact, that is, if the society is closely integrated, the tension will be great. If the society is loose (as was, for example, the world society during the nineteenth century) such intiatives originating in different and widely separated nations may create little tension. It is also true that if the groups or nations within the society from which the inconsistent initiatives emerge are small and weak, tension will be less than if they are great and powerful.[9] In the present world of decreasing social distances, initiatives emerging from such different and inconsistent ideologies as democracy and communism, respectively supported by such great powers as the United States and the Soviet Union, can be expected to cause great tension.

Tension is more likely to develop into violent conflict if it is intense and if regulatory arrangements are ineffective.[10] The United Nations is a more effective regulatory arrangement than was the system of diplomacy of the nineteenth century, but tensions are so much greater today that serious conflict is more probable. Once conflict develops, the process by which anxiety and power accumulate in each of the conflicting groups tends to result in war.

The phenomena of inconsistency, tension, conflict, and war within a society may thus be considered distinct, but they constitute a series in which each succeeding term includes those that precede it. In war, each inconsistent value system has integrated itself in order to maintain its position against the other; tensions have rise, the situation is recognized as conflict, and open violence is used or projected.[11] Relations of logical inconsistency in social ideas or institutions are likely to generate tension, which in turn leads to conflict and frequently to war.[12]

However, this progress is not inevitable. Social inconsistencies can coexist without tension, and tension can exist for a long time without conflict, just as conflict may be resolved without war. If regulatory procedures such as diplomacy, mediation, conciliation, consultation, arbitration, and adjudication are available and efficiently operated, then accommodation, adjustment, and settlement may be achieved at any point and the process stopped. If, however, tensions rise above a certain level, these procedures are likely to prove ineffective.

CONFLICT AND COMPETITION

Conflict, defined as opposition among social entities directed against one another, is distinguished from *competition* defined as opposition among social entities independently striving for something of which the supply is inadequate to satisfy all. Competitors may not be aware of one another, while the parties to a conflict are. *Rivalry*, half-way between, refers to opposition among social entities which recognize one another as competitors. Conflict, rivalry, and competition are all species of *opposition*, which has been defined as a process by which social entities function in the disservice of one another. Opposition is thus contrasted with *cooperation*, the process by which social entities function in the service of one another.[13]

These definitions are introduced because it is important to emphasize that competition between organisms is inevitable in a world of limited resources, but conflict is not; although conflict in some form – not necessarily violent – is very likely to occur, and is probably an essential and desirable element of human societies.

Many authors have argued for the inevitability of war from the premises of Darwininan evolution – the struggle for existence among organic species from which only the fittest survive. In the main, however, this struggle of nature, is competition, not conflict. *Lethal* conflict among individuals or groups of animals *of the same species* is rare. Birds and some mammals monopolize nesting and feeding areas during the mating season and fight off intruders of the same species. Males of such polygamous species as seals, deer, and horses fight other males to maintain their harems. Social animals, such as monkeys and cattle, fight to win or maintain leadership of the group. The struggle for existence occurs not in such combats, but in the competition among herbivorous animals for limited grazing areas, for the occupancy of areas free from carnivorous animals; and in the competition among carnivorous animals for the limited supply of herbivorous animals on which they prey. Those who fail in this competition starve to death or become victims, not of attack by their own, but by other species. The lethal aspect of the struggle for existence does not resemble human war, but rather the business of slaughtering animals for food, and the competition of individuals for jobs, markets, and materials. The essence of the struggle is the competition for the necessities of life that are insufficient to satisfy all.[14]

Among nations there is competition in developing resources, trades, skills, and a satisfactory way of life. The successful nations grow and prosper; the unsuccessful, decline. It is true that, because nations are geographically circumscribed and immovable, this competition may induce efforts to expand territory at the expense of others, and thus lead to conflict. This, however, is a product of civilization. Wars of territorial conquest and economic aggrandizement do not occur among animals of the same species or among the most primitive peoples. They are consequences of large-scale political and military organization and of legal relations defining property and territory. Even under conditions of civilization, however, it cannot be said that war-like conflict among nations is inevitable, although competition is.[15]

CONFLICT AND COOPERATION

Lethal conflict among individuals or groups of the same species, or war in a very general sense, is not a necessary factor of either animal or human life. Most psychologists seem to be in agreement on this.[16] However, opposition – both in the sense of conflict and of competition – is a necessary factor of human society no less important than cooperation. A society has been defined as a group manifesting sufficient cooperation internally and sufficient opposition externally to be recognizable as a unity.[17] This definition raises the question: Can there be a *world* society unless contact is made with societies in some other planet to which it can be opposed? It is perhaps premature to say there cannot be a society existing without external opposition and manifesting itself only by the cooperation of its members to achieve common ends. It would be difficult to discover such an isolated society among either primitive or civilized peoples; but, even in such an isolated society, there would be internal opposition because a society implies that its members have interests of their own as well as common interests, and in these individual interests they not only compete but also, on occasions, conflict.

Communism seeks, like the ant colony, completely to subordinate the individual to the society and thus to eliminate all oppositions within it. In a communist society – whether through heredity, education or central control – all divergent initiatives of individuals and sub-groups have been destroyed and all are, in theory, in complete harmony. There is no historic illustration of such a society, and it is probably inconsistent with the psychological characteristics of man. Among colonial insects guided by instinct, it is perhaps possible; but among man, having taken the road of reason, which is a function of the individual human mind, such a complete subordination of the individual to the group is impossible.[18] Human societies exist by the cooperation of individuals and subgroups, and the existence of the latter implies that they have some initiative, some autonomy. They cannot exist unless each defends some sphere of freedom. Such a defense implies conflict. A society in which there was no internal conflict would be one in which no individual or subgroup could formulate its own purposes and act to achieve them. A society of that character would be an entity guided by a single purpose and a single method. In short, it would not be a society at all. It would not even be a machine, because in a machine gears and other parts are opposed to one another. It would rather be an undifferentiated mass moving toward a single goal – perhaps more like an inflamed mob than any other social manifestation.[19]

Democratic societies, in accepting human rights, freedom of association, and a multiplicity of political parties, have institutionalized opposition. They regard it as no less important than cooperation. In England, "His Majesty's Loyal Opposition" is an essential feature of parliamentary government, and its leader receives a salary out of the annual budget. American party leaders recognize an opposition party as an essential, though sometimes unpleasant, feature of the

Constitution.

Psychologists have suggested that the ability to consider conflicting alternatives of action at the same time distinguishes man from the animals. This mental conflict creates the possibility of choice, thus permitting man to escape the necessity of following a single course of action to which minds incapable of such internal conflict are bound.[20] The hesitancy of man, suddenly faced by a wild bull and by the choice of fleeing to a fence, taking to a tree, or facing the animal and dodging may save his life, provided he chooses rapidly and adequately. In the field of politics, the democratic state, within which the opposition of parties continually suggests alternatives of policy, has possibilities of choice and progress denied to the one-party state. The same is true in the economic field. Competition among many firms offers the consumer choices that may be denied the citizen under a totally planned economy.

Too severe and enduring conflicts in the individual mind may create neuroses, and over-intense conflicts can disrupt societies. Even democratic societies must keep their internal oppositions within bounds, or they will become anarchies. In general, they prohibit fraud and violence. The competition of business firms must be by fair methods, and the conflict of political parties must avoid violence. Although a society cannot exist without competition and conflict, and cannot progress without a good deal of both, it can exist without violence and war. However, even in the best regulated societies, eternal vigilance is the price of avoiding these disruptive manifestations of opposition.

TYPES OF CONFLICT

As already noted, conflict can take place among different sorts of entities. *Physical conflict* in which two or more entities try to occupy the same space at the same time must be distinguished from *political conflict* by which a group tries to impose its policy on others. These two types of conflict can be distinguished from *ideological conflicts* in which systems of thought or of values struggle with each other, and from *legal conflicts* in which controversies over claims or demands are adjusted by mutually recognized procedures.[21]

War in the legal sense has been characterized by the union of all four types of conflict. It is manifested by the physical struggle of armies to occupy the same space, each seeking to annihilate, disarm, or capture the other; by the political struggle of nations to achieve policies against the resistance of others; by the ideological struggle of people to preserve or extend ways of life and value systems; and by the legal struggle of states to acquire titles, to vindicate claims, to prevent violence, or to punish offenses by recognized procedures of regulated violence.[22]

Is this identification of different sorts of conflict in a single procedure expedient? Might it not be wiser to deal with legal conflicts by adjudication; ideological conflicts by information, education, and persuasion; political conflicts by negotiation or appeal to international agencies, such as the United Nations Security Council or the General Assembly, leaving to war only resistance to armed aggression? Such discrimination is the objective of the United Nations, as it was of the League of Nations before it, the Hague system before that, and of customary international law even earlier. Practice has indicated that such a segregation of the aspects of conflict is difficult to achieve, but the effort should nevertheless be made.[23]

TENDENCY OF CONFLICT

It has been emphasized by Clausewitz that there is a tendency for conflict to become war, and for war to become total and absolute in proportion as the parties are equal in power and determination, and are unaffected by outside influences. This tendency has four aspects – the unification of policy, the garrison state, total war, and the bipolar world.

The legal claims of the state come to be conceived as inherent in the value system and way of life of the people. These claims come to be formulated as national policy, and armed forces are developed as the only certain means of achieving this policy. Policy in the legal, moral, political, and military field becomes integrated at the national level.

This integration of policy, and of military preparation to maintain it, tend to integrate the state. Public opinion and moral values, as well as economic life and the maintenance of law and order, are placed under central authority; institutions of deliberation, freedom in the formulation and expression of opinion and the exercise of individual rights, are subordinated to the demands of national policy, of military preparation, and of national loyalty. The garrison or totalitarian state emerges in which the individual is in a large measure subordinated to the group.[24]

In such unification of the state, restraints on war tend to be abandoned. These restraints have existed because of the presence of religious, moral, aesthetic, economic, and legal opinions and interests that are independent of the government and have been influenced by similar opinions in outside countries. Once all elements of the state are united behind the national policy and the effort to achieve that policy by war, internal and external influences for moderation cannot penetrate the crust of the gigantic war machine in motion. War becomes unrestrained and total.[25]

Integration, however, does not stop with the nation, since alliances and coalitions are formed until the entire world is drawn in on one side or the other. Absolute war is fought in a bipolar world. There are no neutrals, and the forces of the world concentrated at two strategic centers lunge at each other in unrestrained fury, each demanding total victory and the annihilation or unconditional surrender of the enemy.[26]

This expansion of war is in fact but an aspect of the movement of conflict from the individual mind. The Constitution of UNESCO declares that wars begin in the minds of men. The psychologists assert that conflict in the individual mind is a human trait. Instead of the simple sensory-motor circuit of animals, whereby a stimulus of the senses at once induces appropriate action developed in the instincts or the experience of the animal, the circuit is interrupted in man at the seat of consciousness in the brain. Here ideal alternatives of action are set against one another, their advantages considered, and eventually a decision is made and action proceeds on the chosen course. Sometimes, however, decision fails; and the indecision gives rise to ambivalence, especially when each of the conflicting alternatives is highly charged emotionally. Such conditions are characteristic of the child who loves his mother as the source of material comforts and yet, at the same time, hates her because she disciplines him to teach him the requirements of social life. To escape this ambivalence the child displaces his hatred upon a scapegoat – perhaps the father, perhaps the neighbor's child; but the habit of displacement to solve apparently insoluble conflicts is established. As the child becomes an adult in a local group he tends to find a scapegoat outside the group so that all can be harmony within. So with consciousness of the nation, all citizens displace their hatreds and animosities upon an external enemy who conveniently serves as scapegoat. Similarly when coalitions are formed their maintenance depends in no small degree upon displacement of all sources of conflict among the allies upon the enemy. While the United States and Russia were desperately fighting the Axis [powers], they could displace the hatreds causing differences among them on the common enemy.

The mechanism of displacement tends to enlarge conflicts from the individual mind to the bipolar world, and the mechanism of projection tends to augment the vigor of these conflicts. Once group conflict develops, each group is stimulated by its anxieties about the other group to build its armaments and to prepare for strategic action. Its own preoccupation about the favorable conditions of attack is projected upon its antagonist. It sees every move of that antagonist as preparation for attack. This stimulates its own preparation. The enemy similarly projects his own aggressive dispositions, armaments mount, and eventually war emerges.

The tendency toward the expansion and intensification of war is further developed by the rational pursuit of balance of power politics. Each of two rivaling great nations seeks allies to maintain the balance, and smaller nations seek protection of one or other of the great. The number of uncommitted declines. Finally, all power in the world is gathered about one or the other pole. Once the world is bipolarized, each center of power anticipates war and begins to calculate the influence that time is having on its relative power position. There is a strong urge for the power against which time is running to start the fight. This may entail risk, but the risk may be greater if hostilities are postponed. Thus, psychological and political factors conspire to extend, enlarge, and integrate conflicts, and to precipitate war.[27]

METHODS OF CONFLICT

Conflict may be carried on by methods of coercion or persuasion. The former usually involves violence and has the character of physical conflict; the latter need not involve violence, though violence may be utilized as a method of persuasion, and is characteristic of political, ideological, and legal conflict.

In employing purely coercive or physical methods of conflict, each party may seek to destroy the other, to control him, or to occupy his territory. In war, the destruction or disorganization of the enemy's armed forces, communications, and sources of supply; the capture of his materiel and the imprisonment of the personnel of his forces;

and the driving of the enemy from strategic points or from productive territory and the occupation of that territory are operations of this character, constituting what may be called the military front in war. These methods are also used by governments in conflict with criminals and by international organizations in operations of collective security.

Non-coercive or moral methods of conflict involve efforts by each party to isolate the other, to persuade him to change his policy, ideology, or claims, or to defeat him in accordance with the rules of the game. In war successful efforts to cut off the enemy's external trade and communications, to create an opinion opposed to him in other countries and governments, and to deprive him of allies, make for his isolation. Such efforts constitute the economic and diplomatic fronts in the war. Military methods may also contribute to such isolation – such as naval blockade and the destruction of the instruments of external trade and communication.

Persuasion may be conducted by propaganda utilizing symbols to influence the minds of the enemy's armed forces, his government and his civilian population. In war, propaganda constitutes the psychological front. Persuasion is, of course, used in many types of conflict other than war, such as diplomatic conversations, political campaigns, and parliamentary debates.

In a certain sense, however, all methods of war, unless the total destruction of the enemy's population as well as his power is contemplated, are aimed to persuade the enemy's population and government. The object of war is the complete submission of the enemy. It is assumed that military methods aimed to destroy or control his armed forces and occupy his territories, economic measures designed to starve his population and reduce his resources, and diplomatic measures designed to destroy his hope of relief or support will, when sufficient, induce the enemy government and population to change their minds and submit to whatever terms are demanded.[28]

Defeat means formal abandonment of effort by the losing party to the conflict. It implies that all parties to the conflict have accepted certain rules and criteria by which victor and vanquished can be determined. In games such as chess, bridge, football, and tennis defeat is thus conventionalized, although in some, such as football, the conventions may permit coercive methods resembling war, but with less violence. Chess is a highly conventionalized war in which available forces, strategies, and tactics are strictly regulated by the rules. War itself may have a conventional character. Rules of war may prohibit certain kinds of action, and custom may even decree that forces or fortified places ought to surrender in certain circumstances even though such action is not physically necessary. War among primitive peoples often has a highly conventional character not unlike a game; and in the wars of the *Condottiere* in fifteenth century Italy and the sieges of the eighteenth century, war was highly conventionalized in Europe and regulated so as to moderate losses. In most wars, the formalities of surrender instruments, armistices, and peace treaties register defeat and victory symbolically, usually after the application of military, economic, diplomatic, and psychological methods have persuaded one side that further resistance is hopeless. The degree of formality, regulation, and symbolic representation in conflicts varies greatly from games to total war. However, the extent to which war has been conventionalized at certain periods indicates possibilities of limitation and avoidance of the trend toward absolute war by means of rational considerations and suitable social organization.[29]

Under suitable conditions, war might be decided by highly intelligent generals without any bloodshed. Each would calculate the best utilization of materials and manpower, the best strategy and maneuvers of armed forces both for himself and the enemy, each assuming – as in playing a game of chess – that the other would similarly calculate and would follow the plan most in his own interest. According to such calculations, victory for one side and defeat for the other might be certain, and the defeated would surrender without any hostilities. However, it is highly improbable that war will ever be so conventionalized that incalculable factors like courage, morale, faulty intelligence, accidents of weather, and new inventions can be eliminated. The party whose defeat seems certain by logical calculations may yet believe it can win because of these factors, and so will not surrender without a trial of strength unless indeed the disparity in strength is very great, as in interventions by a great power in the territory of a very weak power. In the course of time, such disparity may be presented by the United Nations in its operations of collective security or international policing; but, as the Korean episode indicates, the United Nations cannot yet be certain of overwhelming power against a dissident member. Even national federations cannot always muster sufficient power to discourage rebellion, in which case their policing operations assume the character of war – as witness the American Civil War.

Consideration of the variety of methods by which conflict is conducted suggests that appraisal of national power or capacity to win wars cannot be based on any simple analysis. Capacity to win allies and persuade enemy and neutral opinion by propaganda is no less important than capacity to create a powerful war potential including the command of large armed forces. Capacity to invent and to produce, which depends upon a high development of science and technology, is no less important than capacity to plan the strategy of campaigns and tactics of battle. Perhaps most important in statecraft is the capacity to analyze conflicts, to distinguish the important from the unimportant aspects, to view the world as a whole, to appreciate the influence of time and opinion, and to synthesize this knowledge in order to forward the interests of the nation and of the world without resort to violent methods, which often destroy more than they create and which settle fewer conflicts than they initiate.

SOLUTION AND CONFLICT

None of the methods by which conflict is carried on necessarily ends the conflict – unless, indeed, the conflict is completely conventionalized as in a game. Even total defeat in war may not remove the causes of conflict, and after a time the defeated may revive and renew the conflict.

A conflict is solved by *definitive acceptance* of a decision by *all* parties. In physical conflicts where all but one party are totally destroyed such decisions may be absolute; but if the conflict concerns ideas, policies or claims, the words "definitive," "acceptance," and "all" have to be taken relatively. The rejected ideas, policies, or claims may be presented again. A decision may be accepted in a different sense by different parties. Finally, the direct parties to a controversy may not be the only parties interested. In the modern situation of wide-spread interdependence and general vulnerability to military and propaganda attacks from distant points, solutions of a dispute may not stand unless accepted by many states and groups in addition to the formal litigants.

In democracies, the relative character of decisions and settlements is both acknowledged and approved. In the United States, defeat of the Republicans by the Democrats in an election is accepted by the Republicans only on the assumption that they will have another chance in which the decision may be reversed. The opponents of legislation adopted by Congress often hope to acquire a majority and to repeal the law later. Democracy seeks to avoid once-for-all decisions which permanently reject certain alternatives, but rather seeks to facilitate temporary and relative decisions achieved by methods which avoid violence by keeping alive the hope of those defeated that eventually they may triumph. Only by the maintenance of such hope can minorities be persuaded to submit easily and can a spirit of tolerance be maintained.

Dictatorships that seek final decisions find it necessary to suppress minorities by force and are likely in time to be overthrown by revolution. Democratic institutions maintaining – at least to some degree – freedom of thought, expression, opinion, and association are not designed to suppress conflicts within the society but to encourage advocates of all policies, ideas, or claims to think that eventually they may win sufficient support to achieve their objectives.

Psychologists have discovered, however, that unresolved conflicts in the individual human mind may cause neuroses, incapacitating the individual for social life, or produce a displacement of animosities upon scapegoats resulting in serious social conflicts. A mature human personality is one which poses alternatives of action, reflects upon such conflicts, but eventually decides and acts, abandoning the rejected course after commitment.[30]

It may be that while the definitive settlement of conflict is a vice in societies, it is a virtue in the individual mind. A more accurate description would perhaps avoid the dichotomy between psychic and social conflicts and would recognize that socio-psychological conflict may occur at a number of different levels. It may occur in the individual mind, in small societies like families, clubs, trade unions, and corporations, in large societies like nations, and in supranational groups like alliances, regional arrangements, international organizations and the world community. It is perhaps a safe generalization that the smaller the group, the more necessary is decision; the larger the group, the more dangerous is decision. In the world as a whole, in which differences of religion, ideology, culture, economic system, and policy exist and are to be expected for a long future, definitive decision of conflicts that may arise because of these differences seems to be both improbable and undesirable. Variety is the essence of a progressive and interesting world. However, so long as these differences exist conflict is possible.[31]

There are four ways in which social conflicts can be relatively solved: (1) by negotiation and agreement resulting in settlement or adjustment in accord with the will of all the parties; (2) by adjudication and decision in accord with the will, perhaps guided by legal or moral principles, of an outside party; (3) by dictation or decision in accordance with the will of one party to the conflict; and (4) by obsolescence through agreement to disagree which may in time, as new issues arise, sink the conflict into oblivion and result in a settlement according to the will of no one.[32] It may be that while negotiation and obsolescence are least likely to result in speedy and definitive decisions, yet, for that very reason, they may be most suitable for dealing with controversy among the nations and alliances of the international community. In practice, settlement by dictation usually involves violence; and while it brings about social change and settles some conflicts, at least for the time, it is likely to precipitate new ones. Adjudication in the form of arbitration and judicial settlement has been used in international affairs; but has, on the whole, proved capable of settling only controversies in which both parties base their claims on formal principles of law and in which vital interests, such as national power and survival, and policies supported by widespread and intense public opinion, were only slightly involved.

With these considerations in mind, it is well for those responsible for the foreign policy of a nation in the presence of any conflict to ask in what degree decision is desirable, and to adjust the methods employed to conclusions on that point.

CONFLICT AND CIVILIZATION

This discussion should indicate that conflict is a complicated subject and presents complicated problems to individuals, group leaders, and statesmen. Conflict is related to competition and to cooperation, but differs from both. There are many types of conflict – physical, political ideological, and legal – but there is a tendency for conflict to become total and absolute, and to split the community of nations into halves which would destroy one another in absolute war. The shrinking of the modern world under the influence of new means of communication and transport, and the increasingly destructive methods of warfare culminating in the air-borne atomic bomb, have augmented this tendency, and have made war ominous for the future of civilization.

Conflict is carried on by many methods – coercive and non-coercive – and there are various procedures for settling conflicts; but among large groups no final decision of most conflicts is likely to be absolute, and it is perhaps undesirable that it should be.

It may be suggested that all champions of civilization, particularly of the American type, should earnestly and hopefully search for means to obstruct the natural tendency of conflict under present-day conditions to integrate policies, to centralize authority both geographically and functionally, to bipolarize the world, and to precipitate absolute war between the poles. It is difficult to question the existence of that tendency manifested in two world wars and in the present "cold war." It is possible to describe the psychological, technological, sociological, and political factors which account for this tendency, but it is difficult to stem the tide. Nevertheless, the effort to do so is called for by our culture and may be required for the salvation of our civilization. It is worth recalling that, when faced by conditions resembling those of today, most civilizations have begun a fatal decline ending in death to be followed, after a period of dark ages, by a new civilization.[33] Since our civilization, differing from others, is worldwide, and therefore without the roots of new civilizations on its periphery, the situation may be more ominous.

The object of such efforts should be to diffuse conflicts by increasing the number of centers of initiative. Overcentralization is dangerous. Many small conflicts are less serious than one great conflict. Perhaps if the West were less willing to accept the alleged Soviet thesis that all communist states are necessarily satellites of the Kremlin and that all other states are necessarily in opposition to them, it would be discovered that states other than Tito's Yugoslavia have within them strong nationalist roots and resist integration into the Kremlin pattern of ideology and policy; and that states other than Nehru's India, while not wishing to become satellites of the Kremlin, may also hesitate to accept American leadership completely.

American policy, while creating situations of strength and containing Soviet expansion, might also encourage communist states to emanicipate themselves from complete subservience to the Kremlin. Perhaps the national interest of China in resisting Soviet absorption of Manchuria, Mongolia, and Sinkiang is not wholly dead even in the communist government of Mao-Tse-tung. Perhaps the age-old love which the Chinese peasant has for the "good earth" will check his enthusiasm for the Kremlin pattern of collective farms. It may also be that a zone of states manifesting different patterns of nationalism, and reluctant to follow blindly the leadership either of the United States or of the Soviet Union can in time establish third, fourth, and fifth forces in the world thus multiplying centers of initiative between the two great poles and providing the conditions for a more stable equilibrium of power and a more effective international organization.[34]

Conflicts can perhaps be analyzed and certain of their aspects dealt with by non-violent methods, thus weakening some of the urge toward unified policies and total war. Perhaps, also, a more careful examination of the roots of social and political conflict in the individual mind will suggest methods of education in personal decision making which, when widely practised, will moderate the tendency to displace hatreds and project aggressive impulses upon scapegoats. Such education of the kind attempted by UNESCO, but up to this time rather ineffectively, might reduce the ultimate springs from which great conflicts arise.

Undoubtedly wider appreciation of the complexity of most international conflicts, of the inevitability and desirability of some conflict in the world, of the value of a broad spirit of toleration in our complex world, and of the possibilities of coexistence of divergent cultures, systems, ideologies, and policies, may offer effective obstacles to the development of the fatal tendency toward a new world war.

NOTES AND REFERENCES

1. Quincy Wright, *A Study of War* (Chicago: University of Chicago Press, 1942): 699, 956.
2. Wright, *A Study of War*: 8, 341, 891. See also Wright, "Neutrality and Neutral Rights Following the Pact of Paris," *Proceedings*, American Society of International Law (1930): 86; "International Law and International Politics," *Measure* (Spring 1951).
3. Wright, *A Study of War*: 9, 685.
4. Kurt Singer, "The Meaning of Conflict," *Australian Journal of Philosophy* (December 1949); *The Idea of Conflict* (Melbourne: Melbourne University Press, 1941): 13ff.
5. Majid Khadduri, *The Law of War and Peace in Islam* (London: Luzac, 1940): 20.
6. Naval War College, International Law Documents (Washington: Government Printing Office, 1917): 17, 220.
7. George Fort Milton, *The Eve of Conflict: S. A. Douglas and the Needless War* (New York: Houghton Mifflin Co., 1934): 608. "There is no scientific validity in the phrase 'inherent contradiction' and 'inevitable conflict.' In so far as they are not just untrue, they merely express a pessimistic conviction that human beings will always fail to find a sensible method of resolving a dangerous situation." R. H. S. Crossman, "Reflections on

the Cold War," *The Political Quarterly, XXII* (January 1951): 10.
8. Quincy Wright, "The Importance of the Study of International Tensions," *International Bulletin of the Social Sciences*, UNESCO (Spring 1950): 90.
9. Wright, "The Importance of the Study of International Tensions," and Wright, "Measurement of Variations in International Tensions," in L. Bryson, L. Finkelstein and R. M. MacIver, *Learning and World Peace*, 8th Symposium on Science, Philosophy and Religion (New York, 1948): 54.
10. Wright, *A Study of War*: 959. On factors making for extreme tensions, see 1107ff.
11. Wright, *A Study of War*: 684ff.
12. Wright, *A Study of War*: 1410ff. This process is illustrated in various forms of the duel.
13. Wright, *A Study of War*: 1439. See also R. E. Park, and E. Burgess, *Introduction to the Science of Sociology* (Chicago: University of Chicago Press, 1924): 574ff; W. F. Ogburn and M. F. Nimkoff, *Sociology* (New York: Houghton Mifflin Co., 1940): 346, 369. Kurt Singer defines conflict as "a critical state of tension occasioned by the presence of mutually incompatible tendencies with an organismic whole the functional continuity or structural integrity of which is thereby threatened, "The Resolution of Conflict," *Social Research*, XVI (1949): 230.
14. Wright, *A Study of War*: 42ff., 497ff.
15. Wright, *A Study of War*: 11, 36ff.
16. Wright, *A Study of War*: 277, 1198. John M. Fletcher, "The Verdict of Psychologists on War Instincts," *Scientific Monthly*, XXXV (August 1932): 142ff.
17. Wright, *A Study of War*: 145.
18. Henri Bergson, *Creative Evolution* (New York: Macmillan, 1944): 453.
19. Wright, *A Study of War*: 517, 957; Georg Simmel, "The Sociology of Conflict," *American Journal of Sociology*, IX (1903): 490; Park and Burgess, *Introduction*: 1, 583; Robert Waelder, *Psychological Aspects of War and Peace*, Geneva Studies, X (May 1939): 7ff.
20. Singer, "The Meaning of Conflict": 5, 21ff; Park and Burgess, *Introduction*: 578.
21. Singer, *The Idea of Conflict*: 14.
22. Wright, *A Study of War*: 698.
23. Wright, *A Study of War*: 750ff, 1227ff, 1332ff.
24. H. D. Lasswell, "The Garrison State," *American Journal of Sociology*, XLVI (1941): 455; *National Security and Individual Freedom* (New York: McGraw Hill, 1950); see also Wright, *A Study of War*: 306.
25. Wright, *A Study of War*: 307ff.; John U. Nef, *War and Human Progress* (Cambridge, Mass.: Harvard University Press, 1950): 464.
26. H. D. Lasswell, "The Interrelations of World Organization and Society," *Yale Law Journal*, LV (August 1946): 889ff.
27. Wright, "The Importance of the Study of International Tensions"; "Some Reflections on War and Peace," *American Journal of Psychiatry*, CVII (September 1950): 161ff.
28. Wright, *A Study of War*: 317.

29. Nef, *War and Human Progress*: 464; Hoffman Nickerson, *Can We Limit War?* (Bristol, 1933).
30. Singer, "The Meaning of Conflict"; "The Resolution of Conflict," *Social Research*, XVI (1949): 230ff.
31. In a communication to the author dated 12 January 1951, Kurt Singer writes: "I am in fact inclined to emphasize the dangers of identifying conflicts within the mind and within a society still more than you do . . . But even a modern democracy organized in an 'agnostic' state must be based on decisions – it requires a consensus and common fund of values and norms, and even the agreement to disagree on the rest and on the mode of settling such differences requires a decision of a very higher order . . . On the other hand I would not equate the individual personality with a monolithic structure and its decision with rigid centralization. In the richest personalities of our culture, Dante, Shakespeare, Goethe, Unity (*Gestaltung*) harbours more differences (e.g., Antique and Christian values) than any democracy could hope to manage and which are never reconciled once forever." Singer emphasizes the differences of "decisions" in a complex situation with respect to explicitness rather than with respect to duration. The latter distinction is also important. It may be the essence of science, as of democracy, to accept any solution only tentatively. Scientists know that in time new observations will force reconsideration of the best verified "laws;" and politicians know that in time new opinions will force legislation superseding established "laws."
32. Singer suggests that conflicts may be resolved by (1) integration and constructive action, (2) by sublimation and withdrawal, (3) by resolute contention and fighting, and (4) by regression and yielding ("The Resolution of Conflict": 230ff).
33. Arnold J. Toynbee, *A Study of History* (Oxford: Oxford University Press, 1935) vol. I: 129ff; vol. III: 167.
34. Dewitt C. Poole, "Balance of Power," *Life Magazine*, XXII (22 September 1947): 76ff.

2 Future Directions in Conflict and Peace Studies
Kenneth E. Boulding*

It is now 21 years since the *Journal of Conflict Resolution* was founded, which is at least an excuse to ask ourselves if we have reached any kind of maturity. The peace research movement, of which the *Journal of Conflict Resolution* was an important component, goes back of course earlier. It is hard to put a date on it; perhaps we can regard Quincy Wright and Lewis F. Richardson in the 1920s and 1930s as the forerunners and perhaps Ted Lentz's book, *Towards a Science of Peace*, in 1952, as a conception. So a brief attempt at appraisal and a cautious look to the future may be appropriate.

A modest pessimism about the actual consequences for society of the peace research movement may be in order. It is very small, indeed minuscule, compared with the gigantic apparatus of organized conflict; the $300 billion a year that goes into the war industry; the continuing and perhaps increasing danger of the breakdown of nuclear deterrence and the high incidence of conventional war, particularly in the tropics. Nevertheless, I think we can claim that the peace research movement has produced a discipline, which goes by a number of different names, but is perhaps most commonly called "conflict and peace studies." This is more, incidentally, than the movement for general systems has done. General Systems, which started about the same time as Peace Research, has not succeeded in institutionalizing itself in the teaching process, and even after 25 years it still survives precariously in universities, mainly as an eccentricity of people who are paid primarily to do other things.

There are perhaps three tests of a discipline: Does it have a bibliography? Can you give courses in it? And, can you give examinations in it? A fourth criterion should perhaps be added: Does it have any specialized journals? On all these four counts, conflict and peace studies can certainly claim to be a discipline. By this time

* From *Journal of Conflict Resolution*, 22(2) (1978): 342.

it has a large bibliography, it has established itself as a teaching unit in close to 100 colleges and universities. At least one or two Ph.D.s have been given in the field. One can certainly give examinations in it. And it has a number of professional journals, including the *Journal of Conflict Resolution*. It has an international association, the International Peace Research Association, sponsored by UNESCO. There is a private, but very lively international association, the Peace Science Society (International), founded and guided through the years by Professor Walter Isard of the University of Pennsylvania. In North America we have had a Consortium on Peace Research, Education and Development for eight years, which holds annual meetings, puts out a newsletter, and has a variety of other activities. There is no doubt, therefore, that conflict and peace studies has arrived as a discipline and that it is likely to continue to be one.

The name "conflict and peace studies" expresses a certain dilemma which I think has been present in the discipline from the very beginning. A discipline centered around conflict makes a good deal of sense, for conflict is a virtually universal phenomenon in all social and indeed some biological systems. Patterns of conflict have some similarity in many different situations, whether within the family, within the organization, in industrial relations, in the church, in science, between nations, and even within the personality itself. A discipline which abstracted the study of conflict from the general field of social systems, therefore, would seem to make as much sense as, say, economics, which abstracts the idea of exchange and exchange-ables from the general field of social systems. The French and the Dutch indeed have given this discipline the name of "polemologie."

One could perfectly well suppose a discipline of polemology as a positive science studying conflict in all its aspects, which had no normative implications. Peace research, however, has always been normative, in the sense that it has been practised by people who are deeply conscious of the pathologies of conflict and who want to make it as cheap and productive as possible. I always wanted to call this aspect of the subject "irenics," but the name never caught on. The expression "conflict resolution," however, was invented by Professor Robert Angell and myself to describe both the positive aspects of the discipline as it studied conflict, but also a certain normative interest for the resolution of conflict. In the light of hindsight I think perhaps we should have called the "Journal", the *Journal of Conflict Management*, as I think frequently conflicts are not, and perhaps should not be, resolved, but should be managed, at least to maximize the total gain to both parties, no matter what the distributional outcome. Conflict management is to polemology then somewhat as welfare economics is to positive economics. It is an attempt to derive what might almost be called a "minimal normativeness." Peace and conflict studies then would include both polemology as a positive discipline and conflict management as a normative discipline, very much as economics also includes both positive and normative aspects.

In regard to polemology one can make a good case that the last 25 years or so have seen important contributions and the development of something like an integrated body of theory, even though some of this was developed outside the peace research movement proper. There is, first, Quincy Wright's[1] identification of war and peace as a segment of the long historic process of the human race, so beginning the systematic descriptive study of this segment. Then we get Lewis F. Richardson's[2] theoretical and mathematical models of arms races, and of war moods as dynamic interactive processes; arms races being very much like the theory of discontinuities and systems involving sudden shifts, like icebergs overturning. Richardson's theory of war moods, as a matter of act, is a precursor of catastrophe theory, which has aroused so much interest in recent years. Richardson also pioneered in statistical analysis of historical data in *Statistics of Deadly Quarrels*.[3] His pioneering work received very little attention at the time when it was written, and indeed was not fully published until a whole generation after it was written. It was reading Richardson in microfilm, however, at the Center for Advanced Study in the Behavioral Sciences at Stanford in 1954–5, that awakened my own interest in conflict and peace theory. It would be interesting indeed to see how many of the "founding fathers" of the peace research movement had read Richardson in microfilm!

The next great contribution to conflict theory was, of course, game theory, coming ironically enough from two of the most hawkish, if also the most brilliant, intellectuals of their day, von Neumann and Morgenstern.[4] Game theory did for conflict theory what the marginal analysis did for economics. Indeed in many ways it was an extension of microeconomic theory, and it is certainly no accident that Morgenstern was a distinguished economist. Zero-sum and *n*-person game theory, on which the early work concentrated, turned out to be more interesting than useful; zero-sum games are actually very rare in practice. Positive-sum game theory, as developed for instance by Rapoport and his associates[5] and many followers, has not only been of great interest theoretically but has also been a remarkable field of empirical research, which has illuminated many of the actual processes of conflictual interaction.

Other insights about conflict processes have also come out of social psychology, particularly in regard to conflict processes in groups. The work of Sherif[6] and of Kelman[7] is of particular interest in this regard. The work in social psychology has been translated dramatically into actual proposals, or at least a scheme for making proposals, by Professor Charles Osgood, with his idea of graduated, reciprocated international tension-reduction (GRIT), a principle of course which would apply far beyond the international order. There are at least some signs that this idea played a modest role in the development of the detente between the United States and the Soviet Union, though whether the people who made the policy had read the research is a matter of considerable doubt.

I have a strong impression that the last ten years or so in conflict and peace research have been one of consolidation and what Kuhn calls "normal science" in the United States, without any striking new ideas or new lines of development, whereas in Europe the whole peace research enterprise has been diverted along ideological lines, which impress me as having been very unfruitful. This development had a number of origins, some more legitimate than others. Opposition to the United States war in Vietnam united two groups of people of very different motivations, those who were primarily interested in peace and conflict resolution as such and those who were primarily interested in the victory of communism. Somewhere in between there is a group of European peace researchers particularly represented by Johan Galtung of the Oslo Peace Research Institute, a man of great brilliance and energy, and the unquestioned leader of the European peace research community.

Galtung is very legitimately interested in problems of world poverty and the failure of development of the really poor. He tried to amalgamate this interest with the peace research interest in the more narrow sense. Unfortunately, he did this by downgrading the study of international peace, labeling it "negative peace" (it should really have been labeled "negative war") and then developing the concept of "structual violence," which initially meant all those social structures and histories which produced an expectation of life less than that of the richest and longest-lived societies. He argued by analogy that if people died before the age, say, of 70 from avoidable causes, that this was a death in "war" which could only be remedied by something called "positive peace." Unfortunately, the concept of structural violence was broadened, in the word of one slightly unfriendly critic, to include anything that Galtung did not like. Another factor in this situation was the feeling, certainly in the 1960s and early 1970s, that nuclear deterrence was actually succeeding as deterrence and that the problem of nuclear war had receded into the background. This it seems to me is a most dangerous illusion and diverted conflict and peace research for ten years or more away from problems of disarmament and stable peace toward a grand, vague study of world developments, for which most of the peace researchers are not particularly well qualified. To my mind, at least, the quality of the research has suffered severely as a result.

The complex nature of the split within the peace research community is reflected in two international peace research organizations. The official one, the International Peace Research Association (IPRA), tends to be dominated by Europeans somewhat to the political left, is rather hostile to the United States and to the multinational corporations, sympathetic to the New International Economic Order and thinks of itself as being interested in justice rather than in peace. The Peace Science Society (International), which used to be called the Peace Research Society (International), is mainly the creation of Walter Isard of the University of Pennsylvania. It conducts meetings all around the world and represents a more peace-oriented, quantitative, science-based enterprise, without much interest in ideology; COPRED, while officially the North American representative of IPRA, has very little active connection with it and contains within itself the same ideological split which divides the peace research community in general. It has, however, been able to hold together and at least promote a certain amount of interaction between the two points of view.

Again representing the "scientific" rather than the "ideological" point of view, we have SIPRI, the Stockholm International Peace Research Institute, very generously (by the usual peace research standards) financed by the Swedish government, which has performed an enormously useful service in the collection and publishing of data on such things as the war industry, technological developments, armaments, and the arms trade. The Institute is very largely the creation of Alva Myrdal. In spite of the remarkable work which it has done, however, her last book on disarmament[8] is almost a cry of despair over the folly and hypocrisy of international policies, the overwhelming power of the military, and the inability of mere information, however good, to change the course of events as we head toward ultimate catastrophe. I do not wholly share her pessimism, but it is hard not to be a little disappointed with the results of this first generation of the peace research movement.

Myrdal called attention very dramatically to the appalling danger in which Europe stands, as the major battleground between Europe, the United States, and the Soviet Union if war ever should break out. It may perhaps be a subconscious recognition – and psychological denial – of the sword of Damocles hanging over Europe that has made the European peace research movement retreat from the realities of the international system into what I must unkindly describe as fantasies of justice. But the American peace research community, likewise, has retreated into a somewhat niggling scientism, with sophisticated methodologies and not very many new ideas.

I must confess that when I first became involved with the peace research enterprise 25 years ago I had hopes that it might produce something like the Keynesian revolution in economics, which was the result of some rather simple ideas that had never really been thought out clearly before (though they had been anticipated by Malthus and others), coupled with a substantial improvement in the information system with the development of national income statistics which reinforced this new theoretical framework. As a result, we have had in a single generation a very massive change in what might be called the "conventional wisdom" of economic policy, and even though this conventional wisdom is not wholly wise, there is a world of difference between Herbert Hoover and his total failure to deal with the Great Depression, simply because of everybody's ignorance, and the moderately skillful handling of the depression which followed the change in oil prices in 1974, which, compared with the period 1929 to 1932, was little more than a bad cold compared with a galloping pneumonia.

In the international system, however, there has been only glacial change in the conventional wisdom. There has been some improvement. Kissinger was an improvement on John Foster Dulles. We have had the beginnings of detente, and at least the possibility on the horizon of stable peace between the United States and the Soviet Union, indeed in the whole temperate zone – even though the tropics still remain uneasy and beset with arms races, wars, and revolutions which we cannot really afford. Nor can we pretend that peace around the temperate zone is stable enough so that we do not have to worry about it. The qualitative arms race goes on and could easily take us over the cliff. The record of peace research in the last generation, therefore, is one of very partial success. It has created a discipline and that is something of long-run consequence, most certainly for the good. It has made very little dent on the conventional wisdom of the policy makers anywhere in the world. It has not been able to prevent an arms race, any more, I suppose we might say, than the Keynesian economics has been able to prevent inflation. But whereas inflation is an inconvenience, the arms race may well be another catastrophe.

Where, then, do we go from here? Can we see new horizons for peace and conflict research to get it out of the doldrums in which it has been now for almost ten years? The challenge is surely great enough. It still remains true that war, the breakdown of Galtung's "negative peace," remains the greatest clear and present danger to the human race, a danger to human survival far greater than poverty, or injustice, or oppression, desirable and necessary as it is to eliminate these things.

Up to the present generation, war has been a cost and an inconvenience to the human race, but it has rarely been fatal to the process of evolutionary development as a whole. It has probably not absorbed more than 5 per cent of the human time, effort, and resources. Even in the twentieth century, with its two world wars and innumerable smaller ones, it has probably not accounted for more than 5 per cent of deaths, though of course a larger proportion of premature deaths. Now, however, advancing technology is creating a situation where in the first place we are developing a single world system that does not have the redundancy of the many isolated systems of the past and in which therefore if anything goes wrong everything goes wrong. The Mayan civilization could collapse in 900 AD, and collapse almost irretrievably without Europe or China even being aware of the fact. When we had a number of isolated systems, the catastrophe in one was ultimately recoverable by migration from the surviving systems. The one-world system, there-fore, which science, transportation, and communication are rapidly giving us, is inherently more precarious than the many-world system of the past. It is all the more important, therefore, to make it internally robust and capable only of recoverable catastrophes. The necessity for stable peace, therefore, increases with every improvement in technology, either of war or of peace.

In the light of these desperate necessities, therefore, where do we go from here in the field of conflict and peace research? We must recognize first of all that war is a result of human decisions made in a framework of human institutions. The decisions are a result of the images of the world and the values by which these images are judged on the part of the decision maker. The institutions are very important because they create role structures, play a considerable part in creating the images and the values on which decisions are made, and determine the power distributions in the society. The power to make war is in the hands of very few people, which introduces elements of indeterminacy and instability into the international system, particularly as the institutions for the filling of powerful roles have strong random elements in them and also are subject to perverse processes. I have argued elsewhere indeed that there is a "dismal theorem" of political science, which states that all the skills which lead to a rise to power unfit people to exercise it. Institutions can certainly be devised to offset this principle. But we have thought so little about this problem that we have not even begun to propose solutions.

An area of human behavior which has been very much neglected in conflict and peace studies is that of the development of taboo and its impact on human behavior. We have been so obsessed by what people do that we have neglected to study what they do not do. The study of taboo has been relegated to anthropologists – and even there largely of a previous generation. Indeed, in a world of uncritical liberationism it has been assumed that all taboo is irrational and therefore hardly worth the attention of a serious social scientist. This seems to me to have been a great mistake. Economists have tended to assume that economic behavior is limited only by some possibility boundary, which defines what a person cannot do – that is, which divides those positions in the field of choice which are possible from those that are impossible. In a great many aspects of human behavior, however, there is a taboo line well within the possibility boundary, which divides the field of possible behavior into three regions: the lowest region, things we both can and may do; the next region, separated from the first by the taboo line, which includes all those things we can do physically but which we do not do because of the structure of taboos; this is further separated by the possibility boundary from the third region, those things we cannot do because they are physically impossible. Thus, there are no physical impossibilities about spitting in our neighbor's drink at a cocktail party, but it is a very rare person who does it. The number of people who could get away with murder far exceed those who actually do, and most of them are inhibited not only by the fear of legal sanctions but also by a habit of mind which puts that kind of behavior "beyond the pale," the "pale" of course being precisely the taboo line.

These concepts are of great importance in the study of the international system and indeed of all conflict systems. Insofar as these systems exhibit two phases, war and peace – often with quite sudden transitions from one to the other – the transition from peace into war is characterized by a sudden outward shift of the taboo line, so that many things which are taboo in peace are not taboo in war. Similarly, the transition from war to peace represents an inward shift of the taboo line. After peace is declared, many things which are not taboo before now become taboo. The peace research community has paid remarkably little attention to this phenomenon, perhaps first because the more scientific section of it has tended to be obsessed by continuities and has failed to devise a theoretical apparatus which could handle the fundamental discontinuities of the peace–war system. These problems have perhaps been neglected by the radical wing of the movement because they have been obsessed by liberation and have regarded taboo as something always irrational and to be destroyed.

Concern with this problem indeed is much older than the conflict and peace studies enterprise of the last generation. It goes back to a discussion of the just war from St Augustine on, which is very closely related to the question as to what should be taboo and what should not. In the last generation, however, the study of taboo has been singularly neglected, and it is surely time for a revival of it. We understand very little about how taboos are generated, how they are eliminated, and the critique of taboo – that is, the study of what taboos are rational and lead to human betterment, and what taboos are irrational and unnecessary and lead to a worsening of the human condition – has still hardly been born in the modern world.

Very closely related to the problem of taboo is people's concept of their own identity. Large numbers of people refrain from stealing even when they have the opportunity and they could get away with it without sanctions, because their own image of their identity does not include the identity of a thief. Similarly, the image of identity of a pacifist does not include the identity of a soldier or other member of the armed forces. Under stress, of course, and under erosion these identities can change. Yet we know very little about how they change and what are the institutional environments under which they change. Conversion is another aspect of the process, in which a person takes on a different identity and therefore a different set of taboos. The interactions between the self-image of identity of the powerful and of leaders with that of the powerless and the led is also a problem of great importance that has been studied very little. Sometimes a change in the image of identity of the leaders produces a widespread change in the image of identity of the led. Sometimes the reverse happens and the movement of identity change among the led eventually produces a change in the leaders. But we understand the nature of these processes very little.

Another problem which is highly relevant to the study of conflict but which has received very little attention is the study of "interests" – that is, of the impact of particular policies or decisions or frames of reference on the distribution of human welfare among individuals and groups, whether as "perceived" welfare or in some sense "objective" welfare. This problem is highly relevant to conflict theory because conflict is frequently visualized as an organized attempt to change the distribution of welfare. It was in the second issue of this journal that Jessie Bernard[9] made the distinction between "issue conflict," which is about something (presumably that something being a redistribution of welfare) and "no-issue conflict," which is irrational in the sense that it results from the interaction of the parties and results in a diminution of aggregate welfare, with its distribution being determined by largely random factors. Psychologists have rather tended to see conflict in terms of this irrational dynamic. Radicals – and especially, of course, Marxists – have tended to see conflict almost exclusively as "issue conflict" with great importance attached to who wins.

Not very much solid research has been done on the dynamic principles that underlie changes in the distribution either of power or of human welfare. This is perhaps one of the greatest gaps, not only in social sciences generally, but it is a gap of particular importance to the study of conflict. One could almost identify two poles of conflict theorists: theorists at the one pole interpret all human behavior in terms of interests, which they regard as something essentially simple and easy to discover and well-known by everybody, and regard such things as affect, emotions, identities, identifications, and so on both as deep mysteries and essentially peripheral to the ongoing dynamics of the system. At the other pole we have those, among whom I find myself, who regard interests as a deep mystery simply because of the vast ecological complexity of the total system, which means that pressure applied at one point will produce often completely unexpected and counter-intuitive effects elsewhere. Even if people knew what their interest was, they would find it extremely difficult to act on it, so that the actual dynamics and changes in the distribution, both of power and of human welfare, are the result of vast misunderstandings and delusions about the actual effects of particular actions, and very little the result of rational choice.

Another profound difficulty cannot, however, be brushed aside when we attempt to distinguish between perceived welfare and some concept of "actual" welfare. Perceived welfare we can at least ask people about. Most people have at least some idea, for instance, as to whether they are worse off or better off than they were last year. On the other hand, we cannot rule out the proposition that people's perceptions of their own welfare may be in some sense illusory, though if we are to define this illusion we must have some standard by which perceived welfare can be compared with some more objective indicator. Economists, of course, have indicators like real income, which is certainly not meaningless for large variations, although it excludes many things which can legitimately be regarded as a part of total welfare. Marxists have always had a strong belief that welfare is in some sense objective, not subjective, although they have never been very clear as to how it should be measured. Whatever these objective measures, there are also subjective, reevaluations of the perceived welfare of the past, or of the perceived welfare of others. Statements of the type: "I thought I was well off last year, but in the face of my values I see I was not as well off as I thought I was," or "A thinks he is well off but I think he is deceiving himself," are by no means meaningless, and can certainly be investigated.

As economists know, even a concept like real income is very shaky, especially when compared over long periods because of change in the commodity mix and of assessing alternatives in terms of constant prices. What, for instance, was the value of a color television set in 1920? With all the severity of the measurement problems, however, we are convinced that human welfare means something and that its distribution means something and that it should be possible to study the changes in these things, even though it may be hard to associate them unequivocally with particular decisions and policies in the light of the famous ecological principle that everything depends on everything else. So great is our ignorance in this field that I have formulated a proposition which I call the "law of political irony," that almost everything we do to help people hurts them and almost everything we do to hurt people helps them. One can at least find a number of examples of this principle. How universal it is would be a magnificient field for research.

It is something of an open question, however, as to whether improved knowledge in this field would increase or diminish the intensity or even the cost of conflict. Suppose, for instance that we were able to make a "distributional impact statement" about every law, regulation, decision or historical event, stating who was injured, who was benefited, and who was unaffected, with some suggestion as to how much. This would divide the world into what I call "interest classes." Even if we could only identify five interest classes altogether (1) all those people who are benefited a lot; (2) all those people who are benefited a little; (3) all those people who are not affected much either way; (4) all those people who are injured a little; (5) all those people who are injured a lot, we would have some very important information which would substantially affect the perceptions of the world on the part of conflicting parties. If there is widespread information, for instance, to the effect that winning a war injures the winner and that losing a war benefits the loser, this might play havoc with culture of the military, who always have to assume that winning a war will benefit the people on behalf of whom they think they are fighting. If we find on the whole that radicals injure the poor and conservatives benefit them, which is at least a researchable proposition, the impact on political ideologies might be very severe. It may be that these problems are too difficult for research with the tools that we now have. But it may be better to do bad research on important problems than good research on unimportant ones.

Perhaps the highest priority of the conflict and peace studies discipline in the future is to rewaken concern with peace policy. Peace and war are still too much regarded, both in the circles of the powerful and in those of the people, as a random element almost like the weather. Even in the Great Depression, however, economists talked about "economic blizzards," as if unemployment too were something like a bad hailstorm. In the international system the situation is even worse than that, for our preparations against bad weather do not usually bring it on, though in these days of cloud seeding one is not quite so sure. Umbrellas and raincoats are perfect examples of wholly defensive weapons which diminish the impact of bad weather but do nothing either to produce it or to make it cease. In the international system, however, our nuclear umbrellas and our organizations of defense actually increase the probability that the bad weather of war will occur. It is as if our umbrellas brought down the lightning upon us.

No government at the moment has anything remotely resembling a policy for peace. All of them have a policy of defense, but that is something quite different. If the peace research community would devote a major effort to inquiring as to what a policy for peace, even on the part of a single government, would look like, and what world institutions would make it more probable, we might be able to lift ourselves out of this slough of sterility and impotence into which we seem to have fallen.

NOTES AND REFERENCES

1. Q. Wright, *A Study of War* (Chicago: University of Chicago Press, 1942).
2. L. F. Richardson, *Arms and Insecurity: A Mathematical Study of Causes and Origins of War* (Chicago: Quadrangle Books, 1960).
3. L. F. Richardson, *Statistics of Deadly Quarrels* (Pittsburgh: Boxwood Press, 1960).
4. J. von Neumann and O. Morganstern, *The Theory of Games and Economic Behavior* (Princeton: Princeton University Press, 1944).
5. A. Rapoport and A. Chammah, *Prisoner's Dilemma: A Study in Conflict and Cooperation* (Ann Arbor: University of Michigan Press, 1965).
6. M. Sherif, *In Common Predicament: Social Psychology of Inter-group Conflict and Cooperation* (Boston: Houghton Mifflin, 1966).
7. H. C. Kelman (ed.), *International Behavior* (New York: Holt, Rinehart & Winston, 1970).
8. A. Myrdal, *The Game of Disarmament: How the United States and Russia Run the Arms Race* (New York: Pantheon, 1976).
9. J. Bernard, "Parties and Issues in Conflict," *Journal of Conflict Resolution*, 1 (1957): 111–21.

II
Crisis

Chapter 3   The International Relations Discipline: Asset or   51
             Liability for Conflict Resolution?
             Michael Banks
Chapter 4   Paradigms in Conflict: the Strategist, the Conflict   71
             Researcher and the Peace Researcher
             A. J. R. Groom

3 The International Relations Discipline: Asset or Liability for Conflict Resolution?
Michael Banks*

This chapter seeks to place the growing discipline of international conflict resolution in the wider context of international relations theory.

There are two themes that I wish to put forward. First, I am convinced that there is a pattern in the development of international relations thinking and research. It has culminated in what I shall call pluralist thinking. This involves very considerable shifts of attitude by comparison with ten, twenty, or fifty years ago in the study of international relations. If we consider international relations as a whole – as a body of thought over the centuries, as a collection of research findings, as a conventional wisdom, as a set of disciplined propositions about the world and the way it works – then we find that a message is waiting for us. It is a distinctive message about behavior in the world, and *ipso factor*, about how to approach and analyze conflict.

The second theme is that there is a developing gap between theory and practice. The discipline is emerging as a critique, a sort of alternative international politics to that which actually goes on in the real world. There is a disjunction between what the academics say and what the practitioners are doing. This presents questions for us. How clear-cut is what we have to say? How useful is it? How practicable is it? How solid is it? Are we speaking in ideologies? Are we just presumptuous social scientists meddling in the real world to express our own values? Or are we actually implementing ideas which have in fact a firm intellectual basis?

If we ask the question, "What is the relationship between theory

---

* From E. Azar and J. Burton (eds), *International Conflict Resolution: Theory and Practice* (Brighton, England: Wheatsheaf, 1986).

and practice?", then there ought to be three possible answers, or at least two clear-cut answers plus one complex one.

One possible answer to the question is that practice dominates theory. On this view, the job of the academic is to be passive: to record what the practitioners do in the real world. We are basically archivists: we inductively store and retrieve, in some sort of ordered form, a record of the actions of decision makers. If we believe that practice dominates theory our job is to note what goes on, then sort it into patterns and when an inquiry is made to stand ready to report and explain what has been happening in the world. That is a positivist view of the relationship between theory and practice. It is objectivist. It is empiricist. It is, I think, a comfortable position – as long as one does not think too deeply about what the implications of it are, because it is based on a questionable assumption. That assumption is that it is possible to paint an accurate picture of reality, avoiding all wishful thinking and prejudice, simply by being a bystander who tracks down what has been happening, takes note of it, and imposes order on the data.

The reverse position in answer to the question "What is the relationship between theory and practice?" is that theory is more important than reality. Now, unlike the objectivist–positivist position which is popular in the United States, this position has a long tradition in Europe. It is very widely held there now. It is certainly much more influential in Britain today than it was twenty years ago. The argument here is simply that men make their own history, and that they do this on the basis of ideas and passions: their ideologies, their values, their belief systems, the theories they hold about cause and effect. People in politics are trying to teach each other lessons all the time on the basis of their own commitment and understanding, within general world views, of current issues in politics and society.

Now, doing research on that assumption is very different from the positivist position because it is subjectivist. We are not studying what people do. We are, instead, studying what people *think* they are doing. That, of course, is much more difficult. It creates a far more activist role for the academic because the focus is on ideas rather than institutions and policies. The creation of ideas is, of course intellectual activity. It belongs, therefore, in the domain of the academic and of the thinker. It means that we cannot stand back and be dispassionate archive keepers, because we are participants. We are all in politics, and that means that all disciplines are to some degree themselves political. They are a part of the world that we live in. They helped to create it, and now sustain it. As scholars in international relations, we are all contributors to the ongoing formation of politics in the world. That is a very extreme position, of course, one that is sometimes known as the structuralist position.

Both those positions, that practice dominates theory, and that theory dominates practice, should be treated as ideologies. They are extreme positions, and most middle-of-the-road academics take a compromise position: one that is less self-assured. They say: on the one hand, we cannot be whole-hearted positivists because there are lots of well-known problems in that position. We have to modify it a bit. On the other hand, we cannot be wholehearted subjectivists either, because we are forced to recognize that there is a real world out there. There are decision makers, and military–industrial complexes, and jingoistic nationalism, and powerful economic forces. The crises are happening and we need to know about them. So what we must conclude on the theory-versus-practice question is that a moderate position is inevitable, rather than one of the two extreme positions.

This conclusion sets the context for an activist approach to work in conflict resolution. There is indeed an international relations system out there, and its institutions and organizations are real enough. But the real world is also made up of habits and practices and theories of how it all works. The theories are, to some degree, self-fulfilling and self-perpetuating. They help to create the reality that we have to deal with. We do need to recognize that the existing system is shaped and conditioned by ideas. As writers and teachers, we may not be responsible for making policy, but we are most certainly responsible for creating and maintaining the climate of opinion within which policy is made.

The lesson to be drawn from looking at the theory–reality relationship is that this real world of ours is not inexorable. If it was made by people, it can in principle be remade by people. The moral for conflict resolution as an intellectual movement is that we are in the business of reformist interventionism. We need to inject ideas into the international political system and its subsystems in order to unmake and replace some of the institutions, habits and practices which our own ancestors and predecessors have helped to instill and to reinforce in the real world. Not just in practical terms, but intellectually as well, there is an opening here. There is an ecological niche for conflict analysts, if we can take possession of it and use it in a way that is academically sound and socially responsible. Our

values are those which we set for ourselves and which we are prepared
to defend by reference to our knowledge of human aspirations and
behavior.

This means that we can take a semi-optimistic position. International politics presents a truly awful set of facts. Studying it is like
working in the pathology department of a hospital. The positivist
position, for that reason, is fatalistic and depressing – recording
mainly horrid events. The structuralist position, in contrast, is unduly
optimistic because its exponents have their own Utopia which they
try to force upon everyone else. We cannot be either that optimistic,
or that arrogant, but we can be semi-optimistic. There are opportunities for us to act. Put that way, the argument sounds modest and
bland. When we look at its implications, however, in relation to the
recent history and development of international relations theory, we
find that it is actually bold and dramatic.

I want to turn now to the history of ideas in international relations,
in order to show that a description of the situation we now find
ourselves in requires a strong vocabulary. It includes the words
contradiction, anomaly, crisis and paradigm shift. We are in a
changing discipline, and today I am more confident about what
scholars have to say than I have ever been before.

I would argue, when looking back over the history of thought in
international relations, that our discipline, in our century, has
undergone a lengthy flirtation with empiricism. Empirical work has
succeeded. It has produced findings, and explanations of a sort, and
even intuitive insights. But these very successes are forcing us away
from empiricism. Having passed through a phase in which facts have
dominated theory, the logic of our scholarship is carrying us into a
phase in which theory dominates facts. In this new situation, we have
not just an opportunity but an obligation to criticize and to prescribe.
At the same time, we need to accept fully the moral and political
responsibility that we could safely, in the past, deny as long as we
claimed "scientific objectivity" for every statement.

To justify this argument, I must survey the evolution of thought in
the field. There have been three so-called "great debates" which
have arisen during the history of the discipline. First, there is the
realist v. idealist debate that has permeated the last four centuries.
Second, there was the brief behavioralist–traditionalist debate of the
1950s and 1960s. Third, there is the inter-paradigm debate of the
recent past, the 1970s and 1980s. To refer to these is simply a way of
organizing the material chronologically. When one looks back at all

that has ever been written and said, about international relations and how the system works, it becomes apparent that these three debates encapsulate the major issues. I consider each of them in turn and then review the present situation of the discipline.

The debate between the realists and idealists is classical in the sense that it goes all the way back to the medieval diplomats and religious theorists. It goes back to the Westphalia Settlement of 1648 which formalized the institution of sovereignty and formulated the state system as a set of ideas.[1] It goes back to the notion that there are governments which have total control over their peoples, but must do business with each other even while each retains separate responsibility for security in a system that has no world authority. It goes back to the cynical relationships of the great dynasts of the seventeenth and eighteenth centuries in Europe. They created the world of power politics and its associated theory that has been so important ever since. The realist–idealist debate goes back also to the Natural Law tradition: to the philosophers of the middle ages and the seventeenth century who created the ideas which lie behind our present thinking about such issues as just war, human rights, humanitarian intervention, justice and decent conduct between groups of civilized people.

These philosophers, thinkers, lawyers, practitioners, and proto-scholars produced fundamental theories and doctrines about international politics which remain important today. In particular they made three observations which have conditioned our understanding down to the present time.

First, they noted that we live in a condition of international anarchy: there is no world government. This creates conflict between states, because states are in a competitive position. They then spun out elaborate theories about what this circumstance implied for the conduct of foreign policy.

But second, they noticed that we also live in a world of cooperation and law. This is so, not because of any inherent altruism in human nature, but because of the doctrine of sovereignty. Sovereignty is a claim: "This is mine." To make any claim in society is to concede a reciprocal obligation. In practice this results in a network of rights and obligations, expressed in law. Effectively, it creates a worldwide community of sovereign states. The community is limited, but its implications for the interpretation and practice of politics are far reaching.[2]

Third, the classic writers noted that states were not the only politically significant features of the world. There was also a latent unity of mankind even though it was both subjugated by the sovereigns and split apart by the state system.

Out of those three observations, three schools of thought and three quite distinct traditions of thinking about international politics grew into existence. The first contained thinkers who believed that the anarchy was what mattered. In their view, from the competition between states everything we needed to know of importance about international politics was observable. These were the people we know as "realists." The second group, by contrast, emphasized inter-state community. They stressed the enforced, reciprocal set of obligations between states: the cooperative relationships. These were the people who came to be known as liberals or "idealists." Third, there were the people who emphasized global unity. For them, shared humanity, however interpreted, counted for more than the integrity of the states. These included the people who became truly creative thinkers, revolutionary thinkers, radical thinkers: people like Karl Marx who thought about social class, people like Immanuel Kant who contemplated the destiny of the human spirit and its implications for politics, and many others.

The scholarly community is still divided among these three attitudes, and most of us find a home in one of them. Of the exchanges between them, the realist–idealist debate is the most significant because it gave us structures and institutions which still operate. It also endowed us with a durable vocabulary, some of which has become extremely damaging. Such notions as reason of state, balance of power, and national security dominate our thinking and cripple our creativity.

It is unfortunate that we seem to have retained the worst of the realist–idealist argument and lost the best part of it. The main division between the schools of thought reduced itself, in essence, to sterile argument about whether human beings are naturally conflictual or competitive. We may never know that, and certainly we do not know it now. All that we can observe is that in practice people exhibit both tendencies. The proper focus for the debate is, therefore, the conditions under which people are conflictual or competitive. Modern social science has sought this understanding which, I suggest, transcends the traditional discourse, and can give us some assistance in our task of looking at conflict resolution.

The best part of the old debates was the rich set of insights produced by the balanced nature of the exchange between the liberals on the one hand, and the realists on the other. The liberals insisted upon a full consideration of norms, values, morality, ideology, reform, law, progress and peaceful change, along with all of the concepts and proposals put forward by the realists. But this entire set of liberal–progressive–idealist ideas has been neglected in our own time.

In the years between World War I and World War II, there was a brief period in which the liberals, or Utopians as they were often (wrongly) called at the time, dominated thinking as a result of reaction to the disaster of World War I. The Great War had called into question the old mechanisms of international politics: alliances, arms races, secret treaties, and the closed diplomacy of the old elites. Theories of stable equilibrium, crisis management and great power hegemony went out of fashion.

A similar pattern, but reversed, occurred in the aftermath of World War II. That war destroyed faith in all the liberal analyses and prescriptions.

Our task now is to redress the balance. But constructive ideas in our time will need to have a more secure foundation than those which were so much discussed and to some extent implemented in the 1920s and 1930s: collective security, open diplomacy, majority voting, economic sanctions, intellectual cooperation, and all the rest. It was too easy for those fragile institutions to be discredited by Hitler, the Japanese military and the Italian Fascists. When we look back over this meandering river of thought which has been so heavily influenced by real world events, particularly the dramatic events of major wars, we can see the risks involved in the changing fashions. John Burton's *Dear Survivors*[3] now suggests that only the prospect of another traumatic event – nuclear war – might enable us to accept a really progressive theory and, therefore, improve the practice of international relations.

The controlling ideas today are a legacy of the 1940s and of the 1950s, when we switched completely from liberalism to realism. That period was an intellectual disaster zone. If we look back at those Cold War decades and examine the way international relations was studied then, especially in Britain and in the United States, three particularly distressing features of it stand out; it was a period of realist dominance, without any liberal balance, and without the refreshment of radical thinking.

If we spell that out specifically, we can see what happened. Consider the intellectual capacity of realism to explain the world, to predict it and to provide prescriptions that would enable decision makers to control it and to deal with problems. Individually, scholars knew that capacity to be well short of 100 per cent. But collectively, we allowed the policy-relevant utility of realism to be overrated and distorted. There was no full-scale criticism of it from a liberal perspective. There were no major liberal spokesmen. There were no influential books written by liberals, idealists, Utopians, reformists, progressives. The discipline had become intellectually totalitarian, dominated by one school of thought.

In addition, realist theory became intermixed with superpower ideology. Much of the work in international relations was a vested interest of those who advised the foreign policy establishments of the great powers, particularly in the United States. The comments of Stanley Hoffman[4] on this matter are interesting and powerful. Many scholars began to see it as their job to give advice to government on how to maximize the values that represented American interests in world politics: international order and stability, alliance cohesion, counter-insurgency, the effective use of military force and all the rest. These became major concerns in the discipline, but they are not explanatory theories of how the world as a whole works; they are merely the perceived policy needs of one status quo actor in a dynamic and complicated system.

Furthermore, conformism meant that we lost the stimulus of the revolutionists, the people who saw visions of what might be in world politics, the thinkers who were so subversive of orthodoxy in previous centuries. Consider the sheer quality of some of the old radical thinking. We had the integration theory of such people as David Mitrany in the inter-war period. We had the great classical works of Schumpeter and Hobson, Marx and Lenin, Mill and many others on social structure, class systems, imperialism and foreign policy. We had the work of Rousseau and of Kant on the nature of peace, or their more gentle equivalent in St Pierre and the Quaker/pacifist tradition. We had the medieval just-war theologians, pondering moral obligation, decency and civilized conduct.

All these were ignored in the 1950s and 1960s. Instead we put our minds to supposedly key questions such as, "Are we more safe in a bipolar world or a multipolar world?" We studied escalation in nuclear warfare. We analyzed all the things that were wrong with the United States, and why individual persons could not be subjects of international law. Our training was in a field that had lost the humanism and breadth of the classic writers in international relations.

It had instead become narrow and, in a real ideological sense, self-serving – a travesty of the great tradition of international relations.

I come now to something more technical, the second of the great debates, traditionalism v. behavioralism. This occurred in the 1950s and 1960s, mainly in the United States, but also in Western Europe. It consisted of an attempt by a "Young Turk" movement to make international relations more scientific, more professional, more effective. It resulted initially from the appearance of younger scholars in the discipline who were true professionals, the first generation to be trained in it. There was also a powerful impact from the behavioral movement in other branches of social science. The new arguments were not concerned with values and policy implications, as the realist–idealist debate had been. They were concerned with methods, with proof, testing, with the structure of theories, and with the quality of explanations that could be regarded as satisfactory in international relations.

This second "great debate" produced a great deal of contention. There was a very sharp division in the field from the 1950s to the 1970s. Despite protests from the traditional side, there was a wave of scientific research inspired by the vision of positivism that I referred to earlier. There was energetic use of quantification, systematic data gathering, computer work and simulation. Elaborate new theories were put forward, stimulated by vigorous interdisciplinary activity that introduced new concepts and analytic frameworks. The whole would-be revolution created extravagant hopes: we could have a positive value-free science. We could have a unified social science in which the entrenched distinction between international relations and domestic politics would disappear.

Today that second great debate is over. Through the corrective lenses of the post-behavioral period, we can see that behavioralism was at its peak about twenty years ago. It was not a failure, but its success was very functionally specific. It was a genuine debate, clearly, because it clarified important issues. It taught us things that we had never considered before, things that we needed to know about methodology and research techniques. It introduced novel categories of analysis in international relations – perception, system, decision – and for those alone, I suggest, it can fairly be called a revolution.

But it was not the most important of the historic debates in the field. As time goes by, it seems rather less important, even undesirable, because it diverted the central focus of the discipline. That focus should be on general theory: on how to build a constructive vision of the world as a whole and the way in which it all fits together. Consider for a moment the decades of the 1950s, 1960s and 1970s and recall what students read in their textbooks, what professors said in their lectures, and what we all thought we knew about the world in each period.

In the 1950s we all *knew* what the world was like. We talked in a confident way about international politics and how to interpret conflict and other things within that framework. We had our nice solid theory of power politics and sovereignty, summarized in Morgenthau's famous text.[5] We thought that in a very broad way, we could predict events and understand them. Then came the behavioral revolution. Its immediate effect was that we dropped that general theory and, in the 1960s, nothing officially replaced it at all. We all had a creed. We were going to have open minds and a thousand flowers were to bloom. We would look for ideas in psychology and anthropology and biology. We would test everything we said, which meant we had to operationalize our propositions and thus make them specialized and technical.

The result was that instead of having a general view of the world, we had little fractions of ideas which we came to call "islands of theory." The point about islands is that they stand in an ocean, in this case an ocean of ignorance. Although the behavioralist credo of precision, rigor and the systematic use of quantitative data was in itself wholly admirable, it prevented us from making generalized assumptions about the world at large. So, as we moved from the 1960s to the 1970s, beyond the behavioral attack on the old mainstream thinking, we found ourselves with no general theory at all – or at least none that leading scholars would admit to.

That situation was both unfortunate and unreal. It was unfortunate because people in the discipline, recognizing this problem, stopped talking about the world as a whole. Instead, the discipline of the 1970s became one of specialists, diffuse and fragmented. A smaller and smaller proportion of all scholars in the field looked at the grand questions. This meant that their work, excellent though it often was, was conducted in a vacuum. There were numerous technical studies of arms control unenlightened by any deeper consideration of the larger problems of peace, war and security. Area studies burgeoned, producing a rich – but necessarily ephemeral – literature. Multinational companies were subjected to exhaustive analysis, but there was no comparable advance at all in the much more significant and lasting questions of fundamental political economy, involving the basic relationships between economic, political and social processes and their implications for the distribution of wealth and the achievement of security and human welfare. By the mid-1970s, it was very hard to find general theories in international relations at all. One paper[6] captured the mood precisely: "Where Have All the Theories Gone?" In this respect, the effect of the behavioral movement was unfortunate.

Its effect was also unreal. The apparent loss of faith in the general theory of international relations was merely an illusion. It is simply not possible to talk about the world without having a general theory, however tacit or implicit. What really happened in the behavioral revolution was that the preexisting dominant theory, realism, was not abandoned at all. It just went underground. We now have a magnificent study of that period, by John Vasquez, called *The Power of Power Politics*.[7] It is probably the best single product of the whole behavioral revolution, because Vasquez demonstrates beyond doubt that the behavioral "islands" were actually linked to a continent of theory. Quantitative behavioral research was, of course, very fine work. It consisted of laborious, painstaking, Kuhnian normal science.[8] It involved systematic gathering of information, precise specifying of hypotheses, exhaustive testing, careful exclusion of uncontrollable variables and so on. But what the behavioralists did was to use, unconsciously in many cases, the realist paradigm to guide the research. Its achievement was to provide proof that the realist paradigm does not properly either describe or explain the world.

As Vasquez points out, we must now find a general theory that makes sense, fits together, and explains the data better than the realist paradigm did in that very long period of realist domination from E. H. Carr[9] to Morgenthau,[10] in the 1940s and 1950s, and onward to the behavioralists in the 1960s and 1970s. We now know that we need to have a better theory.

The search for a better theory forms the third debate. It was developing in the 1970s, and has become in the 1980s a major focus of attention among those people who take the risk of thinking about the general theory question. The debate is about what Kuhn called paradigms; those who do not like Kuhnian language about the structure of scientific revolutions can simply call them "perspectives," "frameworks," "world views," or "attitudes" towards world politics as a whole. They are emergent rather than fully developed. But they are certainly identifiable and the interchange between the schools of thought is potentially the richest, most promising and exciting that we have ever had in international relations. The three perspectives are: realism, still alive but only, I think, among people who have not read Vasquez and have not yet looked at the implications of his work; structuralism, also known as Marxism or dependency theory; and the world society perspective, or pluralism.

How did they emerge? Realism, as has been explained, has always been a part of the discipline. Structuralism has existed at least since the nineteenth century among the radical fringe, although many people (including some of the world's present leaders) studied in the great universities of the English-speaking world in the 1940s and 1950s without learning anything beyond a caricature of it. But it has been reinvigorated in the 1980s by dependency theory in the Third World, by "world system theory" in the USA,[11] and by the resurgence of Marxist thinking in Britain and Western Europe.

Pluralism, however, is relatively new. It is possible to regard pluralism as a successor, in a direct linear sense, to classical liberalism. But I see it more as the product of the behavioral revolution because it is based on empirical findings produced in that very solid period of critical scholarship and quantification in the discipline. The findings consist of things that scholars have observed in the world, technical findings from technical studies which do not fit realism and cannot be explained by the old paradigm.

Thomas Kuhn, in his study of the structure of scientific revolutions, has the right word for these vitally significant observations. He calls them "anomalies," a term which aptly suggests the problems which are raised when something happens that does not fit a body of agreed propositions. An anomaly is inexplicable. Faced with it, one must either ignore it or change one's most fundamental assumptions. International relations today has, as we are only now beginning to realize, an unacceptable quantity of significant anomalies. Vasquez[12] lists a large number of them, Burton's work has long been concerned with them,[13] and there are useful overviews in two recent collections of papers, one edited by Maghroori and Ramberg[14] and introduced by James Rosenau, and the other a set of essays in honor of John Burton.[15]

The most perceptive scholars in the field, naturally, have been aware of anomalies for many years. Consider, for example, the work of Arnold Wolfers, the distinguished Swiss realist who taught at Yale. As far back as 1951, he mused upon the odd fact that intelligent, well-informed people can take such diametrically opposed positions as the liberals and the realists persistently do take on the question of the-state-as-actor. Was there, he asked, "some unexplored terrain lying beyond their controversy?"[16] For him, it was right to treat states as "billiard balls" – hard objects bouncing off one another on a smooth surface – because that conveniently simple assumption permits us to build plausible-looking theories. But what if states are not billiard balls? We can now see that Wolfers had the insight of a prophet, despite the fact that he himself had nothing further to add. It was left for others to enter the unexplored terrain, and different scholars have attempted it in different ways.

Initially, many of us thought that the most far-reaching benefits to be gained from exploring the Wolfers anomaly would be produced through foreign policy analysis. Like many of my peers, I was greatly encouraged by the appearance, in 1954, of the celebrated Princeton research paper on the decision-making framework.[17] The new sub-field, rapidly developed by a swelling coterie of researchers, raised a whole series of pertinent questions. What do we find if we open up the billiard ball and inquire how foreign policy is made within the state? Does the concept of national interest still have a role to play? How do perceptions fit in? In what way do domestic politics and foreign policies interact?

An impressive body of work followed, and as we look back at it from the perspective of 1984, there is genuine cause for disciplinary pride because we now know some of the answers. We know that states are not particularly rational actors, but are better thought of as creatures of habit that learn slowly.[18] We know that the external postures of states are heavily influenced, to say the very least, by the internal machinations of bureaucratic politics.[19] We know that subjective attitudes and false perceptions play a major role.[20] Above all, we know how complex and varied states can be in their behavior.[21] The entire picture carries the message for us that states are anything but unitary rational actors in the way that realism requires them to be. On the basis of foreign policy analysis, one of the central pillars of the realist paradigm has come tumbling down.

But also we know that foreign policy analysis cannot itself provide a better theory. Little work of significance has been conducted in that subfield in the past decade. Clearly, it has run out of steam. The reason is obvious, and it takes us back to Wolfers: foreign policy analysis is imprisoned by its starting assumption, that states are the principal actors in the international system. Maybe they are, but we cannot explain everything that states do, still less everything else that happens in the world, if our analytic framework concentrates exclusively on the means by which governments reach decisions. We must find some way of including the sources of the pressures that so burden the practitioners of politics, especially those that involve the risk and the activity of violent conflict. We need to allow for actors other than governments, for trans-national processes, for liberation movements, for ethnicity and ideology. In the state-centric perspective of foreign policy analysis, these matters are too easily overlooked.

Exponents of the subfield are coming to recognize that their own past successes are now leading them back toward the need for a wider theoretical framework, as James Rosenau, for example, has noted.[22] There is an echo here, in Rosenau's call for a multi-actor analytic scheme, of J. David Singer's[23] famous recognition of the anomaly known as the "levels of analysis" problem in international relations. As Singer shows so clearly, the state-centric focus of realism, with its primary concern being the explanation of government decisions, could never accommodate insights and theories derived from an exploration of processes at work on non-governmental levels of societal action.

Overall, it would seem that the most productive legacy of our Wolfers anomaly is to be found not in the foreign policy analysis field, but in the much less well-developed efforts of a scattered and uncoordinated group of pioneers to coax the general theory of international relations in a pluralist direction. In place of the billiard ball metaphor, they have substituted the image of the interconnecting cobweb.[24] Instead of the focus on decision makers, they have suggested that we concentrate our attention on the newly presented (or perhaps just newly discovered) interaction patterns of economic interdependence.[25] Rather than continue to assume that security can be achieved only by the threat of force, they have put forward the idea – based on observed evidence – that integration may be an equally effective, perhaps much more effective, means of achieving the same objective.[26] Contrary to the realist doctrine that states are always masters of their own destiny where international law is concerned, they have begun to tabulate and spell out the contemporary existence of international "regimes" involving collaboration and agreed procedures of a kind implicit in the naturalist legal theory written by Grotius 350 years ago.[27] Where the realist paradigm stresses the high politics of elite diplomacy, a few of the most daring pluralist thinkers[28] have begun to trace out the ways in which a participative, almost populist, form of international politics may be both possible and even beginning to happen. So far, all these contributions are piecemeal and incomplete. A full-scale synthesis is needed, perhaps building on the kind of scheme set out in Mansbach and Vasquez's *In Search of Theory*.[29] And given the continuing strength of the competition from the realist and structuralist devotees, there will no doubt be constructive criticism to help the synthesizing task along its way.[30]

An anomaly of a very different kind was set before the discipline in 1966 by Martin Wight, a contemporary of Arnold Wolfers. "Why," he asked, "is there no international theory?"[31] It was a sad paper. Like virtually all the prominent figures of his generation, both his academic conclusions and his emotional convictions held him firmly in a realist framework, but he fought to escape from it. For him, the word "theory," when applied to society and politics, should properly mean political philosophy. He was no crude empiricist, and he bemoaned the coarseness of international relations theory: it was a body of knowledge concerned with means but not with ends. Power politics, he argued, was merely a theory of survival, not a theory of the good life. Why, he asked, can we not have a coherent political theory of a normative kind of world politics? What about justice, human rights and progress? Why can we not provide navigation points, beacons more constructive in their function than what he called the "casuistry of reason of state,"[32] to help guide the decision makers?

Wight himself could not resolve his anomaly, falling back wearily on what he saw as "the recalcitrance of international politics to being theorized about,"[33] and rejecting the argument that scholars should just go ahead and compose normative theory, with the harsh comment that "it is surely not a good argument for a theory of international politics that we shall be driven to despair if we do not accept it."[34] Luckily for the discipline and indeed for humanity at large, other scholars of the calibre of David Mitrany, John Hobson, Karl Deutsch, Quincy Wright, Richard Falk, Johan Galtung, Kenneth Boulding, Anatol Rapoport and many others have all – in different ways – implicitly recognized and acted upon the Wight anomaly without sharing his gloomy conclusion.

It is clear, then, that we have anomalies in plenty in international relations. Empirically, things have been happening in the real world that are not predicted by our existing theory; normatively, questions are being raised for which the theory has no answers. What can we expect in this situation? Kuhn is helpful on this point.[35] He makes three predictions, based on his analysis of past revolutionary shifts in other fields of study. First, he suggests, anomalies are universally present; all disciplines have some and at all times, but they do not matter as long as they are neither numerous enough, nor significant enough, to undermine general faith in the discipline. Scholars can say: despite these anomalies, we have a useful paradigm, so we are going to carry on with what we are doing. Paradigms, in other words, are tenacious, not so easily shrugged off; they are world views that form part of the identity of the persons that hold them. The stability and persistence of a well-founded theoretical base is, in any case, what makes normal science possible. If progress is to occur, paradigms need to be durable, and generally that is what they are.

Kuhn's second prediction of a discipline's response to the presence of anomaly follows from the first. If anomalies contradict existing assumptions, then mental health requires that the contradictions be accommodated. This is done by rationalization. We "explain away" the irritating and embarrassing observations by all the methods with which we are so uncomfortably familiar: making exceptions, adding qualifications, ridiculing the alleged counter-instance, stretching the fundamental theory without abandoning it.

Take a look, for example, at today's average international relations textbook. It represents our collective wisdom. "Dear student," it says, "here is international relations. Basically it consists of power-politics theory, which specifies that the need for security makes states behave aggressively. Their aggressive behavior forms stabilizing patterns which we call balances of power, and enables big states to dominate lesser ones, which is why all those obedient minor powers have signed the non-proliferation treaty. We know, dear student, that there are numerous exceptions to these propositions; we shall call them special cases. The theory predicts that law, morality, ideology, religion and similar social forces are unimportant, but they exist and so we have put chapters on them in our textbook anyway. You must understand, dear student, that states are inherently compelled to respond rationally to their national interests; but world politics is also subsystem dominant, which means that states often disobey that systemic imperative. Conflict, dear student, is caused by the clashing of state interests. However, much research has shown that international conflict spills over from domestic disputes – that is, conflict within states rather than between them – so we have included some discussion of that too. The whole system is, of course, essentially political and not economic, but so much fuss has been made about economic forces in recent years that we have included sections on interdependence, the North–South dialogue, energy and the multinations. We, the scholars, perceive all the contradictions but we cannot resolve them; you, the student, must do your best." It is small wonder that our subject tends to confuse its undergraduates. My judgement is that our tendency to add the anomalies to pre-existing theory, rather than to rethink the theory, has gone far enough.

The third prediction in the Kuhnian account of paradigm change is that any paradigm which is riddled with anomalies must eventually enter a crisis stage. It will then collapse. In due course it will be replaced by a new paradigm which accounts for the anomalies in a satisfactory fashion. Self-reform in this way, Kuhn points out, is painfully difficult to any discipline. Usually the reconstruction of basic ideas must come from new people, perhaps operating in new institutions. Choosing and testing the replacement paradigm is no easy matter, because paradigms are incommensurate. It will not be possible to assess the worth of any candidate aspiring to the throne of academic world politics by the only method that comes easily to most of us, namely the application of what we instinctively think of as "realistic" tests. Our notions of what is and is not "realistic" are fundamentally conditioned by our professional training in what we must now see as an outmoded set of ideas. Instead, following Kuhn, we must decide what are the most significant questions that our discipline needs to answer, and select from the competing ideas the ones which most persuasively deal with those questions. Only then can we proceed to build a normal science, testing and checking.

Can we do this? It seems that we will have to. As I have sought to demonstrate in this review of the academic study of international relations, we are not starting from scratch in our attempt to make a constructive contribution to the resolution of conflict. The discipline does have assets. Some are to be found in the classical tradition, especially on the liberal side of the realist–idealist debate and in the radical insistence that political consequences do follow from the common humanity of people everywhere. Other assets are to be found in more recent scholarship, especially among the writings of those researchers whom I have identified as pioneers (by implication if not explicitly) of the pluralist approach. And the most important assets are to be found in the specialized studies of conflict resolution itself, from the foundations laid by Boulding[36] and Johan Galtung in his many papers in the early years of the *Journal of Peace Research*, down to the most recent work reported in Azar and Farah,[37]

Mitchell,[38] Kriesberg,[39] Banks,[40] and many others.

The task, then, is to draw upon these assets. With them we can satisfy Martin Wight's criterion for progress: that any new perspective must be founded upon reason, because emotional impulse alone is not enough. Our assets provide the resources needed to undertake what Kuhn described as "the reconstruction of the field from new fundamentals, a reconstruction that changes some of the field's most elementary theoretical generalizations."[41]

But as I have also argued, the international relations discipline is today weighed down by heavy liabilities. This means that its scholarly output must be employed only with the greatest of caution when the purpose is to find a theoretical basis for conflict resolution. Ideologically, many writers on international relations hold status quo views. These views incline them more towards the partisan manipulation of a conflict than towards its impartial mediation, and discourage altogether any sympathetic inquiry into means for the achievement of justice. Intellectually, there is a pervasive rigidity of attitude which holds back the spontaneous creation of new ideas within the discipline. It also obstructs an open-minded discussion of ideas that originate outside it. Taken as a whole, the discipline has become a processor that is expert in the recycling of old analytic formulas to fit the succession of new problems presented by the real world.

These ideological and attitudinal handicaps are intensified by the theoretical precepts of realism which operate to the systematic disadvantage of any attempt to build a powerful theory of how to analyse and resolve conflicts. The most basic premise of realism stipulates that violent conflict between states must be assumed to be inevitable. From that premise it is logical enough to deduce that the changes of violence are reduced by preparation for it, and that stability will best be assured in a heavily armed world run by experts in the controlled use of force.

That basic premise must be challenged if progress toward a stable and peaceful world society is to be made. And that is why a pluralist theory of international relations is so important in the construction of a viable approach to peaceful resolution of conflict.

NOTES AND REFERENCES

1. Terry Nardin, *Law, Morality and the Relations of States* (Princeton: Princeton University Press, 1983): 57–62.
2. James Mayall (ed.), *The Community of States: A Study in International Political Theory* (London: George Allen & Unwin, 1983).
3. John W. Burton, *Dear Survivors* (London: Frances Pinter, 1982).
4. Stanley Hoffman, "An American Social Science: International Relations," *Daedalus* 106(3) (Summer 1977): 41–60.
5. Hans J. Morgenthau, *Politics Among Nations: The Struggle for Power and Peace* (New York: Alfred A. Knopf, 1938).
6. Warren R. Phillips, "Where Have All the Theories Gone?" *World Politics* 26(2) (January 1974): 155–88.
7. John A. Vasquez, *The Power of Power Politics: A Critique* (London: Frances Pinter, 1983).
8. Thomas S. Kuhn, *The Structure of Scientific Revolutions* (Chicago: University of Chicago Press, 1962).
9. Edward Hallett Carr, *The Twenty Years' Crisis* (London: Macmillan, 1939).
10. Morgenthau, *Politics Among Nations*.
11. William R. Thompson (ed.), *Contending Approaches to World System Analysis* (London: Sage Publications, 1983).
12. Vasquez, *The Power of Power Politics*.
13. John W. Burton, *International Relations: A General Theory* (London: Cambridge University Press, 1965); Burton, *Systems, States, Diplomacy and Rules* (London: Cambridge University Press, 1968); Burton, *World Society* (London: Cambridge University Press, 1972); Burton, *Dear Survivors*; Burton, *Global Conflict: The Domestic Sources of International Crisis* (Brighton, England: Wheatsheaf; College Park, MD: CID, University of Maryland, 1984); Burton *et al.*, *The Study of World Society: A London Perspective* (Pittsburgh, PA: International Studies Association, 1974).
14. Ray Maghroori and Bennett Ramberg (eds), *Globalism Versus Realism: International Relations; Third Debate* (Boulder, CO: Westview, 1983).
15. Michael Banks (ed.), *Conflict in World Society: A New Perspective on International Relations* (Brighton, England: Wheatsheaf; New York: St Martin's, 1984).
16. Arnold Wolfers, *Discord and Collaboration: Essays on International Politics* (Baltimore: Johns Hopkins Press, 1962): 82.
17. See Richard C. Snyder, H. W. Bruck and Burton Sapin (eds), *Foreign Policy Decision Making* (New York: Free Press, 1962): 14–185.
18. Karl W. Deutsch, *The Nerves of Government* (New York: Free Press, 1963); John D. Steinbruner, *The Cybernetic Theory of Decision: New Dimensions of Political Analysis* (Princeton: Princeton University Press, 1974).
19. Morton H. Halperin, *Bureaucratic Politics and Foreign Policy* (Washington, D.C.: Brookings Institution, 1974).
20. Robert Jervis, *Perception and Misperception in International Politics* (Princeton: Princeton University Press, 1976).

21. James N. Rosenau, *The Study of Global Interdependence: Essays on the Transnationalization of World Affairs* (London: Frances Pinter, 1980).
22. Rosenau, *The Study of Global Interdependence*: 3.
23. J. David Singer, "The Level-of-Analysis Problem in International Relations," in Klaus Knorr and Sidney Verba (eds), *The International System: Theoretical Essays* (Princeton: Princeton University Press, 1962): 77–92.
24. Burton, *World Society*; Richard W. Mansbach, Yale H. Ferguson, and Donald E. Lampert, *The Web of World Politics: Nonstate Actors in the Global System* (Englewood Cliffs, N.J.: Prentice-Hall, 1976).
25. Edward L. Morse, *Modernization and the Transformation of International Relations* (London: Collier Macmillan, 1976); Robert O. Keohane and Joseph S. Nye, *Power and Interdependence* (Boston: Little, Brown & Co., 1977).
26. Arend Lijphart, analyzing the work of Deutsch in "Karl W. Deutsch and the New Paradigm in International Relations," in Richard L. Merritt and Bruce M. Russett (eds), *From National Development to Global Community* (London: George Allen & Unwin, 1982): 233–51.
27. Stephan Krasner (ed.), *International Regimes* (Ithaca, N.Y.: Cornell University Press, 1983).
28. Burton, *World Society*; C. Alger, report of an address given in Yokohama in 1982 in Burton, *Global Conflict*: 74–82.
29. Richard W. Mansbach and John A. Vasquez, *In Search of Theory: A New Paradigm for Global Politics* (New York: Columbia University Press, 1981).
30. R. J. Barry Jones and Peter Willetts (eds), *Interdependence on Trial: Studies in the Theory and Reality of Contemporary Interdependence* (London: Frances Pinter, 1984).
31. Herbert Butterfield and Martin Wight (eds), *Diplomatic Investigations* (London: George Allen & Unwin, 1966).
32. Butterfield and Wight (eds), *Diplomatic Investigations*: 24.
33. Butterfield and Wight (eds), *Diplomatic Investigations*: 33.
34. Butterfield and Wight (eds), *Diplomatic Investigations*: 28.
35. Kuhn, *The Structure of Scientific Revolutions*.
36. Kenneth E. Boulding, *Conflict and Defense: A General Theory* (New York: Harper & Row, 1963).
37. Edward E. Azar and Nadia Farah, "The Structure of Inequalities and Protracted Social Conflict: A Theoretical Framework," *International Interactions* 7(4) (September 1981): 317–35.
38. Christopher R. Mitchell, *The Structure of International Conflict* (London: Macmillan, 1981).
39. Louis Kriesberg, *Social Conflicts* (Englewood Cliffs, N.J.: Prentice-Hall, 1983) 2nd edn.
40. Banks, *Conflict in World Society*.
41. Kuhn, *The Structure of Scientific Revolutions*.

4 Paradigms in Conflict: the Strategist, the Conflict Researcher and the Peace Researcher

A. J. R. Groom*

The purpose of this chapter is to compare three approaches to conflict, those of the "strategist," the "conflict researcher" and the "peace researcher." Strategic studies, our starting point, are usually seen exclusively within the framework of power politics and the manipulation of threat systems. This approach to conflict is clearly of great importance, especially as it is the one most frequently adopted by decision makers. It is not, however, the only possible approach, and the lineage of each of the three approaches can be traced back to antiquity.

Several caveats seem to be in order before we broach our subject. The statements of the views (used here as a rough synonym for "approach," "conceptual framework" and "paradigm") of the strategist, conflict researcher and the peace researcher are composite ones and they do not reflect the position of any one writer. Moreover, in order to make them clear, the differences are emphasized, but not intentionally to the point of setting up mere straw men. Also, the use of terms is somewhat idiosyncratic, reflecting a lack of consensus on usage in the literature where there sometimes seem to be as many differing approaches and terminologies as there are analysts.

Our approach is predominantly conceptual since nothing is as practical as a good theory. Whether we have good theories in the sense of being able to make highly probabilistic statements about human behavior in conflict and war is a more controversial question. But the fact of the matter is that we cannot think without a theory: facts do not speak for themselves, we impose meaning on them. Decision makers and practical men of affairs ignore this at their peril. This alone is justification enough for a conceptual approach comparing

---

* This chapter is taken from a work on which the author is presently engaged.

paradigms in conflict so that, in a domain in which the very future of humanity may be at stake, we can be a little more aware of the subjectivity and derivation of our interpretations. As J. M. Keynes once remarked

> Practical men, who believe themselves to be quite exempt from any intellectual influence, are usually the slaves of some defunct economist. Madmen in authority, who hear voices in the air, are distilling their frenzy from some academic scribbler of a few years back. I am sure that the power of vested interests is vastly exaggerated compared with the gradual encroachment of ideas. Not, indeed, immediately, but after a certain interval – for in the field of economic and political philosophy there are not many who are influenced by new theories after they are 25 or 30 years of age, so that the ideas which civil servants and politicians and even agitators apply to current events are not likely to be the newest.[1]

Keynes' "practical men," insofar as international relations in general and conflict and war in particular are concerned, have usually acted within one paradigm – that of the realist. But there are alternative views which have a history as long as realism, and which compete with it as modes of interpreting contemporary international relations.

The three paradigms which now dominate the study of international relations in the English language – and, to a large extent, in all Western universities – are the realist, world society and structuralist paradigms, although the nomenclature can vary. While this division is far from being universally accepted,[2] it serves our purpose of examining the implications for the study of conflict of the conceptual framework that is adopted. Moreover, it does not do irremediable violence to the different tendencies of thought that can be traced historically.

THE "REALIST" APPROACH

The realist approach is based on the assertion that the study of international relations is primarily concerned with inter-state rela-tions. States are the dominant actors and they are conceived to be well integrated internally and to act externally as a clearly defined unit. Non-state actors are considered to be of little consequence since, ultimately, they are controllable by states. Non-state, or private, transactions are largely ignored for the same reason that the state can, if it wishes, act as a gatekeeper controlling their direction, content and rate of flow. A more fundamental reason for ignoring both non-state actors and transaction is that the primary concern of this school is power politics. Although states are formally equal in their mutual relations and fully sovereign in the disposition of their internal affairs, the realist denies that sovereign equality exists in practice. Both sovereignty and equality are severely circumscribed by an amalgam of pressures known as power. Indeed, there is a hierarchy of states with the great powers collectively, through the medium of the balance of power, acting as the guardians of world order. Lesser powers are obliged to act within those constraints or suffer the consequences. Those at the top of the hierarchy are assumed to have the power and the responsibility to impose their will, whereas minor powers and non-state actors are more likely to be the objects of power politics than independent actors within the system.

Power politics is thus seen as fundamental and nowhere has this view been more forcefully put than by Hans Morgenthau. Morgenthau's *Politics among Nations* has had an enormous influence in the English-speaking world as the Bible of realism. It was not the first major work setting out this position, both E. H. Carr and Georg Schwarzenberger had preceded him,[3] but Morgenthau's work has greater salience today. While the sharpness of his exposition was somewhat blunted in successive editions, he states the basic premise of the realist position:

> . . . it is sufficient to state that the struggle for power is universal in time and space and is an undeniable fact of experience . . . The drives to live, to propagate and to dominate are common to all men . . . The tendency to dominate, in particular, is an element of all human associations.[4]

For Morgenthau, the "key concept" is "interest defined as power" which "is indeed the essence of politics and is unaffected by the circumstances of time and place . . . Power may comprise anything that established and maintains the control of man over man."[5] Thus "international politics, like all politics, is a struggle for power. Whatever the ultimate aims of international politics, power is always the immediate aim."[6]

The starkness of this view is, however, softened by Morgenthau himself since "Two conclusions follow from this concept of international politics. First, not every action that a nation performs with respect to another nation is of a political nature . . . Second, not all nations are at all times to the same extent involved in international politics."[7] Power politics does not therefore engulf everything, and we get a glimpse of a spectrum of relationships which stretches from those based on power to those which are legitimized, that is those based on criteria freely and knowingly acceptable to all the parties without coercion in any form. For the most part, however, the realist model concerns itself with states interacting in a system of power politics.

States acting in a power framework give rise to a hierarchical system in which each seeks to dominate. Threats and other coercive devices are the chief modalities of the system which emerges from the eternal dialogue between status quo and revisionist actors. These result frequently in a balance of power which can have the effect of creating a semblance of order and stability, and also, and not least, of maintaining the independence of the major actors. Peace, other than a temporary absence of violence, cannot exist. For if each state seeks to dominate there will be a situation in which if some are to be successful others will have to fail. The latter will accept their inferiority for only as long as they are constrained to do so by the prevailing balance of forces. When the balance of forces changes the dominated will seize whatever opportunities may present themselves to reverse the relationship – hence the eternal dialogue between status quo or dominating powers and the revisionist or dominated powers. The alternative is the balance of power which may for a time codify and stabilize a stalemate in the form of a distribution of relative dissatisfaction.

THE "WORLD SOCIETY" APPROACH

The world society paradigm, like that of the realist, has no official or consensual credo. However, it does have some commonalities. In the first place it treats the role of states as an empirical question rather than as being axiomatic. States may on significant occasions be the most important actors, but this is not necessarily so. Nor are state boundaries necessarily the fundamental dividing line between intra-state consensus and inter-state anarchy. Intra-state relations can be anarchical and inter-state relations highly consensual. States are not alone in having effective means of self-help and the self-arrogated right to make use of them. Moreover, important systems of transactions, both qualitatively and quantitatively, both of a coercive and a legitimized nature, transcend state boundaries in ways which are not amenable, actually or potentially, to governmental control, even as a "gatekeeper." Furthermore, states themselves, and especially their governments, frequently do not act as cohesive, hierarchically organized, well-integrated units commanding the full loyalty of their citizens. Indeed, government departments may frequently be at odds with each other, and even seek alliances with like-minded departments of other governments in a network of transgovernmental relationships such as can be seen between treasuries, defense ministeries and foreign offices in NATO countries or similar phenomena in organizational settings such as the European Communities. Moreover, non-governmental organizations [NGOs] can play an important world role and even inter-governmental institutions can, usually through their secretariats, have an impact which escapes the control of their member states. Greenpeace, Amnesty International, the International Olympic Committee, the World Council of Churches – to name a random selection – illustrate, in contemporary world politics, the active and frequently independent role of NGOs, and many of them operate in an a-territorial manner. So, too, do many multinational corporations whose ability to mobilize financial, technical and human resources may rival or surpass that of many governments. A range of such actors may come together to form a regime which thereafter acts as a constraint on their behavior. In short, the state is a penetrated society. It can be *a* nodal point, *an* actor, *a* potential gatekeeper, but when and the extent to which it is must be an empirical question and cannot be assumed.

But if the state is not necessarily a basic unit of analysis, although it may often be, what can take its place? In the world society model the emphasis is put on transaction so that the notion of system – a set of patterned interactions – is the basic unit of analysis. In this approach the level of analysis is not crucial (inter-state, intra-state, individual), nor is the status of actors. To analyse a phenomenon it may be necessary to include the activities of actors as widely disparate as a particular individual and the UN Security Council. Since an adequate explanation cannot be given at one particular level, say inter-state relations, it is necessary to go beyond that level. By mapping transactions and determining where marked discontinuities occur, both qualitatively and quantitatively, a systems analysis emerges. Such systems develop properties which have a durable and independent existence as, in their different ways, regime theorists, structural-functionalists and general systems theorists would argue, but the world society approach is, in general terms, a systems approach which does not necessarily imply far-reaching normative considerations. Yet if international relations goes beyond the inter-state system, where does it stop? Does world society include everything? Surely not, for then it would be of little use.

To some the final resting point is the individual. John Burton, one of the most influential figures in the development of the world society model, has come to believe this.[8] Burton's position is an escape from those institutional values that have permeated thinking about international relations. Politics was about structures, be they states, empires or dynasties, and people were frequently merely a concomitant property. Individuals were thus seen as the temporary guardians of the structure and made important essentially by their role in that structure or as part and parcel of it, an object to be disposed of as the leadership thought fit. To start with the individual is, therefore, as far as International Relations is concerned, something of an innovation. It takes Burton beyond the world society or pluralist framework of which he was one of the pioneers.

The starting point in the world society framework is a question, a problem or a phenomenon to be explained, and the approach to it is to map transactions in a systemic framework. This gives an added dimension to the conceptualization of social science. Confining the analysis to one level, such as the inter-state, is too constraining and so is a limitation to one facet of behavior, be it economic, legal, sociological, or political. Interdisciplinary research therefore became fashionable since few questions, problems or phenomena are exclusively, say, economic, or could reasonably be treated as such. Hybrids came to the fore, or reappeared, such as political anthropology, political psychology, political sociology or political economy, throughout the social sciences. Interdisciplinary research teams and centres were established. But the results were often disappointing. The reason for this lay frequently in the non-cumulative nature of the work of members of the team: an economist would look at the problem from the perspective and within the paradigm of economics and others likewise from their differing paradigms. These paradigms were not easily made compatible and therefore interdisciplinary research did not cohere – it lacked a discipline.

A solution to this problem is to reverse the process from a discipline to a problem by making the problem, question or phenomenon itself the starting point. Thus conflict, security, integration, participation, identity and the like become themes that cut across both levels of analysis and academic disciplines. Conflict, to take our particular concern, has economic, legal, psychological and other disciplinary dimensions. It manifests itself at different levels between individuals, between states, in industry and across all these levels. But conflict (and the other themes) also has a coherence of its own so that, whatever the idiosyncracies of level and discipline, general statements can usefully be made. The problem, question or phenomenon in the world society framework is located within, and acts as the fulcrum of, three dimensions – level of analysis, discipline and theme (Figure 4.1).

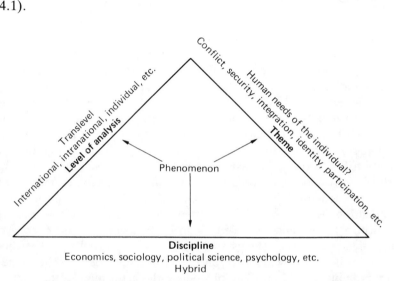

Figure 4.1   Three dimensions: level of analysis, discipline and theme

Besides suggesting that the world is increasingly non-state-centric in character, adherents of the world society approach would acknowledge that man is not driven by an instinct to dominate. Thus aggressive behavior at all levels results from other factors and notably as a learned response in certain environmental conditions. Peace, in the sense of being more than the mere absence of overt violence, is therefore possible. Indeed, transactions in any social system can be located on a spectrum between a pole of power politics and one of legitimized politics.

Realists view all politics as being necessarily power politics. Even ostensibly cooperative relations are merely "power politics in diguise," in Schwarzenberger's phrase, because there are inevitably asymmetries in relationships which can be manipulated. Since the parties know this they take it into account even in their "cooperative" behavior. Thus they do not view transactions within the purviews of international relations as being situated on a spectrum between power politics and legitimized politics. In so doing they limit themselves unnecessarily, since some degree of legitimization must always exist as it is impossible to coerce all of the people all of the time. Moreover, the idea of a continuum between a pole of power and a pole of legitimacy, rather than the realist's usual sharp distinction between intra- and inter-state politics may be a more accurate reflection of the empirical world even in a cold war. Prescriptions based on such a sharp distinction could therefore give rise to self-defeating policies.

However, the notion of a continuum requires a criterion by which the transactions can be situated along it, and this is the degree of acceptability of the transaction to the parties concerned. If it is acceptable then it is legitimized, if it is not, then it is situated towards the power end of the spectrum. The operational definition of what is acceptable is a matter for the researcher, and it is a function of the problem in which he is interested. As a rule of thumb a legitimized relationship is one in which the behavior of the actor is based on criteria fully and freely acceptable to it without coercion either overt, latent or structural. The essential element is not overt behavior but motivation. Motivation – that is, acceptance by an actor of the criteria on which its behavior is based – can be free and without coercion only if, among other things such as a low opportunity cost if the behavior is rejected, the actor has "perfect knowledge" of the range of possibilities. Without that knowledge the actor may be the victim of structural violence. Of course transactions rarely fall at either extreme end of the spectrum. At the power end the example of Rome and Carthage, the Nazis and European Jewry or Pol Pot are, happily, not the usual case, while at the legitimized end, of the spectrum the Bible refers to the "peace that passeth all understanding." However, transactions can cluster consistently towards one or other end of the spectrum. Consider Franco–German relations from 1870–1950 at the power end or, towards the other end, Nordic country relations. The realist would, however, deny that the spectrum could venture much further from the power pole than a situation of non-war or cold war. The conception in the world society framework, on the other hand, is to envisage the full spectrum and to try and account for a basic shift along it. Why, for example, have Franco–German relations had such a shift towards the pole of legitimized politics since 1950 or Soviet–Chinese relations moved in the contrary direction? A degree of power or legitimacy is simply a label to indicate the nature of a transaction. Because power relations tend to be dramatic and traumatic they monopolize the attention, but without the all-pervasive fabric of legitimization there can be no social order. Moreover, even theorists who see the struggle for power as being universal in time and space usually accept some socialization of this instinct in the form of a limited degree of consent. Their rationalization of legitimized relationships ultimately depends on a truism, or they are excluded by definition.

Nevertheless, the study of perceived power-dominated relationships is the domain of the realist – and at its sharp end that of the strategist. He seeks to understand the mechanisms of power relations, much as he may personally abhor them. The domain of the world society analyst is wider in that he is interested in shifts between the pole of power and the pole of legitimacy. Most realists treat the parameters of power politics as axiomatic – where there is politics there will be a struggle for power. They do not recognize politics as a process in which goals and roles are assigned on a basis which may be power *or* legitimization. If the notion of the legitimized allocation of goals and roles is eschewed, then the only way in which the political process can function peaceably is when it is based upon the premise of retribution against those who do not accept the rules. Thus, like Hobbes, realists see a need for a Leviathan or "common power." Being realists they can conceive of little possibility of such a Leviathan at the world level. They therefore see the only hope for peace in the creation of balances to deter or punish deviant behavior. Politics for them is essentially a zero-sum game, and many of them bitterly regret that it should be so.

The world society model acknowledges that the political function may be perceived in power terms, but it does not allow that this need necessarily be so. The reasons for this lie in a different conception of the nature of man. Behavior is a rational response to the environment as the actor sees it, so that changing the environment can elicit different, more cooperative behavior. It is the old story of the predominance of either nature or nurture. The realist (and strategist) points to the ground rules being set by the former and the world society analyst (and conflict researcher) the latter. But what of the structuralist, in our third principal paradigm?

THE "STRUCTURALIST" APPROACH

This paradigm has had but a fitful recognition in the study of international relations in English language universities and we are the poorer for it. Its classical formulation in political philosophy – by Hegel and Marx in particular – came perhaps somewhat later than the intellectual antecedents of the other paradigms. Yet it received a powerful statement by Lenin which was part of a major debate on imperialism during the founding decades of International Relations. But, apart from Hobson, it was a debate that had its intellectual roots in Central and Eastern Europe and was somewhat alien to the intellectual climate of the English-speaking world. Moreover, it was an approach that became associated with a particular state – the Soviet Union – which was treated as a diplomatic pariah and lay at the basis of a political doctrine – Marxism–Leninism – which was feared, denigrated and reviled by Western elites. Until recently the advocacy of structuralism was a passport to exclusion from the mainstream in the Western study of International Relations.

The starting point of structuralism is simple. An emphasis must be given to the whole since this has an impact greater than the sum of its parts and must therefore be taken into consideration in any empirical theory of behavior at whatever level. As Richard Little puts it

> Structuralists assume that human behaviour cannot be understood simply by examining individual motivation and intention because, when aggregated, human behaviour precipitates structures of which the individuals may be unaware. By analogy, when people walk across a field, they may unintentionally create a path. Others subsequently follow the path and in doing so "reproduce" the path. The process of reproduction, however, is neither conscious nor intentional.[9]

Structure thus takes on a life of its own and determines future behavior and individuals (or states) find it difficult either to escape from such constraints or to create new ones more to their liking.

At the political level Marx, like Harrington before him, pointed out that unless a society's economic and political systems were consonant with each other there was likely to be a revolution. If the holders of political power were not also the holders of economic power then the latter would oust the former. It is a good historical explanation of the emergence of the bourgeois capitalist state from feudalism. Lenin applied this general notion to the international relations of the late nineteenth and early twentieth century to explain imperialism and especially the inevitability of a war between the capitalist powers who were necessarily imperialist and for whom the Great War was thereby ineluctable. Thereafter structuralist thought moved out of the Western mainstream and we are only now beginning to perceive its strengths and to feel its impact upon the other paradigms.

The neo-realists, led by Waltz,[10] claim to have rediscovered the structuralist wheel, but Morgenthau himself, while formulating his six principles of political realism from an actor's perspective, did consider the structure of the international diplomatic system, regretting the movement from multipolarity to bipolarity in the post-war period.[11] Systems thinkers, for their part, came easily to thinking in terms of wholes since it is implicit in the very nature of their basic unit of analysis, but the resurgence of structuralism has forced them to consider more carefully the durable aspects of systems' structures. More generally, structuralists have had recently a significant impact upon the conceptual, empirical and prescriptive agendas to the extent that we are all to some degree impregnated with structuralist ideas. The interdependence of politics and economics is now widely recognized and theories of *dependencia* and centre–periphery models have a cogency and relevance for the understanding of contemporary international relations. Wallerstein's[12] notion of a single world system that has emerged with capitalism and continues to this day, although the hegemon may have changed, has brought to the forefront not only structural factors, the unity of the world system and centre–periphery analysis but a heightened awareness of the need for historical depth – a trait he shares with Marx. Nevertheless, as in the other paradigms, there is no unison and not always harmony among structuralists since some view inter-state politics as trivial in the context of all-pervasive structural factors which shape behavior and, above all, outcomes, while others are giving a crucial role to the state as a structure. However, perhaps the most important impact that the structuralists of every hue have had is that no one is now likely to ignore the effect of structural factors when considering questions of conflict and change, which is our principal concern. Whatever its merits, "structural violence" is now part of every scholar's conceptual lexicon.

These sketches of the three main paradigms in contemporary International Relations form the background for a brief description of the conceptual framework of the strategist (in the realist paradigm), the conflict researcher (in the world society paradigm) and the peace researcher (in the structuralist paradigm). The term "peace researcher" can be confusing and it often arouses political passions which produce more heat than light because it infers that peace is the prerogative of a particular paradigm which others would strongly – and in the case of conflict research rightly – contest. The positions outlined do not, let us repeat, reflect an official credo, nor do contemporary writers always fall neatly into the respective categories, but these descriptions may be helpful as conceptual "navigation points."

THE STRATEGIST, THE CONFLICT RESEARCHER AND THE PEACE RESEARCHER

While these three approaches to the phenomenon of conflict clearly derive from long-standing traditions stretching back beyond the formal recognition of International Relations as an academic discipline in Western universities, their contemporary manifestation is a post-war phenomenon. Peace and security courses, which paid a good deal of attention to the League of Nations and United Nations, began to be supplemented by courses on strategic studies in the 1950s as the impact of the nuclear revolution became more keenly felt, giving rise to institutions such as the (International) Institute for Strategic Studies. In the 1960s the extraordinary intellectual migration from other social and natural sciences into studies of conflict and war was a catalyst for the separate emergence of conflict studies. This migration of scholars meant that conflict studies did not owe so much to the principal intellectual forebears of International Relations – international law and diplomatic history. The Vietnam war was an inspiration, both in Western Europe and North America, for a reconsideration on the part of some, first in the guise of "post-behaviouralism," which later led to the resurgence of structuralism which has continued to grow in importance. Let us examine the three approaches separately before trying to compare them.

Strategic studies

War and violent coercive activity are the sharp end of power politics and the domain of strategic studies. Strategy is concerned with the manipulation and application of threats either to preserve or to change the status quo. There is an acceptance of the realist paradigm since states are seen as the principal actors and their relationships are predominantly, perhaps exclusively, coercive, either actively or in a latent fashion. To put it at its strongest, if the drive to dominate cannot be eliminated, as it is instinctive, it can only be channelled into tolerable forms by the threat of sanctions. States are the major actors since they have a plenitude of means of coercion available to them and the right to go to war and defend their interests. They are the principal actors in high politics. However, the manipulation and application of threats is pursued not only to secure domination for one state, it is also the currency for preventing the domination of other states or for seeking a period of order based on a stable and recognized balance of forces. In a nuclear world it is more than ever in the interests of everyone to manipulate threat systems to ensure that conflict does not escalate to engulf the system, hence a quest for stability through arms control and the like. Elements of this philosophy lie at the conceptual base of most strategists, diplomats and journalists in their concern with "high politics." The military balance is thus a prime focus for it is a measure of the state of play in countervailing threat systems. Peace, in any sense other than the absence of overt violence, is a chimera: peace is merely whatever propensity to non-violence and stability the current balance of forces induces and it is unlikely to sustain itself since the balance will change sooner or later in a significant manner.

Developments in the empirical world have caused strategists to modify considerably the state-centricity of their thinking in the areas of revolutionary warfare and bureaucratic politics. The multitude and magnitude of revolutionary wars since 1945 forced strategists gradually to widen their concern from the world of nuclear deterrence and high politics between superpowers to include the "poor man's war" in which many of the principal actors are non-state actors. Moreover, the dominant mode of violence is guerrilla warfare or civil violence. The strategist has thus had to modify his state-centric model to account for transnational linkages and to delve into theories of modernization and development and consider concepts such as relative deprivation, status disequilibrium and structural violence.

Strategy now encompasses intra- as well as inter-state relations and this has given rise to a burgeoning literature by academics and practitioners from different sides of the political fence.[13] The strategist here needs the skills and the paradigm of a political sociologist which is a far cry from his earlier concerns with nuclear deterrence and inter-state high politics.

Developments in another direction – arms control – have also contributed to the partial dethronement of the state-centric model among strategists. As the negotiations for arms control got under way in the late 1950s it became clear that the view of the state as a monolithic national actor did not fit the empirical world. Slowly strategists have come to terms with bureaucratic politics,[14] as various substate actors jostle to get the upper hand in deciding official state policy on a particular issue. The systems of interaction may well spill over a state's frontiers to include similar actors in allies and even adversaries. Many of the developments in decision making theory such as disjointed incrementalism, role behavior, and satisficing are central to the strategist's attempts to understand the decision making process in defense. The strategist thus finds himself deeply involved in some of the major issues and developments of political and administrative science which are seemingly far removed from the concerns of the strategic balance, but nevertheless clearly relevant to it. However, strategists, as a group, are not in the forefront of new developments in the study of international relations, since the overwhelming majority remains within the domain of state-centric high politics, concerning themselves with analysing defense policies and problems in a traditional manner. Moreover, they often do this from the point of view, or even at the behest of, particular actors.

The strategist is, to a lesser or greater degree, an activist. Most strategists write from the point of view of one side or another and they tend to advocate policies designed to enhance or protect the interests of one or other of the parties. Indeed, many strategists undertake work on contract for governments or become civil servants for a period. This influence of strategists on decision makers, which is often more apparent than real since the decision making process is usually difficult to influence or the decision makers are only looking for a rationale for policies which have already been decided upon, has been strongly criticized.

The fear is that strategists are too pro-status quo and that they are not peace-oriented. Strategists from the academic world have had the greatest degree of contact with decision makers in the United

States and it is there that the protests have been greatest, with good cause in that the independence of some universities has been somewhat compromised through direct government funding for military purposes of a substantial proportion of all the research undertaken. Over time such direct funding could mean that both the subject of research and even the research findings deviate from the traditional liberal university ethic. Moreover, in such circumstances strategists may become disturbingly ethnocentric.[15] Strategic studies risks becoming an applied science, a mere adjunct of state power, dependent upon the value orientation and policy premises of governments in their struggle with each other and with parvenu non-state or potential government actors. For this, in comparison with those in other approaches, strategists are well paid and their programs and institutes well funded. Strategic studies, insofar as it reveals such tendencies, puts its academic status at risk as a pure science concerned with the best approximation it can get to knowledge. Fortunately some strategists are not *parti pris* – SIPRI, for example, tries to fulfill an international vocation. As Lawrence has so bluntly put it,

> Strategic Studies faces a stark choice. It can either particularize itself as an ideology tied to state power, or it can frame its theories in the context of human interests which are universal.[16]

Conflict research

The world society paradigm is the one in which the conflict researcher sits most easily and congenially. This is particularly so because the conception of conflict embraces many different levels, crosses disciplinary boundaries without compunction and, because it is non-partisan in spirit, is supportive of all the parties without exception, so that a movement may take place towards a resolution based on a new set of legitimized relationships which are self-supporting. For example, in the Cyprus conflict it is as relevant to know about political relations within the Greek Cypriot community as in the UN Security Council and insights useful for the resolution of that conflict may come from industrial conciliators as well as from international mediators. And clearly, as the failure of the 1960 settlement showed, the Cyprus conflict cannot be resolved without the full participation of both Cypriot communities.

The conflict researcher does not accept that the cause of conflict is an instinct in man – a drive to dominate. Rather, conflictual behavior is a response to an actor's perception of the environment. It is a learned behavior triggered by circumstances and, to the extent that the environment can be manipulated, so can conflict behavior which is dysfunctional. Thus threats are not the only form of social engineering, although, in deep rooted structural conflicts, this implies profound changes which are very difficult to achieve on a non-partisan basis. Conflict researchers may also see conflict as functional, or rational, in that it is intended to serve a useful purpose. However, if the purpose being served is outweighed by the costs of the conflict then, it is argued, conflict behavior will end. But such a rationalistic and simplistic approach creates difficulties, in that those that pay the costs are not always those that get the benefits or take the decisions. Yet, despite such problems, in terms of the three approaches under consideration this view of the origins of conflict is the most hopeful one in regard to its resolution, for it suggests that the decision making process of the parties is amenable to a cost–gain calculus that is not restricted to the parameters of power politics.

Differing views on the nature of conflict require further comment. Like the strategist, the conflict researcher sees conflict as ubiquitous, but for different reasons. He notes that the world consists of a very large number of separate decision making centers. Since each center has a measure of independence, it is likely that outputs from the various centers will, on a random basis, be incompatible. As such, conflict is endemic, since it is virtually inconceivable that every decision-making center's output will fit snugly into an appropriate niche in the environment. Conflict of this sort is neither intentional nor the result of a drive.

Feedback to the decision making center may, if it is correctly interpreted, indicate the clash of policies generated by the initial output and the actor may or may not decide to respond to the feedback by adjusting its policy. In the normal way such adjustments occur in a routine fashion since conflict handling mechanisms have been institutionalized. They require no special thought and are not considered to be conflict. At the personal level we can illustrate the argument by observing people in the concourse of a railway station or the foyer of a hotel. They are all pursuing their separate purposes, but rarely do they bump into each other. They steer, literally, successfully and without thinking. Conflict, which has been generated by a host of decision making centers, in this case individuals, is unnoticed because our cultural and socialization procedures have generated an internalized set of conflict handling mechanisms for moving about in a crowd. But sometimes people do get angry on a station concourse or in a hotel foyer, voices are raised, and there is shoving and pushing. Such situations may be exacerbated if there are significant asymmetries between the actors. The routinized conflict handling mechanisms have failed and conflict in the everyday meaning of the term has begun. It is now clearly intended conflictual behavior. Conflict in this sense arises from an actor imposing the burden of change on the environment either through a faulty interpretation of feedback or through an unwillingness to respond to negative feedback. Incompatible behavior is now evident and power politics have begun. The cause, however, is not an inherent power drive but the breakdown or absence of an acceptable conflict handling mechanism short of power politics.

To the conflict researcher conflicts are subjective, although they may appear to the participants to be objective. An objective conflict is one in which the gains of one party are directly related to the losses of the others. If, for example, the dispute is a territorial one, then if one side controls practically all of the territory the other side can control practically none. In the realist paradigm all social relations are ultimately of this sort, since all actors seek to dominate and only some can. However, the strategist is well aware that in the struggle there may be no winner in any meaningful sense, as in nuclear war. Therefore the goal of the analyst in this case is to ensure safe and orderly rules for this struggle. It is to ensure that a positional zero-sum game is kept within limits to thwart the threat of mutual disaster.

This view of the human condition is rejected by the conflict researcher. He allows that the parties to a conflict may perceive their relationship as objective, and act upon that basis, but he holds that this belies the underlying structure of their relationships. Only if an actor is pursuing just one value, and one alone, or if the range of values of the parties and the relative preference schedules are the same and immutable, or change in exactly the same way, can an objective conflict exist. All other conflict is subjective, in structure if not in perception. This is because the parties can change their goals, and the importance of one value in terms of other actual or potential values is always, at least theoretically, subject to reassessment. Moreover, the conflict researcher will argue that the two genuine cases of objective conflict never occur in practice, except among the insane or as freaks of nature. Conflict is objective only because the parties choose to see it as such and their perceptions are subject to change. Thus, non-war based on threat systems is not the only form of social management. While it may have its place to hold a situation in the short term, the conflict analyst looks to a condition of self-sustaining peace as his goal. In self-sustaining peaceful circumstances actors are willing to steer to ensure that the totality of their values is fulfilled, and that totality is potentially infinite.

To be sure, such a situation is utopian since it would require perfect information, perfect costing mechanisms and a perfect decision making process. But it is not an impossible dream to move in that direction. The reasons for this lie at two levels. The first concerns rational decision making to ensure that the opportunity cost of any desired want in terms of other desired wants is minimized, and the totality of goals is brought to the fore, so that there is an overall maximization of wants. This needs to be conceived in the context of the wants of others. But others may respond to this in a non-legitimized manner, and power politics therefore ensues. In the short term such a response can mean that power politics will pay for the coercer to the detriment of the coerced, but not in the long term since the cost of long-term coercion tends to be prohibitive (although this may be of no great solace to particular actors here and now).

An inducement not to pursue this eventually costly short-term track is that basic social needs are not necessarily in short supply. If we postulate, at least insofar as contemporary world society is concerned, that values such as security, identity, participation, development and esteem are ubiquitous, or nearly so, then their supply is such that all actors can partake of them to their full satisfaction. In many circumstances today not all actors are able to do so, but there is no immutable barrier to their doing so. The sense of identity – individual, ethnic, racial or whatever – of one man need not necessarily be at the expense of another although, lamentably, it often is in today's world and it gives rise to complex protracted conflicts. It is the job of the conflict researcher, as an activist, not only to analyze such situations but to provide a supportive framework whereby they can be rectified. Conflict researchers have developed techniques precisely for this purpose.[17] To the extent that this satisfaction of basic social needs can be accomplished then the allocation of scarce resources of a material or positional nature is more likely to be on a legitimized rather than a power basis. As John Burton has put it

> Where there are important values at issue, as distinct from negotiable interests, the use of coercion or pressure in any form,

to force an opponent party to compromise is likely to be dysfunctional in that it will tend to promote protracted conflict, even after
a settlement.

It is only in respect to interests – quantities, roles, advantages,
privileges – that power bargaining has a role. Moreover, it needs
to be noted that in a power bargaining situation . . . what appear
on the surface to be interests frequently are a manifestation of some
basic fears and values that have not, because of the requirements of
bargaining, been admitted, perceived or defined.[18]

For at least some conflict analysts, these are conceptual notions that
provide a guide to analysis and prescription.

STRATEGY AND CONFLICT RESEARCH: CONTRASTS AND COMMONALITIES

In common parlance settlement and resolution are often used as
synonyms. However, they are used here to express an important
difference between strategic thinking and the conflict research
approach. The strategist, because of his assumption of a ubiquitous
drive to dominate or the prevalence of power politics, cannot envisage
any more than the settlement or stalemate of a conflict. Such a
settlement or stalemate is based on deterrence or coercion by a victor
or a third party without which the conflict would resume since the
behavior of some actors is decided on criteria not acceptable to them.
Thus, an order based on non-war backed by a threat system is the
best, in terms of peace, that society can expect. The conflict
researcher, however, argues that the resolution of conflict is, in
theory, possible even though in practice men may need to be
restrained in particular circumstances. By resolution is meant a
situation in which relationships between the parties are legitimized
and self-sustaining without the intervention of third parties and
without the imposition of behavioral patterns. There are, in addition,
long-term expectations that the relationship will continue on that
basis. With resolution the parties to a dispute accept the relationships
between them and base their behavior on criteria fully acceptable
both to them and to the other actors in the system.[19]

In seeking resolution the conflict researcher is apt to take much
more of a bird's eye view of a conflict than a strategist. Indeed, this
in part stems from his willingness to treat all parties to a conflict as

undifferentiated participants and his refusal to take a judgemental role. Thus, once recognized as a party, an actor's position must be accommodated on terms acceptable to it if the dispute is to be resolved. There is no penchant for the government side, as in the case of the strategist, nor for the underdog, as in the case of the structuralist. The difficulty, however, lies in deciding which actors are parties to a dispute, and to what extent.[20] Nevertheless, the conflict researcher is also an activist, but on behalf of all the parties. In his active role he seeks to provide a supportive framework for the parties to work towards the resolution of their dispute. He has no particular outcome in mind except for one to which the parties give their free assent. It does not seem that such an approach is inherently biased towards either the status quo or the revisionist side given the equal status of the parties. In practical terms not a great deal of work has been done using this approach at the inter-state level. It is, however, widely applied at other systems levels, such as industrial relations and in social work. In all these fields, as in international or inter-communal conflict, the prime focus of attention is upon relationships in a systemic framework among actors whose principal motivation can often be traced back to a quest for the satisfactory fulfillment of basic social goals such as security, identity and the like.

However, both the strategist and the conflict researcher have some points in common which, because of the greater importance they give to the individual actor, they do not share to the same extent with the structuralist. Both the strategist and the conflict researcher believe that conflict behavior has alterable components. They agree that perceptions can be modified and images changed, that external conditions can be influenced to alter the environment of an actor which in turn may be reflected in its behavior, that the process of selecting goals and the means to achieve them from a wide range of possible values is not necessarily preordained and that the costing procedures relating to different policy options are in some cases subject to manipulation. In short, behavior is neither random nor preprogrammed. While for the strategist a drive to dominate may underlie the behavior of all social actors, its manifestation in particular circumstances is mediated by a variety of factors. In effect, therefore, the strategist is able to agree with the conflict researcher that behavior is not given and that an attempt can be made to influence it. There, however, the agreement ends for as we have seen the strategist seeks to influence behavior through the manipulation of threat systems, whereas the conflict researcher adopts the supportive approach.

The former deals primarily in negative sanctions while the latter concentrates more on positive sanctions.[21]

A second area of agreement is that both assume decision making by the parties to a dispute to be rational. By rational is meant the notion that in the mind of the actor there are some criteria by which goals are set and policies adopted for their achievement. This rationality may not, of course, be evident to an observer, but since it is assumed to be there, observers – and, more importantly, parties – seek it out and try to understand it so that, in the latter case, they can influence it. Rationality in this instance does not refer to a normative system of rules which behavior must try to match, nor does it necessarily involve any notion of consensus about the appropriate way to do things. Rationality as used here merely asserts that actors behave in a purposeful way and that their actions are neither random nor predestined. However, this is in no way intended to suggest that actors always make the right decisions to achieve their ends: they may choose to follow self-defeating policies, although they do so unwittingly. Both strategists and conflict researchers must assume this degree of rationality if they are to approach the parties with a view to influencing their behavior. Random or completely programmed behavior cannot be influenced: it can only be changed by destroying the decision making center from which it emanates. Despite these commonalities, differences abound between strategists and both conflict researchers and peace researchers, as their respective paradigms presage.

PEACE RESEARCH

The conceptual world of the peace researcher is very different, since it is not the subjective element in the nature of relationships that is important for him, but the deep rooted structure which gives rise to them. The analysis of conflict which gives great emphasis to structure is Marxist in tradition, although it goes back to Kant and beyond. However, it came to the fore in Western universities, and especially on the continent of Europe, at a time when the post-behavioralists were calling for a greater emphasis on future-oriented, politically relevant, value promoting research.[22] To be sure empirical research was not eschewed but it was rightly pointed out that research grew out of a social consciousness and that it constituted political action. If it merely described the present then it had a tendency to put blinkers on the vision of alternative, better worlds (and also, by inference, less favorable worlds). Research, or part of it, had, therefore, self-consciously to be future-oriented so that universal humane values would be promoted. As Galtung put it:

> The *values* that can be derived and developed from the general concept of peace should be our basic guide to the future, not *data* from a highly unpeaceful world. Concretely, peace research should not only be concerned with the evaluation of the peace policies of the *past*, but at least equally much with social critique of the present (criticism) and with the presentation of proposals, even whole blueprints, for the future (constructionism). Only by escaping that prison of the past which is the essence of empiricism can the peace researcher make a meaningful contribution to an ever transcending world. The implication of this is far-reaching: to conceive of science as an activity that brings about a new world (i.e. *new* data) more similar to our values – not only a theory more similar to the old data (i.e. the old world).[23]

But the question is, a new world based on whose values? While it is not difficult to concede that any social thought is a political act and that we must therefore be aware of our values and of the consequences of the act so that in a sense we are all activists, it is an entirely different matter to assert that all research should be aimed at the eradication of one particular interpretation of the principal ills of our society.

Besides alerting us to the value implications of our work, the peace researchers in the structuralist mode have also focused our attention to the notion of structural violence. What the term lacks in elegance, and in its apparent contradiction since only people can behave in a violent manner, it makes up for in its salience as an academic "buzz word." Structural violence connotes a situation in which overt violence is absent but in which structural factors have virtually the same compelling control over behavior as the overt threat or use of force. In a society prone to structural violence an actor or group is prevented, by structural constraints, from developing its talents or interests in a normal manner, or even from realizing that such developments are possible. A glaring example in contemporary world society is the role of women or class, race and religious discrimination.

It matters little to the peace researcher that the victims of such structures may not be unhappy with their lot – to him they would then be happy slaves – since he holds that a legitimized relationship is not incompatible with structural violence. His complaint about the conflict researchers is that they do not acknowledge this fully. A society without structural violence is the only peaceful society because it is the only just society. What then constitutes a just society if it is not the satisfaction of its participants as denoted by legitimized role differentiation?

To this some peace researchers admit confusion, others espouse an unthinking egalitarianism, whereas still others grope for some neo-Marxist millennium as they strive to elaborate an objective essentialist definition of justice. Such a definition is, of course, impossible, but an inter-subjective consensus on what constitutes justice at a particular time and place and in particular circumstances is not. If, for example, slavery is considered universally to be abhorrent apart from one society of literally happy slaves, then it could be argued that these slaves too are victims of structural violence. The concerns of the conflict and peace researchers would then converge, but so long as the peace researchers treated structural violence as an objective phenomenon they cannot.

Like the strategists the structuralists argue that conflict is an objective phenomenon. It emerges from a real clash of real interests rather than a perceived clash of interests, although actors may not perceive who their real enemies are. Unfortunately, no definition of an interest is given, as is also the case in the power approach, and thus, since interests are not self-evident, we are left with a subjective definition of interest and, therefore, also of conflict. This argument the peace researcher does not hold to be valid since he assumes his definition of interest to be objective and he is thereby able to maintain his view of conflict as being a situation in which incompatible interests are built into a structure. If this proposition is accepted then it is logical that conflict can be resolved only by structural change and to the extent that such structural change is necessary the peace researcher is a revolutionary. This also helps to explain the peace researcher's activist proclivities and his taking of sides in a conflict.

How can structural change be brought about? Like the strategist the peace researcher resorts to threat systems and rejects the supportive approach. He does not attempt to increase behavioral or attitudinal integration. On the contrary, he seeks to polarize conflict and to make it manifest. Once those who benefit from the structural violence are forced to uphold the situation by the use of overt violence there can be little doubt where the interests of the contending parties lie. To attempt to defuse a situation of structural or actual violence is actually to support the top dogs. Rather the peace researcher sees his role as aiding the underdogs in the struggle to change the power relationships between the top dogs and the underdogs so that the system breaks down. With the onerous structure destroyed by the successful exercise of power, the peace researcher, who is by now less of a revolutionary, can put his knowledge and research to the building of a new structure about which there is, among peace researchers who think in these structural terms, perhaps understandably, little consensus and few clear ideas. The goal of the peace researcher is a revolutionary peace and the means to its attainment is power politics including, if necessary and appropriate, the use of force. In many respects the peace researcher is an inverted strategist.

As Helge Hveem put it:

> Whereas many peace researchers [conflict researchers in our parlance] would maintain that the means to make peace must be non-violent in themselves, others [peace researchers in our parlance] would hold that [physical] violence should be used in order to abolish [structural] violence. A primary task of a peace research institute according to this latter line of thought is to study and offer guidance in how to make conflicts manifest, and how to polarize antagonists to take sides in the conflict and to fight the opponent by guerrilla warfare.

Hveem thus distinguishes between "constructivist" and "criticist neo-Marxian" peace research. Constructivists, like the conflict researcher, see peace as the "absence of physical and structural violence," whereas the criticist sees peace as the "absence of structural violence but not necessarily of physical violence." In terms of loyalty that of the constructivist is "to the individual in a world society and the victims of violence," but that of the criticist is "to the proletariat of the world, fighting against structural violence." The latter's unit of analysis is therefore that of class. While the constructivist has a blend of "normative theory and empiricism," the criticist indulges in "*a priori* thinking, normative theory." Thus the primary means of peacemaking which is advocated in the constructivist's case is "social transformation." Non-violence is "preferred, but not a dogma."

Mediation is possible only in a symmetric conflict since in an asymmetric conflict there must be "support for the under dog" together with "radical social entrepreneurism." For the criticist the class struggle must prevail, if necessary with "physical violence as a means to abolish [structural] violence" giving rise to a "socialist revolution."[24] The constructivist, in Hveem's formulation, thus leans heavily towards the conflict researcher as we have described him, but not wholly so. Despite some convergencies peace researchers in general have some other serious reproaches to make to the conflict researcher.

PARADIGMS IN CONFLICT

The reaction of the peace researcher to the conflict researcher's activism is to castigate the latter for being the witting or unwitting tool of the status quo parties.[25] By persuading parties to a dispute to resolve their conflict, the peace researcher argues, the conflict researcher "cons" the underdog into playing the top dog's game since, while there may be reform, essentially it will be cosmetic as the structure, which is the foundation of the top dog's position, will remain. For the peace researcher the destruction of oppressive structures is the goal. The conflict researcher's riposte is that there can be no resolution of conflict while such oppressive structures remain. Moreover, given the long-term cost of power politics to a top dog, it will be in everyone's interest to dismantle such structures, especially as basic human needs are not in short supply. Human relations for the conflict researcher are essentially non-zero-sum. Thus the conflict researcher, incrementally and by agreement, may help the parties to create a revolution, while the peace researcher is willing to make the revolution by whatever means are available, including the use of organized violence. On the other hand, the only essential difference between the peace researcher and the strategist lies in their values. They are on opposite sides of the barricades, whereas the conflict researcher is trying to make barricades unnecessary.

A further point of significant dissension lies in the asymmetric nature of conflict. Parties to a conflict are, almost always, asymmetrical in some significant ways. The peace researcher argues that in such circumstances the analyst and activist should side with the underdog in order to empower that party to overthrow the oppressive structures that benefit the top dog and thus to enhance the cause of social justice. The conflict researcher rejects such partisan behavior since his approach is both non-judgemental, highly participatory for all the parties and seeks to impose no guidance in the form of a clear suggested outcome. On the contrary, it is not empowerment that the conflict researcher seeks, but disempowerment. The parties and their relative coercive capability are not his central concern. His lodestone is the problem and in the context of the problem all the parties are equal. His approach, therefore, is, in effect, to make the parties symmetrical.[26]

CONCLUSIONS

Our purpose had been to sketch three main approaches to the study of conflict in order to provide a primitive map whereby the exposition and analysis of strategic studies, conflict research and peace research can be seen in a broader context. Bearing in mind the full plenitude of our initial caveats a brief summary can be made (see Figure 4.2).

	Strategist	**Conflict researcher**	**Peace researcher**
Conceptual framework	Realist	World society	Structuralist
The world is	State-centric	Non-state-centric	Class or world system-oriented
Conflict is	inherent in man	endemic	incompatible interests built into structures
and is therefore	objective	subjective	objective
Approach to conflict stresses	manipulation and application of threat systems	supportive techniques	revolution
The role of the analyst	partisan (top dog)	non-partisan	partisan (bottom dog)
The focus is on	capability, hardwear and tactics	relationships	structural violence
The goal is	order and stability based on balance of forces	legitimized resolution of conflict	post-revolutionary peace

Figure 4.2   Three approaches to the study of conflict

Individuals in the real world cannot be so crudely categorized, and would rightly resist such an attempt, but the justification for this rough map is that it may set some useful navigation points further to explore approaches to conflict in the contemporary world. In so doing we need to know what we are doing. Conflict, its causes, modalities, outcome and effects, is a matter central to each of the three approaches which characterize for the most part the study and practice of international relations in the English-speaking world today. What we think causes conflict determines what we think we can do about it. And both are a reflection of our conceptual framework for studying world society. It matters, too, if we are to survive.

NOTES AND REFERENCES

1. J. M. Keynes, *The General Theory of Employment, Interest, and Money* (London: Macmillan 1936): 383.
2. For an alternative formulation see Hayward Alker and Thomas Biersteker, "The Dialectics of World Order: Notes for a Future Archaeologist of International Savoir Faire," *International Studies Quarterly* (June 1984). For a further elaboration of the paradigm adopted here see Michael Banks, "The Inter-Paradigm Debate," in Margot Light and A. J. R. Groom (eds), *International Relations: A Handbook of Current Theory* (London: Frances Pinter, 1985).
3. E. H. Carr, *The Twenty Years' Crisis: 1919–1939* (London: Macmillan, 1981), and George Schwarzenberger, *Power Politics* (London: Stevens, 1964).
4. Hans J. Morgenthau, *Politics Among Nations* (New York: Alfred A. Knopf, 1959): 30–1.
5. Morgenthau, *Politics Among Nations*: 8.
6. Morgenthau, *Politics Among Nations*: 25.
7. Morgenthau, *Politics Among Nations*: 26.
8. Burton first set out his conception of world society in three works, *Systems, States, Diplomacy and Rules* (Cambridge: Cambridge University Press, 1968), *World Society* (London: Cambridge University Press, 1972), *The Study of World Society: A London Perspective* (Pittsburgh, International Studies Association Monograph, No. 1, 1974). His more recent views stressing the role of the individual as the basic unit of analysis can be found in *Deviance, Terrorism and War* (Oxford: Martin Robertson, 1979), *Dear Survivors* (London: Frances Pinter, 1982), and *Global Conflict* (Brighton, England: Wheatsheaf, 1984). For a brief overview see J. W. Burton in Light and Groom (eds), *International Relations* (London: Frances Pinter, 1985).
9. Richard Little, "Structuralism and Neo-Realism," in Light and Groom (eds), *International Relations*: 76.
10. See Kenneth Waltz, *Theory of International Politics* (London: Addison-Wesley, 1979), and Robert Keohane (ed.), *Neorealism and its Critics* (New York: Columbia University Press, 1986).
11. For a telling critique of neo-realism see Richard Ashley's contribution to a "Symposium on the New Realism," in *International Organization*, 38 (Spring 1984).
12. For an analysis of Wallerstein and the *dependencia* literature see Chris Brown, "Development and Dependency," in Light and Groom (eds), *International Relations*.
13. See Chalmers Johnson, *Revolutionary Change* (Boston: Little, Brown, 1966), Samuel P. Huntington, *Political Order in Changing Societies* (New Haven: Yale University Press, 1968), Harry Eckstein (ed.), *Internal War* (New York: Free Press of Glencoe, 1964), Ted. R. Gurr, *Why Men Rebel* (Princeton, N.J.: Princeton University Press, 1970), Che Guevara, *Guerrilla Warfare* (Harmondsworth, England: Penguin, 1969), Sir Robert Thompson, *Defeating Communist Insurgency* (New York: Praeger, 1966), Carlos Marighella, "Mini-manual of the Urban Guerrila"

(London, International Institute for Strategic Studies, 1971), appendix; Frank Kitson, *Low Intensity Operations* (London, 1971), to name some who first moved in this direction.

14. See Morton H. Halperin, *Bureaucratic Politics and Foreign Policy* (Washington D.C.: Brookings Institution, 1974).

15. See Ken Booth, *Strategy and Ethnocentrism* (New York: Holmes & Meier, 1979).

16. Philip K. Lawrence, "Nuclear strategy and political theory: a critical assessment," *Review of International Studies*, 11(2) (April 1985): 118.

17. See A. J. R. Groom, "Problem-Solving in International Relations," in Edward E. Azar and John W. Burton (eds), *International Conflict Resolution: Theory and Practice* (Brighton, England: Wheatsheaf, 1986).

18. J. W. Burton, "The Means to Agreement: Power or Values?" (Washington, D.C., March 1985): 23, mimeo.

19. Burton has set out the differences clearly in tabular form from the analytical point of view in the practical terms of the intervention in a conflict by a mediator or facilitator. See John W. Burton, "About Winning," *International Interactions*, 12(1) (1986): 87–91.

20. For a discussion of these problems see A. J. R. Groom, "Conflict Analysis and the Arab–Israeli Conflict," in James Barber, Josephine Negro and Michael Smith (eds), *Politics between States: Conflict and Cooperation* (Milton Keynes: Open University Press, 1975).

21. In his interesting article on positive sanctions David Baldwin discusses their comparative neglect in international relations and strategy as well as analyzing their means of application and their effect. See his "The Power of Positive Sanctions," *World Politics*, XXIV (1) (October 1971), and more recently his *Economic Statecraft* (Princeton, N.J.: Princeton University Press, 1985).

22. For synopses of the behavioralist and post-behavioralist positions see David Easton in James C. Charlesworth (ed.), *Contemporary Political Analysis* (New York: The Free Press of Glencoe, 1967), and David Easton, "The New Revolution in Political Science," *American Political Science Review*, LXIII (4) (December 1969).

23. Johan Galtung, *Essays in Peace Research*, vol. I (Copenhagen: Christian Ejlers, 1975): 256.

24. Helge Hveem, "Peace Research and its Institutionalization," Fourth General IPRA Conference, Bled, Yugoslavia (October 1971): 8–9, mimeo.

25. For an example of this general approach see Hermann Schmid, "Politics and Peace Research," *Journal of Peace Research* (March 1968). For a penetrating comment see Bernice A. Carroll, "Peace Research: The Cult of Power," *Journal of Conflict Resolution*, XVI (4) (December 1972).

26. See A. J. R. Groom and Keith Webb, "Injustice, Empowerment and Facilitation in Conflict," *International Interactions*, 13 (3) (1987).

III
Analysis

Chapter 5   The Individual, the Group and War   101
            Bryant Wedge
Chapter 6   Legitimacy and Human Needs   117
            Paul Sites
Chapter 7   Protracted International Conflicts: Ten   145
            Propositions
            Edward E. Azar
Chapter 8   A Critical Assessment of the Power of Human   156
            Needs in World Society
            Jerel A. Rosati, David J. Carroll and Roger A.
            Coate

5 The Individual, the Group and War
Bryant Wedge*

LEVELS OF BEHAVIORAL ANALYSIS

A fundamental issue in the analysis of behavior is the level of focus to which attention is directed. Psychoanalysis concerns itself largely with intrapsychic forces within the individual person as these are patterned by the internalization of his *intimate* history; second, psychoanalysis concerns itself with the expression of these forces in the behavior of the individual person. A political scientist, J. David Singer,[1] has shown that consideration of behavior of the national systems requires scarcely any appreciation of these intrapsychic forces, while the level of analysis of the international system needs none at all. Yet, there is no doubt that the manner of operation of the national and international levels of human organization depends ultimately on the participation or at least the consent of the individual persons whose aggregated behavior constitutes organized action – including war. Might we not, then, consider how the person relates to these larger contexts, how the various levels of transaction may serve to integrate the demands of drive-expression with environmental possibilities in ways that are not too threatening to survival or to such lesser expressions of love as self-esteem.

Professors Karl Deutsch of Harvard and Dieter Senghaas of Frankfurt distinguish seven identifiable levels of behavioral analysis – each linked transactionally with the others but each involving behavioral forces and mechanisms peculiar to the organizational level. These are:

1. Individual traits (intrapsychic processes expressed behaviorally).
2. Personality as a whole.
3. Small group levels.
4. Large interest groups (political parties, industrial organizations,

---

* From H. Z. Winnick, B. Moses and M. Ostrow (eds), *Psychological Bases of War* (New York: Quadrangle Books, 1973).

mass media, bureaucracies, etc.).
5. The nation-state.
6. Regional and international systems of organization (government relations including international bodies and non-governmental relations including trade and traffic patterns).
7. Humanity as a whole (virtually hypothetical as a construct but, nevertheless, the level of the "processes" of civilization of which Freud spoke so hopefully, if mystically).

Even with respect to the first two levels on which psychoanalysis focuses its principal attention, there are undoubtedly shortcomings in our formulation of the sources of personal aggressiveness and particularly of methods of training and management that would encourage the diversion of aggressive drives and affects from violent expression. Especially, we have neglected the analysis of "obedient aggression" which is fundamental to the conduct of war. It has been shown experimentally, for example, that subjects will frequently administer what they believe to be painful and even killing electric shocks to a screaming "victim" under the command of an experimenter.

For psychoanalysis to contribute fully to the analysis of the roots of personal violence it will be necessary to work together with experimentalists. Certainly there is nothing sacred about the practice of drawing knowledge *only* from patients on the couch; the methods of analytic reconstruction are equally applicable to associative materials from specific experience. We could learn and classify, for example, the kinds of experience which lead some persons to be more ready to be violent than others, what elements of "innate" or competitive aggression find outlet in specific violent acts, how defensive anxiety turns to willingness to harm others, and what kinds of frustrations promote aggression. More important, perhaps, we could learn how violence-inducing fear or frustration or obedience or competitiveness could be reduced by social circumstances and how social training could aid the ego toward finding non-violent means to relieve the aggressive impulse.

I will comment on the next three levels of analysis, those of the small groups, the large-interest group, and the national state as instances of group membership which, although there are decided differences between the levels with respect to unit behaviors, call forth broadly similar responses from the ego. Freud, of course, was fascinated by group psychology which he considered "the oldest human psychology" in his *Group Psychology and the Analysis of the Ego*.[2] In that essay, Freud recognized the profound impact of group participation on the behaviour of individuals; while he attributed this in part to the re-arousal of infantile family complexes and asserted the releasing-from-repression effects of group participation, he noted the role of multiple levels of group membership on the formation of personal aspirations and on the structure of the ego-ideal.

First, let me call attention to observations by social psychologists of the behavior of small groups in conflict and cooperation which I am certain would have fascinated Freud. Muzafer Sherif[3] and others have shown that whenever small groups of persons are brought together in common and shared circumstances for a length of time, over a few days they invariably develop a distinctive identity, a decided social structure with patterned interaction and mechanisms for accomplishing tasks and a sense of pride and loyalty in belonging. All of these phenomena are considerably heightened when the groups are faced with tasks that require working together to attain a common end – whether it is eleven-year-olds fixing a camp site or psychoanalysts establishing training criteria.

The next range of observations is even more striking. If, when such a group has formed, it is brought into contact with other groups with which there is a possible conflict of interest, there follows a process of invidious comparison. One's own group is seen as superior in a variety of ways – cleaner, bright, more honest, etc., while the other group(s) is/are seen as harboring undesirable traits and elements. Social distance is established between ingroup and outgroup members.

If such established groups are then brought into competition – for example, competing on a group basis for prizes, honor, or recognition – the invidious images become rapidly stereotyped. The structure of these stereotypes is remarkably constant among all sorts of experimental groups and remarkably consistent with the view held in such nationally-occurring groups as nations in conflict. I shall borrow from an analysis of such images in Ralph K. White's *Nobody Wanted War: Misperception in Vietnam and Other Wars*[4] to describe the sorts of stereotypes that are found. These studies are psychoanalytically fascinating, especially since their observations are wholly empirical and innocent of contamination by psychoanalytic formulations but are remarkably consistent with the language and predictions of psychoanalytic psychology.

White lists six principal components of the images held by the people of nations in conflict – pointing out, incidentally the "mirror-image" character of the stereotypes has been noted by Urie Bron-fenbrenner[5] in the views that Soviets and Americans hold of one another. I will discuss the implications of these components.

THE DIABOLICAL ENEMY IMAGE

Regularly, the outgroup that is seen as threatening some goal or value of the reference group becomes perceived as personifying a clever and amoral force bent on damaging one's own group as a principal purpose. It is supposed – and evidence can always be adduced in support of the supposition – that the "enemy" has no sense of decency or fairness, indeed, has proclivity for sneaky and underhanded methods. Further, the enemy is diabolically clever and plays on the morality of the group as though this were a weakness.

A group of eleven-year-old boys in Sherif's famous Robber's Cave experiment, for example, supposed that the competing group would mess up their swimming place and, having decided this, concluded that there were more stones in the water than before.

I found that professional diplomats in the American Embassy after the Dominican Republic uprising of 1965 were convinced that communist groups were plotting to create incidents that would require military suppression and, indeed, a number of accidental encounters were interpreted in terms of this theory; the young Dominican revolutionaries, in turn, developed identical images of American purposes and similar interpretations of accidental incidents. The psychoanalyst will recognize the familiar mechanism of projection in these views although, as I will discuss later, this is normal to members of groups in conflict rather than a pathological ego defense measure. The well-known reciprocal views of "expansionist, atheistic, subversive, totalitarian communism" held by whole groups of otherwise sane men in the West and the image of "lackeys and running-dogs of capitalist imperialism bent on destroying socialist development" held by otherwise mentally healthy people in the communist states represent similar tendencies which vastly complicate examination of the actual nature of the competing groups.

A VIRILE SELF-IMAGE

Groups in competition regularly develop a kind of anxious concern for their status and prestige manifested by the double symptoms of assertion of strength and fear of humiliation if there should be any retreat. Eleven-year-old boys bragged about their strength, skill, champions, and heroes *within* their groups, and chastized members who advocated retreat or peacemaking gestures. The obsessive concern of United States leadership about the consequences for American "credibility" of any retreat from what have long been recognized as impractical objectives in Vietnam is another case in point; here, the disparities in real power between the parties in conflict make the threat so ludicrous that it requires extensive rationalization to sustain.

THE MORAL–IMMORAL IMAGE

Another component of misperception is the "moral" self-image and the correspondingly "immoral" enemy image. A particularly common variant of the moral self-image is the "black-top image" of the competitor, at least in times of non-violent competition. The members of the competing group are good people who are misinformed and misled by an immoral leadership. Whether it is the "hidden ruling circles" that the Soviet Union sees in the United States or the "totalitarian dictatorship" that Americans see in the Soviet Union, the sources of evil are localized especially in places that are difficult to identify as humane.

SELECTIVE INATTENTION

Selective inattention is a major dynamic of misperception that sustains these invidious group images. As conflict escalates, there is a striking tendency to perceive only those items which would sustain the enemy image and to be blind to evidence that would contradict such views. This tendency is so powerful as to bring much punishment to serious scholars of the enemy's society; in extreme cases even a nation's accredited ambassadors are disbelieved when they report a disposition toward reasonableness on the part of the opposing leadership. Robert North,[6] at Stanford, has shown that this happened on nearly every side at the approach of the First World War. In short, woe to him who would oppose a stereotyped image of a competing group with evidence; he is certain to become a victim of the selective inattention that suppresses unpopular truths.

ABSENCE OF EMPATHY

Absence of empathy is notable because a psychological function that normally enables men to make judgements about the intentions of others becomes seriously impaired. The capacity to view the world and oneself from the other's point of view, to put oneself empathetically in the other's shoes, normally allows one to anticipate the impact of one's own behavior. But, when groups come into conflict, the capacity is lost; it is assumed that others will see things as one does oneself. The United States Administrations, for example, have been saddened and amazed that their allies and even many of their own people have perceived the Vietnam action in terms of a large nation bullying smaller ones – in fact, official announcements after five years of persistent criticism on this point continue to emphasize America's strength and power in such a way as to actually promote the unwanted image in others' eyes.

It is of course, exceedingly difficult to hurt or kill someone who is identified as another human being, and identification is a large component in empathy. It is, therefore, an ego-protective mechanism to dehumanize persons defined as enemies which, as Jerome Frank[7] has pointed out, is even easier in modern technical war than in previous military encounters. In any case, dehumanization of the enemy causes loss of empathy and, therefore, of the capacity to judge the other side's response to one's actions. This is a principal cause of miscalculation in intergroup conflict.

The question for the psychoanalyst, then, is: How can empathy be maintained in the face of group conflict? For it is certain that whatever reduces miscalculation and whatever sustains recognition of other persons' human qualities will reduce one's inclination to violent action or to the unwitting provocation of violence.

MILITARY OVERCONFIDENCE

Finally, in White's listing of sources of misperception in conflicts, comes military overconfidence. He notes that, "It is paradoxical but true that exaggerated fear can be combined with military overconfidence."

Regularly, *before* athletic contests, Sherif's eleven-year-old subjects bragged about how they would "destroy" the other side. Regularly US military leaders have miscalculated their effectiveness in Vietnam, including Secretary of Defense McNamara's famous estimate – made after full review of the most complete and detailed evidence – that the United States could begin to withdraw its forces in the Spring of 1966 with the military conflict under control. Today the statements of a Sadat or a Dayan bear earmarks of a similar dynamic in the Middle East conflict.

There is evidence that military overconfidence is particularly likely among professional soldiers – although it may at times affect whole populations and leaderships – and this is almost always on the basis of technical calculations that ignore the human response capacities of the enemy. As it happens, one of the tragic facts of international life is that military instrumentalities and military advice become especially prominent in times of international crisis, thus bringing to the foreground of decision making precisely those persons who occupy roles that demand an occupational absence of human empathy.

Now, before remarking on how psychoanalytic study might illuminate these regularly occurring group phenomena, I will briefly describe how cooperation has been induced between competing groups. Two elements appear to be essential: the establishment of direct human contact between members of the groups and the discovery of common goals that require cooperation to achieve ends desired by each interacting group. Outside these factors, only exhaustion, defeat, or subordination seem to limit cycles of intergroup conflict interaction.

Sherif and others have shown that direct contact in non-competitive circumstances – for example, the two groups of eleven-year-olds viewing films together – does not, by itself, markedly reduce intergroup hostility but that such contact allows the less violent expression of hostility. When, however, the necessity for cooperation to attain commonly desired "superordinate" goals is introduced, there is a rapid decrease in intergroup tension. For example, the eleven-year-olds found that *both* groups had to pull a rope to start the food truck and that both had to cooperate in eliminating a stoppage in the camp water supply. In such circumstances, the stereotyped images melt, and a variety of friendly interactions begin.

Between larger natural groups, I have found that tension can be materially reduced in applying this formula in ways modified by the fact that large natural groups are not subject to experimental manipulation. In the Dominican Republic, for instance, I undertook to reduce hostility between the grouping of revolutionary Dominican youths and the United States diplomatic mission. There, contact was established in steps, first by meeting personally with each group as a neutral outsider interested in scholarly issues, some time later introducing to both sides groups of distinguished international scholars concerned with university development. This paved the way for direct contact between leading members of the United States Embassy and the Dominican University Community with the general purpose of finding means to cooperate in university stabilization and development which, we had determined, was wanted by both sides.

The first direct meeting was arranged carefully; it took place at the home of the University Rector, and a number of neutral persons – the visiting scholars, the Papal Nuncio, a Bishop, and the Mexican Ambassador – were present as buffers between twenty leading persons from both groups. In this real-life experiment, the findings of the laboratory were astonishingly confirmed. Group members paired off with their counterparts and argued their respective cases with considerable vigor. By the end of an evening no minds had been changed nor had any opposing argument been accepted. *But*, the leaders of each group concluded that the other side was reasonable (if mistaken in its views), serious in purpose, and capable of cooperation. They then proceeded to joint planning and have worked together ever since.

Here, again, in a national setting as in the laboratory, tension reductions followed direct contact and a variety of superordinate goal definition. I consider this to be one model for contributing to a process of peace: contact by intercession followed by direct contact followed by joint planning for common goals – which I term partial superordinate goals, since the immediate aim is not a peace treaty or high level settlement of outstanding problems but merely learning to work together on limited issues requiring cooperation. I believe that a series of such arrangements between groups in conflict, regardless of their scale, can inhibit the conflict cycle and reduce the disposition toward misperception, miscalculation, and violence.

POSSIBLE PSYCHOANALYTIC CONTRIBUTIONS

I have chosen to summarize a range of validated observations that have been made in complete innocence of psychoanalytic models of psychological functioning and which still lack the sort of explanation which would permit intervention in intergroup conflict with the purpose of reducing hostility and violence. I consider that all the phenomena described are subject to psychoanalytic interpretation and that such interpretations can be refined and validated by direct and indirect examination of participants in both experimental and real-life circumstances. What I am proposing is that the community of psychoanalysts support and encourage some of its members in detailed and scientific work on the psychological dynamics of group behavior. This would require close collaboration with behavioral scientists using other methods *and* it would require that psychoanalysts both sanction and fund specific investigations relevant to understanding of the war problem. We might here recall that Freud would surely have pursued this subject further and that even the founder of psychoanalysis had to appeal to humanitarians for funds to carry on his work; those analysts who have benefited personally and professionally from this work might well repay their indebtedness by a more active role in extending their science.

Here, I shall remark only on the most general dynamic that appears to operate in the production of group behavior. This is what the psychoanalyst Charles Pinderhughes of Boston has described as "the resolution of ambivalence by (normal) group paranoia." Pinderhughes's investigations of racial feelings have led him to conclude that perceptions of one's own body and of physiological processes which are associated with unpleasant feelings are readily linked with images and representations of other significant persons and memories. These "normal" projective processes are particularly liable to activation by group involvement, especially since group members reinforce one another in their "delusional" interpretations which are, moreover, insulated from reality testing by the limitations of contact with members of the despised outgroup.

In [this] setting . . . I cannot forbear to report an example of this dynamic in the Middle East. Ten years ago, during a visit to a Kibbutz, I observed a play-therapy setting in which one of the toys was a doll in Arab costume. When I asked the therapist how Israeli children treated this toy it was explained that they playacted all their rejected impulses with the Arab doll, including theft, violence, and sex. The psychologist deplored this tendency, already evident at the age of $2\frac{1}{2}$ years, but soon afterwards the same psychologist warned me against visiting a certain Arab village: the inhabitants might well rob and possibly kill me as they were so hostile and unscrupulous. The psychologist asserted he would never go there himself without adequate protection. Needless to say, the Arab villagers proved to be warm hosts but were equally and even more overtly convinced of the evil purposes of their Jewish neighbors – and were so instructing *their* children.

It appears to me that this general dynamic is operative in all the phenomena that I have summarized. This does not imply psychological disorder but is a normal manifestation of group life: every human person constructs his own interpretation of reality in the context of his association with unique groups of others. It is, however, an extended task to trace the development of each of the empirically observed items of group psychology at the different levels of analysis: notice, for instance, the complete inversion of psychological interpretation in the "black-top image" of the enemy as contrasted with attribution of identity of structure (intrapsychically and socially) implied in the diabolical enemy image.

Interventions aimed at the reduction and correction of intergroup delusions would surely be made more effective by the development of an adequate formulation of the dynamics on which the delusions depend. For example, my own interventions in the Dominican conflict were materially assisted by recognition of the Americans' overestimation of the presumed hostility of the unruly revolutionaries and of the Dominicans' identification of the Americans with tyrannical superego structures. What is needed then, is the construction of psychoanalytically-based formulations of group psychology that are as elegant and confirmed as are the interpretations of the development of the neuroses – and their treatment.

STEPS TOWARD WAR

We now come to the study of the specific manifestation of human aggression in the institution of war. In the first place contemporary war is an exclusive property of national state behavior; as Freud noted, the national state monopolizes the exercise of killing violence against the human person, most particularly those forms of organized deliberate and systematic killing of the people of other national states. Second, the whole process of war is highly institutionalized; a large variety of formal conditions must be satisfied before the national state can successfully engage in military violence. In these characteristics war is thoroughly unlike all other forms of human aggression, mayhem, murder, riots and civic uprising; here the ego and the superego join with the drives in the aim of killing.

It is well to recall here that the contemporary national state is a very recent development in the history of man, scarcely four hundred years old in the judgement of Hans Kohn,[8] a preeminent historian of nationalism. And the war behavior of national states is distinctly different from that of earlier forms of warfare – so different as to be essentially discontinuous in social and psychological as well as political form with such anachronistic events as tribal conflict or the Greek and Roman imperial campaigns. Earlier, individual leaders, small elite groups, or large special interest groups could decide on and prosecute military campaigns as a matter of assumed prerogative, while national state warfare absolutely requires the sustained mobilization of the sentiments of the entire citizenry to the national purposes of war. The national state is truly a new level of analysis of human behavior, itself a product of the process of cultural learning and its global diffusion.

The institution of war is, of course, much older, as earlier forms were evolved and codified in the dim prehistory of the race. The national state has simply preempted the use of the institution and, in the process, substantially modified it. I emphasize this point because a vast amount of political scholarship has clarified these issues since Freud wrote and since any analysis of the institutions of contemporary war must necessarily be directed to the specific group level of behavior; it is exceedingly easy to confuse precedent from historic periods or from other levels of violent actions when, in fact, entirely distinctive psychological and political dynamics are involved.

When one focuses on the issues of contemporary war in these terms as a good deal of scholarship has been focused, it rapidly becomes apparent that a very large number of conditions must be satisfied for a national state to engage in overt war and that going to war is therefore a *process* involving distinctive stages or phases of escalation. While there are a number of formulations of the stages in the production of war, I will here only mention some of the steps as outlined by Senghaas. He points out that within any national body some individuals must first be convinced of the virtues of engaging in war and must set about recruiting many others. Then, large interest groups must find the idea compatible with their purposes. These forces can engage the sanction of the dominant elite of the nation which, in turn influences the mass media toward mobilization of mass opinion. At this point the national political system and the specific regimes become involved and undertake the recruitment of the government organization and bureaucracy to war readiness. Only at this point do national policies and strategies become involved and these must be reconciled with the war purpose. Since adversary nations are now certain to be responding to the growing threat posed by the mobilizing nation, the necessity arises for crisis decision making which generally reverts to a small group within the regime. At this point there is a real risk of the process getting out of control both internally and externally and this leads to an escalation of commitments. For example, even when Serbia had capitulated to Austrian demands, there was no stopping the momentum of the aroused war-making impulse that precipitated the First World War. Finally, into this process enters the role of the wider environment, the actions and accidents that may restrain or encourage the opening of military engagements.

As a case in point, we might notice national state behavior at the tenth stage, that of crisis decision making. As I have noted, the decision process becomes localized in a small group of leaders and advisors at this point and one can analyze the forces at work in such a group. All the rules of small group behavior certainly operate in a complex environment. For example, perceptual distortion in viewing the nature and intentions of the enemy and even of the nation's own population is certain to enter in, in accordance with some of the dynamics of group image that I outlined. Then, there is the phenomenon of the "risky shift;" it has been experimentally demonstrated that group members tend to reinforce one another toward risk taking beyond the degree that the individual members would have considered individually. Military overconfidence is a decided risk, as President Kennedy learned with the ill-fated Bay of Pigs misadventure and President Johnson learned in relation to Vietnam.

Analysis at these critical stages in the production of war is well advanced in the fields of political and psychological study but has scarcely been touched psychoanalytically although there is a vast range of material available for such study. What could be made, for example, of the consequences of Stalin's image of "Mother Russia, beaten down and dragged in the mud" and requiring the defense of her sons as compared with President Johnson's "manly" image of "bringing home the coon-skin to nail on the wall."

Here, of course, I have touched upon another critical question: that of distinctive national psychologies and their dynamic consequences. In the final analysis, it can be seen, the elimination of the war menace will require a case-by-case study of the psycho–political dynamics of specific peoples and groups in specific encounters.

At this point, however, we can already envision broad strategies for war-preventing action. At each level of analysis and at each stage of war production an adequate study of the psycho–political processes involved would lead to the formulation of interpretations which would indicate how man's aggressive energies could be diverted to other channels than war making. It is very difficult for national states to be aroused to the point of war participation. It ought to be relatively possible to intervene at various points in the process if serious citizen scientists were to mobilize energies to that purpose. Personally, I have chosen to intercede at the levels of international and national governments for the most part and have invariably found a powerful preference for peaceful solutions *if* any practical way could be found.

A GENERAL STRATEGY FOR PEACE

So far in this chapter, I have only spoken of the first five levels of analysis, but the two broader discernible levels of organization of human systems are the locus of culture change from which Freud and all of us can find hope for the elimination of war.

Regional and international groupings and linkages, among both government and private participants, certainly serve to restrain the war making impulse. When members of different nations establish and institutionalize programs of cooperation for any purpose, trade, scientific exchange, or cultural enrichment, these serve to act as third systems or intersystem systems that then exert influence on the respective governments and nations in order to maintain their own programs. Numerous such linkages between any set of nations have the effect of "tying down Gulliver" – that is, of constraining gigantic forces with many small threads and connections.

While the psychological needs of such intergroup groupings have been studied quite largely in the sphere of the social ego, there are undoubtedly points in the history of each such development that involve such individual strain as to open the way for the eruption of infantile impulses; until psychoanalytic observation has been applied to such developments, it is impossible to guess what sources of static and breakdown spring from the operation of unconscious forces.

It is at the final level of analysis of mankind as a whole, that exceedingly profound changes can be discerned, however dimly. What can be observed on a worldwide scale is the failure of the established and traditional forms of authority relationship to contain or manage the energies and aspirations of subjects. This is true between governments and people – one hardly speaks any more of the ruler and the ruled – between institutions and members and between parent and child.

A psychoanalytically sophisticated political scientist, Manfred Halpern of Princeton University,[9] has pointed out that the hierarchical authority relationship has passed through several stages from that of acceptance by mutual assumption, through various forms of physical repression, isolation and boundary establishment to avoid conflict, direct bartering and contest of power, to a new phase, that of mutual transformation between parties in relationship. This formulation accords with that of John Spiegel,[5] perhaps the only psychoanalyst to have undertaken the systematic study of human violence, who also points out the failure of hierarchical or linear forms of social organization to meet contemporary demands for social change and advocates the strengthening of capacities for "collateralism" of relationship. Here, indeed, is a challenge to psychoanalytic psychology.

There is no doubt at all that profound changes in intrapsychic organization will accompany the sort of alteration in models of relationship between parent and child that must, perforce, accompany a sweeping reorganization of social authority processes. I personally believe that the influence of psychoanalysis in the lifting of social repression of sexuality in the West has contributed materially to what could be characterized as cultural change of revolutionary proportions. In any case, just as psychoanalysts have observed a striking shift in symptom manifestation from the neuroses of crude repression to those of character and relationship, I believe that we are now seeing a still further change in which studies of neurotic preoccupation and symptom formation will be centered around the relations of men to their societies. I have no question at all but that the central methods and statements of psychoanalysis will assume growing importance in the understanding of man; the question is, whether the community of psychoanalysts will apply those methods in changing circumstances or will insist on definitions of man based in part on kinds of authority relations that are being modified by culture change.

I believe that Freud was correct in observing that war is an outcome of the exercise of suppressive force but I think he was wrong in recommending the same model on a broader level – that is, the development of a global authority – as a prescription for eliminating war; indeed, it seems probable that the use of violence or threat of violence to enforce authority at any level is apt to produce violence at all levels. Rather, his observation that cultural change might eliminate war would seem more likely of realization in the down-grading of the authority principle in human organization and relation-ships. I think that this is taking place and that whatever helps us understand and recognize and accommodate to these changes will assist in avoiding that last disastrous spasm of a dying era in human relations that could end the whole human venture.

Psychoanalysis can study these new forms; we can assist in the recognition of their consequences and limitations. We can provide some guidance to the social change process based on an understanding of the intrapsychic requirements of the human species. With certainty, psychoanalytic study at each level of behavioral analysis during each major stage of the war production process would illuminate the hidden psychological causes of war and contribute to developing practical steps to abort the process and to divert the aggressive energies of man to less self-destructive channels.

Few professions and sciences are in a position to contribute to the "superior class of independent thinkers" that Freud thought might guide mankind out of the suicidal habit of war; psychoanalysis is in that position and now, thirty-five years after Freud wrote, could enrich mankind and the profession itself by an active and systematic – Freud wrote "fervent" – participation in the peace process that is now as clearly recognizable as is the war cycle.

NOTES AND REFERENCES

1. J. David Singer (ed.), *Human Behavior and International Politics* (Chicago: Rand McNally, 1965).
2. Sigmund Freud, *Group Psychology and the Analysis of the Ego* (New York: Boni and Liveright, 1920).

3. Muzafer Sherif, *Intergroup Conflict and Cooperation: the Robber Cave Experiment* (Normon, O.K.: University Book Exchange, 1961).
4. Ralph K. White, *Nobody Wanted War: Misperception in Vietnam and Other Wars* (Garden City, N.J.: Prentice Hall, 1968).
5. Urie Bronfenbrennen, *Two Worlds of Childhood: U.S. and U.S.S.R.* (New York: Russell Sage Foundation, 1970).
6. Eugenia V. Nomikos and Robert C. North, *International Crisis: the Outbreak of World War I* (Montreal: McGill–Queen's University Press, 1976).
7. Jerome D. Frank, *Sanity and Survival* (New York: Random House, 1967).
8. Hans Kohn, *The Idea of Nationalism* (New York: Collier, 1967).
9. Manfred Halpern, *The Morality and Politics of Intervention* (New York: Council of Religion and International Affairs, 1969).

6 Legitimacy and Human Needs
Paul Sites*

The past decade or so has produced a great deal of scholarly dialogue about a crisis in legitimacy. The events which are seen as having produced this crisis are variously discussed by different authors and include the following: (1) the student ferment of the 1960s and early 1970s; (2) the disillusionment produced by Stalin and the failure of the socialist experiment; (3) the non-tractable dependency of third world nations; (4) the reemergence of ethnic identities challenging the hegemony of entrenched majorities; (5) the challenge to patriarchal dominance by the women's liberation movement; (6) the failure of the welfare state; (7) the growth of evangelical religions indicating a dissatisfaction with existing secular order; (8) the problem of homelessness and the inability (unwillingness) to deal with this; (9) the increased use of drugs by the middle and upper class, not seen as a problem when restricted to the ghettos; (10) the emergence and growth of neo-conservatism; (11) the crisis in health care; and (12) the growth of outright greed and corruption during the Reagan years.

These events, most of which either occurred or were recognised after World War II, challenged the prevailing theory of legitimacy among sociologist and political scientists based primarily upon the work of Parsons[1], whose work[2], in turn, was based primarily on a synthesis of the work of Max Weber and Emile Durkheim even though others were included in this early volume. Parsons was probably the last of Enlightenment thinkers. Even though he said he rejected rationalist solutions to the problem of order, this is belied by his veiled belief in progress, and his explicit belief in the inevitability of universal democracy. He may have seen the real world around him but he could not force himself to believe what was happening. We need to look briefly at the Parsonion view of legitimacy and show why it failed. This will involve looking at Weber's treatment of legitimacy and a brief mention of Durkheim's conceptual bias. What follows is not meant to be an exhaustive treatment of the work

* This chapter was written at the request of the editors for the purposes of this collection of essays.

117

of any of these scholars.

There is little doubt that Weber's thought set the stage for the modern treatment of legitimacy. In his theory of action, Weber was a subjectivist in the sense that he was concerned with the meaning action had from the point of view of the individual actor. Thus, for him, legitimacy is based on the *belief* among people that an order is legitimate. This is to say, in Weber's terms, that an existing order is what it ought to be from the point of view of the actor.[3] Since considerations of "oughtness" presuppose a basis of judgement, Weber provides three basic types of legitimate orders. An order may be seen by an actor as valid if it rests on tradition (traditional order) or if it rests on the teachings of a charismatic leader (affectual order) or if it rests on value or instrumental rationality (legal order). This yields three types of corresponding authority; traditional, charismatic and legal rational.

Weber was clearly aware, however, that obedience does not always rest on a belief in the legitimacy of a ruler:

> It is by no means true that every case of submissiveness to persons in positions of power is primarily (or even at all) oriented to this belief. Loyalty may be hypocritically simulated by individuals or whole groups on purely opportunistic grounds, or carried out in practice for reasons of material self interest. Or, people may submit from individual weakness and helplessness because there is no acceptable alternative.[4]

This recognition, along with the fact that he saw types of religious orientation as class-based, did not sway him from his types of legitimacy based on belief. It thus becomes an empirical question as to the number or percentage of people who must submit to a given order based on belief compared with those who submit for the reasons listed in the above quotation. If a majority submit out of belief, an order is supposedly legitimate. It is this type of "division" in Weber's thought which, in more recent years, led some sociologists, with a conflict persuasion, to place Weber in the conflict rather than the functionalist tradition.[5]

Before going on to a brief discussion of Durkheim, a word needs to be said about the ambiguity of Weber's concept of authority. As D. Sites[6] makes clear, the concept of legitimacy as used by Weber and consequently many other political scholars is superfluous: indeed, a contradiction. A differentiation is made between power which is coercive and/or manipulative and authority which is seen as legitimate power based on belief or consensus. But as he points out, "Power makes sense only when there are cleavages which resist being combined or committed as a whole."[7] This is to say that power is never expressed unless there is other power resisting it. Thus, if people are willing to go along, for whatever reason, the use of power is not necessary. Given this, to define authority as the legitimate use of power makes no sense. The use of power, by definition, can never be legitimate. As he points out, there may often exist a tyranny of the majority (dominant group) where the concept of legitimacy is used as justification for such tyranny but minorities obviously would not see such tyranny as legitimate. One then wonders if this is not typically the case in many societies – e.g., blacks in The Union of South Africa and in the USA, Arabs under Jewish control and Armenians in the USSR to name but a few. In spite of this problem of definition, we will maintain the concept of legitimacy as the designation of a valid system but will introduce a different criterion for the judgement of such validity (legitimacy).

As typically interpreted,[8] Durkheim's[9] somewhat rigid sociologism left him with little concern for the individual. The primary concern which runs throughout, even though tempered somewhat in this latter work, is social solidarity and the social facts that increase or decrease this solidarity and/or change its type. Even though Durkheim is aware that crime or other types of "deviant behavior" such as suicide may be seen as either abnormal or normal, depending on the type of society in comparison with other societies of the same type in which they occur, he is not generally concerned with why such deviant behavior is a normal reaction to existing conditions. The big exception to this is his study of the rates of suicide.[10] He bases his explanation of suicide, however, on the degree of solidarity experienced by the individual and/or present in society, rather than basing it on some type of (say) overall "misery index" related to individual existence. If the degree of social solidarity is high, he would be interpreted to say that a system is legitimate. Anyone or anything that threatens this solidarity is therefore illegitimate. Given this it is not expected that Durkheim would have much to say about the use of coercive power or sectional interests, and he does not.

As [already] indicated, Parsons synthesized his interpretation of the work of Weber and Durkheim in his *The Structure of Social Action* which became the basis for much of his work which followed. In doing this, Parsons paid scant attention to the possible bases of conflict in Weber's work. Thus, even though he used Weber's ideas of action and his idea of consensus based on belief, it was Durkheim's collective conscious as a basis for solidarity that was to underpin his major work. The collective conscious became culture based upon "ultimate values." Using Freud's idea of introjection, he has individuals introjecting these values in the socialization process. This automatically produces a continued belief in these values from generation to generation so that consensus is guaranteed. Like Durkheim, he had little concern for the basic needs of individuals even though he was aware of their existence. He was forced by the logic of his theoretical system, however, to get rid of this extraneous variable. What he calls "viserogenic" needs, following Freud, are transformed into need dispositions which match the normative demands of the system so that "people come to want to do what they have to do."[11] In this, he pays little attention to the possible disruptive forces contained in Freud's "id" even though he was aware of this in Freud's work. To maintain the logic of his theoretical structure deviant behavior is seen as caused by a need disposition toward deviance.

Culture and socialization are the keystone of his theory, as this relates to our concern, so that in terms of political theory, political socialization or the acquisition of political culture became the basis of political thought in terms of legitimacy by mid-century, accepted by most sociologists and political scientists. People supposedly accept any regime as legitimate because they internalize the values which support its continuance. Most political scientists and sociologists concerned with consensus legitimacy use Parsons as their theoretical source.[12]

CRITICISM OF THE "DOMINANT IDEOLOGY" THESIS

Abercrombie, Hill and Turner[13] criticize the consensus thesis as naive in relationship to historical facts. Their position is that a dominant ideology as a basis for consensus legitimacy had little credence either during the feudal period or the period of early capitalism. A dominant ideology had use only in terms of integrating members of the elite in both periods. In the feudal period, peasants, isolated in rural areas, had little interaction with the church and its teachings which provided the basis of ideology in that period. Their religious life was much more likely to be based upon "pagan" beliefs and rituals and their real concern was the routine of everyday life. In the early capitalist period, otherwordly religion was the mainstay of the masses as exemplified in the teachings of early Methodism. Thus, even though there may have been a consensus among elites produced by belief in a dominant ideology, the masses marched to the tunes of different drummers. They were more concerned with survival than anything else and what meaning they had came from differing religious orientations.

As they point out, and as indicated above, religious beliefs for Weber were class-based and these beliefs differed significantly among the various classes. In interpreting Durkheim, they point out that Durkheim[14] saw the collective conscious (culture) becoming less and less of an integrating force as the division of labor becomes increasingly more complex. It might be added that Durkheim's ideas concerning the abnormal division of labor also speak to the alienation from a dominant ideology. Thus, Parson's views as these are related to these two scholars are highly selective and do not square with historical facts. In spite of this, the consensus view of legitimacy came to be the prevailing view.

THE DEPRIVATION THEORY OF LEGITIMACY

Even though Easton[15] accepted much of the consensus orientation in the sense that diffuse support of a system can come only through socialization, he did recognize a contingent component: the necessity on the part of elites of meeting the demands of citizens. Easton, like many others, sees the political system as the mechanism that allocates various values. When people feel deprived in their realization of one or more of these values, they make demand for redress. A system that continuously responds to such demands maintains its legitimacy. But as Bay[16] has pointed out, "uncritical acceptance of our allegedly democratic order does not jibe with [add up to] what political scientists know about the power of elites, or the techniques of mass manipulation." Not only do elites attempt to formulate and maintain values which are in their interests, they also manipulate populations by the manner in which values are allocated. Piven and Cloward[17] have demonstrated this conclusively in their classic *Regulating the Poor*. When the poor make demands, relief programs are allocated but when the poor become less demanding, the allocation is taken away. The same has been the case with blacks: cities which had riots in the 1960s received more allocations than cities that did not.

Furthermore, when blacks stopped making demands, many of the gains which they had achieved were lost. The demands of one group are usually played off against the demands of another.

Elites are also masters at making all deprivations appear relative so that demands will not be made. For example, people who are hungry in the American society are asked to compare themselves with people in Africa who are starving. Or people who feel insecure are asked to compare themselves with people in police states where secret police engage in constant terror tactics to control populations. People with low incomes are asked to compare themselves with people in third world nations who makes even less. Furthermore, the fact that there are large differences within a nation makes some better off than many and cools demands since those with very little fear they might be worse off under changed conditions.

RATIONAL MODELS OF LEGITIMACY

Following Easton, Rogowski[18] constructs a rational model of legitimacy based on the axiom that "people's preferences among alternative governments, and their decisions to accept or to oppose existing governments, result from rational choice."[19] As in exchange theory, rationality is based on the calculation of costs and outcomes based on probabilities among possible *extant* alternative values. Here again values may be constructed and maintained by elites to serve their own interests rather than providing a fuller range of choice. People are typically asked to choose alternatives within the framework of *existing* values since people in power do not permit other values to be seriously considered. For example, Americans are not given a choice among alternative economic systems based on different values. Nor are they given a serious choice is terms of alternative medical delivery systems. Indeed, there is a concentrated effort on the part of elites to keep systems based on different values from even being worthy of consideration. "As a matter of fact, the definition of alternatives is the supreme instrument of power."[20] It finally boils down to this. Since reason *qua* reason provides no basis for judgement, any system of legitimacy based on rational choice must base such choice on extant values, at least in the absence of a charismatic leader, and these extant values may be inadequate to the task of a truly valid order.

POST-MODERN AND POST-STRUCTURALIST THOUGHT

Some of the events set forth at the beginning of this chapter also produced what has come to be called post-modern and post-structuralist thought. Even though we will not take the space to treat this body of thought in any depth, two ideas embodied in this thought – the death of essences and the questioning of reason – are relevant to the discussion. These thinkers take the position that we can no longer rely on "essences" as a basis for judgement since none can be demonstrated. These were the "essences" for which traditional philosophy searched and, for our purposes, upon which traditional legitimacy was supposedly based. As Schaar[21] says, ". . . a claim to political power is legitimate only when the claimant can invoke some source of authority beyond or above himself." He goes on to quote Arendt[22] ". . . legitimacy derives from something outside the range of human deed; it is either not man-made at all . . . or has at least not been made by those who happen to be in power." Schaar gives such examples as "immemorial custom, divine law and the law of nature." Thus elites have evoked a variety of external essences in an attempt to legitimate their use of power with the divine right of kings being perhaps the most obvious as this relates to the political order, and Adam Smith's natural law of supply and demand as this relates to the economic order in capitalist societies.[23] The American civil religion might also be considered here.[24]

What post-modern/post-structuralist thinkers are saying in regard to our concern is that essences are becoming increasingly flimsy as a basis for judging the validity of an order. If this is the case, a belief in an essence – e.g., Parsons' "ultimate reality" which stands behind power to "legitimate" its use or misuse – is decreasingly feasible. This not only leaves the emperor without clothes but also increases the probability that others, in addition to children, will tell him he is naked. If this is the case, what then can serve as a basis for the judgement of the validity of an order; perhaps reason?

Weber saw this problem being solved in the modern world by a reliance on instrumental rationality as a basis for legitimacy. In this type (*zweckrational*) both means and ends may be manipulated. But this is the problem facing the modern world once this is realized since *explicit* manipulation denies any basic ontology or essence upon which decisions may be made. Since this is the case, instrumental rationality comes to be based not on the validity of ends but on the validity of means with the judgement of validity based on efficiency: where there is efficiency, there is legitimacy. In practice this comes to be a series of procedures, the strict following of procedural means to arrive at an end. Thus, justice, for example, becomes procedural justice, and judgements within a bureaucratic organization are based on the correct following of procedures in spite of what this may do to people. If the correct – that is to say, efficient – procedures are followed, that is all that is required. Thus, a truly innocent person becomes guilty by definition in a court of law if correct procedures are followed and a person may be "justly" fired, without recourse, within a bureaucracy, if correct procedures are carried out. In neither case can there be any consideration of real or absolute justice since there is no absolute basis for judgement. In the former case, laws are also established by procedures and in the latter bureaucratic rules are established by procedures. The affirmative action procedure might also be noted. Thus, "legitimacy" under instrumental rationality, is reduced to an infinite regress of procedures. Interestingly enough, Weber was aware of this as indicated by his concern for the "iron cage of rationality" which denies basic humanity but he still called it a type of legitimacy. In all this, it is obvious that only the individual, not the system, may be blamed since it is only system procedures which make it "work."

Too many fail to see that reason cannot be its own guide; reason *qua* reason can provide no basis for judgement in terms of the ultimate validity of ends. Because of this, as indicated above, ends may be manipulated, along with means. As Lyotard[25] says, "there is no reason, only reasons." Reasons given typically differ only on the basis of sectional interests.

> *Given (1) that essences, the supposed traditional basis of judgement, are being held up to questions; (2) the knowledge that beliefs can be manipulated along with the increasingly contingent nature of social life; and (3) that reason* qua *reason cannot provide a basis for judgement, there is perhaps only one final basis upon which judgements in regard to legitimacy might rest and this is the nature of the individual: on human needs.*

As Touraine[26] says, "Isn't it high time to recognize that humans are not located in front of nature but in it?" He goes on to say:[27]

> The traditional thought of industrial societies has conceived needs as the simple replication of economic growth. Engle's famous law meant to show that a rise in revenue augmented the share of

optimal consumption and lowered that of basic staples. Today we are seeing a violent rejection of this quantitative conception of needs, a rejection that takes the form of an appeal to deep, fundamental and natural needs. Now these are all notions that do not have a clear sociological meaning, but they are indicative of a will to oppose another mode of life and other preferences to the technocratic modeling of demand.

Many other recent scholars have questioned the validity of the technocratic path of production and consumption as being the *only* path.[28] As indicated, Touraine has suggested fundamental human needs as a point of beginning and others have suggested this as well, and this will be discussed below. First, it seems necessary to establish this type of thinking within a tradition or traditions of thought since this is not the first time human needs have been suggested as providing a basis for judgement in evaluating the legitimacy of systems. This was the case for the social contract thinkers, along with Marx and others.

THE CLASSICAL THINKERS AND MARX

Hobbes began with individuals in a state of nature. Following his assumption that these individuals' [lives] were by their nature "solitary, poore, brutish and short" social order was impossible: there was only chaos. The only alternative to the "war of all against all," given this basic nature, was that of entering into a social contract and the appointment of a sovereign with unlimited power to lay down rules which would end the chaos. Once the contract was made it could not be broken since breaking the contract would, by definition, destroy the only basis of order and bring about once again a condition of chaos. Even though Hobbes had a very negative view of human nature, along with a solution that few today would find acceptable, at least his view of legitimacy takes the nature of the individual into account in the formulation of a solution.

Locke's view of human nature is nearly the opposite of Hobbes's in that, by nature, humans are capable of achieving a decent humanity without government; they are inherently moral. Thus, for Locke, the role of government is legitimate only if it guarantees to people what nature has already bestowed upon them. People have the right to overthrow governments which do not meet this legitimating responsibility. Final sovereignty thereby lies with the people since it is their nature that society is protecting. Again, we find that legitimacy is a logical outgrowth of Locke's view of the nature of the individual.

Rousseau's view was close to that of Locke even though he saw his assumption of the basic nature of the species as a hypothetical construct. His famous dictum: "man is born free; and everywhere is in chains" is a prologue to his view of sovereignty and the state and thus his view of legitimacy. Thus, in his *Social Contract* he sees liberty and equality as the greatest goods and the perpetuation of these as the legitimate end of any system of rule, insisting that true liberty cannot exist without equality. Legitimate governments must protect what people *by nature* most desire: freedom, equality and happiness.

In summary, we find that the views of these early scholars concerning legitimacy are unequivocally based upon what they viewed as the basic nature of individuals. None saw the needs of governments or requisites of systems taking precedent over the needs of individuals. But as we have seen, this line of thought was not to continue as modern theorists turned their attention to the needs or requisites of systems rather than being concerned with the needs of individuals. Marx's view was closer to those of earlier scholars.

Even though Marx was somewhat prone to accept the dominant ideology thesis as indicated by his treatment of false consciousness, he was aware that the dominant ideology did not produce a valid legitimacy. One focus of Marx's[29] early work was the nature of the human species. He isolated two basic differences between the human species and other species. The uniqueness of the human species is the potential for creativity and the possibility of constructions made in the mind before they are made in actuality. Thus, people make their own history even as they are made by history. Any system which denies this creative potential on the part of all people is, by definition, illegitimate since it alienates people from their species-nature. In this regard, Marx's later work cannot be divorced from the early since his later work, devoted primarily to the critique of capitalism, is based upon this earlier insight. In short, Marx's basic critique of capitalism was that it denied the nature of the human species.

Since space does not permit a complete discussion of Marx's true need/false need conceptualization to which much of the discussion of human needs can be traced,[30] let me provide one brief quote from Marx which not only shows the basis of the problem but also summarizes much that has been said above. In contrasting the implications of socialism and capitalism for human needs, he says concerning the latter:

> Under private property their significance is reversed: every person speculates on creating a *new* need in another, so as to drive him to fresh sacrifice, to place him in a new dependence and to seduce him into a new mode of *enjoyment* and therefore economic ruin. Each tries to establish over the other an *alien* power, so as thereby to find satisfaction of his own selfish need. The increase in the quantity of objects is therefore accomplished by an extension of the realm of alien powers to which man is subjected, and every new product represents a new *potentiality* of mutual swindling and mutual plundering . . . Subjectively, this appears partly in the fact that the extension of products and needs becomes a *contriving* and ever-*calculating* subservience to inhuman, sophisticated, unnatural and *imaginary* appetites. Private property does not know how to change crude need to *human* need.[31]

MORE RECENT THOUGHT ON HUMAN NEEDS

Before going on, it is useful to state why the consensus thinkers have not been concerned with human need. This tends to spring from an assumption that human infants are infinitely malleable so that the process of socialization can mold them into what they *must* become in order to live in any type of human society. In Parsons's terms, the biological organism provides *only the energy* which is molded by socialization agents using cultural information: his cybernetic hierarchy of control. In this, little attention is paid to the possible damage done even though this is somewhat obvious in non-conforming behavior, from crime and mental illness to revolutions. The point here is that there must be something about the nature of the human species that cries out for gratification under certain types of social structure. Were this not the case, and assuming complete socialization, what is called deviant behavior, alienation and a variety of other behaviors would not occur. At base, the problem comes down to this. Can social science more adequately explain the total behavior of individuals and the way in which societies are ordered and changed by understanding the basic nature of individuals or is socialization enough? In terms of legitimacy, presupposing we want to keep the concept, we are faced with the problem of judgement. We must

specify the conditions under which we are willing to say that an order
and its political system are legitimate. This is a judgement call, and
it does have obvious implications.

Before the Enlightenment, Christian thought saw the nature of
humans as basically evil with Christ being the only hope of salvation.
Enlightenment thought rejected this idea and replaced it with the
view that humankind, unencumbered by any remnant of an animal
nature, could save itself through reason. Even though the social
contract thinkers raised the possibility of a basic human nature, as
noted above, this view did not catch hold until the nineteenth century
in the work of Marx and Freud, both of whom came to have a
renewed concern with human nature and, therefore, with human
salvation. Marx, of course, saw the possibility of eventual salvation
of total humanity through the play of social and economic forces.
Freud saw only the possibility of individual salvation through therapy
but this could produce only normal neurosis or a normal degree of
unhappiness given the basic nature of psychic forces. Scholars dealing
with human nature and human needs in modern times are the
intellectual heirs of either Marx or Freud or both. Freudian-based
thought has attempted to "flesh out" the "id" by specifying more
completely, with a listing of needs a more specific "content" for this
hidden "force." Marxian-based thought has attempted to flesh out
the social conditions necessary for the realization of the basic human
potential.[32] Most use Freud, in one way or another to specific the
"if" and Marx to specify the "then." That is, if people have certain
basic needs, then social conditions should be of a certain type in
order to gratify these needs.[33] In the area of political theory and
legitimacy, Bay,[34] using Maslow's listing of needs, is the best example
of this latter approach. The approach taken here is also of this nature
but hopefully going beyond others in that needs are based on a firmer
foundation.

In an earlier work,[35] I constructed a listing of human needs, basing
these on the results of conditioning during the primary socialization
process. This was an attempt to give needs an ontological grounding
in the sense that the socialization agent *must* (it is ontogically
necessary to) provide such things as security and consistency of
response if the infant is to become human. Based on conditioning
principles this creates the needs for security and meaning, for
example. This was picked up by John Burton[36] and became part of
the theoretical basis for what might be called the Burton School
of conflict resolution.[37] Other political scholars[38] have become

concerned with human needs in recent years with most being concerned with social policy considerations of one kind or another. Some sociologists[39] have also turned to needs as a necessary explanatory concept in their theories. In most of these cases, however, listings of needs are not given a firm ontological grounding so that these scholars are accused of being arbitrary or ideological. As Jean-Jacques Rosa says:[40]

> The very widespread idea that the consumer is alienated, that false needs are imposed upon him, contrary to his true interest, by advertising and distorted information has an obvious weakness: How does one draw the line between true needs and false ones? Where is one to draw the line between them? And who is going to draw it? There cannot be any absolute or objective hierarchy, because everybody makes different choices. There can only be desires and preferences.

This quotation summarizes many of the criticisms on the part of the many who take a position against the possibility of establishing universal human needs, and many of the criticisms are warranted. But if needs can be reduced to desire and preferences which are relative to societies and thus, in large part, nothing more than the result of socialization, this leaves no place to turn as a basis for judgement concerning the validity of a social order or a system of power. An argument to the contrary follows.

EMOTIONS AND HUMAN NEEDS

Nearly everyone concerned with human needs, from Marx to the most recent authors, would agree that there are physiological needs for such things as food and shelter. Unless these needs are gratified there is human suffering and perhaps death. This is the case because of the physiological nature of the organism. Changing my earlier position which based needs on conditioning, in a more recent paper,[41] I made the argument that food and shelter are not the only needs that are physiologically based and which, if not gratified, also end in human suffering. The argument is that human needs are analogues of primary emotions and since the primary human emotions are ontologically given, so are human needs. Let me briefly restate the case.

Scholarly work on emotions tends to be split in the same manner as scholarly work on needs. The constructionist view of emotions[42] takes the position that all human emotions are constructed within the framework of social life, usually during socialization, which is a view similar to those who would reduce human needs to socially produced wants, desires or preferences. At the extreme, the constructionist view would take the position that if emotions were not constructed in social life, there would be no recognizable emotions: they are not an essential part of the human species. The other approach to emotions, even though not rejecting all constructionist ideas, takes the point of view that some, the primary emotions, are innate even though their expression can obviously be masked by culturally-based display rules[43] in the early socialization process and later. This view parallels the view of those need theorists who claim that emotions are ontologically given.

Another scholarly split in the study of emotions is between those who take a diffuse point of view and those who take a specificity point of view. The former believe it is impossible to link a given emotion to specific autonomic patterns while the latter believe it is possible. Kemper[44] is a non-constructionist in terms of the primary emotions and provides good evidence for specificity. His is the view used by this author for the simple reason that the weight of empirical evidence which he draws on along with other evidence, indicates his view is the more correct in both instances.

Kemper[45] posits only four primary emotions; fear, anger, depression and satisfaction (happiness, joy). In doing this, he shows that many scholars, using a variety of different approaches, have isolated nearly the same primary emotions even though some add a very few others and/or use different terms in naming the same ones. He then makes a convincing case for the existence of his four primaries in terms of evolutionary value, ontogenetic primacy, *cross-cultural universality* and differentiated autonomic patterns. In short, he is saying, and many others agree with him on this, that even though there are many other emotions which come into existence in the socialization process and later, the four listed above are primary in the sense that they can be directly connected with specific autonomic patterns and they came into and remained in existence in animals and humans because they had survival value. Even if Kemper's position concerning autonomic specificity, the weakest part of his position, turns out to be incorrect, this would not render what follows wrong.

My argument is that the four primary emotions are present in humans not only as these relate to the physiological organism but also, and more importantly, as they relate to the self once the latter is developed in the socialization process. In terms of human needs a need for security becomes the analogue of the fear emotion; a need for meaning the analogue anger emotion; a need for self-esteem the analogue of depression; and what I called a need for latency (rest, relaxation), which can come only if the other needs are sufficiently gratified, the analogue of the satisfaction emotion. Each of these emotions in the human are related to the survival of the physiological organism but for our concern the survival of the self as well.

It is interesting to note in all this that most social scientists are willing to accept the capacity for reason as part of human nature. The belief in reason has been the hallmark of philosophy and social theory since the Enlightenment. At the same time, too, few have been willing to accept emotion as part of human nature even though there is considerable evidence that the animal limbic system, the major seat of animal emotion, remained relatively unchanged in humans with the evolution of a larger cerebral cortex.[46] The point is that the primary emotions (their need analogues) posited, along with the human capacity for reason (cognitive constructions and interpretations) make a more complete model of the nature of the human species than does the latter alone. Gazzaniga's[47] modular model of the mind makes a contribution by showing that cognition and emotion always work together. On the one hand, if we have a certain feeling state, an interpretation (a theory) to explain this is developed. On the other hand, as we form a certain cognitive interpretation based on perception, this triggers and is influenced by a certain feeling state based on past experience.

The position here is *that the human needs posited provide reason a basis for judgement in terms of the legitimacy of an order*. When people are hungry they suffer but they also suffer when they lack security, when they have no meaning in their lives, when their self-esteem is damaged and thus when latency cannot be achieved. In this, there is only one value judgement made: a social order (or the use of power) that produces human suffering is wrong and thereby illegitimate. I must hasten to add that a value position is inherent in all theories of legitimacy. In consensus theory, for example, the value position is that a social order or the use of power which does not follow the consensus of the people is wrong and thereby illegitimate. The difference in a theory of legitimacy based on human needs as analogues of human emotions is that it is more objective, leaving less room for manipulation. It is difficult to convince people to the contrary when they are experiencing real suffering: (1) that they are secure when they are experiencing fear; (2) that their lives are meaningful when they are angry because implicit or explicit promises by others have not been kept; (3) that they have self-esteem when they are experiencing depression. In short, that they are fully satisfied or happy when they are troubled by nagging emotions.

Given this, it becomes easier to understand why and how people have been and may be controlled and even how people might come to exhibit consensus concerning certain systems of order over which they have little control and which may not be in their total self-interests as specified by the nature of basic needs. All this is to say that people can be controlled only because they have needs whether or not they agree with the mechanisms of such control. Social sanctions work only because people have needs whether these needs are for food and shelter or the needs based on emotions listed above. We can now see why there may be seeming consensus, which has passed for legitimacy, even though this consensus is a long way from producing a total system of justice. This will hopefully add proof to the case being made and, at the same time, show that the needs discussed are interrelated.

THE FEAR EMOTION AND THE NEED FOR SECURITY

It has not been unusual in history for a powerful chieftain or king to guarantee physical security from the perceived or real threat of hostile enemies in return for the compliance of subjects. This was true in ancient Rome[48] and it served as the basis of feudalism during the Middle Ages. This remains the case among contemporary nation-states. As is well known, national security and therefore the security of the citizen is used and misused as a reason for a variety of state actions and many citizens willingly comply with these actions. If people did not experience fear, had no need for security, this could hardly be the case. Thus, the need even for physical security has been of high importance in controlling the masses.

The need for security as it relates to the survival of the self is also important in compliance. Persons in many interaction situations have at least some fear that they will do or say the wrong thing and thereby produce reactions from others which will damage their self-concept. Thus, as Goffman[49] points out, a great deal of care is taken in the staging of performance to keep this from happening. There is little doubt that people in many work situations are more motivated by the fear of losing their job and/or losing the approval (the basis of self-esteem) of their fellow workers than by loving the work they are doing. Thus, in all social situations there is a great deal of "going along without complaint" even though a person may at the same time be suffering. It is not unusual for persons to sacrifice the integrity of self and even self-esteem for security, even though some remain unwilling to do so.

THE ANGER EMOTION AND THE NEED FOR MEANING

The historian of religion, Eliade[50] indicates that primitive people, more than anything else, feared chaos. Given the loss of instinct in the human species, the social can be, has been and is "ordered" in a variety of ways. This ordering, at least historically, tended to be validated by appeals to "essences," as indicated above. In this ordering, charisma was highly important in that it grounded order, as Arendt indicates, in something outside of human experience, thereby supposedly removing it from arbitrary sectional interests and giving it validity. In Eliade's terms it was typically based in the supernatural in one way or another and was thereby conceptualized as being at the "center" of the society, the place where the temple was built. It is interesting to note that this idea of the "center" is still somewhat with us[51] although if "essences" are weakening, this idea of the "center" is also weakening.

As noted, Weber's types of legitimate authority correspond to his types of order so it is the principle of order, in the last instance, which is important. It is those who have the power (not authority) to establish an order through charisma, force or fraud that set the stage for human action. Since, as indicated, there are few, if any, viable alternatives outside an existing order, once established, people tend to *go along* (conformity does not necessarily imply consensus) even if they suffer in doing so. Concerning the latter, it is interesting to note how inventive elites have been in the creation of ways to rationalize human suffering and sacrifice, ranging from being necessary for salvation as in Weber's Protestant ethic and other religious practices to sacrificing oneself for the "national" honor. Thus, the necessity of order in the overcoming of chaos or existential uncertainty[52] has tended to set the stage in many regimes as a basis for what is called legitimacy. Historically, people in a given society were "forced" to comply with a particular order because it was, for them, the only order possible; there were no viable alternatives. It was either an existing order as a basis for making sense of the world (meaning) or chaos. This is perhaps somewhat different in more modern differentiated societies since in these there may be a variety of ways of making sense of the world.

In all this, however, there usually has been a sacred order along with a secular order in societies where these have not been coterminous. If a person could not make sense of life in the latter, she/he could turn to the former. This is what bothered Marx about religion. He wanted people to change the secular order in order to make it truly legitimate rather than spending time attempting to make sense of their existence within the sacred order which he saw as an opiate. It is obvious that this sacred order has great resilience, however, as evidenced by the growth of the evangelical movement since the 1950s, along with the religious fervor which is currently found in some other nations. In this, it appears to be obvious that if the secular order provided a vibrant sense of meaning for individuals, these movements would hardly be occurring. The same could also be said for a variety of other "opiates" used by large numbers of people in the form of other types of drugs which probably mask anger and disillusionment with an existing order of things, or the outright anger expressed by some in such things as wife and child abuse, membership in gangs and a variety of other types of violent behavior. If individual experiences more closely paralleled what should be the meaning-given experiences or everyday ordering, these kinds of behaviors would hardly be expected. Yet, most political theorists would say that ours is a legitimate order. Most people may agree (but see below) even though if all forms of behavior are added up, including religious behavior, which belie this, the vast majority of the population would be included.

THE EMOTION OF DEPRESSION AND THE NEED FOR SELF-ESTEEM

It is difficult to separate the need for self-esteem from the need for meaning since the former need can be gratified only within the framework of a meaningful order. Since those who have great power control the framework of this order and thereby the means of intellectual and emotions production,[53] they obviously control those processes in a society which provide the basis for self-esteem. It has been many times the case that people attempted to experience self-esteem vicariously (and thus attribute legitimacy because of this) through the creation of heroes with whom they could "identify." Historically this may have been kings or queens (note even today the deference Princess Diana receives in the UK) or gallant knights. Today is it movie stars and sports heroes and occasionally political leaders. These heroes merely take the place of external essences in one way or another but provide little real self-esteem. Ernest Becker's[54] treatment of hero systems is instructive in terms of this.

If self-esteem cannot be gained in the real world, an individual may attempt to gain it through what is called deviant behavior. Others have made essentially the same case.[55] R. D. Laing maintains in much of his work that mental illness is a rational response to existing conditions: "the experience and behavior that gets labeled schizophrenic is *a special strategy that a person invents in order to live in an unlivable situation.*"[56] It is difficult to make a case for real legitimacy in a nation which has 600 000 of its citizens, roughly 1 out of 175 adults, locked up in prisons. The fact that many of those locked up are black says a great deal about the legitimacy of the system. The position taken by many using older models of legitimacy would be that those who are deviant should be punished since there is a majority consensus but even this can now be contested.

In the 1989 Harris poll, 57 per cent of white Americans and 75 per cent of black Americans agreed with the statement, "Most people with power try to take advantage of people like yourself." In addition, 54 per cent of whites and 65 per cent of blacks agree that "The people running the country don't really care what happens to you." More than three-quarters of the respondents also agree that "The rich are getting richer and the poor are getting poorer." Harris's "index of alienation" also finds a majority of Americans alienated in the 1980s as compared with 29 per cent the first year this was measured (in 1966). When people are questioned in the privacy of their homes, where they are much more likely to express their true feelings, they obviously question the legitimacy of the prevailing order of power relationships.

MAKING THE ARGUMENT CLEAR

Before going on I want to make clear what is being said about human nature on the one hand and culture and society on the other. It seems rather obvious, given what we know about feral children and the process of socialization, that there is no "humanity" outside the framework of society. There is neither a good nor a bad human nature on the one side and on the other, neither a good nor a bad culture or society outside the framework of human judgements. Nor is there an acceptable religious or secular eschatology. Just as culture and society make no sense without individuals, the latter make no sense without the former. The argument is that as the self comes into existence, the emotions that are attached to the physiological organism and help to insure its survival become attached to the self to help insure its survival. Since the individual is self-conscious and has the capacity to interpret feeling states, the individual is consciously aware of suffering when the emotions of fear, anger, depression are triggered. Once the self is constructed in interaction, the individual has an overall need to alleviate this suffering. In order to be more specific this overall need is broken down into the four needs discussed above.

Since humans are social creatures, needs as they relate to self can be gratified only in interaction with others. This is to say in specific terms that the security of the self and any estimate concerning the worth of self, can come only from others. In addition, the need for meaning can be gratified only by values which are socially constructed, usually interpreted as within the realm of culture. It is these values that people use in attempting to make sense of their existence. But because individual experiences differ and because others may not reward the individual when she/he thinks rewards should be forthcoming, the individual's world may be rendered meaningless. The same is true of the need for security as this relates to the self. If the person feels that the self is being threatened by others, the emotion of fear is triggered, and if the individual's behavior and claims of being a certain kind of person are ignored, depression occurs. In the real world of social experience, these needs are obviously connected together in a variety of ways and can be separated only for purpose of analysis. Since values are central to much of this, a brief discussion of values is in order.

VALUES

Most theories of legitimacy have, of course, taken values into account in one way or another. As noted, Easton and others see the political system as the mechanism in a society that allocates values, and social order is based on values of one kind or another. As Becker[57] has pointed out, people value what they need or see themselves as needing. It is obvious that if elites can manipulate people to accept certain values and convince people that they need these values, they can perpetuate their differential power.[58] This has obviously been the case throughout history, and is thus the production of false legitimacy, but the basis nevertheless of the theory of legitimacy based on value consensus. This is related to the discussion directly above in the sense that elites implicitly know this. Thus, for example, since security is needed and therefore valued, rulers can manipulate people by providing a security from either real or contrived threats. No one really knows, for example, the degree of real threat which exists on the part of either the USSR or the USA in their relationships with each other. My guess is that it is minimal but the use of one by the other permits the possibility of continued control of the respective populations. The same is true in terms of the legitimacy of economic systems. If the basis of self-esteem can be relatively restricted to how much money one has and thus what one can buy, as in capitalist nations, populations can be controlled by the perpetuation of capitalist values.[59] Since values order meaning systems, the same is true here as well. If priests can get people to value an afterlife and if priests hold the keys to this valued "kingdom," priests can control congregations. The charismatic leader has power because the message makes sense to followers within the framework of their life experiences.

The problem through much of history has been that the values created and/or perpetuated by elites and rulers are scarce values in the sense that their realization by many is not fully possible. This maintenance of scarcity is necessary for the perpetuation of power since scarcity breeds continued dependency. As Emerson[60] has pointed out, the power of one person over another equals the dependency of the other. Thus, those who control the allocation of values which gratify needs, either real or created (desires, wants), control the social world.

VALUE DOMAINS AND PLURALISM

Even though Emerson,[61] like all exchange theorists, bases values on reinforcement schedules, his idea of "value domains" is useful. Using the concept of marginal utility, he says that "Any two valued things are in the same *value domain* if acquisition of one reduces the unit value of another."[62] From our point of view, which bases values on needs, this helps to see that the realization of many different social values, *may* gratify the same need. This, of course, has always been known from cross-cultural comparisons but, as indicated above, elites within nations have tended to restrict the gratification of a particular need to a specific value. Thus, for example, people within a nation have been expected to gratify their need for meaning by embracing the prevailing value upon which an order is based. Or, they have been expected to gratify their need for self-esteem by pursuing a single value – e.g., money. Other values may have been pursued (e.g., sacred values) but these have typically been relegated to second-class standing, thereby making citizens that pursue them second-class citizens.

Since individual life experiences differ and since people have different abilities and skills, a truly legitimate system must be based on value pluralism without ranking. Under value pluralism a variety of values may be pursued for the gratification of a particular need. Thus, following Marx, a person may want to be an architect in the morning, raise cattle in the afternoon and discuss philosophy in the evening, all for the purpose of gratifying the same or different needs, depending on the person. There is no reason why discussing philosophy should be seen as better than raising cattle.

POWER AND CONTROL

It was noted early in the chapter that defining authority as the legitimate use of power makes little sense. This being the case, what becomes of power under the suggestion made here that we move to human needs as a basis for judging the legitimacy of systems? The answer is somewhat obvious and is based on an additional ontological fact given the nature of the species along with what must occur in the socialization process. The human self comes into existence as the individual produces effects upon the environment and others. If an individual did not produce effects on others, thereby permitting the possibility of differentiating self from others, an autonomous self could not and would not be constructed; a self is, in part, that which produces effects on others. This can be demonstrated in a variety of ways but is simply summarized in Mead's[63] account of "taking the role of the other." We take the role of others before acting in an attempt to control others' responses, thus social interaction is based upon each attempting to control the behavior of others.

This is additionally demonstrated by the theoretical and research work on helplessness. This work shows that if people have no sense of control over their environments, dire consequences from childhood to old age occur.[64] Sites[65] made an additional case for this by showing that the socialization agent must control the infant's and child's behavior. This teaches the child, through conditioning and later cognitive learning, that the attempted control of one person by another is the very essence of social life. People attempt to control others for the gratification of the basic needs discussed and, as indicated, this is why sanctions work. Some people have greater power to sanction than others, indicating that those with greater power have a value of one kind or another which they are attempting to protect through the use of such sanctions. They are attempting to protect this value and the power it bestows upon them from others who have different values, as exemplified in behavior which triggers the use of a sanction. Some behavior that triggers the use of sanctions may, of course, be impulsive in nature and not based on any recognizable value even though this is rarely the case if traced sufficiently. If people value what they need and if need gratification is frustrated by the use of a certain value, an impulsive response based on emotion may occur.

Power or the ability to control events is typically maldistributed, making it possible for some to gratify their needs at the expense of others thereby producing non-legitimate relationships. Thus, sectional interests on the part of parties with more power win out over the interests of people with less power. A truly legitimate order would therefore, by definition, be an order in which the power to control events is equally distributed. Since this could not happen operating under a scarcity of values, value pluralism is again called for if a system is to be judged as legitimate.

SUMMARY AND CONCLUSION

As the old saying goes, "there is nothing new under the sun." Marx's view of what society must be if it is to be considered legitimate is quite close to what has been said here. His critique of capitalism was that it continued to produce needs (really wants and desires) that could not be realized by all people. If we add to this modern technology, it remains the critique since the ability to buy new products becomes a central basis of self-esteem, meaning and the security of self. But this never ends, in his view, since new "needs" are constantly being created: Marcuse's[66] "one dimensional man." Under this condition the need for latency can never be gratified and the emotion of satisfaction or happiness truly experienced. *Commodities come to be fetishes giving a sense of control but not real control.* All Marx really wanted was a system where the basic necessities for the maintenance of physical life were secured so that people could get on with gratifying their species-nature, in our terms, their basic needs.

As indicated, people attempt to control their worlds in one way or another in their attempt to gratify basic needs. The fact that people have been forced to "trade" self-esteem for security, or security for meaning, etc. is an indication that few, if any, societies have achieved a full measure of legitimacy which can be instituted only under relatively equal control on the part of all individuals. Power has been and remains maldistributed in all societies thereby providing more opportunity for need gratification on the part of some at the expense of others. From Marx's point of view, so long as a state is anything more than an administrative apparatus this will continue to be the case. In short, so long as the state represents sectional interests rather than common interests, thereby creating cleavages, *the use of differential power, not authority*[67] will, by definition, remain the ordering principle and the needs of many citizens will go ungratified.

There is not a crisis in legitimacy, even though there is a crisis in the use of the concept; there is a crisis in the manner in which power is distributed, masked and used. This crisis has always been present but it has been hidden behind a variety of external "essences" and/or negative ideologies and political theorists have masked it with the concept of legitimacy. As these misuses are recognized, the state will either become increasingly coercive and/or manipulative and continue to serve sectional interests or become only an administrative structure serving the common interest. If the common interest is to be served, it must first be recognized. It has been the intent of this essay to provide a basis for such recognition, basic human needs, and thus a basis for judging the legitimacy of an order.

Let me close by saying that I am not so naive as to believe that all this is about to happen. I have doubts that it ever will and the theory presented gives the reasons why it is doubtful. People who have the power to protect extant values which designate certain essences or beliefs as values and under which they can gratify their own needs will not readily give these up. Furthermore, people who are experiencing some gratification of one need or another are not likely to engage in radical movements or revolutions for fear of losing what gratifications they are relatively assured of under an existing order. The least we as social scientists can do is to stop calling social orders and structures of power legitimate when they are not!

NOTES AND REFERENCES

1. Talcott Parsons, *The Social System* (Glencoe, Ill: The Free Press, 1951).
2. Parsons. *The Structure of Social Action* (New York: McGraw-Hill, 1937).
3. Max Weber, *The Theory of Social and Economic Organizations*, Talcott Parsons (trans.) (New York: Oxford University Press, 1947): 327.
4. Weber, *The Theory of Social and Economic Organizations*: 326.
5. E.g. Randall Collins, *Conflict Sociology* (New York: Academic Press, 1975).
6. Danny Sites, "Power, Exchange, and Authority" (unpublished Master's thesis, Kent State University, 1977).
7. Sites, "Power": 12.
8. But see Whitney Pope, "Classic on Classic: Parsons' Interpretation of Durkheim," *American Sociological Review*, 38 (1973): 405–20.
9. Emile Durkheim, *The Division of Labor in Society* (New York: Macmillan, 1933).
10. Durkheim, *Suicide* (New York: The Free Press, 1951).
11. Talcott Parsons and Edwards A. Shills (eds), *Toward a General Theory of Action* (Cambridge, MA: Harvard University Press, 1951).
12. Lucian Pye, *Politics, Personality and Nation Building* (New Haven: Yale University Press, 1962); Gabriel Almond and Sidney Verba, *The Civic Culture: Political Attitudes and Democracy in Five Nations* (Princeton: Princeton University Press, 1963); H. Eckstein, *A Theory of Stable Democracy* (Center for International Studies, 1961); Seymour Lipset, *Political Man* (New York: Doubleday, 1960).
13. Nicholas Abercrombie, Stephen Hill and Bryan S. Turner, *The Dominant Ideology Thesis* (London: George Allen & Unwin, 1980).
14. Durkheim, *The Division of Labor*.

15. David Easton, *A System Analysis of Political Life* (New York: John Wiley, 1965).
16. Christian Bay, "Needs, Wants and Political Legitimacy," *Canadian Journal of Political Science*, 1 (1968): 241–60.
17. Frances Fox Piven and Richard Cloward, *Regulating the Poor: The Function of Social Welfare* (New York: Pantheon Books, 1971).
18. Ronald Rogowski, *Rational Legitimacy* (Princeton: Princeton University Press, 1974).
19. Rogowski, *Rational Legitimacy*: 35.
20. E. E. Schattschneider, *The Semisovereign People* (New York: Holt, Rinehart & Winston, 1960): 68.
21. John N. Schaar, *Legitimacy in the Modern State* (New Brunswick, N.J.: Transaction Books, 1981): 20.
22. Hannah Arendt, "What Was Authority?" in Carl J. Friedrich (ed.), *Authority* (Cambridge, MA: Harvard University Press, 1958): 83.
23. Margaret Archer, *Culture and Agency* (New York: Cambridge University Press): 173.
24. Robert Bellah, "Civil Religion in American," in Bellah, *Beyond Belief: Essays on Religion in a Post-Industrial World* (New York: Harper & Row, 1970).
25. Willem van Reijen and Dick Veerman, "An Interview with Jean-Francois Lyotard," *Theory, Culture and Society*, 5 (1988): 277–309.
26. Alain Touraine, *Return of the Actor*, Stanley Aronowitz (trans.) (Minneapolis: University of Minnesota Press, 1988): 112.
27. Touraine, *Return of the Actor*: 110.
28. Herbert Marcuse, *One Dimensional Man* (Boston: Beacon Press, 1964); Schaar, *Legitimacy in the Modern State*.
29. Karl Marx, *Economic and Philosophical Manuscripts of 1844* (New York: International Publishers, 1964).
30. Agnes Heller, *The Theory of Need in Marx* (London: Allison & Busby, 1976); Patricia Springborg, *The Problem of Human Needs and the Critique of Civilization* (London: George Allen & Unwin, 1981); Kate Soper, *On Human Needs* (Atlantic Heights, N.J.: Humanities Press, 1981).
31. Springborg, *The Problem of Needs*: 95.
32. Heller, *The Theory of Need in Marx*; Ivan Illich, *Toward a History of Human Needs* (New York: Pantheon, 1978); William Leiss, *The Limits of Satisfaction: An Essay on the Problem of Needs and Commodities* (Toronto: University of Toronto Press, 1976).
33. Erich Fromm, *The Sane Society* (New York: Holt, Rinehart & Winston, 1955); Jean-Paul Sartre, *Being and Nothingness*, Hazel E. Barnes (trans.) (London: Methuen, 1969); Sartre, *Between Existentialism and Marxism* (London: New Left Books, 1974); Marcuse, *One Dimensional Man*; Abraham H. Maslow, *Motivation and Personality* (New York: Harper, 1954).
34. Christian Bay, *The Structure of Freedom* (Stanford: Stanford University Press); Bay, "Needs, Wants."
35. Paul Sites, *Control: The Basis of Social Order* (New York: Dunellen, 1973).

36. John W. Burton, *Deviance, Terrorism and War: The Process of Solving Unsolved Social and Political Problems* (New York: St Martin's Press, 1984).
37. Roger H. Coate and Jerel A. Rosati (eds), *The Power of Human Needs in World Society* (Boulder, CO: Lynne Rienner, 1988).
38. Katrin Lederer (ed.), with Johan Galtung and David Antal, *Human Needs: A Contribution to the Current Debate* (Cambridge, MA: Oelgeschlanger, Gunn & Hain, 1980); David Braybrooke, *Meeting Needs* (Princeton: Princeton University Press, 1987).
39. Anthony Giddens, *The Constitution of Society* (Berkeley: University of California Press, 1984); Jonathan Turner, "Toward a Sociological Theory of Motivation," *American Sociological Review*, 52 (1987) 521–7; Turner, *A Theory of Social Interaction* (Stanford: Stanford University Press, 1988); Anthony Giddens and Randall Collins, "Toward a Microtheory of Structuring," in Jonathan H. Turner (ed.), *Theory Building in Sociology* (Newbury Park, CA: Sage, 1989).
40. Quoted in Braybrooke, *Meeting Needs*: p. 12.
41. Paul Sites, "Needs as Analogues of Emotions," Chapter 1 in John Burton (ed.), *Conflict: Human Needs Theory* (New York: St. Martin's Press, 1990).
42. Rom Harre (ed.), *The Social Construction of Emotions* (New York: Blackwell, 1986).
43. Paul Ekman, "Expressions and the Nature of Emotions," in Klaus R. Scherer and Paul Ekman (eds), *Approaches to Emotions* (Hillsdale, N.J.: Lawrence Erlbaum, 1984).
44. Theodore Kemper, *A Social Interaction Theory of Emotion* (New York: John Wiley, 1978); Kemper, "How Many Emotions Are There: Wedding the Social and the Autonomic Components," *American Journal of Sociology*, 93 (1987): 263–89.
45. Kemper, "How Many Emotions."
46. Richard Restak, *The Mind* (New York; Bantam, 1988).
47. Michael S. Gazzaniga, *The Social Brain: Discovering the Networks of Mind* (New York: Basic Books, 1985); Gazzaniga, *Mind Matters* (Boston: Houghton Mifflin, 1988).
48. Ramsey MacMullen, *Corruption and the Decline of Rome* (New Haven: Yale University Press, 1989).
49. Erving Goffman, *The Presentation of Self in Everyday Life* (Garden City, N.Y.: Doubleday, 1959); Goffman, *Interaction Ritual* (New York: Doubleday, 1967).
50. Mircea Eliade, *A History of Religious Ideas* (Chicago: The University of Chicago Press, 1978).
51. Sean Wientz (ed.), *Rules of Power, Symbolism, Ritual and Politics Since the Middle Ages* (Philadelphia: University of Pennsylvania Press, 1985).
52. Jean Lipman-Blumen, *Gender Roles and Power* (Englewood Cliffs, N.J.: Prentice-Hall, 1984).
53. Giddens and Collins, "Toward a Microtheory."
54. Ernest Becker, *The Denial of Death* (New York: The Free Press, 1973).
55. Albert K. Cohen, *Delinquent Boys* (Glencoe, Ill.: The Free Press, 1955); Burton, *Deviance, Terrorism.*

56. R. D. Laing, *The Politics of Experience* (New York: Ballantine Books, 1967): 115.
57. Howard Becker, *Through Values to Social Interpretation* (Durham, N.C.: Duke University Press, 1950).
58. Gerhard Lenski, *Power and Privilege* (New York: McGraw-Hill, 1966).
59. See Thorstein Veblen, *The Theory of the Leisure Class* (New York: Macmillan, 1899).
60. Richard M. Emerson, "Toward a Theory of Value in Social Exchange," in Karen S. Cook (ed.) *Social Exchange Theory* (Beverly Hills, C.A.: Sage, 1987).
61. Emerson, "Toward a Theory of Value."
62. Emerson, "Toward a Theory of Value": 15.
63. George H. Mead, *Mind, Self and Society*, Charles W. Morris (ed.) (Chicago: The University of Chicago Press, 1934).
64. Martin Seligmann, *Helplessness* (San Francisco: W. H. Freedman, 1975); Ellen J. Langer, *The Psychology of Control* (Beverly Hills, CA: Gunn & Hain, 1983).
65. Sites, *Control.*
66. Marcuse, *One Dimensional Man.*
67. See D. Sites, "Power, Exchange and Authority."

7 Protracted International Conflicts: Ten Propositions
Edward E. Azar*

I wish to set down ten related propositions on protracted social conflicts. These propositions have been generated by monitoring conflictual and cooperative events in world society over a decade. I will then show how these propositions throw light on conflicts generally and, also, on the theory and practice of conflict resolution.

I am using the term "protracted social conflict" to suggest the type of on-going and seemingly unresolvable conflict that is our current concern, whether it be a conflict such as in Lebanon or Soviet–USA relations. I am not concerned with low-level conflicts which are part of the normal processes of change, and adjustment to it, which all persons and societies experience in relations with others.

1. Protracted social conflicts have typical characteristics that account for their prolonged nature. In particular, they have enduring features such as economic and technological under-development, and unintegrated social and political systems. They also have other features that are subject to change, but only when conditions allow for far-reaching political changes. These include features such as distributive injustice which require the elimination or substantial modification of economic, social and extreme disparities in levels of political privilege and opportunity. Any "solutions" that do not come to grips with these features are solutions that must rest on law enforcement, threat, or power control by the more powerful party to the conflict. Conflict is likely to erupt once again as soon as there is any change in the balance of forces, in leadership, or in some other significant ecopolitical conditions.

2. These observable features provide the infrastructure for intrac-

* From E. Azar and J. Burton (eds), *International Conflict Resolution: Theory and Practice* (Brighton, England: Wheatsheaf; Boulder, CO: Lynne Rienner Publishers, Inc., 1986).

table conflict: multi-ethnic and communal cleavages and disin-
tegrations, underdevelopment and distributive injustice. The
re-emergence of conflict in the same situation, a particular
characteristic of protracted social conflicts, suggests to anyone
monitoring events over a long period that the real sources of
conflict – as distinct from features – are deep rooted in
the lives and ontological being of those concerned. Now
and again this is confirmed in statements, as when some Turkish
Cypriots once asserted that they were "nameless people"
because they could not issue their own passports. Those
involved in protracted social conflicts seem to have difficulty
in articulating what it is that leads them to violent protest and
even war.

We are led to the hypothesis that the source of protracted
social conflict is the denial of those elements required in the
development of all people and societies, and whose pursuit is
a compelling need in all. These are *security*, *distinctive identity*,
social recognition of identity, and *effective participation* in the
processes that determine conditions of security and identity,
and other such developmental requirements. The real source
of conflict is the denial of those human needs that are common
to all and whose pursuit is an ontological drive in all.

3. It is difficult to detect, to define and to measure a sense of
   insecurity and distributive injustice and other such deprivations. On the other hand, ethnic and communal cleavages
   and the political structures associated with them are more
   conspicuous. The fact that ethnic and communal cleavages as
   a source of protracted social conflicts are more obvious than
   others does not make ethnicity – used here to refer to identity
   groups that make up a polity – a special case. Ethnicity is an
   important case, though not a special one, because it draws our
   attention to a need that is fundamental. The study of ethnicity
   and the drive for ethnic identity enables us to understand the
   nature of conflicts generally. It is the denial of human needs,
   of which ethnic identity is merely one, that finally emerges as
   the source of conflict, be it domestic, communal, international
   or inter-state.

4. Situations of protracted social conflict in the world, of which
   there are more than sixty now active, are not unique events.
   To the participants – and to external observers who do not

follow events over long periods – they appear to be unique, because local circumstances, histories and attitudes give them individuality. In fact, they are not accidental combinations of circumstances, but have certain behavioral and structural characteristics in common. They are predictable for this reason. Some conflicts may be accidental and short-lived – though tracking events suggests that these are probably few. Protracted social conflicts universally are situations which arise out of attempts to combat conditions of perceived victimization stemming from: (1) a denial of separate identity of parties involved in the political process; (2) an absence of security of culture and valued relationships; and (3) an absence of effective political participation through which victimization can be remedied.

5. Tracking conflict, negotiations, temporary settlements and the outbreak of further conflicts (a sequence which is a characteristic of East–West relations no less than regional conflicts such as in the Middle East) draws attention to the reality that human needs and long-standing cultural values, such as those to which I have referred, will not be traded, exchanged or bargained over. They are not subject to negotiation. Only interests which derive from personal roles and opportunities within existing political systems are exchangeable and negotiable. Agreements that come out of negotiations that may give certain advantages to elites, but do not touch upon the underlying issues in the conflict, do not last.

6. Conflictual and cooperative events flow together even in the most severe of intense conflicts. Cooperative events are sometimes far more numerous than conflictual ones even in the midst of intense social conflict situations. However, conflictual events are clearly more absorbing and have more impact on determining the consequent actions of groups and nations. Cooperative events are not sufficient to abate protracted social conflicts. Tension reduction measures may make the conflict more bearable in the short term, but conflict resolution involves a far more complex process than mere conflict management.

7. The most useful unit of analysis in protracted social conflict situations is the identity group – racial, religious, ethnic,

cultural and others. It is more powerful as a unit of analysis than the nation-state. The reason is that "power" finally rests with the identity group.

I wish to deal with this proposition at some length, because in my experience this is the key to research and to conflict resolution.

For the purpose of describing, explaining and predicting the dynamics of a protracted social conflict situation, the identity group is more informative than the nation-state. Most nation-states in our contemporary international system are unintegrated, artifically grouped or bounded, and totally incapable of inspiring loyalty and a civic culture, despite the strength of nationalism and the sophisticated strategies of communication. This is a reality with which we must come to terms.

Since [the Peace of] Westphalia, nation-states have been legal fictions of the international system. They perpetuate the myth of sovereignty and independence as instruments of control. There are times when national interest and group interest overlap, but these are becoming less obvious in the world.

Just as the rise of the nation-state since Westphalia has perpetuated the fiction that groups are not natural political units and will wither away and melt into the larger and more efficient and "natural" unit, the nation, so has the rise of the individual in the last century perpetuated the fiction that all relevant political action deals with the satisfaction of all sorts of personal needs and wants of the discrete and smallest unit of social analysis, each separate individual. What is of concern are the *societal needs* of the individual – security, identity, recognition and others.

I realize that it is difficult for a student of international relations to get involved with empirical work on identity groups and their behavior. The international institutions and system are biased in such a way that we often cannot find reliable data on ethnic or religious groups, whereas we do find data on national variables. Because some states are made up of apparently homogeneous groups and others are not, one experiences disincentives for comparative analysis. Our focus on nation-states and their individual actions has deflected our attention from the study of ethnic, religious and other identity group conflicts within these territorial entities.

The professional debate over the question of the appropriate unit of analysis has dwelt on the differences between focusing on the individual, state or system and their implications.[1] It has ignored the group totally. Our protracted social conflict research has impressed upon us the need to re-examine this issue of the unit of analysis and to correct this deficiency in the international politics literature.

The group appears to be a competitor to the nation or system. Scholars in the field of international politics seem to have accepted the view that a legitimate role of the state is its historical role of suppressing the group. Furthermore, the group as a unit disturbs the neatness of the models at hand. We had no motivation to generate data and study the consequences of the actions of groups.

In my own work on events research and data banking, I took the most commonly accepted unit, the nation-state. My present familiarity with the phenomenon of protracted social conflict has led me to feel very strongly that we need to build data banks on ethnic, religious, cultural and other groups if we want to understand better the phenomenon of needs, interests and motivations of parties in protracted social conflict situations.

8. Many internal and external relations between states and nations are induced by the desire to satisfy such basic needs as I have been describing. The unit of analysis is the identity group that makes this possible, be it the state, the nation or some more intimate group. The origins of international conflict are, therefore, in domestic movements for the satisfaction of needs and in the drives of nations and states to satisfy the same needs. Thus, distinctions made between domestic and international conflicts are misleading.

I have argued earlier that groups as actors in protracted conflict situations initiate plans, actions, reactions and strategies in order to accomplish the goal of satisfying individual societal needs or of reducing and eliminating need deficiencies. For these purposes the domestic and the international are only arenas. In whatever arena the actors behave, they do so to satisfy their needs. The motivations for action are internal, not systemic or international.

Empirically, we have found that in protracted social conflicts actors seek to placate others, and seek alliances and do all the things they see as serving their interests, as they set out to accomplish the task of satisfying their basic needs. Of course, there are many other variables which affect the behaviour of groups and their leaders, but the basic motivation to act is internal, whereas the arena can be more extensive. In the conflict situations between 1979 and 1984 which we have examined, elites and their leaders show a serious contempt for international and regional arenas. They see these arenas as mere opportunities for scoring points with their own domestic constituencies. Self-image and perception of self by others are important needs to be satisfied and, therefore, they can be a source for action and influence. In this sense, the regional and international environments are important, but only in a very limited way. Ultimately, actors behave in order to satisfy domestic social needs and not international ones.

To separate domestic and international is artificial – there is really only one social environment and its domestic face is the more compelling: thus, there are international and national interests which actors manipulate and exchange in return for the opportunity of satisfying domestic needs, but not the other way around.

9. It follows that protracted social conflicts in multi-ethnic societies are not ameliorated peacefully by centralized structures. For conflicts to be enduringly resolved, appropriate decentralized structures are needed. These structures are designed to serve the psychological, economic and relational needs of groups and individuals within nation-states.

Traditional and contemporary political theory is weak in this respect. We have few models of decentralization that would ensure the pursuit of human and societal needs. Western political theory, for example, favors the centralized state and its legitimate monopoly of violence. In recent years attempts have been made to address the needs of minorities by human rights guarantees, as in the original Cypriot Constitution, and by "power sharing," as attempted by the British government in Northern Ireland. Within the analysis I have made, neither could succeed. No compromises are possible when societal needs are at issue. We have to evolve non-power models.

The concept of a unified and centralized power entity has

been mistaken for a socially integrated political unit. In protracted conflict situations, highly centralized political structures are sources of conflict. They reduce the opportunity for a sense of community among groups. They increase alienation and they tend to deny to groups the means to accomplish their needs.

Societies which have undergone decades of violence and hate retain very little trust for any sort of government – local or central and distant. They become cynical. They transform even benign systems into deformed political and economic entities and they show very little inclination to participatory politics. Decentralized political structures promise to provide the sort of environment which permits groups to satisfy better their identity and political needs. They promote local participation and self-reliance. They give the groups involved the sense of control over their affairs.

In general, decentralized political systems permit the local authorities control over their educational system and their social concerns. They increase the sense of identity, participation and security in the broadest sense of these terms. Decentralized political systems have shortcomings such as parochialism, they foster autocratic rule, they do not address inequality across regions and groups and generally tend to be inefficient. But the benefit might outweigh the costs. Conflict resolution in protracted conflict situations necessitates an understanding of the importance of open, participatory and decentralized political structures as opposed to centralized, dominant and exclusive structures.

It is here that international relations theorists have a contribution to make. The international system is governed on a fuctional basis, and is remarkably orderly. There are a large number of function agreements observed even in times of high tension and war. They cover communications, navigation, health, and even the treatment of prisoners in war. It is this functional model that could be applicable to situations such as in Cyprus and Lebanon, where each community seeks the security of its identity and independence, yet values its wider relationships within the state.

10. My tenth and final proposition is that, not only have we been mistaken in taking the state as the unit of analysis in

international relations and thus failed to perceive the continuity between domestic and international, but that we have, as researchers, failed to perceive the continuity over time of what appear to be discrete conflicts. I wish to communicate a perspective derived from monitoring events over a long period.

There is a strong tendency in international relations theory that leads us to regard conflict actions as discrete, delineated by time and space, and differentiated in terms of the actors, targets and issues involved. Conflict is thus perceived as a phenomenon found in the natural unity of action events which can empirically be isolated, formalized and studied. Each situation is seen as a unique one. No patterns or common features are related to common causes. The number of wars each year can be counted; but each one is taken as a separate event to be studied separately.

This is a confused point of view. What happens is that we the observers select events which we call conflict events and others that are not. We devise intellectual criteria to define conflict. It is important to emphasize that the set of events that we take as conflictual are always preceded and followed by a stream of events. The start and end points are established by the external observer, generally the researcher.

Furthermore, those events we designate as conflictual are also part of a set of observable relationships, economic, social and political "cooperative" ones as well. We draw the conclusion that conflict is the result of a mix of factors, accidental and inevitable, a part of human organization, about which little can be done.

Because conflicts fluctuate in intensity over time, we tend to make assertions about starting and end points which may be of limited utility for an understanding of the inertia embedded in some conflict situations. Curves depicting change and stability in social relations over time may lead us to a poor understanding of the role of intervention, management and conflict resolution.

This view of the natural unity of the flow of events has led to a systematic omission of the notion of protracted social conflict from the domain of empirical research. I did not pay attention to this phenomenon of protracted social conflict until I began, as mentioned earlier, to look for patterns and to deal with the existential experience of Lebanon and the Middle

East situation. Such conflicts linger on for a substantial period of time, sometimes interrupted by relatively low-level coexistence and even cooperation. On the other hand, they play a significant role in reshaping the societies involved, and have a considerable spill-over effect into the international society.[2]

We have thought that there are epoch-long changes involving social conflicts, and that the episodes which reflect the character of these changes are protracted social conflicts. However, when we try to formalize the beginning and end of these episodes which reflect the epoch-long phenomena, we find ourselves on very thin ice. The difficulty arises when we try to determine the start and end points and what we consider continuous, discontinuous and intermittent interactions. Does a conflict start at the moment of an act of aggression, at the installation of a conflict structure, or only at the moment of violent interactions? The main thing that we are finding useful at this stage of our intellectual development is that in studying protracted social conflict situations we benefit more from looking at historical sweeps or the episodes than from searching for specific starts or end points. This historical outlook is lacking in the recent traditions of political, sociological and social–psychological research on empirically based conflicts because of the dangers embedded in historiographic categories. Romantic overtones, which influence our impressions of these categories, have distanced social scientists from history.

CONCLUSIONS

What brief observations can be made on the handling of conflict situations from these propositions?

The outbreak of identity-related conflicts and crises has been on the increase since World War II, particularly in the Third World. Currently it is possible to identify more than sixty cases. Most are identity-related – that is, they involve tribal and cultural rivalries which can be traced to colonial boundaries and migrations. Examples are Lebanon, Sri Lanka, Northern Ireland, Ethiopia, Cyprus, Iran, Nigeria and Zimbabwe. The "class struggle" is not a prime cause, though the existence of class itself creates conditions that promote identity struggles based on a common sense of deprivation and injustice.

Each conflict invites the intervention of great powers, thus complicating even further the relationships of those powers and complicating, also, the already difficult ethnic relationships of each situation. The result is that all of these seemingly intractable and protracted conflicts exhaust the resources of those directly and indirectly involved, further deform the economy and thus accentuate underdevelopment. The increase of state-sponsored terrorism and the disruption of trade and commerce are a by-product of these conflicts, thereby making their resolution all the more important.

These conflicts appear to start with one set of stated goals, primary actors and tactics, but very quickly acquire new sub-actors, new goals and new types of resources and behaviours. In Northern Ireland and in the Middle East, the protest movements broke down into many factions as new leaders came to the fore with slightly different emphases. Thus conflicts that commence as a clear confrontation between one authority and an opposition become complicated with many parties and issues that make the process of resolution all the more difficult.

How can breakthroughs be achieved? What can conflict and peace research contribute?

The Richardson thesis[3] and the normative perspectives attached to it by Norman Alcock of the Canadian Peace Research Institute,[4] namely that war is a function of the availabity of large stockpiles of arms in the hands of selfish and sometimes unstable leaders, who are bound to use them simply because they are there, is too simplistic. Certainly, the quantity and sophistication of arms have a lot to do with the maintenance and severity of conflicts, especially in southeast Asia and the Middle East, and if the world could find a way to reduce the availability of arms, then nation-states might be able to do something about the perpetuation and spiralling of violent conflict. It is more likely, however, that the level of arms can be reduced only when they are no longer felt to be needed. The problems of perceived threat and of conflict have to be resolved first.

In the Third World, war and poverty combine to demoralize entire populations and reduce their capacity to search actively for conflict resolution. War and poverty, which are dramatically obvious to the observer and the main cause of human physical suffering, are but symptoms of underlying structural conditions. The notion of protracted social conflicts provide a deeper insight into the issues of conflict – motivations of those involved, authority roles, political and social structures, behavior patterns, needs and interests, and other aspects. It draws our attention away from the obvious and the superficial toward the underlying conditions that create conflict situations. It directs our attention, finally, to the means of resolution.

It follows from the above that conflict resolution requires a face-to-face exploration into the needs of the opposing parties and the ways and means of satisfying them. This analytical step appears to be the first and most essential in the resolution of protracted conflicts. Legal frameworks and negotiations over interests are useful efforts if they follow the analytical identification of needs and need-satisfaction mechanisms. Bargaining over interests should not be mistaken for the analytical phase of need identification.

What has become clear is the need for structural change as part of the process of conflict resolution. One of the most devastating predicaments in the world today is the simultaneous occurrence of conflict and underdevelopment. These two processes feed on each other and make it difficult for societies to overcome either condition alone. In protracted conflict situations, trying to resolve conflict without dealing with underdevelopment is futile. The two have to go together.

Reducing overt conflict requires reduction in levels of underdevelopment. Groups which seek to satisfy their identity and security needs through conflict are in effect seeking change in the structure of their society. Conflict resolution can truly occur and last if satisfactory amelioration of underdevelopment occurs as well. Studying protracted conflict leads one to conclude that peace is development in the broadest sense of the term.

NOTES AND REFERENCES

1. Kenneth Waltz, *Man, State and War* (New York: Columbia University Press, 1959); David Singer, "The Level of Analysis Problem in International Relations," in Klaus Knorr and Sidney Verba (eds), *The International System: Theoretical Essays* (Princeton: Princeton University Press, 1961):77–92.
2. John Burton, *Global Conflict: The Domestic Sources of International Crisis* (Brighton: Wheatsheaf; College Park, MD: Center for International Development, 1984).
3. Lewis Richardson, *Statistics of Deadly Quarrels* (California: Boxwood Press, 1960).
4. Norman Alcock, *War Disease* (Oakville, Ont.: CPRI Press, 1972).

8 A Critical Assessment of the Power of Human Needs in World Society

Jerel A. Rosati, David J. Carroll and Roger A. Coate*

Human needs approaches to the study of international relations rest on the basic assumption that human needs are a key motivational force behind human behavior and social interaction. According to this perspective, there exist specific and relatively enduring human needs which individuals will inevitably strive to satisfy, even at the cost of personal disorientation and social disruption. As human needs theorists point out, there is empirical support for this assumption in a developed body of literature in the social sciences, both experimental and documentary, which demonstrates clearly that individuals have fundamental human needs such that if they are deprived of those needs, especially in the early years of development, they will suffer physically and psychologically.

As human needs theorists, we locate the foundation of politics, including global politics, in the interaction of individuals and groups striving to satisfy their needs in the social contexts that surround them. We see international relations in world society (or global politics) as consisting of the consequences and actions of the networks of social relationships that are created as individuals and groups go about their pursuit of needs satisfaction. This approach allows us to exploit the key insight of the human needs perspective – that human needs are a fundamental underlying source of political and social interaction in world society – at a time in which it is becoming more and more apparent that many of the new issues on the global agenda defy explanation in terms of traditional approaches to international relations. In addition to issues of war and peace, the global agenda now includes hunger, poverty, terrorism, human rights abuses, resource scarcity, economic dependency, financial indebtedness,

---

* A modified form of a chapter in R. A. Coate and J. A. Rosati (eds), *The Power of Human Needs in World Society* (Boulder, CO: Lynne Rienner, 1988).

pollution and ecological decay, etc. As these problems grow in complexity and intensity, it will be increasingly important for international relations theorists and practitioners to acknowledge the role of human needs in social change.

One way in which human needs theorists highlight the role of human needs in the emergence of such problems and in social change is by focusing on the impact that human needs deprivation has on the long-term legitimacy and stability of political and social systems. That is, given the existence of human needs which individuals will strive to fulfill, human needs theorists argue that social systems must be responsive to individual needs if they are to maintain their legitimacy and survive intact in the long run. Social systems that fail to satisfy human needs will inevitably grow unstable and be forced to undergo some sort of change (e.g., through violence or conflict). This does not mean that human needs will necessarily be fulfilled, but rather that individuals will strive to fulfill them. Societies in which human needs are not satisfied may survive (and even grow more powerful) for long periods of time. Ultimately, however, social change will be brought about due to the interaction of individuals and groups in pursuit of needs satisfaction. This simple observation is both important and "realistic" since it enables international relations theorists to account simultaneously for individual human behaviour as well as the ebb and flow of historical social change.

Our understanding of human social relations, including international relations, will remain incomplete – if not flawed – until it is recognized that human needs are a fundamental underlying source of political and social interaction in world society. Human needs theorists thus face the important task of promoting a wider recognition and acceptance of the value of a human needs approach. A large part of this task is to demonstrate the power of human needs in explaining individual and group behavior across a range of applications in international relations. This was one of the principal purposes of our work in *The Power of Human Needs in World Society*.[1]

A related, but perhaps more difficult and enduring aspect of the task, is to critically examine the value of a human needs approach to the study of world society. This chapter makes an initial effort in this regard by conducting a self-critical review of the weaknesses, promises, and future of the approach. In order for a human needs perspective to be part of the study of world politics it is not enough to demonstrate the promise of its strengths. Its weaknesses also need to be highlighted and addressed in order to determine the potential contribution and future agenda of a human needs approach to the study of international relations.

PERCEPTIONS AND HUMAN NEEDS REALISM

Clearly, there are a number of problems and unanswered questions, both empirical and theoretical, concerning the viability of a human needs approach in international relations. Some of these deal with the difficulty of "proving" empirically the existence of human needs, and the link between these needs and actual behavior. Since these reflect very real concerns which must be addressed, we will consider them at some length below. Before doing so, however, we would stress that perhaps an even greater obstacle to the process of establishing a human needs approach is the prevalence of simple misconceptions about the term "human needs" itself: in the eyes of all too many theorists and practitioners of international relations, the concept of "human needs" smacks of idealism and of some kind of sentimental attachment to the worth of human beings – laudible as an idea, yet unworkable and impractical as a "scientific" or "realistic" approach to the study of international relations.

While some critics may likewise label the generalizations of a human needs approach as far-fetched and idealistic, we believe that to a large extent this type of reaction is due to preconceived (and misconceived) notions of the term "human needs," rather than due to any failings of the approach itself (of which there are undoubtedly many, as will be discussed below). Certainly, the concept of human needs may appear at first glance to [those unacquainted with it] as overly simplistic and idealistic. But the inherent complexity of the concept and the range of applications found for it in, for example, political theory and development should dispel many of these concerns.[2]

Individuals who use a human needs approach in their work, by and large, harbor no idealistic illusions concerning the inherent goodness of human nature, nor about easy paths to harmony and peace in human social relations and international relations. On the contrary, they seek to underscore the very *complexity* of human nature as a fundamental source of human behavior. To the extent that attention is brought to this important yet complex source of human behavior an important goal has been achieved. More important, however, such work generates a more realistic and comprehensive treatment of human behavior and social relations.

Thus, a major objective of many needs theorists has been to suggest simply that the concept of "human needs" provides social scientists with an important conceptual tool that will facilitate a more comprehensive and realistic understanding of the sources of motivation that underlie micro-level behavior. Moreover, the notion of human needs can serve to guide the development of empirical theory at the macro-level. That is, by generating a set of deduced assumptions regarding micro-level human needs, the human needs approach builds a foundation upon which social scientists can formulate more powerful macro-level theoretical explanations.

Developing this major strength of the human needs framework draws attention to the distinction between inductive and deductive analysis. Inductive analysis derives theory on the basis of empirical observations of human behavior. Deductive analysis, on the other hand, develops theory based on a set of fundamental assumptions about human behavior (which are derived to a greater or lesser extent from empirical observations). As we will see below, inductive analysis in the human needs framework faces numerous epistemological problems due to the difficulty of directly linking human needs to observed individual behavior and patterns of social relations. Deductive analysis in the human needs approach, however, is much less problematic. Although questions of overall validity can be raised, the human needs approach to world politics allows for the development of powerful theory that transcends the limits of conventional approaches to the study of international relations. In order to arrive at a thorough and well-balanced assessment of its value, the human needs approach, like any other paradigm or approach, should be evaluated in terms of its potential (dis)advantages for both inductive as well as deductive analysis.

The major advantages of deductive analysis based on assumptions of human needs flow from the explicit attention that is thus drawn to the impact of human needs on human behavior. This is especially important, since questions about the linkages among human needs, human nature, and political behavior have been overlooked in many, if not most, of the work in international relations. A large and respected corpus of theoretical and empirical literature in international relations scholarship has simply assumed, *a priori*, that human nature is evil and aggressive. The range of human needs is thus circumscribed to the pursuit of power, security, and prestige.

This basically aggressive and egoistic characterization of the individual, when reified in the form of the nation-state, has served as a causal force underlying many of the "realist" writings in international politics.[3] The so-called "neo-realists" have tried to avoid these simplistic individual level assumptions by reifying the "international system" so that the forces flowing from the structural characteristics of this system account for state behavior.[4] Yet here, too, an atomistic view of nation-states as unitary, rational actors underlies the approach, so that ultimately the question reverts to reification of egoistic state actors.

The human needs perspective proposes, among other things, to replace this fundamental simplifying assumption of human nature used by "realists" (and so-called "neo-realists") with a more realistic set of assumptions and to open up these assumptions to detailed investigation and analysis. It suggests that examining human needs can actually help shed light into the "black box" that surrounds our understanding of state and international behavior. In this way the approach points toward a more comprehensive and realistic understanding of human behavior, both in terms of individuals and in terms of larger social aggregates, including various social and political groups and organizations, as well as states. In this light, therefore, a strong current of realism – "human needs realism" as it were – should be acknowledged. Focusing attention on the complex composition of human needs motivation, which leads individuals to join into various groups in pursuit of needs and values satisfaction, should be recognized as a "realistic" and responsible approach to analyses of social and international relations.

Certainly such an approach is more realistic than simply assuming, *a priori*, that humans by their very nature are fundamentally evil and aggressive (or conversely, human nature is fundamentally good). Such assumptions are belied by common everyday experiences which demonstrate mankind's complex and contradictory nature, combining at various times benevolence and altruism with evil and selfishness. Moreover, even the greatest of philosophers have been unable over the ages to agree upon a single concept of human nature. It would thus seem both naive and pretentious for scholars of international relations to continue to rely on such singular and simplistic notions of human nature.

In order for the merits of the human needs approach to be fully exploited, however, a wider acceptance and utilization of the concept has first to be brought about. Only when a significant number of serious scholars and practitioners begin to accept the validity of the human needs concept, and utilize the insights it generates, will the full potential of the approach be realized. Therefore, the reluctance of many analysts of international relations to even consider the potential importance of the concept and approach of human needs is clearly a problem. As suggested earlier, we believe that this hesitation is due in large part to the intellectual rigidity that pervades the field of international relations.[5] A major goal of this paper, then, is to help dispel unfounded misperceptions about the realism and potential of a human needs perspective, as well as to reflect self-critically on such an approach.

In addition to the obstacles posed by such misperceptions and intellectual rigidities, it seems clear that the lukewarm reception given to the human needs approach can also be traced, at least in part, to the inability of human needs theorists themselves to build an appealing and intellectually coherent paradigm, one that is clearly superior, in the Kuhnian sense, to existing ones. There is no question that a number of difficult issues need to be more thoroughly resolved before a new approach incorporating human needs assumptions could be realistically considered of value as an addition to the predominant approaches. However, we believe that these problems, to a large extent, are confined to human needs approaches that rely on inductive analysis. In order to establish a firm empirical micro-level basis for inductive analysis, major progress will have to be made in addressing these concerns. Nevertheless, we are optimistic since we feel that the merits of human needs perspective are compelling, especially in the case of deductively-derived theory and research.

Thus, it would seem appropriate to step back and critically examine the weaknesses and limitations of needs theory. An intentionally self-critical assessment of these problems, and the potential ways that they might be overcome, or circumvented, can help in clarifying the prospects for integrating human needs into international relations research. In fact, it is probably the best way squarely to confront the questions that loom regarding the practicality and likely success of research employing a human needs approach, both inductively and deductively.

WEAKNESS AND LIMITATIONS

The crux of the human needs approach, as applied to international relations, can be found in the work of John Burton. Burton claims that over time all societies experience conflicts between the institutional values and structures of society on the one hand, and human needs at the level of the individual on the other hand.[6] Individuals, in striving to meet their needs, will interact with other individuals. As a result of this interaction, individuals identify with, and join in, various associations that might facilitate the satisfaction of their needs. The requirements of maintaining certain social institutions – that is, political structures – are often inconsistent with individual human needs, since social institutions tend over time to express the bargaining power of elites and higher status groups. Societies that thus fail to meet the needs of their members eventually become unstable over time. If they are to survive and be seen as legitimate by the vast majority they will ultimately be forced to undergo change. Global politics thus are a function of the processes of legitimization and delegitimization in world society, which result from individuals and groups pursuing needs and values.

Seen in this human needs perspective, the social networks of relationships that individuals enter into, and that are salient in terms of important needs and values, become important objects of inquiry. It is at the level of such social networks that individual need satisfaction is determined. Intergovernmental networks have traditionally been the almost exclusive concern of scholars of international relations. Yet, with respect to political processes through which needs are satisfied or deprived, intergovernmental relations are but one type of relevant social relation in world society. Perhaps even more important for a substantial portion of the world's people are non-governmental networks and institutions, including for example those involved with global trade, investment, and finance.

Assuming that one accepts the validity of this human needs approach on the face of these deductive arguments, a number of important questions nevertheless begin to arise, especially in so far as questions of empirical analysis are concerned. Indeed, almost every strength in the theory of human needs pointed to by the supporters of the approach has a corresponding downside which raises problems that cast doubt on the practical utility of the approach. This represents a dilemma for those would-be adherents of the human needs perspective who allow immediate empirical problems to overshadow the richness of the theory's set of fundamental assumptions. The most immediate, and perhaps the most important question in this regard, concerns the concept "human needs" itself.

THE CONCEPT OF HUMAN NEEDS

In trying to apply the abstract concepts in the discussion above regarding human needs to some real world situations, we are confronted immediately with the problem of determining *exactly* what human needs are. No consensus exists at present regarding this crucial definitional question. Are human needs, for example, to be defined and understood as some minimum set of universal needs common to all individuals everywhere, as John Burton suggests? Or, are human needs better understood as culturally relative, varying across diverse cultural contexts?[7] This question is a vitally important one since the way human needs are defined will clearly affect our understanding of behavior: if the pursuit of human needs do in fact vary across cultures – due to the interaction of needs and values – then it should be expected that needs will in fact be "seen" differently by peoples of different cultures. That is, if values rooted in culturally relative contexts serve as "filters" through which underlying human needs are funneled, then an expanded set of behavioral modes becomes possible. Different means or satisfiers might be employed in the pursuit of the same individual needs, and varying levels of need satisfaction and varying sorts of need-pursuing behavior could be recognized as "normal" or "legitimate," as one moves from culture to culture.

The need for identity that Burton and others have discussed, for example, might be radically different in Eastern cultures, or for that matter in Native American ones, than the identity need as understood by Westerners. The former tend to stress the collectivity as a source of identity, whereas in the latter, a greater emphasis is usually placed on the individual. A number of similar examples could be cited as evidence of the types of problems that arise in situations where cultural values have a strong imprint on the conception of human needs.

A related, and perhaps prior, concern is the question regarding the degree to which needs are determined by society and the process of socialization, as opposed to being ontological, universal needs, such that all individuals share a fundamental set of needs due to the very fact of their human-ness. There are well-established schools of thought in psychology that believe that human behavior (and perhaps by extension, human needs as well) is largely a function of the social environment to which individuals respond. This concern is only heightened if we conclude that needs, as related to human behavior, are culturally relative, since the socialization process will vary across cultural contexts as well. Indeed, if needs are to a large extent a product of the socialization process, and thus not very different from "learned" values and desires, and if what is "learned" changes from one society to another, then what the concept "universal human needs" contains becomes very small, in effect merely a residual concept.

All of these concerns revolve around the key question of the degree to which human needs, as they interact with values, are changeable, both across time as well as across space (both physical and cultural). Although it would seem that the human needs approach requires us to assume a very limited degree of variability in human needs, this might not necessarily be the case. Ramashray Roy, for example, argues that industrialization and technological progress tend to produce over time a gradual proliferation and change in human needs. He sees this as a negative, even dangerous, development since such a seemingly unending expansion of human needs threatens the long-term harmony and stability of man's relationship with society and nature. Thus, Roy calls for Ghandian self-restraint, and for the "reform of man himself" to control and reshape human needs.[8] Obviously, Roy's conception of human needs is dynamic and variable. But again, this is not necessarily inconsistent with the fundamental assumptions of the human needs perspective. As long as it can safely be assumed that some set of fundamental universal human needs exists, such that changes in these only occur over very long periods of time (and over relatively great cultural-value distances), human needs theorists can still be credited with important and valid insights.

Yet even if these issues were somehow addressed at a general level, important underlying questions would then have to be resolved. Assume, for example, that it could somehow be established that some set of universal human needs do in fact exist. Assume, further, that beyond this it could also be established that socialization (varying in its form, content, and intensity across cultures) plays an important role in determining exactly how human needs are perceived, how these needs interact with cultural values and, consequently, how these needs are acted upon. At this point it becomes important to know a number of other things, such as: the precise nature of human needs; whether a hierarchy or priority of needs exists; how human needs are different from (and related to) interests, values, and desires; and how other factors, such as ideologies, intervene between needs, interests, values and behavior. Social scientists are thus impelled to conduct extensive empirical research aimed at answering these questions. But such research faces a number of obstacles that could prove insurmountable in the long run. In short, in order fully to develop a major strength of the human needs approach, a score of problems will inevitably arise. If inductive analysis in the human needs approach is to be fruitful these will have to be resolved in one manner or another. In the next several sections, we will briefly explore the kinds of problems that will almost certainly hound social scientists in their attempts to give empirical grounding to the concept of human needs.

WHAT IS THE NATURE OF HUMAN NEEDS?

That some set of universal human needs does exist is something we can accept as almost self-evident, arising out of the very fact of mankind's human-ness. We can assume further that these ontological human needs contain both physical (minimum survival requirements) and psychological elements. This is not at all unreasonable, especially when one considers the store of empirical historical and experimental evidence, surveyed by James Davies (or, for example, compiled by Johan Galtung regarding development).[9] Yet, the *exact* mix of elements that make up these universal needs is something that may prove impossible ever really to determine, since social scientists cannot "see" human needs empirically.[10] Rather, the existence of needs is something that at present can be only hypothesized, and then "observed" via some sort of *indirect* means.

We can hypothesize, for example, that a given set of universal needs exists, and then deduce the extent to which these needs are being met on the basis of the types of behavior in which individuals engage. In a similar vein, the absence or presence of what Galtung and Lederer call "need-satisfiers" could serve as indicator of human needs.[11] Nevertheless, the fact remains that at our present state of knowledge, these epistemological problems will preclude any *definitive* identification of human needs, or any consistent separation of human needs from interests, values, and desires.

These sorts of methodological limitations are admittedly troubling in light of the types of propositions that a human needs approach generates, which tend to focus on the degree of need satisfaction and on various kinds of needs hierarchies and prioritizations. In fact, a key insight into human behavior offered by the human needs perspective is based on the proposition that behavior is a function of the level to which human needs are satisfied as related to the relative priority placed on those needs. But, since the degree to which human needs are met cannot as yet be determined with any degree of confidence (let alone the fact that the concept itself is very difficult to ground empirically), it is not surprising that critics often question the practical utility of the approach.

HUMAN NEEDS HIERARCHIES

Obviously, these sorts of epistemological problems also undermine attempts to establish empirically the existence of needs hierarchies. Yet, as we noted above, the distinctions that such needs hierarchies reveal can be very important for building needs-based theories. James Davies, for example, points out that what is often considered "irrational" behavior might actually be better understood as completely rational once a prioritization of human needs is recognized.[12] In essence, Davies is arguing here that "rational" behavior can be defined only in relation to individual behavior and to the level of human needs satisfaction. John Burton builds a similar argument about what is usually labeled "deviant" behavior, as do other important theorists of human needs.[13]

It should be pointed out that the work along these lines by both Davies and Burton also stresses the fact that human needs theory inherently incorporates an element of purposive behavior and self-interest into its conception of human nature. Human nature is not seen merely as some abstract set of human needs. Instead, building on the work of Abraham Maslow, needs theorists often envision some sort of hierarchy of needs, which together with the degree of need-satisfaction and a variety of other intervening variables (interests, values, desires, etc. – see below) set the parameters for the range of "rational" behavior that is ultimately decided upon. This emphasis on purposive behavior – within the context of a hierarchy of human needs – further underscores the "realism" of the human needs approach. In addition, it suggests that "human needs realism" is actually quite compatible with many existing approaches to international relations, including rational actor models and approaches that stress the role of perceptions in understanding human behavior.

Assumptions about rationality as grounded in needs hierarchies, however, can at times be confounded by situations in which behavior appears deviant, or "irrational," even in the context of a hierarchy of needs. Numerous examples of self-sacrificing and intentional need deprivation could be cited as evidence of this possibility. Cases like Ghandi or Martin Luther King Jr, in which certain needs are intentionally subordinated to the promotion of other needs, are clear examples of this type of situation. But these cases do not necessarily contradict the basic importance of needs hierarchies for explaining variations in what can be considered "rational," since individuals will generally tend to emphasize the satisfaction of certain human needs more than others. However, it is important to recognize that such "hierarchies" are not so rigid as to predetermine individuals actions in all cases.

Moreover, it should be noted that needs hierarchies are not a crucial element of all human needs approaches. Galtung's appeal for a human needs approach to international development, for example, is actually critical of current developmental approaches based on needs hierarchies.[14] Compatible with arguments by Burton in this regard, Galtung argues that such needs hierarchies tend to emphasize a set of policies that are more oriented toward the needs of Western elites than the needs that must be promoted to further human development. Furthermore, he suggests that humanity in all its cultural manifestations is too diverse, so much so that constructing some universal hierarchy of human needs becomes almost impossible, and not all that useful. Instead, Galtung favors a more modest research agenda that would encourage the investigation of a rich and diverse set of needs corresponding to the cultural diversity of mankind. Galtung's approach highlights the fact that human needs based theory can generate interesting and provocative ideas, regardless of whether or not needs hierarchies are considered important.

HUMAN NEEDS VERSUS VALUES, INTERESTS AND DESIRES

Besides trying to delineate the nature of human needs and needs hierarchies, future empirical research must also attempt to distinguish these relatively unchanging phenomena from what Azar has suggested are the more time-bound notions of values, interests, and wants (or desires).[15] Values, interests, and desires, more so than needs, are closely tied to socialization and to the political, social, economic, and cultural environment. As such, they reflect the impact of social and cultural institutions and norms, as well as the influence of a multitude of more specific social groupings and relationships of which an individual may be a part. While the social relationships particular to certain individuals play a much larger role than the more general societal values, both will have an impact on determining how an individual acts upon his/her human needs.

At the same time, however, it must be remembered that in the long run of history there is a dialectic interplay between individual human needs and the larger societal values and interests that society promotes. This, again, is the "historic process" of social change to which Burton makes reference. Both Sites and Burton suggest that society itself, and hence societal values, comes about only as a result of the long-term existence and pursuit of individual human needs.[16] Thus, the existence of human needs causes individuals to come together into various social groupings which aggregate at some level to create "society." Yet society itself, plus the myriad of lesser social relationships in turn, shape and limit how individuals interpret and act on their needs.

Distinguishing an individual's needs from one's values, interests, and desires, therefore, is a complicated task. Nevertheless, it is not a major barrier to working with the human needs approach. Since human needs are more enduring (even though some variability across social and cultural space might be recognized), these should be distinguishable from the more variable patterns of individual values, interests, and desires. And, since the latter are largely derived from the specific network of social relationships in which one interacts, research could examine how social relationships create and transmit values and interests, so as to help in the task of identifying an individual's values, interests, and desires. In a sense, research in this area should not be foreign ground to scholars of international relations and politics. On the contrary, the study of values, beliefs and opinions constitute major areas of traditional concern in these disciplines. Ronald Inglehart's analysis of value change in Western Europe (from materialism to post-materialism) is one good example of empirical political research that exploits the theory and concepts of human needs and needs hierarchies.[17]

What is new is the emphasis placed on uncovering the links between the pursuit of human needs, especially in the context of social relationships, and the more conventional concepts of power, values, and interests. The human needs perspective recognizes the importance of power and the related concerns of traditional political realism. But it tries to treat these concepts within a larger framework which directs attention to the fundamental sources of human motivations. Thus, the focus is not on the attributes, capabilities, and interests of state actors. Rather, it is on the specific social relationships which give rise to influence, control, and authority. Furthermore, attention is also directed to the link between these various social and political relationships and the underlying individual human needs which serve to motivate individuals to enter into these relationships in the first place. This, once more, points to the intellectual sophistication of "human needs realism."

HUMAN NEEDS, IDEOLOGY, AND THE PROCESSES OF LEGITIMIZATION

Examining the role of values, interests, and desires, which intervene between underlying human needs and actual human behavior also brings attention to the importance of ideology. Like values and interests, ideologies are related to the variety of social and economic forces that envelop the individual, especially those social relationships and economic forces that are salient to the individual in terms of satisfying needs. Similarly, ideologies occupy an intervening position in the chain that links fundamental human needs to individual behavior. The exact empirical relationships between individual needs, ideology, and behavior also remains problematical.

A matter of special interest to social scientists is the role ideologies have on an individual's awareness or perception of his/her level of need satisfaction. This in turn influences the degree to which individuals participate in socio-political relationships and the extent to which associated social and political structures are viewed as legitimate sources of authority (that is, to what extent they are valued because they satisfy needs).

Historically, ideologies have often served to reinforce the dominant social institutions and values developed by elites. In attempting to shift attention away from unmet needs within society, communist ideology, for example, focuses attention on certain unmet needs in capitalist societies, while liberal ideology directs attention to the neglected needs in communist or socialist societies. Furthermore, as Ashley notes, liberal "laissez-faire" ideology attempts to create an image in which the productive economy is a sphere of reality discrete from the political realm, so that no political responsibility is found for economic inequality and deprivation.[18] Thus, the political foundation of economic relationships highlighted by writers as diverse as Carr and Gramsci is obscured.[19] Alternatively, ideologies can dramatically alter an individual's awareness and perception of needs, possibly "awakening" individuals to the fact of need deprivation or to ways in which such a situation can be realistically countered.

It is also possible that ideologies might create "false" needs (false consciousness, as it were), so that individuals perceive and act on "needs" that are not really needs ontologically. "Needs" in this light are often seen as created by various political and economic elites via their control over communications and advertising as a means of manipulating the masses (possibily to buttress sagging legitimacy). A case can be made, for example, that the television and radio media have fostered the development of the "need" to consume. In addition, a tendency to conform to the "legitimate" authorities and to be more passive and apathetic is condoned by these media, since the outside world seems to be overpowering, and yet at the same time distant.

Thus, ideology not only colors how individuals perceive their needs; in addition, it might help to explain why it is that needs can at various times change from "latent" to "active," or vice versa. This is important since we can point to scores of cases throughout history in which it would seem that individuals' needs were not being met, yet in which no significant challenge in the form of "deviant" behavior was mounted. Why is it, for example, that serfs in feudal societies, or slaves in a variety of other societies, did not always attempt to change the structure of society or the nature of the social and economic relationships that tied them to others in society? Although a complex range of factors are most likely at work in any single situation, one answer would be that serfs' basic needs were not being deprived to the extent to which it would be "rational," in terms of the anticipated costs and benefits and chance of "success," to actually attempt to undertake such actions. Given the overwhelming power of lords and other elites who controlled social institutions, it would seem likely that there was often no real possibility to expect to bring about change.

Another possibility, however, is that such action or non-action is more a function of the extent to which individuals are truly conscious of their socio-economic and political situations, and the possibilities for participation or action these circumstances hold. Ideologies may work to alter an individual's consciousness of needs deprivation and at times reveal the exploited power in their situations. They may even change the perceived costs and benefits associated with actions to change the status quo and delegitimize reigning sources of authority. These are topics of great importance which, admittedly, are difficult empirically to link to the concept of human needs.

HUMAN NEEDS, PARTICIPATION, AND SOCIAL NETWORKS

In spite of the problems discussed above regarding the difficulty of empirically grounding the concept of human needs and the problem of differentiating needs from values, interests, and ideologies, the human needs approach is a critical navigation point for focusing on social relationships as important objects of inquiry. Building theory with a human needs approach does not require that we first achieve a comprehensive and problem-free empirical understanding of human needs. A similar lack of consensus has confounded realists with regard to defining and using the concept of "power;" yet such difficulty has not prevented the development of a large body of thought and practice. If the needs concept has potential for allowing us to understand and explain much of international activity, in particular many of the new issues on the global agenda, then we should work with it to attempt to develop it further.

In a human needs approach, social networks of individuals and groups are the units of analysis, since it is through these networks that human needs are pursued and where values, interests, and power arise. Clearly, a human needs approach to the analysis of the nature and dynamics of social relationships will encounter difficulties similar to those discussed above. How, for instance, do we know that an individual's participation in a given social relationship or organization reflects underlying human needs? Similarly, how can it be determined whether or not participation in such a relationship has, or has not, served to satisfy the needs that we assume give rise to participation, in the first place? How can we actually know, or somehow measure, the level and impact of needs deprivation and satisfaction? These, again, are empirical and epistemological problems to which no easy answer exists. Nonetheless, this should not stop creative and forceful minds from utilizing the insights that human needs assumptions offer to forge theoretical generalizations that improve our understanding of the human condition.

Theorizing about the nature of social networks and relationships based on a human needs approach does not require explicit and definitive empirical linkages. The development of theory and a research agenda is not dependent solely on inductive, empirical analysis, but is also heavily dependent on deduction. There is already sufficient empirical evidence to allow one to conclude that individuals have human needs which motivate and affect human behavior. Although there is no consensus as to the specific nature of these needs and their specific relationship to values, ideology, interests, there is a growing consensus as to their existence and their importance. Thus, one is on firm ground in deductively theorizing about human behavior based on assumptions about individual human needs.

An area where the human needs approach would seem to hold out special promise is in linking theory and research at the micro-level to that at the macro-level. As we argued in *The Power of Human Needs in World Society*, three key factors (or concepts) – groups, values, and social networks – can enable us to build up from the level of the individual to macro-level collectivities.[20] Individuals participate in groups and become part of different social networks in order to pursue their needs and values. Each of these social networks can correspond analytically to a specific system of social relationships definable in relation to the particular issue or problem under investigation.

The work of Quincy Wright and others in social field theory some thirty years ago provides the basic conceptual and analytical tools for examining the characteristics of, and the relationships between, various social networks.[21] Thus, social networks, and the groups of which they are comprised, can be treated as systems of action within a social field consisting of various characteristics (such as capabilities, value orientations) which correspond to those factors important in the context of the issue at hand. As we aggregate the virtually infinite array of possible social networks of relationships into larger collectivities, the entire range of processes that relate to value allocation, as well as need satisfaction and deprivation, comes into view. In effect, then, this framework could afford analysts the opportunity to look into any and *all* social relationships that make up the substance of politics in world society, in any of its forms or levels – local, national and international.

This is reinforced by Rosenau's work on "roles" and his treatment of the individual "as a composite of identifiable and competing roles."[22] Focusing on roles expands the range of units that can be analyzed as existing in social fields by allowing scholars to breakdown the individual into analytic subparts, corresponding to the various roles an individual occupies within a set of groups, institutions, and social networks. Rosenau seems content to utilize the concept of "role" without dwelling on the question of what motivates individuals to assume these roles in the first place. The human needs perspective assumes that the entire set of roles which an individual occupies are largely functions of the individual's efforts to pursue needs and value satisfaction. This is entirely compatible with Rosenau's analysis, yet goes beyond it by delving into the underlying human needs that motivate individuals to assume the variety of roles that they do.

Thus, the study of human behavior at the macro-level by focusing on groups, values, and social networks due to assumptions of individual human needs comes close to reflecting the complexity of world society. Reliance on deduction for the development of theory, based on assumptions of human nature and behavior, is no different for needs theory than for so-called realist theory (or for that matter, almost any body of thought). However, where realist assumptions about human nature go unexamined, the concept of human needs has received a considerable amount of study and analysis over time. Furthermore, not only is needs theory inductively and deductively derived, when applied to the study of world society through the concepts of groups, values, and social networks, the micro–macro gap is directly addressed and minimized.

RESTORING RELATIVITY OF THOUGHT TO REALIST ANALYSIS

An important idea in the writings of E. H. Carr suggests that international relations theory is not a static and absolute conceptualization of an unchanging world, but rather a dynamic and relative one, evolving over time in dialectic interplay with real world circumstances that surround the theorist.[23] Theory, like all thought, is relative. It is historically conditioned by currents in the intellectual world and in the world of political and social relations in which it develops. As the world changes and as man's knowledge and understanding of his world develops, theory evolves.

In some ways, human needs theorists envision their efforts as a contribution to the progressive evolution of theory in international relations and related disciplines. In response to a range of developments in the twentieth century that have placed a new emphasis on problems and actors that more traditional approaches to international relations cannot adequately comprehend, the disparate strains and long historical roots of a human needs approach are gradually coming together into a coherent whole. Human needs theorists' focus on the interaction between individual needs and culturally relative values in a group context sheds a different light on these problems and actors that are so intractable for traditional state-centric approaches.

As such, the insights and assumptions of a human needs approach complement a whole range of recent writings in international relations theory, ranging from the issue area and regime frameworks found in the writings of authors such as Mansbach and Vasquez, Keohane and Nye, to structural and world order approaches typical of Galtung, Mendlovitz, Falk and others.[24] Together, with a score of other writings, such as the work of scholars like John Burton, Quincy Wright, and James Rosenau cited above, the human needs approach is peeling away those overly rigid assumptions of traditional realism that now appear to many as unwarranted, outdated, and unworkable. As part of this effort, scholars are beginning to take note of the potential benefits of inter-paradigm borrowing as a mechanism to advance the evolution of international relations theory.[25] We believe that the central assumptions of the human needs approach can constitute a significant element in this interplay and development of international relations theory.

Fundamentally, it is individuals that drive world society. Thus, in order realistically to analyze world society, scholars must consider what are the underlying motivations that cause individuals to enter into social relationships, as well as the processes through which this occurs. A framework that proceeds from the assumption that one of the primary sources of human motivation is the existence of some set of human needs provides a realistic foundation for subsequent theoretical and empirical work. Indeed, we feel that this is the primary strength and contribution of the human needs approach. Its set of fundamental assumptions, logically deduced from the existence of individual human needs, provides a firm basis for research and practice in international relations.

Beyond this key contribution, there are four other general areas in which a human needs approach has the greatest promise of contributing to the study of international relations. First, as noted above, a human needs approach should allow us to address the micro–macro problem by focusing on the aggregation of individuals into groups and social networks, thus accounting for global actors and structural relationships, while at the same time allowing for the disaggregation of local, societal, regional and global relationships back to the individual.

Second, a human needs approach should allow us to examine the implications and impact of international institutional arrangements on individuals and groups. Most of the work in the study of international relations has focused on large aggregate "actors" at the national and global level, such as nation-states and international organizations. A human needs approach, however, makes it clear that international relations have an impact on individuals and groups of individuals, regardless of whether individuals and groups are active participants, or "passive" ones, unaware of their roles within larger environmental contexts.

Third, a human needs approach can help us explain international relationships and their consequences over time, since the satisfaction of needs and the associated legitimization of social (read "political") institutions is the key to the dynamics and evolution of world society. Thus, a human needs perspective can provide an important foundation for understanding continuity and change in world society. It allows us to understand the sources of global problems and issues that have already developed and that are still developing.

Finally, the human needs concept has heuristic value for evaluating the extent to which social institutions and structures fulfill human needs. For theorists and practitioners of international relations – at least for those who are in agreement with the normative implications of the concept – it can serve as a yardstick with which to evaluate the desirability and efficacy of real world policies and political events in terms of promoting progressive social change. The power of human needs will become increasingly apparent as the world enters the twenty-first century – for the future will be a time of greater challenges to, as well as opportunities for, the fulfillment of individual human needs.

CONCLUSION

The preceding sections have shown that theory grounded in assumptions of human needs can both complement and enrich our understanding of the complex social problems and relationships of world society. Thus, critics who label the concept of human needs unworkable and who claim that this problem poses an insurmountable obstacle to practical research in international relations are quite premature in writing off the approach. Clearly, there are major epistemological problems and basic disagreements concerning the empirical content of human needs concepts. These are hurdles that cannot be dismissed lightly. On the other hand, it is only through basic research designed either to resolve such issues – or, where required, to work around them – that real progress will be possible.

Difficulties and debate over the problem of how to define one of the core concepts of political science – power – have not prevented political scientists from utilizing it as a basic guidepost in their work. Scholars of international relations would be well advised to take clearer notice of this. More scholars need to acquaint themselves with the human needs perspective, and make use of its set of assumptions in building theory and conducting empirical analysis. This should be especially useful since many of them rely on implicit, but unexamined, assumptions concerning the same general motivational phenomena.

As we have seen, numerous problems will doubtless confront empirical research guided by a human needs orientation, especially when such research emphasizes an inductive approach. Empirical investigations directed specifically at discerning the nature and content of human needs may ultimately reveal crucial limitations of the human needs concept. Nevertheless, such analysis could point the way to a dramatically improved understanding of international relations, and social relations in general.

Deductive theory, however, founded on the assumptions of human needs, can proceed in spite of epistemological questions. "Human needs realism" can enrich our understanding of the world around us by forcing analysts to investigate, both theoretically as well as empirically, what are often unexamined assumptions. In this light, the assumptions of "human needs realism," which are anchored in a heightened awareness of the sources of individual behavior, respond to the need for theory to adjust to the social and political problems of the day.

Indeed, the more "realistic" world view provided by a needs approach is perhaps its most important contribution to the study of world politics. Political processes and outcomes in world society are not based fundamentally on the anarchic relations of state actors; they are based in an inherent entropic order, created by the complex interdependence which results as individuals and groups go about the day-to-day process of satisfying needs and values. This resulting order not only severely constrains the range of options for all participants interacting in world society (including those individuals and groups who are acting in the name of states) but, more importantly, provides, in varying degrees, systems of governance over these relationships. Thus, a human needs approach moves us much closer to the realism of world society toward which students of international relations have long been striving.

We are not arguing that human needs will be fulfilled – only that individuals strive to fulfill them. It is the conflict between individuals, in a group and social context, attempting to fulfill human needs in social structures, that results in the dynamics of politics at all levels. Thus, a human needs approach offers students of international relations a realistic foundation for understanding the sources of individual behavior, a basis in which to analyze social change and continuity, and a standard by which to evaluate the progressiveness of changes occurring in world society.

NOTES AND REFERENCES

1. Roger A. Coate and Jerel A. Rosati (eds), *The Power of Human Needs in World Society* (Boulder, CO: Lynne Rienner, 1988).
2. In political theory, see David Braybrooke, *Meeting Needs* (Princeton: Princeton University Press, 1987); Ross Fitzgerald (ed.), *Human Needs and Politics* (Oxford: Pergamon Press, 1977); Michael Ignatieff, *The Needs of Strangers* (London: Hogarth Press, 1984); Alkis Kontos, "Through a Glass Darkly: Ontology and False Needs," *Canadian Journal of Political and Social Theory* 3 (Winter 1979): 25–45; and Patricia Springborg, *The Problem of Human Nature and the Critique of Civilization* (London: Allen & Unwin, 1981). In development, see Johan Galtung, "The New International Economic Order and the Basic Needs Approach," *Alternatives* 4 (1978–79): 455–76; Katrin Lederer (ed.), with

Johan Galtung and David Antar, *Human Needs* (Cambridge, MA: Oelgeschlager, Gunn & Hain, 1980); Han S. Park, *Needs and Political Development* (Cambridge, MA: Schenkman, 1984); and United Nations University, *Human Development in Micro to Macro Perspective* (November 1982).

3. See, for example, Hans Morgenthau, *Politics Among Nations: The Struggle for Power and Peace* (New York: Alfred A. Knopf, 1978), and Raymond Aron, *War and Peace: A Theory of International Relations* (New York: Praeger, 1966).

4. See Kenneth N. Waltz, *Theory of International Politics* (London: Addison-Wesley, 1979); Robert Gilpin, *War abnd Change in World Politics* (Cambridge: Cambridge University Press, 1981); and Stephen Krasner, *Cultural Conflict: The Third World against Global Liberalism* (Berkeley: University of California Press, 1985).

5. Perhaps, a part of this rigidity can even be traced, as Ashley suggests, to the desire of some analysts of international relations to serve as advisors to state elites who are mainly concerned with maintaining the status quo. Richard K. Ashley, "Three Modes of Economism," *International Studies Quarterly*, 27 (4) (December, 1988): 463–96.

6. John Burton, *Deviance, Terrorism and War: The Process of Solving Unsolved Social and Political Problems* (Oxford: Martin Robertson, 1979).

7. See Lederer, "Introduction," in Lederer (ed.), *Human Needs*: 1–14 for a discussion of this issue.

8. See Ramashray Roy, "Human Needs and Freedom: Three Contrasting Perceptions and Perspectives," *Alternatives* 5 (1979–80): 195–212.

9. James Chowning Davies, *Human Nature in Politics: The Dynamics of Political Behavior* (London: John Wiley, 1963) and "The Priority of Human Needs and the Stages of Political Development," in J. Roland Pennock and John W. Chapman, (eds), *Human Nature in Politics* (New York: New York University Press, 1977): 157–195; and Galtung, "The New International Economic Order."

10. Christian Bay, "Self-Respect as a Human Right: Thoughts on the Dialectics of Wants and Needs in the Struggle for Human Community," *Human Rights Quarterly* (1982): 53–75.

11. For discussions on need "satisfiers," see Johan Galtung, "The New International Economic Order": 55–126, and Lederer, "Introduction": 3.

12. Davies, "The Priority of Human Needs."

13. Burton, *Deviance, Terrorism, and War*.

14. Galtung, "The New International Economic Order."

15. Edward E. Azar and John Burton (eds), *International Conflict Resolution: Theory and Practice* (Brighton, England: Wheatsheaf; Boulder, CO: Lynne Rienner Publishers, Inc., 1986).

16. Paul Sites, *Control: The Basis of Social Order* (New York: Dunellen, 1973): 15, and Burton, *Deviance, Terrorism and War*: 64–5.

17. Ronald Inglehart, "The Silent Revolution in Europe: Intergenerational Change in Post-Industrial Societies," *American Political Science Review*, 65 (1971): 991–1017.

18. Ashley, "Three Modes of Economism."
19. E. H. Carr, *The Twenty Years' Crisis* (New York: Harper & Row, 1939), and Antonio Gramsci, *Selections from the Prison Notebooks of Antonio Gramsci* (New York: International Publishers, 1971).
20. See R. A. Coate and J. A. Rosati, "Human Needs in World Society," in Coate and Rosati (eds), *The Power of Human Needs in World Society*: 1–20.
21. Quincy Wright, *The Study of International Relations* (Appleton-Century-Crofts, 1955).
22. James N. Rosenau, "A Pre-Theory Revisited: World Politics in an Era of Cascading Interdependence," *International Studies Quarterly*, 28 (September 1984): 269.
23. Carr, *Twenty Years' Crisis*.
24. Richard W. Mansbach and John A. Vasquez, *In Search of Theory: A New Paradigm for Global Politics* (New York: Columbia University Press, 1981); Robert Keohane and Joseph Nye, *Power and Interdependence: World Politics in Transition* (Boston: Little, Brown & Co., 1977), Robert Keohane, *After Hegemony: Cooperation and Discord in the World Political Economy* (Princeton: Princeton University Press, 1984); Johan Galtung, *The True Worlds: A Transnational Perspective* (New York: The Free Press, 1979), Saul Mendlovitz, "On the Creation of a Just World Order: An Agenda for a Program of Inquiry and Praxis," *Alternatives*, 7 (Winter 1981): 355–73, and Richard A. Falk, *et al.* (eds), *Studies on a Just World Order* (Boulder, CO: Westview Press, 1982).
25. See Hayward Alker and Thomas Biersteker, "The Dialectics of World Order: Notes for a Future Archaeologist of International Savoir Faire," *International Studies Quarterly*, 28 (2) (1984): 121–42.

IV
Applications

Chapter 9   A Theory of Conflict Resolution by Problem-   183
             solving
             Anthony de Reuck
Chapter 10   Interactive Problem-solving: a Social-   199
             psychological Approach to Conflict Resolution
             Herbert C. Kelman
Chapter 11   Principles of Communication Between   216
             Adversaries in South Africa
             Hendrick W. van der Merwe, Johann Maree,
             André Zaaiman, Cathy Philip and A. D. Muller
Chapter 12   Managing Complexity Through Small Group   241
             Dynamics
             John W. McDonald
Chapter 13   The Emergence and Institutionalization of Third-   256
             party Roles in Conflict
             James H. Laue

9 A Theory of Conflict Resolution by Problem-solving
Anthony de Reuck*

In 1974 an account was published of the use of a technique, devised by John Burton[1] and then called "controlled communication," which functions simultaneously as a research tool and as an instrument of conflict resolution. The technique has since been developed further and is now known as the problem-solving procedure. This paper extends and interprets the results presented earlier.[2]

The essence of the problem-solving procedure is this: that representatives of the parties in a dispute should meet in the presence of a small panel of disinterested consultants, professionally qualified in the social sciences, in order to analyze and possibly also to resolve their conflict, in conditions of total confidentiality. The parties should be enabled by the panel to negotiate not by bargaining in the conventional manner, but by collaborating in the solution of their joint predicament through the discovery of accommodations affording net advantages to all concerned. Their joint predicament is the problem to be solved.

The process is non-judgemental and highly participatory in character. The function of the panel of consultants is to involve all the parties in dispute in an uncommitted exploration of the nature of their predicament and, if possible, of solutions to it that do not require *any* of the parties to compromise their basic interests as they themselves perceive them. The research framework is strictly non-directive in the sense that the consultants are never concerned to advocate particular outcomes.

Because almost all mature conflicts comprise whole hierarchies of issues and of parties with differing but interlocking interests, the procedure involves (a) rigorous analysis of the structure of the dispute which must be conducted by the parties themselves, since their interests are at stake; and (b) conflict resolution in a series of steps,

* From *Man, Environment, Space and Time*, 3(1) (Spring 1983): 53–69.

beginning with the reconciliation of any factions on either side, proceeding to resolution of the conflict at the level of those most affected by it, and thereafter step-by-step up the hierarchy to the highest and most inclusive level of dispute. The highest level might be that involving the superpowers, for example.

The problem-solving approach thus implies, in the general case, a cascade of parties, of issues and of accommodations in a series of successive approximations to a satisfactory analysis on the one hand, and to an acceptable set of resolutions on the other. And a true resolution – as distinct from a compromise or an imposed settlement – implies eliminating or transforming the grounds of dispute and reaching an outcome that is self-supporting in the sense that it is positively advantageous to all the parties involved.

The former account dealt principally with the group dynamics and rationale of the analysis.[3] The present paper offers a sequel in which the theory of conflict resolution by problem-solving[4] is extended in the light of experience. It refers to observations made under the auspices of the Centre for the Analysis of Conflict as a participant observer of diplomatic groups representing countries or communities at war attempting to negotiate a resolution of their conflict with the aid of a team of mediating consultants of whom I was chairman.

Our negotiating groups (sometimes called "workshops" by American colleagues),[5] usually numbered between 12 and 24 members.[6] Assuming, for example, that there are only two parties in a given dispute (there are usually more) and that each is represented by five delegates sitting with a panel of six consultants including the chairman, then we reach a total of 16. Since the objective was to enable a group to develop sufficient confidence, common perceptions and shared vocabulary for joint problem-solving, it seemed best to keep the groups quite small.

The observations were made on the basis of earlier small group studies, mostly conducted during 1965 before the technique of controlled communication had been devised, and employing a modified Bales Interaction Process Analysis.[7]

It was not feasible to record in full the behavior of the diplomatic groups, but data collected by more impressionistic means afforded strong confirmatory evidence that, like the earlier groups studied in detail, they too passed through a succession of three characteristic phases, according to the types of activity then predominating.

The first phase is distinguished by role behavior programmed by the expectations of external reference groups – notably the governments in dispute. Direct communication between the parties is avoided and most exchanges are with the panel. The second phase is reached when the parties, still maintaining their separate boundaries, join with the panel in accepting analytical roles and so begin to respond from time to time to one another. In the third phase, the group attains a fitful and fragile integration, sufficient however for the parties to collaborate in joint problem-solving.

THE THEORY OF PROBLEM-SOLVING GROUPS

As an instrument of conflict resolution, problem-solving has features in common with social "casework" and with the conciliation procedures increasingly employed in handling industrial and communal conflicts. All have in common the absence of enforcement and the encouragement of processes of self-adjustment. Burton draws a clear distinction between what he calls *settlement* and *resolution* of conflict.[8] "Settlement" has the connotation of determination by a third party such as a court or a greater power. It could be a compromise which the parties feel they have no option but to accept. "Resolution," on the other hand, implies a solution freely acceptable to all parties, one that does not sacrifice any of their important values, one that parties will not wish to repudiate when they recover the strength to do so. In effect, settlement merely reduces the level of intensity of conflict behaviour, possibly to zero; whereas resolution removes the very ground of conflict, and eliminates or transforms the conflict situation. Only when conflict is resolved, as distinct from settled, is the outcome self-supporting in the sense that it is positively advantageous to all concerned. This is the aim of problem-solving, which seeks not merely a cessation of hostilities but a dawn of cooperation.

On the other hand, conventional negotiation, even in the presence of a mediator, will almost inevitably result in a settlement – that is to say, bargaining procedures result in parties to a conflict trading losses rather than exchanging advantages. The result is a temporary accommodation representing the smallest concessions that each party will accept from the other, and the greatest either is prepared to suffer.[9]

The difficulty about conflict resolution is that it calls for cooperation between antagonists in searching for outcomes that are advantageous to both. And this is what enemies are least inclined to do. Competitors in a market or a tennis tournament do indeed cooperate in order to engage in ritualised conflict. At one level – win or lose – their interests are opposed: but at a higher level their interests coincide. They share the superordinate goal of maintaining the competitive system – the market or tournament – for its own sake.

But it is one of the diagnostic characteristics of conflict in earnest that enemies have mutually exclusive frames of reference which preclude all cooperation between them. These are the psychological "frames"[10] which predispose enemies to a zero-sum interpretation of their relationship. A gain – or loss – to either is experienced as a loss – or gain – by the other.[11] That it is so makes collaboration equivalent to disloyalty. Mutually exclusive frames preclude resolution of conflict – permitting gains to both parties – just because either's gain is felt as the other's loss. This it is that blocks a cooperative search for constructive outcomes: and it is precisely this block that problem-solving is designed to overcome.

The aim must be therefore to help the parties to redefine their situation so that they both perceive it as a shared predicament to be solved jointly, and to equip them with a common language for communication: it is, in short, to enable the parties to create for themselves a common frame or universe of discourse in order to cooperate. That expresses the matter at a psychological level. Because it is part of our understanding of the process that the psychological and sociological elements are inextricably interwoven, let us review the matter from the point of view of role theory.

One of the major obstacles to the reperception of a conflict situation by the parties, and consequently one of the major blocks to innovative thought about cooperative possibilities for its resolution, arises from the cognitive set induced in the parties by their need to conform to role expectations.

The parties arrive at the conference table in their roles as trustees of their peoples' interests and awareness of their fiduciary status is heightened by confrontation with their adversaries. Their roles demand that they defend the stance adopted by their principals and attack the position of their opponents. The conference table is not regarded by them as a place for innovation, and creative thought implying any change of stance on behalf of their absent principals is not part of their repertoire. To adapt a well-known dictum: settlement of a conflict is all too frequently a continuation of the struggle by other means. Confrontation with their opponents may therefore be an occasion for the exercise of tactical skill, but basic reappraisal of the strategic situation in collaborative terms has the whiff of treason.

Since a true resolution of the conflict implies a joint search for mutual advantage, an essential part of the problem-solving technique must be to divest parties of their inhibitions as adversaries, and to offer them alternative roles, first as analysts and later as partners. How is the block overcome? How are roles translated? What does the presence of a panel do to transform the outcome of a problem-solving exercise?

A minimal answer might be that the panel provides additional information – concerning analysis of conflict behavior or psychology, of social or systemic processes, conflict resolution and other social science concepts – which enables the parties to reach a more "objective" assessment of their circumstances and so to aim at a more "realistic" conclusion. However, there must be more to it than this. It is possible to concede that the panel is likely to be calm, cool and collected because it is relatively disinterested, whereas the passionate commitment of the parties may be expected to distort their perceptions and cloud their judgements. It is not likely to be accepted that the panel members need to be either wiser or better informed than the parties to the negotiation. To assert quite simply that the role of the panel is to inject theoretical ideas into the discussion is to invite the response that in that case it can hardly influence the outcome except conceivably to speed up – or slow down! – the process of reaching it.

Experience shows that the outcome of problem-solving is different from that of direct negotiation between the parties because the roles are different. The function of the conciliating panel is to set the implicit rules of a new game and to recruit the parties as players under the guise of doing something else. It is not a question of concealment: it is a matter of a process which proceeds most easily when it is least self-conscious. "Officially" the parties come to negotiate and the panel comes to analyze. Covert switches from analysis to negotiation and back again are operated by the panel with the tacit connivance of the parties. Whenever negotiations break down, the parties are permitted to retreat into analysis; whenever confidence is restored, negotiation can be resumed.

As this process proceeds through successive alternations of analysis and negotiation, the mode of negotiation progressively changes in emphasis. The frequency and intensity of negotiation in the bargaining mode steadily declines and is little by little replaced by a rising frequency and intensity of negotiation in the cooperative mode. The search for mutual advantage emerges tentatively, proves too stressful at first, slips back into analysis, re-emerges when confidence is restored, and eventually becomes the predominant theme. This is the new game just referred to, the new game whose rules are contrived by the panel but which the parties alone can play. The parties may not be entirely conscious either of the game or of its rules, although they are certainly pleased with the prizes it offers. Once a prize has been won, in the form of a proposal for resolving the conflict, it can be borne home in triumph.

The transition from bargaining to cooperation is accomplished by exploiting the ambiguity between two manifest functions of negotiation and analysis. This ambiguity licenses the parties, from time to time, to slip out of their normal bargaining roles; at the same time, this ambiguity permits the panel to lead the discussion into more constructive channels. Practice in playing the analysis game, when anxiety is allayed and creativity enhanced, offers precisely the experience of cooperation that is needed to initiate the new mode of negotiation. In short, the parties begin by cooperating together in resolving their conflict. Analysis offers the parties not only the intellectual tools for reinterpreting the conflictual relationship between them, but also the immediate experience of joint cooperation in problem-solving.

At a psychological level, this can be expressed by saying that the parties, through the group experience, come of their own accord to redefine their conflictual relationship as a joint predicament to be jointly resolved. At the level of group dynamics, it can be expressed by observing that both the parties are persuaded at first to consider themselves members of a group of which the panel are also members: in due course, they come to consider the opposing party as legitimate members of the group as well. The social boundaries and the intellectual frames dissolve and reform together. It is wholly to be expected that the social structure of the group (patterned behavior) should reflect the acting out of the patterns of ideas (frames) which define their situations for the participants: the group structure and the intellectual frames are mirror images of one another.

THE FRAMING OF ATTENTION AND CHANGES IN SOCIAL STRUCTURE

Let us examine the concomitant transitions between bargaining and cooperation at the psychological level and between adversary roles and collaborative roles at a sociological level.

The intimate connection between the social structure and cultural configuration has been the subject of highly seminal studies by Basil Bernstein[12] and by Mary Douglas.[13] The implications of this connection for learning or for change, however, have not yet received much attention.

It is generally accepted that if social structure is defined in terms of persistent patterns of transactions between role enactors, then there are several distinct social structures – alternative configurations (for example, economic or political or cultural or social) – to which each actor can belong according to his/her role at the moment. One might say that the social configuration of a group at any instant depends upon the definition of the situation it has adopted for the time being. Its social structure for the moment is a function of its shared "frame of mind."

At first sight this may appear to be a surprising assertion to those who have a tendency to reify social structure. Nevertheless if we are careful to conceptualize structure as a process rather than an entity, it becomes almost tautological. Social structure represents a persistent pattern of behavior. Since there are behavior patterns peculiar to say, economic, political, cultural or social contexts, there must be alternative configurations of the social structure appropriate to each context. There are coextant in short, an economic structure, a political structure and many other different structures, in each of which every actor occupies a different role at different times.

To express the matter in another way, let us redefine social structure in terms of the attention that actors accord one another. As Chance[14] has shown, attention within a group is highly structured because some individuals consistently receive more attention than others. Each individual accords and receives attention as a function of his role and status, with high status individuals according less and receiving more attention than those below them. But to whom attention is directed depends upon the context. The social structure of attention within a group at any instant relates to the definition of the situation its members have adopted for the moment. Attention structure is social structure made manifest.

Now it is obvious that changing frames of reference – from, say, a political to an economic context – will result in changing structures of attention or of transaction. Conversely, in the usual social dialectic, a change in social structure must also be accompanied by a changing frame of reference. In particular, any hardening or dissolving of social boundaries and any enlarging or diminishing of groups involves a concomitant change in the definition of their situation for all concerned. In particular such a change involves a reframing of identities for both ingroup and outgroup, and possibly a relocation of the boundary between them.

Thus it is inevitable that social structure (patterned behavior) and frame of reference (patterned ideas) should reflect one another, be mirror images, almost, one of the other, because patterns of behavior (structure) result from the acting out of the patterns of ideas (frame) which define their situation for the participants.

Now the introduction of Gregory Bateson's[15] concept of "frame" (or context) can afford us further valuable insights into the rationale of the problem solving process.

FRAME OR DEFINITION OF THE SITUATION

Cooperation between people for productive purposes has as a minimum prerequisite a state of affairs in which all participants share a common definition of their joint situation. Over the limited field defined by their respective partnership roles – that is to say, defined to cover at least the area within which their activities are interdependent – those involved must share a common universe of discourse, a code for communicating and a model for interpreting all that they experience, their perceptions and motives and their evaluation of events and actions. In particular, they must, if they are to collaborate successfully, share a definition of this shared situation, which includes their respective roles, so that each views the other – in role at least – to some substantial extent as he sees himself.[16]

Thus the audience at a production of Hamlet colludes with the actors to see ghosts or murders where there are only counterfeits, because they both define the situation as a dramatic performance. Indeed in the play within the play where Hamlet seeks to catch the conscience of the king, the audience agrees to see actors acting the parts of actors while the other actors act the parts of an audience upon the stage. What is more, present among the audience-actors is the king upon whose conduct the whole performance of one of the actor-actors is a commentary. That performance for the real audience is a commentary upon a performance: a metaperformance and a metacommentary.

Take a rather different set of circumstances and consider the action of passing coins from one person to another. The meaning of this action can only be understood in terms of its context. For an economic context it might be to buy something, in a political context to make a bribe, in a religious context to offer alms, and in a cultural context it might be a gift from one numismatist to another. In an instrumental context it might be to proffer the coin as a tool to lever open a can.

The differentiation of these circumstances and the disentanglement of roles within roles are carried out by means of "frames" – frames of reference or even frames of mind, one might say. Action and communications are understood only by reading the *content* of each in the light of its *context* (or frame). It is as though every message were a cablegram which bore at the beginning (as most cablegrams do) a further message about who was the sender, to whom it was sent, and the code that should be used to interpret it.

Every frame or context thus represents a metacommunication about the interpretation of the message (i.e., a message about the message) which is essential to make sense of the message itself. Content connotes the semantic meaning of the message, say, reporting a particular state of affairs in the world, and is intended to alter or confirm the orientation to reality of the receiver. Its context includes a code of interpretation asserting what is understood to be "going on" – what game is in progress, who are the players, what are the prizes, what rules have been adopted for the occasion. The frame defines the context within which the content of a message, of the significance of an action, are to be understood.

Manifestly, any concerted activity – any productive collaboration – requires that the parties to it shall share a communicative code and a common orientation both to relevant reality and to their respective roles in connection with the task in hand. A common frame is thus a prerequisite for cooperation.[17]

Complementary roles, like those of buyer and seller or conductor and orchestra, call for complementary self-images in the participants if they are to cooperate in the joint undertaking of making a sale or playing a symphony.

Now it might appear superficially that parties in conflict also share such a common and complementary framework. Each expects the other to adopt a hostile role and to behave in an inimical manner, and in this they are unlikely to be disappointed. It would however be mistaken to say that parties to a dispute have to cooperate in order to conflict. They do not share a communicative code or a common orientation to reality or to their respective roles.

They are on the contrary immersed in mutually exclusive frames of reference which lack a communicative code and adopt incompatible views of reality. In fact, as we have seen, this is the most evident diagnostic feature of conflict *per se* and this is precisely what distinguishes it from competition or from sports wherein the participants do indeed cooperate in order to engage in ritualized conflict. At the level of win or lose their interests are opposed. But at another metalevel their interests are identical, because they share the superordinate goal of competing for its own sake.

Enemies on the other hand have separate frames which impede communication, distort perceptions of reality and lead them to interpret and evaluate their opponent's role in terms unacceptable to her/him. And these separate frames preclude cooperation. They amount in each case to a psychological set which predisposes enemies to a zero-sum interpretation of their relationship – Alter experiences Ego's gain as his loss and vice versa – and by that very token makes collaboration equivalent to treason.

FRAME REFLECTED IN GROUP RELATIONS

Moreover, a common frame is the key to group membership and, insofar as the group serves to identify its members, frame is the key to self-identification. Those and only those who display communicative competence are identified by themselves and others as members of a group. Communicative competence includes a capacity for reflexive communication – that is to say, to make evaluative comments on the efficacy, propriety and rationality of other members behavior. The possibility of these metacommunications gives rise to various paradoxes, pathologies and strategies. As has been so fruitfully pointed out by Beck,[18] these include schizogenic double-binds which simultaneously include and exclude from group membership those to whom certain complex messages are addressed, by implying, for example, (context) that she/he is perfectly entitled as an insider to behave in such and such a way but (content) only an outsider would in fact presume to do so (e.g., demonstrate against the government).[19]

Now the existence of separate frames is – in the usual sociological feedback loop – both a cause and a consequence of the fact that enemies define themselves as belonging to mutually exclusive groups. The parties to a successful problem-solving exercise have in the end to come to conceive of themselves, at least for the purposes of conflict resolution, as belonging in some sense to the same, albeit temporary, group. The antagonists have been invited by the panel to consider themselves members of a group of which the panel are members: in due course, they come to treat their opponents as group members also. This is the process which can be monitored at a group level by interaction analysis; and which is accompanied at a psychological level by the dissolution of the separate (conflictual) frames and by the substitution of a joint (cooperative) frame. The social boundaries and the intellectual frames dissolve and reform together; they are as completely interdependent as mirror images.

The emergence of a resolution to the dispute creates a redefinition of the opponents as partners, if only for the limited purposes prescribed by the resolution formula (whatever that may be).

Put differently, the group can devote its attention to creating a resolution only when it reaches a stage in which it is relieved of the necessity for devoting attention to its internal antagonistic social relations.

The avoidance of mere settlement and the search for true resolution calls for intellectual creativity of a high order. In the circumstances attending a dispute, this goes entirely against the psychological grain. It involves abandoning the security of established stereotypes and embarking on uncharted seas of trust in former opponents. Above all it involves innovation and productivity; it involves replacing the struggle to divide the cake by preparations to enlarge the cake available for division.

Now the most distinctive characteristic, intellectually speaking, of any creative process is a collapse of categories. It resides in the breaking of the familiar mold of thought and the appearance of new forms and new connections between previously disparate concepts. As Arthur Koestler[20] has remarked, this is also the essence of humour. A psychological shift to a higher level, to a metaframe, enables one to see what were formerly two disparate ideas as conflated into what appears suddenly as a single incongruous concept – a flash of insight which may be either a joke or a discovery. The problem-solving situation not only fosters the enlargement of the frame within which the disputants conceive their situation but also breaks down the categories of thought which in bargaining tend to block the conception of constructive outcomes. In short, problem solving offers a creative intellectual environment.

THE LANGUAGE OF NEGOTIATION AND THE STRUCTURE OF INTERACTION

Basil Bernstein's work on "Language and Socialization"[21] led me to examine the different speech forms (*la parole*) that characterize the various phases of problem-solving meetings. In the necessary absence of taped recordings, the evidence was gathered impressionistically and the conclusions are therefore tentative at present.

Bernstein has shown that different forms of social relationship are mediated by different speech forms or codes, since both the relationships and the codes reflect the actors' frames of reference. Social structure influences speech form, and in turn speech forms influence, by tending to reinforce or to restructure, the social relations they mediate.

Bernstein distinguishes between restricted and elaborated speech variants (codes) arising from different constraints placed upon speakers' grammatical–lexical choices by their social and contextual milieux. Everyone has access to both types of code, though with varying facility in use depending upon previous socialization and the immediate social environment in which one is operating.

Elaborated codes orient their users toward universalistic meanings that are not tied to a specific context. They afford access to metalanguages necessary for social reflexivity and structural change and explicitly expose the principles of social control and innovation.

Restricted codes, on the other hand, sensitize their users to particularistic meanings that are group- and context-bound, and relatively implicit. Restricted codes are thus tied to an immediate social circle and obscure the means of access to a reflexive commentary on the possibilities of change in the social order. Bernstein associates elaborated and restricted speech codes with dominant and subordinate social classes respectively.

Elaborated codes are necessary to mediate the interactions of relatively specialized roles, particularly between comparative strangers collaborating in instrumental tasks, or in issuing instructions with explicit clarity: the daily burden of modern life.

Sapir and others have pointed out that the closer the identification of speakers and the greater their range of shared interests, the more probable it is that their speech will assume a restricted form. The range of syntactical alternatives is likely to be reduced and the lexis to be drawn from a restricted range. In such close relationships, the intent of the speakers may be taken for granted as they communicate against a background of common experience, common assumptions and common interests. As a result there is less need to elaborate meanings explicitly. Speech is likely to be strongly metaphorical. What is said may be less important than how it is uttered and silence takes on a variety of meanings.

It has hitherto been taken for granted that the consensus of meanings that evokes a restricted code must generally imply the close ties of an intimate community. It is not necessary to deny this in order to point out that in encounters between enemies (or their representatives) public utterances may be so much more concerned with their diametrically opposed expressive significances for both communities and so much less concerned with their instrumental significance for either side, that their communications too take on some of the attributes of a restricted code. There is a community of meanings and an intimacy of hostility as well as of amity.

This appears to be the case in the opening phase of a problem-solving meeting. In such circumstances speech cannot be understood apart from its context and context cannot be read by mediating strangers. The unspoken assumptions underlying the antagonistic relationship are not explicitly available to those outside the circle. The symbolic form of communication is condensed by the history of the relationship it expresses, whether that relation is friendly or hostile.

But whereas in a family or in a single community, a restricted code is all that is needed within a close nexus of enduring relations, and between hostile communities a restricted code may be adequate to continue hostilities, a more elaborated code is called for if changing relationships are in question. Both consensus and dissensus tend to be perpetuated by restricted codes: building a fresh relationship requires an elaborated code for explicit reflection to the new social order. Only elaborated codes give access to alternative realities.

It is the job of the problem-solving panel to help with equipping the parties with the requisite elaborated code as well as supplying the social milieu for resolving conflict.

During the first phase of the meeting the communication is predominantly by the parties, ostensibly to the panel but substantially it is in fact addressed to their opponents. Because so much of it assumes the community of meanings and intimacy of hostility it takes on the aspect of restricted code.

In the second or analytical phase in which the panel tends to predominate, the restricted and particularistic utterances of the parties are reformulated universalistically in an elaborated code which in due course the parties embrace as well.

The third phase of problem-solving sees the parties in direct communication through their newly elaborated channel. Naturally the restricted–elaborated distinction is a matter of degree. Of course, we are here concerned not so much with a transition from one code to another, but rather from less to more elaborated codes. And from context-bound, particularistic constraints to context-free universalistic premises.

THE FUNCTION OF ANALYSIS

It is excessively difficult to discuss the role of the analysis itself without comparing several instances in such detail as would require a whole monograph. It is vital, however, that the absence of such a discussion should not be taken to signify that a valid analysis represents anything less than the heart of the problem-solving procedure. At this point, we wish only to reflect briefly on the fact that the new definition of the situation which provides the joint frame of reference from which the resolution of the conflict grows must ultimately be derived from the analysis.

The redefinition of the situation is not the work of the panel alone, nor of the parties only, but of the panel and parties in concert. And the warrant for the validity of the definition which is finally adopted is not that it was reached with the aid of an "objective," neutral or independent panel, essential as that may indeed be, but that it is acceptable, that it "rings true" to all concerned, parties and panel alike.

A definition of a situation represents the meaning of that situation and of their actions, for all the actors embedded in it; it is the human significance of what is going on. Manifestly, this is not an "objective" label; it is inherently subjective, a shared frame of mind. The relationship between the interpretations of any situation made by an outsider, say a social scientist, and those made by the actors themselves is *the* problem for phenomenologists.[22] The scientist observing, say, a Hopi rain dance or the Trooping of the Colours in London, or any conflict, must be competent to communicate the theoretical significance of that pattern of behavior to the actors involved. And if it is valid these actors must be able to appropriate to their own use the interpretation of the actions developed by the theorist.

Corroboration of the theoretical interpretation by the actors neither constitutes verification of the interpretation nor is it irrelevant to its verification. At the same time, however, actors must clearly not be led to corroborate or connive in false or distorting interpretations of their situation and behavior. A theoretical interpetation, it seems, can be truly corroborated only by the completion of the self-reflection process. In psychoanalysis, the definition of his situation provided by the patient and that of the analyst successively approximate to one another until they fuse. At this point, the situation is redefined and catharsis achieved. In problem-solving, if the actor, those with whom he interacts and the analyst, all share a common definition of their joint situation, then that definition may be said to be verified or corroborated. The fusion of divergent definitions of a shared situation, the progressive "objectification" of the analysis of their joint predicament, is one of the major functions of the problem-solving process. The role of the analysis provided by the panel is to enable the redefinition to proceed to fusion. The search for an adequate analysis and for communicative competence to secure fusion are integral elements in the problem-solving technique.

NOTES AND REFERENCES

1. J. W. Burton, *Conflict and Communication: The Use of Controlled Communication in International Relations* (London: Macmillan; New York: Free Press, 1969); "The Resolution of Conflict," *International Studies Quarterly*, 1 (March 1972).
2. A. V. S. de Reuck, "A Note on Equity and Distribution," presented at Joint Institute on Comparative Urban and Grants Economics, University of Augsberg (August 1972); de Reuck, "Controlled Communication: Rationale and Dynamics," *The Human Context* 6(1) (Spring 1974): 64–80;
3. De Reuck, "Controlled Communication."
4. L. W. Doob (ed.), *Resolving Conflict in Africa: The Fermeda Workshop* (New Haven: Yale University Press, 1970); Doob (ed.), *The Social Psychological Techniques and the Peaceful Settlement of International Disputes*, UNITAR Research Reports, 1 (New York, 1970); H. C. Kelman, "The Problem-Solving Workshop in Conflict Resolution," *Journal of Peace Research*, 13 (2) (1976): 79–90.
5. Kelman, "The Problem-Solving Workshop."
6. De Reuck, "A Note on Equity and Distribution" and "Controlled Communciation."

7. R. F. Bales, *Interaction Process Analysis: A Method for the Study of Small Groups* (Cambridge, MA: Addison-Wesley, 1950); Bales, "How People Interact in Conference," *Scientific American*, 192 (1955): 31–55; R. F. Bales *et al.*, "Channels of Communication in Small Groups," *American Sociological Review*, 15 (1951): 461–8; J. B. Keller and R. F. Bales, "Comment and Reply," *American Sociological Review*, 16 (1951): 842–3.
8. Burton, *Conflict and Communication* and "The Resolution of Conflict."
9. I. E. Morley and G. M. Stephenson, *The Social Psychology of Bargaining* (London: Allen & Unwin, 1979); G. M. Stephenson and A. Stacey, *The Characteristics of Negotiation and Consultation* (London: Routledge, 1979).
10. Irving Goffman, *Frame Analysis* (New York: Harper & Row, 1973 and Harmondsworth, England: Peregrine, 1975); Alfred Schutz, "On Multiple Realities" (1945), reprinted in *Collected Papers*, vol. 1 (The Hague: Martinus Nijhoff, 1962): 207–59.
11. Morley and Stephenson, *The Social Psychology of Bargaining*.
12. B. Bernstein, "A Socio-Linguistic Approach to Social Learning," in J. Gould (ed.), *Penguin Survey of the Social Sciences* (Harmondsworth, England: Penguin, 1965): 144–68; Bernstein, "A Socio-Linguistic Approach to Socialization," *The Human Context II*: 1 and 2 (1970); Bernstein, *Class Codes and Control* (London: Routledge & Kegan Paul, 1971); Bernstein, "Language and Socialization," in N. Minnis (ed.), *Linguistics at Large* (London: Gollancz, 1971): 225–42.
13. Mary Douglas, *Natural Symbols* (Harmondsworth, England: Pelican, 1973); Douglas, *Cultural Bias* (London: Royal Anthropological Institute, 1978).
14. M. R. A. Chance and R. R. Larsen, *The Social Structure of Attention* (London; New York: Wiley, 1976).
15. Gregory Bateson, "A Theory of Play and Fantasy" (1955), reprinted in Bateson, *Steps to an Ecology of Mind* (St Albans: Paladin, 1973): 150–72.
16. Schutz, "On Multiple Realities"; Peter L. Berger and Thomas Luckmann, *The Social Construction of Reality* (New York: Doubleday, 1966); Goffman, *Frame Analysis*.
17. Goffman, *Frame Analysis*.
18. Henry Beck, "Attention Struggles and Silencing Strategies in Political Conflict," in Chance and Larsen (eds), *The Social Structure of Attention*.
19. Roger Masters, "Attention Structures and Presidential Campaigns," unpublished APSA paper (New York, 1978).
20. Arthur Koestler, *The Act of Creation* (London: Hutchinson, 1964).
21. Basil Bernstein, "A Socio-Linguistic Approach to Social Learning"; Bernstein, "A Socio-Linguistic Approach to Socialization"; Bernstein, *Class Codes*; Bernstein, "Language and Socialization."
22. Berger and Luckmann, *Social Construction*; Masters, "Attention Structures."

10 Interactive Problem-Solving: a Social-psychological Approach to Conflict Resolution

Herbert C. Kelman*

Throughout my professional career, one of my main areas of interest has been the social psychology of international relations. This interest has led, in recent years, to intensive involvement in an action research program on the resolution of international conflicts. My primary and nearly all-consuming emphasis has been on the Arab–Israeli conflict, although I have also done some work on other international and intercommunal conflicts, particularly the Cyprus conflict.

Essentially, my colleagues and I have been evolving and enacting a special kind of unofficial third-party role, utilizing our academic base and our social science knowledge and skills as our unique sources of competence, credibility, and legitimacy. What we are doing can be described as a form of mediation, although we clearly see it as our function not to propose (and certainly not to impose) solutions, but to *facilitate* communication among the conflicting parties themselves so that mutually acceptable solutions can emerge out of their own interaction. Whenever possible, we create contexts and occasions to bring the parties together for direct, face-to-face interaction. Even in those of our activities that do not involve direct communication between the parties, we proceed on the basis of a model that assigns central importance to the interaction process. Thus, for example, when we meet with representatives of a single party, we try to listen so that we can understand (and better communicate) their concerns and perspectives; we try to interpret to them the concerns and perspectives of the other party, as we understand them; and we try to be alert to opportunities for direct interactions between the parties and to encourage and lay the groundwork for such interactions.

* From W. Klassen (ed.), *Dialogue Toward Inter-Faith Understanding* (Tantur/ Jerusalem: Ecumenical Institute for Theological Research, 1985).

The emphasis on interaction in our model of intervention is linked to a social-psychological analysis of conflict itself, which differs from traditional strategic or "realist" approaches in three important ways:

1. It considers a broader range of influence processes in conflict relationships. Thus, it is cognizant of the limitations of strategies based almost exclusively on threats, as exemplified by deterrence theory, and points to the escalatory dynamic of such strategies and to the high probability that the parties will not feel committed to solutions achieved through the use of negative incentives. Instead, it raises the possibility of developing strategies based on the use of positive incentives, as exemplified by Sadat's strategy in his 1977 trip to Jerusalem.

2. Our social-psychological analysis suggests a broader vision of the goals to which negotiations are to be directed. This vision is based on a view of international conflict as a conflict between *societies* and not merely between states. Given such a view, negotiations need to go beyond the achievement of a political agreement to a *resolution* of the conflict – a process conducive to structural and attitudinal change and eventually to reconciliation between the parties and to a transformation of their relationship.

3. Such an analysis focuses on the way interactions between the parties, at different levels, create the conditions for conflict, and help to feed, escalate, and perpetuate conflict. Such an analysis suggests that conflict resolution requires the introduction of different kinds of interactions that are capable of reversing these processes and setting a deescalatory dynamic into motion. Amongst other things, such interactions would enable the parties to discover ways of influencing each other, by exploring what the other needs and what they can therefore offer the other to induce reciprocation.

Interaction in our model is not an end in itself. We do not assume that the conflict could be resolved if only the parties would communicate and understand each other better. Nor is it our purpose merely to bring the parties together so that they can get to know each other as human beings with similar goals and concerns (valuable though such experiences may be, particularly in conflicts between parties whose interactions are limited to hostile confrontations and whose mutual images are thoroughly dehumanized). Rather, our emphasis is on creating the conditions that will make a particular kind of interaction possible – interaction characterized by analysis of the conflict, exploration of mutual perspectives, generation of new ideas, and joint problem-solving. Creative problem-solving in this context searches for ways of redefining, fractionating, or transcending the conflict so that positive-sum, or win/win solutions, which leave both parties better off, can be discovered.

Furthermore, the purpose of the interactions that we try to arrange is to create products – in the form of new knowledge and ideas, altered perceptions and attitudes, and innovative proposals for conflict resolution – that can be fed into the policy process. Thus, while our procedures call for work with individuals, directed at their affective and cognitive processes, the ultimate aim of the intervention is to produce changes at the level of the larger conflict system. Here again – as in our emphasis on social interaction – we are operating within a social-psychological framework. As a social psychologist, I look to the joint operation of psychological and institutional processes in attempting to understand the dynamics of conflict. The stuff of which conflict is made concerns the purposes and goals, the perceptions and images, the expectations and identity concerns of individuals and groups – as these find expression in collective orientations and become translated into national policies. Conflict resolution, in this view, requires changes in individual attitudes and images as a vehicle for and as an accompaniment of changes in official policy and societal action. Our interventions are specifically designed to promote such system-level changes by way of changes in the perceptions and attitudes of influential individuals. This strategy, incidentally, creates certain contradictory requirements, since the specific conditions for maximizing impact on individuals and those for maximizing impact on the system – or, if you will, the conditions conducive to learning and those conducive to transfer – are different and may, in fact, often conflict with each other. To an important extent, therefore, our intervention model is a dialectical process, which takes account of potential contradictions between different requirements and seeks to establish a balance between them.

Another feature of our approach is the special way in which it combines action with research. In most of my work in this area – such as in the problem-solving workshops that I shall describe in a moment – the action requirements have consistently taken precedence over the research requirements. At every stage of the process – for example, in selecting participants, planning the agenda, or making specific interventions – our decisions are based entirely on our judgement of what is necessary to ensure the viability of the exercise and its effectiveness in contributing to conflict resolution. We have not introduced any variations in order to test their effects on the process, nor have we tried out any special procedures in order to observe what would happen.

While we have not been using formal research procedures, however, we are very much engaged in research. Indeed, it is our role as researchers that provides the rationale and legitimacy of our action involvement and that allows representatives of conflicting parties to interact with each other under our auspices in ways that deviate from the norms generally governing their relationship. Our research interest, moreover, cannot be feigned because we would lose credibility very quickly. We must be genuinely interested in learning about conflict in general and about the particular conflict, and we must demonstrate this interest and show what we have learned from our action research program through publications and other means. Thus, our *action* requires involvement in a *research* program just as our *research* requires involvement in an *action* program. The unique advantage of this type of research is that it provides us the opportunity to make rich, detailed observations of on-going processes of conflict and conflict resolution, which would not be accessible to us unless we were engaged in an action program.

To sum up so far, I have described three features of the action research program on conflict resolution in which I have been engaged: it assigns a central role to an interactional, problem-solving process in its model of intervention; it is designed to produce changes in attitudes and perceptions and to generate creative new ideas among influential individuals on the two sides of the conflict, in ways that would maximize direct impact on official policy; and it utilizes social scientists in a special third-party role, based on an integral relationship between action and research.

Let me introduce a caveat at this point. Social-psychological analysis is not a substitute for or an alternative to political analysis. I consider the whole debate about psychological *versus* political factors and about the relative proportions of their influence to be beside the point. Psychological factors do not operate separately from political factors, but suffuse them. Furthermore, psychological conditions cannot be divorced from the objective conditions that underlie the conflict. In intense and protracted conflicts we usually deal with real conflicts of interest and ideological differences that cannot be simply attributed to misperception or distrust. The main significance of psychological factors is that they contribute to escalation and perpetuation of conflict by creating barriers to both the occurrence and the perception of change. Overcoming the psychological barriers does not in itself resolve the conflict. A settlement must ultimately take place at the political level, through political and diplomatic processes. But to the extent that such barriers can be overcome, new possibilities may be created for negotiations on the basis of objective conditions and current interests. As long as these barriers persist, the parties are locked into rigid assumptions and postures rooted in past history.

To make our intervention model somewhat more concrete, let me proceed now to give a brief description of the problem-solving workshops in conflict resolution that we have organized. In our Middle East work, these have mainly involved Israeli and Palestinian participants, although we have also worked with other groupings of Arabs and Israelis. The problem-solving workshop has been the starting point and in many ways the prototype for our work, though it must be seen in the context of a broader approach that can take different forms and operate on different levels. Problem-solving workshops are designed to bring together representatives of conflicting parties in a relatively isolated setting – preferably an academic context – where they can engage, free from diplomatic protocol and publicity, in face-to-face communication in the presence and under the guidance of social scientists knowledgeable about group process and conflict theory.

As I have already indicated in my remarks about the central features of interactive problem-solving, workshops serve a dual purpose: to produce *change* in the participants themselves – to stimulate new understandings, modifications in perceptions and attitudes, new ideas for conflict resolution; and to *transfer* these changes to the policy arena – to feed the new learnings into the political debate and the decision making process within each society. Both purposes are involved in all of our workshops, regardless of the level of the participants and the degree of ready access that they may have to the decision making process. In other words, all of our workshops can be said to have both an *educational* and a *political* purpose, although the relative importance of the one over the other may vary from workshop to workshop. Even when the workshop participants, though politically involved, do not have immediate access to decision makers, we consider their interaction to be politically significant, in keeping with our assumption that conflict is an intersocietal rather than just an intergovernmental affair. In this view, it is important to generate new inputs not only into the decision making process itself, but also into the internal debate within each society.

The participants in the workshops that I have conducted have varied in terms of their level of political involvement and their degree of proximity to the decision making process. Loosely speaking, we can distinguish three types of participants in our workshops, although these categories are overlapping and sometimes participation may be "mixed" in the sense that the same workshop draws its participants from two of these categories:

1. In some of our workshops, the participants are primarily individuals who can be described as "pre-influentials." These have generally been advanced students or young scholars who are already in the United States for a short or long period of advanced study or research. They are selected for participation because they are politically involved and likely to move into influential positions as their careers develop. In workshops whose participants are mostly pre-influentials (which, incidentally, have served as training opportunities for my students, who serve as auxiliary members of the third party), the primary purpose is educational, yet these workshops too have political effects. In the short run, they influence the participants' subsequent political activities and their contributions to the internal political debate; and in the long run, they may have a more direct impact as these individuals become more influential within their own communities. Some participants have also had a professional interest in the enterprise and the experience contributed to their own future work, for example in organizing workshops of their own or engaging in related efforts to promote Arab–Jewish dialogue.

2. The second category of participants can be described as political influentials. These have generally been respected intellectuals – scholars and writers – who are influential in one or both of two ways: as advisors to the decision makers and political leadership in their own communities, and as major analysts and interpreters of the conflict to their own societies through scholarly publications and the mass media. Such participants can often convey the new learnings and new ideas derived from a workshop directly to relevant decision makers. They may also influence the policy process indirectly by their presentation of new ideas in the media, which may have an impact on public opinion and thus on the general climate within which decision makers operate.

3. Finally, the third category of participants can be described as themselves political actors. The best example here would be parliamentarians, political party activists, or representatives of political movements or important constituencies – individuals who are directly (and often professionally) involved in the political process, though they do not personally occupy decision making positions. Sometimes, such individuals may be designated by their political leadership as workshop participants. What such participants learn can be fed directly into the top-level political debate within their respective communities. They are also often in a position to communicate what they have learned in a way that decision makers or political leaders find credible, politically relevant, and compelling. Because the primary purpose of workshops at this level is political, it may at times be necessary to modify their format, but an educational function still remains a central part of their essence: the unique contribution of problem-solving workshops to the political process is their capacity to generate new learnings – new understanding of the adversary, new insights into the nature of the conflict, and new ideas for movement toward conflict resolution.

In general, ideal participants for workshops, in my view, are individuals who are highly influential within their respective communities, but are not themselves in policy positions. Although there may well be occasions when the participation of decision makers themselves would be indicated, I consider non-official but highly influential participants to be most appropriate on theoretical grounds. In view of the dialectical nature of the process that I mentioned earlier, such participants represent the best balance between the requirements for maximizing learning and those for maximizing transfer – i.e., the requirements for maximizing the likelihood of change within the workshop and, at the same time, maximizing the likelihood that the products of the workshop will have an impact on the policy process. Whatever the status of the participants, they come in their private capacities rather than as officially designated representatives. To maximize impact on the policy process, however, it is usually best that they participate with the knowledge and tacit consent of relevant official agencies. Even though the participants are invited as individuals, the composition of the teams and the structure of the situation encourage the members of each party to function as a group with some degree of collective responsibility.

An essential condition for problem-solving workshops, that distinguishes them from official negotiations, is that participants can interact with minimal commitment. The unofficial, private nature of the workshop and its embeddedness in an academic context makes it easier to communicate with the adversary without the implication that one is thereby recognizing and legitimizing them. It thus becomes possible to view communication as a *process*, designed to provide mutual learning and sharing of information, rather than as a *political statement*. The academic, private nature of workshops also makes it easier to enter into them without commitment to any particular set of outcomes. There is, moreover, the understanding that there will be no publicity and that participants will not be held accountable outside of the workshop for what they say in the course of the discussions. Finally, in the event there are leaks resulting in criticism, decision makers, even if they gave their consent to the exercise, can disown it as an academic affair, in which all participants were acting as private individuals.

Setting, agenda, ground rules, procedures, and third-party interventions are designed to counteract the accusatory, legalistic, and conflict-expressive atmosphere that usually characterizes interaction between conflicting parties, and to promote, instead, a task-oriented, analytical approach. The typical face-to-face interactions between representatives of parties involved in an intense conflict take place (when they take place at all) in a context that is almost designed to make it impossible for them to learn anything new about the other party or about themselves. The norms governing such interactions call on the representatives to express their group's grievances and to proclaim its historical and legal rights as firmly and militantly as possible. Their constituencies' and indeed their *own* evaluation of their performance depends on how well they advance and defend the group's position and how strong a case they make. There is little attempt in such interactions to listen to the other, to gain an understanding of the other's perspective, or even to find ways of influencing the adversary. Communications are directed, not to the adversary, but to one's constituencies and to third parties. It is not surprising that such interactions reinforce existing images and strengthen each side's commitment to its original position. Workshops are designed to create a setting governed by a different set of norms in which genuine interaction between the conflicting parties can take place, so that they can come to understand the other's perspective and become aware of possibilities for change – especially of how they themselves can contribute to change through their own actions. To this end, the focus of the interaction is on analysis of the conflict. In particular, participants are encouraged to analyze, with each other's help, how each party perceives itself and the adversary. Such an analytic stance can gradually lead to a collaborative, problem-solving process, conducive to the emergence of creative new ideas for conflict resolution.

Although the focus is on ideas emerging out of the interaction between the parties themselves, the third party plays an essential facilitator role in the process. It brings the conflicting parties together and facilitates constructive communication by providing the appropriate context, norms, and interventions. The functions of the third party can be summarized as follows:

1. We provide a framework in which parties who do not otherwise communicate (or at least do not communicate openly, attentively, and analytically) can come together to talk and listen to each other. In my work, it is the academic context that makes such interactions possible.
2. We select the participants and brief them carefully – both individually, in often intensive conversations that I hold with each participant, and in pre-workshop sessions, in which each party meets separately with the third party for four to five hours.
3. We serve as a repository of trust in the process for both sets of participants. By definition, they cannot trust each other when they come together. Only after some time, and as part of the workshop process, are they able to develop a limited *working trust* in each other, based on the recognition of common interests despite profound differences, which allows them to engage in the work of analysis and point problem-solving. In the meantime, their common trust in the third party enables the participants to proceed with the assurance that their interests will be protected, that their sensitivities will be respected, and that their confidences will not be violated.
4. We establish and enforce certain norms and ground rules, designed to permit and encourage communication oriented to new learning. The academic context is particularly useful in providing an alternative set of norms capable of counteracting the norms that generally govern interaction between conflicting parties. The academic setting encourages, and indeed requires, an analytic approach. Having committed themselves to an academic framework, the

participants feel both obligated and free to abide by its norms. The third party intervenes as necessary – and with restraint – to reestablish and maintain these norms.

5. We propose a fairly broad and loose agenda. In an initial workshop with a groups of participants, we first encourage them to talk about their concerns – about their basic needs that must be satisfied by a solution and about their basic fears that must be taken into account. Only once the two sets of concerns are simultaneously on the table, having been expressed and heard by the other side, do we suggest that participants begin to explore possible solutions that would be responsive to the needs and fears of both sides. We then move to discussion of psychological and political barriers that must be overcome in order to implement such solutions, and to ways in which the two sides can help each other in this effort. The third party encourages participants to adhere to this agenda without, however, cutting off fruitful discussions that might appear to be deviating from it. We intervene on occasion in order to help keep the discussion moving along productive, constructive channels.

6. Finally, we sometimes make substantive interventions, particularly at the beginning and end of sessions. Such interventions may take the form of (a) theoretical inputs, which help participants distance themselves from their own conflict, provide them with conceptual tools for analysis of their conflict, and offer them relevant illustrations from previous research; (b) content observations, which suggest interpretations and implications of what is being said and point to convergencies and divergences between the parties, to blind spots, to possible signals, and to issues for clarification; or (c) process observations *at the intergroup level*, which suggest possible ways in which interactions between the parties "here and now" may reflect the dynamics of the conflict between their communities.

Let me elaborate on the nature of process observations, since this concept may not be familiar to everyone and since this also gives me an opportunity to convey something of the flavor of what can happen in workshops.

The potential usefulness of process observations can be illustrated with two events that took place during our very first workshop on the Israeli–Palestinian conflict, which was held late in 1971.[1] There were many points during the workshop when the Palestinians attacked the Israelis, and attributed imperialism, expansionism, and other negative traits to Israel. The Israelis responded firmly, but they seemed to accept such attacks as a legitimate part of the process. There was only one point during the entire proceedings when the Israelis threatened to walk out – and this was when one of the Palestinians, quite innocently it seems, told a classic anti-Semitic joke. The Palestinians were quite surprised by the intensity of the Israeli reaction. The second event was one in which the Israelis were caught by surprise. They were giving the Palestinians what they considered to be "friendly" advice on how to organize their political movement more effectively. The Palestinians responded with an outburst of anger. Clearly the Palestinians saw the Israeli advice-giving as an act of arrogance and condescension, which underscored their own sense of powerlessness.

These two incidents illustrate in concrete, "here and now" fashion central elements of the national identities of the two parties. They touch areas of special sensitivity for each group by surfacing negative elements of their identities that are of central concern to them. These negative identity elements represent sources of profound humiliation and fear for the groups, reminding them of their current or historical powerlessness and vulnerability. In the case of the Israelis, the reaction to the anti-Semitic joke illustrated the centrality of the Jewish historical experience of persecution and exclusion in Israeli national identity. In the case of the Palestinians, the reaction to Israeli advice-giving illustrated their intense frustration over being unable to control their own fates and their view of Israel as the central symbol and current source of this frustration.

The intense reactions to these events and the fact that, in each case, these reactions were unanticipated by the other party, make them excellent raw material for third-party intervention. Each party can concretely see the intensity of the other's reactions and the genuine and spontaneous nature of that reaction. Moreover, they can see that it was their own actions that produced this response, without intention on their part to be provocative or even awareness that they were touching on sensitive areas. The third party can use such incidents, which are part of the participants' shared immediate experience, as a springboard for exploring some of the issues and concerns that define the conflict between their societies. Through such exploration, they can gain some insight into the preoccupations of the other side, and the way these are affected by the actions of their own side. That these preoccupations, which surfaced so dramatically in the course of our 1971 workshop, play an important role in the relations between the conflicting societies, was illustrated in the Egyptian–Israeli negotiations in 1978. Incidents that contributed most visibly to the souring of the relationship between the two parties were Egyptian actions that Israelis saw as anti-Semitic (such as references in the Egyptian press to Begin or to Israel as "Shylock") and Israeli actions that Egyptians saw as arrogant (such as statements to the effect that Israel does not "need" Egypt's recognition). Thus, interventions that focus on such incidents in the course of a workshop may lead to discussion and analysis of issues that form a significant part of the dynamics of the conflict between the two societies.

It is important that such interventions be pitched at the intergroup level, rather than the interpersonal level. Analysis of "here and now" interactions is not concerned with the personal characteristics of the participants or with their personal relations to each other, but only with what these interactions can tell us about the relationship between their national groups. Experiences within the workshop do provide an especially effective springboard for helping parties gain greater insight into their own and their adversary's concerns and sensitivities because of the immediacy and the emotional strength of the experience. Analysis of intense reactions as they happen is instructive both for those who experience the reaction in themselves and those who observe it in the other. What is particularly instructive for the observers is the opportunity to see directly the impact that they have had upon the other.

To provide the context, norms and interventions that can facilitate constructive interaction, the third party clearly needs to possess certain special characteristics. In our work, our status as academics, social scientists, and students of international conflict provides an important basis for our credibility and legitimacy in the eyes of the parties. There is the presumption that we have the necessary skill, knowledge, and objectivity to perform the third-party function – a presumption that is, of course, continually, put to the test. Much of my work has been carried out as a member of a team of social scientists, consisting of Arab and Jewish Americans. In my experience, such an ethnically balanced team, whose members are intensely engaged in the conflict, has certain advantages over a team that is neutral in the sense of being disinterested. It often conveys greater sensitivity to nuances of the parties, greater alertness to the cultural and social dimensions of the conflict, and greater sympathy for the emotional and symbolic issues at stake. Engagement, of course, must be clearly distinguished from partisanship, which would generally be inconsistent with a third-party role.

In this connection, it would be fair to add that my third-party work does represent a political stance. While the work does not represent a commitment to a particular solution of the conflict, it does imply a commitment to a particular *type* of solution and to a particular process for achieving it. We are dedicated to the search for solutions that are peaceful and just. More specifically, interactive problem-solving is a process geared to the discovery of win/win solutions, in which both parties can feel that their basic needs have been satisfied. Such solutions inevitably require some compromise on both sides, although they are designed to leave both parties better off than they are at present. In my Israeli–Palestinian work, my efforts are geared to helping create the conditions for a negotiated agreement, conducive to reconciliation. Such efforts are not politically neutral, since there are elements on both sides who prefer to maintain the status quo or to fight on to victory rather than accept a solution that calls for any degree of compromise. Moreover, in setting the parameters for our workshops, we must of necessity make certain decisions – such as a decision about the definition of the parties – without which the work cannot proceed. Since there is often considerable controversy around such issues, whatever decision we make, though a technical necessity, does represent a political stance.

Workshops provide the occasion for certain kinds of new learning that are most likely to occur as a result of social interaction in a context that encourages analysis. Workshops are particularly useful in enabling participants to observe directly and to analyze the impact of their own actions on the adversary, and the impact of the adversary's actions on themselves. Some of the learnings that have emerged, for example, from workshops we ran with Israeli and Palestinian participants can be summarized as follows:

1. Participants have learned that there is someone to talk to on the other side and something to talk about – a discovery that may be limited, but is not insignificant in a conflict in which the abiding assumption has been that there is no one to talk to and nothing to talk about.
2. Participants have gained some insight into the perspective of the other party – their fundamental concerns, their priorities, their areas of flexibility, their psychological and structural constraints. Some of the most striking examples of such insights that I have

been able to observe in workshops have focused on the meaning that certain ideological doctrines and central symbols in the conflict have from the perspective of the other. For Palestinians, Zionism tends to have only one meaning – the eradication of Palestinian nationhood; for Israelis, Palestinian nationalism tends to have only one meaning – the destruction of Israel. In the course of their interactions in some of our workshops, participants have come to understand that the destruction of their own nation does not exhaust the meaning of the other's ideology. Palestinians have learned that for Israelis, Zionism may represent a positive vision of national renewal and social change; Israelis have learned that for Palestinians, the quest for a national state – or even for a secular democratic state – may represent a similar vision of a desirable future. This does not mean, of course, that they accept the other's ideology, but the mutual penetration of the other's perspective enables them to think, for the first time, about the possibility of developing a common vision of the future for the land they share, in which fulfillment for one people does not presuppose destruction for the other. The increasing differentiation of what has been a totally demonic image can also manifest itself in other ways in the course of a workshop. Typically, the two parties engage in a variety of exchanges designed to test each other's sincerity and genuine readiness for peace and coexistence. As a result of such exchanges, they may develop a degree of mutual trust, based on the conviction that at least these particular representatives of the opposing camp are genuinely committed to a peaceful solution. They are then startled to discover – usually through the active intervention of the third party – that these individuals, who have passed the tests they imposed on them and whose commitment to negotiation and coexistence they have come to trust, are committed Zionists or dedicated supporters of the PLO, respectively. Such discoveries help to break down the assumption that peace is possible only if the other side undergoes conversion and abandons its own national ideology. They open up the possibility of negotiation based on acceptance of each other's right to nationhood and to commitment to the symbols and institutions expressive of that nationhood.

3. Participants have developed greater awareness of changes that have taken place in the adversary, of the possibilities for change under changing circumstances, and of ways of promoting such change in the other through their own actions – a kind of learning

that is particularly important because the dynamics of conflict create a strong tendency to dismiss the occurrence and the possibility of change on the part of the adversary, which then makes change less likely by way of self-fulfilling prophecy. Of special significance is the discovery by each party of ways in which they could influence the other through the introduction of positive incentives that might create a new situation, setting a process of change into motion. The ability to influence the others is one of the casualties of a conflict relationship, since it is difficult to influence those with whom we are unable to empathize. Workshops can help in recovering this ability.

4. Participants have learned about the significance of gestures and symbolic acts and become more aware of actions they could take that would be meaningful to the other and yet entail relatively little cost to themselves. Of particular importance are gestures that indicate acceptance of the other as a people, or even basic acceptance of the other's humanity. (Note, for example, the powerful response of the Israeli public to Sadat's round of handshakes when he stepped off the plane in Israel in November 1977.) Workshops can be useful in identifying possible gestures that might make a considerable difference to the other, because they reveal areas of sensitivity and vulnerability to which such gestures must address themselves. Such gestures, in turn, can help create an atmosphere more conducive to negotiation.

From our point of view, the different kinds of learning that I have described are significant insofar as they are fed into the policy process, which in turn requires workshop participants who are politically influential.

It should be clear from what I have been saying that I do not view workshops as substitutes for diplomatic or political negotiations; rather, I see them as potentially preparing the way for, supplementing, and feeding into official negotiations. They may provide a unique input into a larger process of conflict resolution by gradually creating an atmosphere conducive to negotiation, or by establishing an appropriate framework for parties that are ready for communication but not for official negotiations, or by allowing the parties to work out pieces of a solution that can then be fed into the formal negotiation process. Workshops can be useful at different stages of the negotiation process; in the pre-negotiation phase, where they can help create the conditions for negotiation; in the negotiation phase itself, where the approach can contribute ideas about the interaction process and where workshops can be arranged alongside the formal negotiation framework in order to work out specific technical or even political issues that require an analytical, problem-solving approach; and in the post-negotiation phase, where they can facilitate coexistence and cooperative efforts, eventually leading to reconciliation and a transformation of the relationship between the parties.

My recent work on the Israeli–Palestinian conflict can essentially be seen as a contribution to the pre-negotiation process. Workshops and related activities can help to create a general atmosphere conducive to negotiation; they can generate ideas and proposals for a framework and a set of principles that can serve as a basis for negotiation – that is, for getting the negotiations started; they can demonstrate the feasibility of negotiated solution; and they can contribute to the creation of a cadre of individuals who have accumulated experience in communicating with the other side and have developed the conviction that such communication can be fruitful.

In this spirit, I have been engaged, over the last few years, in various efforts to bring together politically influential Israelis and Palestinians to address themselves to the question of how they can set a process of Israeli–Palestinian negotiations into motion. Those who agree to participate in such efforts are, of course, individuals who represent the segment of the political spectrum that is interested in a negotiated solution – but these segments of the political spectrum, on both sides, are more numerous and potentially more influential than is often realized. Clearly, workshops or meetings that we arrange for such individuals are not negotiating sessions. Negotiations will have to take place at an official level and in a multi-party context. But they are a promising part of a pre-negotiation process, designed to pave the way for official negotiations. At the moment, the main contribution of such workshops is to provide new input into the political debate within each community and to discover ways in which the elements on both sides who are committed to a negotiated solution can help each other in their respective internal political struggles. I have been greatly encouraged by the extent to which the representatives of the two parties with whom we have been working have been able to discover common ground, to conclude that there are potential negotiating partners on the other side and negotiable issues to consider, to recognize the occurrence of change and the possibility of further change, and to develop the sense of guarded optimism that is required for movement toward conflict resolution.

NOTES AND REFERENCES

1. Stephen P. Cohen, Herbert C. Kelman, Frederick D. Miller and Bruce L. Smith, "Evolving Intergroup Techniques for Conflict Resolution: an Israeli–Palestinian Pilot Workshop," *Journal of Social Issues*, 33(1): 165–89.

11 Principles of Communication Between Adversaries in South Africa

Hendrik W. van der Merwe, Johann Maree, André Zaaiman, Cathy Philip and A. D. Muller*

PRINCIPLES OF NEGOTIATION

1. *Conflict is natural and endemic. It can serve useful social functions and can often be accommodated constructively, provided a rational and sensitive approach is adopted, it is anticipated in advance, and use is made of available insights and expertise.* (Many of these are dealt with in the principles discussed below.)

2. *Under present conditions, fundamental social and political conflict in South Africa can be accommodated or managed but not resolved.*

   Conflict resolution denotes the termination of a conflict through the elimination of the underlying bases or causes of the conflict.

   Although the term is widely used in other countries, we do not favour the use of "conflict resolution" in the present South African context, because of its comprehensive and far-reaching implications. Indeed the majority of conflicts in the world are settled or accommodated rather than resolved. To use the

* Unpublished paper, December 1988, from a manuscript commissioned by the Urban Foundation.

216

term "resolution" loosely could therefore be interpreted as unrealistic, even irresponsible.

We use the term *conflict accommodation* as a generic term to include all methods, practices and techniques – formal and informal, traditional and 'alternative', within and outside the courts – that are used to resolve or settle disputes.

3. *In a situation where gross injustices are built into the major social structures (such as in South Africa) conflict cannot be accommodated constructively and social justice and peace cannot be achieved without fundamental structural change.*

In the political field, this would mean new political institutions for all levels of government on which all population groups, regardless of race or ethnicity, would have direct representation. In Western democratic terms it would mean majority rule.

The need for fundamental structural change is reflected in the recent escalation of industrial action which is directly and indirectly related to political issues that have been taken up by trade unions. This reflects the inability of the existing political structures to accommodate conflict. The changes in industrial relations implemented after the Wiehahn Commission remain relatively minor adjustments within the context of the broad political system. In the absence of political representation, it is inevitable that African trade unions are perceived, in certain sectors, as vehicles for political change. The role that these unions are forced to play and their consequent aims and goals, means that the ensuing conflicts that arise at the workplace cannot be constructively accommodated within the present political structure. Political representation in a common political body is required in order to take the pressure off both management and trade unions.

4. *Coercion and negotiation are complementary aspects of the process of communication between adversaries.*

Coercion and negotiation are not mutually exclusive; coercion, in fact, constitutes an integral part of the negotiations process. Negotiation (the primary concern of the intermediary) should not be seen as a substitute for, or alternative to, pressures for change. Pressures are required to bring about change in South Africa. Negotiation should be seen as a complement to pressure in the communication process between conflicting parties. By improving the quality of communication and understanding, negotiation will ensure more rational and effective pressures and more orderly change. Meaningful and accurate information helps to put pressures in perspective. Third-party facilitiation and mediation should be seen within this wider context.[1]

5. *Violence is a destructive manifestation of conflict, but is part of the communication process between adversaries, and should be interpreted as such.*

   While violence has destructive impact (and probably because of it) it often has significant short-term impact on relations with adversaries. Many forms of violence can be interpreted as attempts to communicate concern for law and order or frustration and anger.[2]

   Human behavior is often motivated by the goal of need-satisfaction and if the satisfaction of a desired need is frustrated, the individual or group will employ "deviant" norms to achieve his/her or their aims if necessary. In South Africa it has become clear that violent behavior in communal conflicts is often the result of frustrated needs-satisfaction and should therefore be seen as largely the expression or the communication of this frustration.

   This is especially true in situations where there is an absence of institutional and acceptable mechanisms to communicate and address these needs and frustrations.

6. *Gross asymmetry of power between contending groups hampers successful negotiations in the sense that the more powerful partner is more likely to benefit.*

   An essential component of successful negotiation is a balance of power – i.e., a situation where both parties hold power, each party is able to exert pressures and inflict cost on the other, and both parties are autonomous. If one party is excessively weak and unable to inflict substantial costs, it cannot in a meaningful way have any impact on the behavior of the opponent and on the outcome of the process.

   When the dominant group perceives a state of stalemated power relations they are more likely to consider negotiations.

7. *Where there is gross asymmetry of power between adversaries, a process of empowerment of the weaker party is essential.*

For meaningful negotiation to take place, there has to be a reasonable balance of power and negotiation skills between the parties, with each party being able to inflict a cost on the other should the need arise. Empowerment is closely related to, but cannot be reduced to, legitimacy and representativeness (discussed in Principles 10 and 11).

Democratic empowerment refers to a process which derives its strength from a grassroots base. Power requires legitimacy and cannot be imposed from outside – e.g., by the investment of authority by government or management.

This principle can be substantiated through the example of industrial relations. A crucial stepping stone in this empowerment lay in the legal recognition of African trade unions. The Wiehahn recommendations thus placed more effective bargaining weapons at the disposal of the weaker party – creating the potential for real and successful negotiations. The recognition of the legality of not only trade unions, but all negotiating parties, is the first crucial step in paving the way towards successful negotiation. The conditions created by the Wiehahn Commission which facilitated this empowerment can be seen in the growth of trade unions since 1979 – in terms of their size, strength, organization and solidarity. Empowerment of the weaker party is not reduced to legal recognition, but this is an unavoidable initial move, which is necessary for organizations relying on non-violent means in a strongly repressive political situation, before there can be any veritable shift in the power balance.

Central to the negotiating process is a movement towards greater power symmetry between the rival parties, and it is argued that the *disempowerment* of the strong will prevent a rising *spiral* of power imbalance; disempowerment of the strong coupled with the simultaneous empowerment of the weak will also lead to the actual reduction of the power distance.

8. *Participation in legal structures can provide organizational and legal space for the consolidation of a power base that can serve to empower weaker participants.*

FOSATU's response to the Wiehahn recommendations clearly illustrates that the utilization of organizational and legal space provided for by negotiations is an important process of growth and empowerment.

The fact that official registration provided recognition, the lack of which had been a serious obstacle in the development of African trade unions, means that the potential was available for using this space to strengthen union organization through the building and the consolidation of organizational power. Opportunity could be made of the new-found negotiating status to move towards real and successful negotiations with the employers.

Organizational space substantiates the principle that incremental steps are not irreconcilable with radical goals. (See Principle 15.) FOSATU's development, post-1979, bears witness to this lesson. It is a significant lesson to be assessed by oppressed groups as a response to the State's "reform" measures – particularly, if such "reform" creates the potential for real negotiation in terms of empowering the weaker party.

It is important to note that, prior to recognition, trade unions had a sufficiently strong and democratic power base to prevent them from being coopted into a bureaucratic structure. As is the case with the trade unions, once a mass base has been established and organized after tenacious struggle, this needs to be sustained over time by achieving short-term goals through negotiation.

Similarly, legitimate mass-based community organizations need to establish a recognized status for themselves as *bona fide* respresentatives in the eyes of the local state, in order to have a sufficiently strong, autonomous and independent power base on which to build.

Thus, negotiations can be used to build power bases and therefore can be seen as a means of empowerment. In the same way, non-constitutional negotiations may facilitate and strengthen working relationships between local constituents of contending national forces.

9. *The process of conflict resolution, accommodation or management needs to be institutionalized.*

By institutionalization is meant the recognition of established usages governing relations based on generally accepted values and norms. The example of industrial relations clearly reflects the dysfunctionality of an unstructured negotiating relationship. The structural weakness in the 1970s (the result of a lack of institutionalized negotiating channels) led to an inability of the state to accommodate industrial conflict.

Industrial relations highlight the need for the institutionalization of conflict within a structure that accepts the legitimacy of both parties as a prerequisite for conflict accommodation and successful negotiation. The Wiehahn Commission laid the potential framework in which real negotiations could take place because, for the first time, African trade unions were recognized as legitimate and representative bargaining partners. The institutionalization of negotiations, as exemplified by industrial relations, is an important and significant principle that needs to be addressed in constitutional affairs.

10. *Institutions created for handling conflict must be legitimate.*
Negotiations can be successful only if the negotiating parties are seen as legitimate representatives. The separation between statutory procedures and labor practices in the pre-Wiehahn period reflected the split between legality and legitimacy. The imposed institutions, though legal, were illegitimate and thus unable to function successfully.

Industrial relations offer good examples of how the old bureaucracy failed to accommodate new developments. Extra-statutory procedures and systems began to develop to meet contemporary needs. Existing institutions such as Liaison and Work Committees failed to meet the needs, largely because they were imposed by the authorities and lacked representatives and legitimacy. The investment of authority in Liaison and Work Committees could not grant them legitimacy. Management started to negotiate with unregistered African unions instead. The increase in extra-statutory communication, whether bargaining or negotiation, led to the institutionalization of newly developed legitimate, though not legal, systems.

Legitimacy implies a perceived satisfaction of the needs of those over whom the authority is exercised. This is the essence of legitimized control. Legitimized control "refers to authority that is derived from those over whom it is exercised."[3] This authority is effective only in so far as it is accepted and regarded as legitimate by the mass base.

The increase in extra-statutory negotiations prior to Wiehahn in industry, and presently in community and constitutional affairs, reflects the need for negotiating bodies which are perceived as legitimate by the constituencies. Successful negotiation can occur only if it takes place between legitimate leaders.

Thus, empowerment and legitimacy are two integrally related concepts. We cannot talk about empowerment if this power is invested by the State into a legal body which is not accepted as the true representative of the people it is professing to represent. Power requires legitimacy. "Power springs up whenever people get together and act in concert, but it derives its legitimacy from the initial getting together rather than from any action that then may follow. Legitimacy, when challenged, bases itself on an appeal to the past, while justification relates to an end that lies in the future."[4]

The state in its long-term interests, needs to allow extra-parliamentary groups the legal space to become strong, legitimate, democratic representative organizations of the people with the ability to negotiate on their behalf.

11. *Participants in negotiation structures and processes must be representative of their constituencies.*

If they are not representative they will not be perceived as legitimate and will be unable to function efficiently. Although not all employers (especially in the public sector) have come to accept this, it is generally appreciated by management. It is, however, not yet appreciated by the government that structures and processes cannot function properly if the people who participate in them do not represent their constituencies.

12. *Fundamental principles need not be compromised by the weaker party through participation.*

Whether or not to participate in state created institutions in the industrial field was a source of deep divisions among trade unions in the past. The dangers of participation were real – that of being coopted, of granting legitimacy to the authorities, etc.

This principle is exemplified by FOSATU's stand on registration. FOSATU decided to register as trade unions but on their own terms – i.e., they rejected racial unionism. Their decision to register was a pragmatic policy decision which did not compromise their fundamental goals and principles concerning trade union rights.

What is required, therefore, is an objective analysis of whether contradictions within the state's reform may be used as potential gains within the state's framework. The principle for negotiation is therefore that oppressed or unrepresented groups should not exaggerate the danger of the State's control in "reform" measures nor underestimate the real gains that might be conceded.

13. *Coercion exerted on the adversary must be constructive and conditional.*

According to Principle 4, coercion and negotiation are complementary. Coercion, however, has to meet certain conditions in order for these processes to be complementary. It has to be as non-violent as possible; it has to be constructive (not punitive), and conditional (that means it has to be eased when certain conditions are met).

14. *The goals of peace and justice are complementary: you cannot have the one without the other.*

The two goals of peace and justice are normally accepted by all parties and by mediators. The unique relationship between these two goals is, however, not always fully appreciated. They are ideal states which can never be fully achieved; they are complementary in the sense that the one cannot be achieved without the other; and the roles of peacemaker (or conciliator) and prophet (or proponent of justice) stand in a relation of tension towards each other.

The peacemaker or conciliator must have credibility on both sides of a conflict. Building and maintaining good relations and creditibility with all parties is not compatible with the exposure of and attacks on injustice and public confrontation with the perceived perpetrators of injustice.

The peacemaker who is trying to make or obtain peace at all costs is likely to underplay injustice and overlook manifestations of injustice. By doing so he/she may be able to arrange some kind of truce or apparent peace, leaving the relations of inequality and injustice unchanged.

In the same sense that peace and justice as goals are complementary, peacemaking and the promotion of justice as means towards these goals are also complementary; the one should not be conducted without the other. An obsession with the promotion of justice at all costs will undermine the foundations of peace and of a stable lasting future society. What kind of justice will it be without peace?

15. *Incremental steps can be reconciled with radical goals.*

Short- and long-term considerations should determine strategies.

Provision should be made for incremental steps within a radical fundamental change programme. It is possible to reconcile gradual and radical change. The demands for radical change should not be contrary to a rational plan of action which, because of its provision for a logical sequence of events, is more likely to assure the achievement of a desired goal than one cataclysmic outburst.

The disagreement about the pace or rate of change is an important genuine one. Quite naturally, whites who do realize that fundamental change, power-sharing and loss of privileges are inevitable, will do whatever is within their power to postpone this transition and to propagate incremental change for that very reason. Those who want to hasten that transition will favor quick change.

But this disagreement is on means and pace of change and not on eventual goals. While differences over means do constitute very severe causes of conflict, they are often more amenable to rational debate than differences over goals. Both parties presumably favor orderly change and the formulation of a reasonable compromise in this particular case should not be impossible.

PRINCIPLES OF MEDIATION

16. *Where negotiation between adversaries is not possible because of rigid stances, inadequate communication or structural obstacles, mediation is required.*

Mediation is closely related to conciliation, an informal process in which the third party tries to bring the parties to agreement by lowering tensions, improving communications, interpreting issues, providing technical assistance, exploring potential solutions and bringing about a negotiated settlement, either informally or, in a subsequent step, through formal mediation. Conciliation is frequently used in volatile conflicts and disputes where the parties are unable, unwilling or unprepared to come to the negotiating table to negotiate their differences.[5] The mediator or conciliator thus (a) facilitates exchange, (b) suggests possible solutions, and (c) assists the parties in reaching a voluntary agreement.

17. *Where formal mediation is not acceptable, informal mediation or facilitation of communication may be successful.*

In situations of extreme polarization where any form of mediation is rejected, informal facilitation of communication between adversaries contributes towards better understanding and paves the way for subsequent mediation.

We want to make a clear distinction between mediation and facilitation. Facilitation is restricted to the first of the three tasks of mediation listed above: the facilitation of *communication* between conflicting parties. The facilitator does not suggest solutions and is primarily concerned with technical rather than moral issues – i.e., the improvement of communication rather than the promotion of solutions.

The mediator is usually motivated by a concern to reach a peaceful solution, consensus, conciliation or some similar goal. He or she can claim neutrality regarding the stands taken by conflicting parties, but not regarding the outcome of the exercise. For the mediator, facilitation of communication is a means to an end.

For the facilitator, facilitation of communication is an end in itself, in much the same way that one can pursue knowledge for the sake of knowledge or develop atomic power for the sake of developing power.[6]

The mediator is relatively more concerned with the use made of new insights gained from reliable communication, while the facilitator is primarily concerned with the fact that the relevant parties gain accurate information, regardless what use they make of it.

For these reasons a facilitator may, in situations of extreme polarization and intense suspicion, be more acceptable to conflicting parties than a mediator. The neutral and almost technical services of the facilitator would appear to be more functional under these circumstances than the services of a mediator who is morally committed to peacemaking. We argue therefore that we should consider facilitation as a first step before attempting mediation between the major contending parties.

Such circumstances call for the quiet, informal services of unofficial diplomats – individuals without status, power, or vested interest. Unofficial or non-official mediators are people not employed by, or responsible to, national governments or inter-governmental organizations. Michael Banks[7] concludes that:

> In recent years, reports of private diplomacy (carried out by Quaker representatives, respected businessmen and others) have shown that there are significant benefits to the parties in the conciliating, go-between role that non-political individuals can create for themselves.

> They have the freedom to be flexible, to disregard protocol, to suggest unconventional remedies or procedures, to widen or restrict the agenda or change the order of items, to propose partial solutions or package deals, to press the case for constructive initiatives or magnanimous gestures.[8]

> The intent of some of the individuals who initiate private efforts is to prepare the way for intergovernmental action, and often they act with the blessing or at least the knowledge of officials of governments or international organizations. When it suits their purposes, governments may support and use private channels.[9]

18. *Parties in conflict must be given the opportunity to change position without losing face.*

In any situation of conflict, and particularly in adversarial politics, parties go out of their way to embarrass their opponents whenever they change policy or admit past errors.

We also need to realize the degree to which politicians refuse to change merely in order to save face, to avoid the appearance of backing down under pressure. For this reason Gandhi always attempted to keep the demands of his campaigns *specific to the local situation* and to convince his opponents that the struggle was *not for victory over them*, but simply for fundamental justice.[10]

Agreements which require shifts in publicly held opinions, attitudes and beliefs can be greatly facilitated if the person or the party is allowed to save face. The facilitator can make a major contribution to face-saving on both sides and this approach allows each participant to change with his/her self-esteem intact.

19. *Private mediation should be supported by public education.*

Not only leaders, but also the masses must come to terms with new arrangements, new situations.

We believe that the Eminent Persons Group (EPG) representing the British Commonwealth maintained a healthy balance between their tasks of private mediation and public education. While many observers described their mission as a failure, we have no doubt that they made an invaluable contribution, not only in formulating common ground between the parties, but especially by making both third-party intervention and a negotiated settlement more respectable in the public eye.

What they have achieved in public may in fact far exceed the benefits of their private negotiations with the respective leaders.

It is also significant to take into account the way that the Wiehahn Commission (in the field of industrial relations) prepared the involved parties (primarily the State, business and the public) for the Wiehahn proposals. The way in which the Commission both sensitized and educated the parties can be seen in their program of preparation. This involved press leakages on their proposals; public lectures; the use of an in-house journal which was attached to the Institute of Labour Relations, UNISA, to explore alternative models of industrial relations; the publication of a labor relations study series to educate industrial relations practitioners and to thereby gain support; and a two-month trip overseas by Wiehahn to sell the report abroad.

These methods of education contributed to the success of the Wiehahn recommendations when compared to those of the Theron recommendations. The education of the public and involved parties needs to be addressed as a contributing factor towards successful negotiations.

20. *The mediator must respect the popular base of elected leaders and acknowledge the tension between privately held views and public stands.*

The sensitive mediator will sympathize with representatives of conflicting parties who are willing to make concessions and who say so in private negotiations, while they proclaim the opposite in public because their constituencies are not willing to make concessions.

Leaders who have agreed to concessions in private negotiations must be assisted with the re-entry process into their
own constituencies – i.e., with selling the agreement to an
audience who may resist.

This process can be facilitated in many ways, such as public
education and through the extension of the negotiating process
to as many levels of the society as possible (instead of merely
the accommodation of elites).

21. *Emphasis in mediation in community conflicts on fundamental
    needs, rather than on values, wants or interests, promotes the
    chances of the resolution of conflict.*

The frustration of basic human needs (such as the refusal to
recognize the authentic representatives of a community) is
causally linked to aggression and destructive violence in our
society. Destructive violence should not only be seen as an
attempt to redress an unacceptable situation, but also as a way
in which the deprived parties express and communicate their
deepest dissatisfaction and frustration.

Sites[11] argues that the individual in the society will pursue
the satisfaction of his/her basic needs within the confines of
his/her environment and the values that are generally held in
such an environment only to the extent that these values or
norms do not inhibit him or her in satisfying these needs.
Should the satisfaction of these needs be frustrated, the
individual will employ means (such as violence) that under
normal circumstances would be regarded as "deviant," in order
to satisfy these basic needs. Under these circumstances, it is
possible that the individual might adapt his or her value system,
to the extent that he/she no longer has any moral problems
with the use of violence. This proposition has severe and
important implications for the potential to resolve the conflict:
the most important being the sufficient explanation of the
weakness of deterrence by threat or coercion for the control
of behaviour. This, for instance, explains to a large extent the
senseless behaviour associated with communal violence in intra-
communal conflicts. Sites[12] remarks:

> We insist, then, that the individual is not a piece of inert
> proptoplasm which is infinitely adaptable to the social
> environment; instead, he becomes self-consciously alive with

certain needs which cry out for gratification.

The theory of needs, as developed by Maslow and others, stresses needs that cannot be curbed, socialized or negotiated. This approach was expanded by academics such as Paul Sites and applied to the field of conflict studies by prominent scholars such as John W. Burton (Centre for the Analysis of Conflict) and John Groom (University of Canterbury). Arguing that the individual has certain basic needs not only in a physical sense (e.g., food and shelter), but also as a social unit (e.g. recognition and security), Burton[13] posits that:

> Needs describe those conditions or opportunities that are essential to the individual if he is to be a functioning and cooperative member of society, conditions that are essential to his development and which, through him, are essential to the organization and survival of society.

This led Sites[14] to develop a realistic appraisal of power in society by attributing effective power to individuals and groups of individuals; and not to governments. He made no reference to interstate conflicts as such, but directed attention to the fact that parties in violent conflict who have *no valued relationships*, for reasons of history and their own behaviour, are *unrestrained* when seeking to pursue such needs. Certain societal needs will therefore be pursued regardless of the consequences.[15]

It is therefore argued that these needs are in a sense *universally* present in all societies and communities but are given *specific* content through culture and interaction. Sites[16] goes on to say that:

> The point we wish to make here is that basic needs do exist and that they are more universal, and thus less specifically cultural, than some behavioural scientists would have us believe.

We argue that the existence of these needs should be recognized; that the existence of needs such as security, recognition, distributive justice and the ability to influence what affects the individual in his or her immediate environment have been sufficiently proved in academic literature and can therefore be accepted on a scientific basis, but that the theory of social needs as posited by Paul Sites requires further development as it does not sufficiently describe and identify these needs.

[Sites] also points out that a clear distinction should be made between needs on the one hand and values, wants and interests on the other. The assumption of universal needs within the human species is not inconsistent with the existence of cultural values. The latter include the specific, local manifestation of needs, as well as the tools or the social norms utilized by that particular society to satisfy these needs. Similarly, wants and interests are cultural-specific phenomena, while needs refer to universal phenomena. In one culture aggressive behaviour might satisfy the same need that is satisfied by cooperative behaviour in another society.

In recent years, in conflict resolution and settlement theory, there has been a shift away from the classical authoritarian approach of confrontation, towards an approach that emphasises the need for *interaction* between conflicting parties. This led to the acceptance of the idea that, in order to be effective, negotiations require some accommodation of the needs of the weaker party in a situation where a power imbalance exists.[17]

As the mediating process unfolds, it often becomes clear that the apparent conflict over interests, wants or values, is in reality a conflict over dissatisfied or frustrated basic human needs.

Concentrating on these needs, rather than on interests, will assist the mediator in finding creative alternatives. This is so, since conflicts over social needs *are not of zero-sum nature*: for example, the increase in the security of the one party will not automatically lead to an equal decrease in the security of the other party or parties. It is more likely that increased security for one party will lead to similar increase for all the other parties, or that increased security for one party might lead to the fulfillment of some other need (e.g., status or recognition) for the other. The chances of finding a *self-sustaining* solution, a win-win solution, are in this way greatly enhanced. Burton[18] argues that:

> The theory of needs led to the development of a new process that enabled parties in conflicts to ascertain hidden data of motivations and intentions and to explore means by which common human societal needs could be achieved. As these

needs of security, identity and human development are universal, and because their fulfillment is not dependent on limited rescourses, it follows that conflict resolution with win-win outcomes is possible.

Thus, it is the *universal* nature of needs and the *independence* of their fulfillment on *limited resources*, that makes conflict resolution with win-win outcomes possible.

22. *The mediator must be neutral/impartial.*

In most cases it is almost impossible for a single person to be completely impartial – one tends to lean towards one or another party. For that reason a team of mediators is often required so that their individual biases are balanced out.

23. *The mediator must be sensitive to the positions and needs of the parties involved and of the situation.*

Different situations require different responses. The mediator must be alert to these challenges.

Although the objective of all third-party intervention is, in the final analysis, roughly the same – namely resolving the dispute and attaining a win-win solution – there are many avenues of approach and the accomplished intervener will utilize the appropriate strategy in the appropriate situation and time.

Our main argument is that intermediaries should at all times, whilst intervening, remain sensitive to the conditions prevailing and to the needs of the parties involved. As the communication process continues, the conditions and needs of the parties are likely to change, and under these circumstances a change in the strategy of the intermediary might become necessary.

Third-party intervention can be of a binding or non-binding nature. Binding intervention normally takes place through government action, where the intervener operates with authority or from a position of power which enables him/her to enforce decisions.

Non-binding intervention is of a more advisory and neutral nature and is normally carried through by individuals. Such strategies of intervention range from repression (the most anti-change or establishment-supporting option) to generating open conflict (the strongest pro-change option), depending on the opinions, attitude and convictions of the intervener.

Third-party intervention should not be seen as a distinct category of behaviour but rather as a series of *roles* assumed in specific situations by certain people. It forms part of a wider continuum of behaviour patterns in which the intervener may have to move between a variety of roles and behaviors.

24. *The mediator must display concern for human suffering rather than cold detachment (concerned impartiality).*

Neutrality and detachment can also be interpreted as lack of feeling, care and concern for suffering, deprived or oppressed parties, parties that believe they have been wronged, or parties that are, or feel, threatened.

Expression of genuine concern is not always easily reconcilable with the very necessary quality of impartiality of the facilitator. Can concern with the oppressed be expressed without sacrificing this impartiality, and without estranging the oppressor? We believe so.

It can be done, provided concern for suffering is distinguished from support for any one party in the conflict. Such concern can be expressed without supporting the particular stands, goals, policies or methods of that party. Adam Curle[19] explains how expressions of shock and horror about atrocities committed may seem to one party to imply sympathy with the enemy.

He suggests: "Perhaps the best approach is to express sorrow, but in a way that suggests no blame except to the practice of war which makes such tragedies, committed by either side, inevitable." This is often possible in situations of extreme violence where both parties are suffering from physical and human losses, as in the case of the violent confrontations between opposing parties in Natal. In most incidents one of the parties suffered greater losses than the other, and the series of incidents offer sufficient opportunities for expression of concern by the intermediary towards both sides. But even in situations where the suffering is predominantly on the one side, as in the case of the oppression of blacks in South Africa, it is now widely accepted in government circles that past policies have been wrong and unjust and have caused suffering with which any person should sympathize.

Injury and death caused by political violence in South Africa give sufficient cause and occasion for public statements by concerned people such as church leaders. But because of the state of polarization, the occasions at which these statements are made and the media through which they are conveyed to the public, their content and tone almost invariably reflect the partisan political stands of these leaders. Conservative or pro-establishment church leaders show comparatively greater horror at the acts of the protests or liberation movements, and concern and sympathy for their victims, while anti-government church leaders express comparatively greater horror at the acts of the security forces and concern and sympathy for their victims. This leaning towards selective expressions of concern does not contribute towards the development of common ground, but towards further polarization.

Examples of selective concern, or horror, are reflected in statements by various parties concerning the increasing number of acts of political violence and counter-violence in South Africa.[20]

Adam Curle[21] argues that it is through concerned impartiality that mediators are able to remain on good terms with both sides.

25. *Mediators must have credibility with the major contending groups.*

Just as no single person can be completely impartial, no single person can have credibility with all groups. For that reason teams of mediators are better than single persons.

26. *Mediators must have expertise in the field of conflict accommodation.*

Conflict accommodation is both an art and a science. The art refers to the more spontaneous and natural inclination to intervene. The science refers to the skills, techniques and expertise acquired through study and experience. Goodwill is not enough; expertise is essential.

The increasing popularity of mediation in industrial relations in the 1980s can be largely attributed to the Independent Mediating Service of South Africa (IMSSA) which has established itself as a credible, professional, and neutral mediating body.

27. *Mediators must suggest or propose possible solutions to the problem and provide incentives to the parties to work towards*

such solutions.

The mediator must help the parties to identify and to confront the issues in an analytical and rational way. He/she must also help to provide favorable circumstances and conditions for confronting the issues.

It seems expedient for parties to a conflict to make things easier for themselves by simplifying issues and, of course, focusing on their own viewpoints, particularly with a view to mobilizing their constituencies and gaining support.

To strip a conflict situation of its complexity is to falsify it. One function of the mediator is to help participants move towards acknowledging that they are enmeshed together in a complex and multidimensional problem.

The facilitator must help to establish such norms for rational interaction as mutual respect, the use of persuasion rather than coercion, and the desirability of reaching a mutually satisfying agreement.

"Fair rules of procedure are valuable in any kind of discussion but are vital in conflicts."[22]

28. *Mediators must be willing to take the blame for negotiations that break down and allow parties to take the credit for negotiations that succeed.*

PRINCIPLES OF LEGITIMACY

29. *Institutionalized (legal) laws should be legitimate – i.e., should reflect social reality.*

Laws which govern the relationship between conflicting parties and lay down the framework in which negotiation between the parties occurs, require *legitimacy*. This legitimacy is derived from the fact that these are "real" or "living" laws which have been developed in social reality.[23]

This substantiates one of the basic principles of the sociology of law as spelt out by Eugen Ehrlich: "The view that law is created by the state . . . will not bear the test of historical analysis . . . The centre of gravity of legal development . . . from time immemorial has not laid in the activity of the state but in society itself . . . The living law is the law which dominates life itself even though it has not been posited in legal provisions."[24] Ultimately, then, the longevity and effectiveness of law depends upon whether it legitimately represents the social reality as opposed to being created and imposed by the State.

The significance of "living" or "real" law is that it is based on *negotiation* at a local and grassroots level. "Real" law in the industrial arena is represented by collective agreements which are binding because of their legitimacy and the negotiation procedure. Self-regulation (i.e., the right to bargain and derive law within this bargaining relationship) is thus a prerequisite for successful and "real" law.

The Industrial Court rulings in South African industrial relations reflect the principle of upholding "real" laws because formal law is made consistent with social reality. The development of social rules was transferred to legal laws after this development had already taken place in social reality. (See Principle 32 for a more in-depth discussion on this point.) *This norm was then ratified by the Industrial Court.* For legal concepts to be effective, they need to be able to change as a result of contact with reality. The Industrial Court rulings exemplify the potential for social forces to shape the law through their involvement in conflict and the resolution of conflict.

30. *Self-regulation is a necessary prerequisite for a living law.*

In order for the principle of self-regulation to be met, the value of collective agreements must be recognized. The case study of the Industrial Court is significant because it is an example of success in this field.

Common law does not recognize the inherent inequality in bargaining power between parties in a contract of employment because it operates on the premise that individuals are equal before the law. Under common law, the employer is free to determine the terms and conditions of employment. Common law endorses the traditional managerial prerogative to fire at will; it does not offer protection against victimization and has no principle which requires employers to recognize or bargain with trade unions. Collective law thus represents an important *redressing of the power balance* and lays the basis for the potential for successful negotiation because of the significant advances with respect to job security, trade union recognition, and the duty to bargain in good faith.

Employees together with employers in collective organizations create extra-statutory legal norms in the form of collective agreements. These agreements often override legal norms established under statute law which tend to contradict social reality. The collective agreements create a body of laws, the practices and processes of which are accepted because trade unions and management negotiated the rules together and these were later ratified by the Industrial Court.

31. *The rule-creating capacity of autonomous collective organizations must be recognized.*

The principles of institutionalization of conflict resolution, empowerment and legitimacy, which were addressed by the Wiehahn Commission, laid the basis for collective bargaining. Thus, the potential for developing self-management or self-rule, in terms of creating binding and acceptable law, lay in the acceptance of trade unions and employer organizations as autonomous rule makers. It is important to stress that only once the state had recognized these organizations as legitimate rule-creating institutions could the collectivist system of labor law arise. We have argued that this is a more effective form of law.

The recognition of the autonomy of collective organizations has resulted in a new kind of law for the exercise of self-government in industry. There is space and potential for addressing a similar principle in community affairs. In order for democratic, local level negotiation to take place, it is a prerequisite that the state, firstly, allows autonomous organizations to legitimately represent their constituencies and, secondly, permits collective agreements to be operationalized between different organizations. The laws governing the negotiation process between organizations and the mechanisms for the resolution of conflict need to be developed on this level.

32. *It is necessary for negotiations to take place in a broad statutory framework.*

The Industrial Court introduced the new concept of the unfair labor practice. The wide definition of an unfair labor practice meant that lawful labor practices might be deemed unfair. The Industrial Court, therefore, is bound neither by common law principles nor common law remedies. Significantly, the state intended that the Industrial Court should have ultimate discretion in developing a body of law relating to fair employment practices. Within the broad statutory framework, *fairness* thus became the guiding principle. This principle is successful because it is based on legitimacy and negotiation. The government set the statutory framework, but then left the development of the *content* of the unfair labor practice to the court. Because self-regulation is allowed, the onus of the rulings is then left to local initiatives.

This presents the possibility for the same potential for dealing with conflict in community, political and constitutional matters. A broad facilitative process should be accommodated to allow conflicting parties to negotiate fairness.

From the lesson drawn from industrial relations, the state should not initiate local negotiations, but should give loose sanctioning to them. Fair practices should be negotiated in self-regulatory ways – they should not be imposed by the state.

33. *Laws must be consistent with negotiated settlements.*
This principle is clearly exemplified and upheld by the Industrial Court. The rulings of the Court have, in most cases, consolidated and supported the rights and procedures negotiated in collective bargaining agreements. Thus, the rights that have been won in the Industrial Court are generally consistent with those that have been determined through self-regulatory collectivism. The rulings of the Industrial Court are accepted because they are based on negotiations between trade unions and management.

Collective bargaining agreements required employers' consent to follow set procedures before dismissal and the decisions made by the Industrial Court uphold these clauses. Thus, the law derives its legitimacy from the negotiated settlement.

CONCLUSIONS

The basic premise of all these legitimacy principles is that the living law which arises necessarily represents the views of the majority. However, it is important to make explicit that this is possible only if the organizations are democratic. Living law implies a free consensus of ideas.

In group decision making, the most representative rules come from a free decision making process – i.e., quality decisions are made in the absence of imposed sanctions. The danger in undemocratic groups is that forces within the group press for uniformity and conformity. In conflict situations in these groups, the natural forces work towards minimizing differences in a way such that conformity is emphasized to the exclusion of any contradictory views. This means that cliches, rather than living law, surface if the atmosphere is not conducive to the democratic expression of ideas and opinions. Thus, superimposed ideas of the ruling clique may dominate and may not necessarily reflect the ideas of the majority.

The antidote to this situation is a truly democratic environment – a situation where the necessity for diversity is recognized and the value of each individual's unique contribution is recognized – i.e., a high premium is placed on the decisions of every member. It is only in such a democratic situation that true consensus can be reached so that the living law which emerges legitimately represents the views of the people.

These principles have significant *implications* for the role of the State if the value of collective law is to be acknowledged. We have argued that this law is effective because it is based on local-level negotiation from which it derives its legitimacy.

Search for common ground

If one asked two people in the midst of a feud what the issue was, one would be likely to get completely different answers, and might be tempted to conclude that the two must be fighting in two different disputes. *But the conflict is shared*, and an understanding and perhaps eventual settling of the matter requires that the participants come to share perceptions of the real issues and of the common ground, regardless of how limited, that is shared.

The development of universal principles of communication between adversaries in South Africa contributes towards the exploration of common ground between them. This exercise also contributes towards the establishment of norms for rational interaction required for the constructive accommodation of conflict.

Multi-role approach

According to Principle 23 the mediator must be sensitive to the positions and needs of parties involved, and of the situation. This suggests that different roles and different strategies are required for different situations.

The same principle would apply to negotiators. Most meaningful communication therefore requires multi-role and multi-strategy approaches.

Monitoring progress

These principles were formulated as an initial experiment . . . some constitute hypotheses rather than principles.

To the extent that any of these can be formulated as firm principles they can serve as criteria for the assessment of the current state of affairs, and as criteria for monitoring progress or regression in the general field of communication between conflicting political groups in South Africa.

NOTES AND REFERENCES

1. H. W: van der Merwe and S. Williams, "Pressure and Cooperation as Complementary Aspects of the Process of Communication between Conflicting Parties in South Africa," *Paradigms*, 1 (1987): 8–13.
2. van der Merwe and Williams, "Pressure and Cooperation".
3. John W. Burton, *Deviance, Terrorism and War: The Process of Solving Unsolved Social and Political Problems* (Oxford: Martin Robertson, 1979).
4. H. Arendt, *On Violence* (London: Penguin Press, 1970).
5. Gabi Meyer, Hendrik W. van der Merwe and Wanita Kawa, *Conflict Accommodation: Towards Conceptual Clarification*, CAPS series, 1 (Cape Town: Centre for Intergroup Studies, 1986).
6. Hendrik W. van der Merwe, "South African Initiatives: Contrasting Options in the Mediation Process," in Christopher Mitchell and Keith Webb (eds), *New Approaches in International Mediation* (Westport, Conn: Greenwood Press, 1988); *Pursuing Justice and Peace in South Africa* (London: Routledge, 1989).
7. Michael Banks, "Conflict Resolution," unpublished paper, London School of Economics (1987).
8. Sydney D. Bailey, "Non-official Mediation in Disputes: Reflections on Quaker Experience," *International Affairs* (1985): 205–22.

9. M. R. Berman and J. Johnson, *Unofficial Diplomats* (New York: Columbia University Press, 1977).
10. Walter Wink, *Jesus' Third Way* (Johannesburg: South African Council of Churches, 1987).
11. Paul Sites, *Control: The Basis of Social Order* (New York: Dunellen, 1973).
12. Sites, *Control*: 10.
13. Burton, *Deviance, Terrorism*: 59.
14. Sites, *Control*.
15. John W. Burton, "The Theory of Conflict Resolution," *Current Research on Peace and Violence*, 3 (1986): 124–30.
16. Sites, *Control*: 7.
17. Dennis J. D. Sandole, "Traditional Approaches to Conflict Management: Short-term Gains Versus Long-term Costs," *Current Research on Peace and Violence*, 3 (1986): 119–23.
18. Burton, "Theory of Conflict Resolution": 128.
19. Adam Curle, *In the Middle: Non-official Mediation in Violent Situations*, Bradford Peace Studies NS, 1 (Leamington Spa: Berg): 19.
20. van der Merwe, "South African Initiatives."
21. Curle, *In the Middle*: 19.
22. M. Deutsch, *The Resolution of Conflict: Constructive and Destructive Processes* (New Haven: Yale University Press, 1973).
23. Sinzheimer in J. Clark, "Towards a Sociology of Labour Law," in Lord Wedderburn, R. Lewis and J. Clark (eds), *Labour Law and Industrial Relations: Building on Kahn–Freund* (Oxford: Clarendon Press, 1983): 81–106.
24. Sinzheimer, in Clark, "Towards a Sociology": 85.

12 Managing Complexity Through Small Group Dynamics
John W. McDonald*

The aim of this chapter is to show that it is possible to achieve global consensus on complex and sensitive international issues such as the environment, population planning or telecommunications policy, to give a few examples, by using the United Nations structure and learning to manage its complexity. One's principal goal should be to narrow the decision making group at an international conference, from the two thousand delegates in attendance, to a very few participants, who have the prestige, influence, skill and trust needed to make a decision and then have their actions accepted by the conference as whole.

THE CONCEPT OF CONSENSUS

When the United Nations Charter was completed in 1945, there were 51 signatories representing the vast majority of the recognized nations of the world and the UN became the world's first universal, global, intergovernmental institution.

The United Nations General Assembly, all of its many Councils, Committees and Commissions, and its more than a dozen Specialized Agencies, such as the International Labour Organization (ILO), the World Health Organization (WHO), the Food and Agricultural Organization (FAO) and the United Nations Educational, Scientific and Cultural Organization (UNESCO), take action at their various international conferences each year, by passing resolutions. Each resolution first describes the background and reason for its existence and then sets forth the actions that should be taken by member states or by the organization's international secretariat to carry out the

---

* This chapter was written at the request of the editors for the purposes of this collection of essays.

purpose of the resolution. None of these resolutions has the power of law – all are only recommendatory in nature. The unwritten rule is that if a nation's delegation votes in favor of a resolution it means that the country so voting agrees to carry out the recommendations in that resolution. There are no sanctions, however, against member states who fail to implement a resolution.

After a resolution is debated a member state has to call for a vote in order to have it adopted. The resolution passes if a majority of nations vote in favor of the text. If no nation calls for a vote the President of the Conference may state, hearing nothing to the contrary, that the resolution is adopted by consensus.

Since only moral suasion can be used on those member countries who vote in favor of a resolution and no action can be taken against those members who vote against a resolution, it soon became clear that major efforts had to be made to reach consensus on all resolutions. This created the optimum chance for a resolution to be implemented by all member states.

The United States strongly supported the consensus process the first fifteen years or so after 1945 and was quite successful in its efforts, because of its totally dominant position in the world. From the late 1950s to the 1970s, the world changed dramatically, in terms of UN membership, with more than 100 new countries coming into being. The old colonial empires had collapsed. There are now 159 member states of the United Nations. What did this new membership surge do to the UN's concept of consensus?

In 1962, the United Nations General Assembly (UNGA) passed a resolution calling for a World Conference on Trade and Development. In the General Assembly's first major effort to manage the complexity of a world conference it assigned every member country to a group:

Group A   consisted of all Asian and African countries
Group B   consisted of the countries of Western Europe, The United States, Canada, Australia, New Zealand and Japan
Group C   consisted of the countries of Latin America
Group D   consisted of the countries of Eastern Europe.

It did not take long for groups *A* and *C* to realize they had a great deal in common and that they might strengthen their position if they combined their forces. They became known as the "Group of 77" because they were the 77 developing countries at that time who were members of the United Nations. Today there are 126 developing countries in the UN, but they still call themselves the "Group of 77" or "G-77".

The G-77 seized upon this first World Conference on Trade and Development, held in 1964, as an ideal opportunity to break the UN's consensus concept and show the developed countries of the West that they now had the power of the voting majority and were going to exercise that power. The G-77 at UNCTAD I, as it later became known, pushed through a number of resolutions, against strong opposition from the West, with overwhelming votes in their favor. The voting results were especially large because Group *D* sided with the G-77 on every possible occasion. This three-month conference was finally concluded with the Third World feeling that it had used the power of the vote to its own advantage in order to compel the West to take action in the field of Third World development.

UNCTAD II took place four years later, in 1968. The first substantive item on the agenda called for all Western delegations to report what they had done during the past four years to carry out the Third World resolutions adopted at UNCTAD I. It soon became clear that the members of Group B had done absolutely nothing to carry out the resolutions they had voted against. The idea of global consensus was suddenly reborn. UNCTAD II again passed a number of resolutions, but this time most were carefully negotiated and then adopted by concensus. The members of Group B returned to their capitals and actually worked very hard to carry out the resolutions the group had supported.

The idea that one could achieve consensus in the midst of north–south diversity was a new one. How had this reversal been achieved at the practical level?

The UN General Assembly had started the process of managing complexity with its group designations. In addition, to make things easier, each group elected a group spokesperson who represented the group's view on the issues at hand. Individual delegations could still speak out, but the group leader had more power and influence and the idea took hold and has proved to be very useful. This system was formally applied, however, only at UNCTAD and later UNIDO (UN Industrial Development Organization) conferences.

Dr Raul Prebisch, the brilliant Argentinean founder, organizer and first UN Secretariat head of UNCTAD, developed another idea which was not contained in the UN's formal rules of procedure. Under his dynamic leadership, he created what he called a "Contact Group." This small committee was made up of two or three leaders from each of the four UNCTAD groups and was called together by Dr Prebisch to try to hammer out draft consensus resolutions. These drafts would then be submitted to the various groups, debated and amended, and renegotiated again in the Contact Group. They were then adopted by consensus at the Plenary Session of the full Conference.

The Contact Group approach was first used successfully on a global scale, at UNCTAD II, under Dr Prebisch's strong and skillful guidance. It often entailed around-the-clock negotiating sessions on the part of those in the Contact Group. This close and intense interaction proved invaluable, because bonds of respect, trust and friendship were forged. These impacted favorably on many future negotiations because the same delegates tended to come back again and again to UNCTAD conferences.

THE SINGLE AGENDA ITEM CONFERENCE

Each year the UNGA meets in New York for three months in the Fall and discusses over 250 agenda items dealing with the numerous political, economic, social, budgetary and legal problems our world is currently facing. In 1968 the Swedish government proposed another model for global deliberations. Their idea was to focus exclusively, for two weeks, on one single subject. The Swedish representative argued that this short time-span would attract the political leadership of member states, force them to concentrate on that one issue and make decisions that would help to solve some of the problems surrounding that particular issue. This model was accepted by the UNGA, and it was agreed to hold the first global conference of governments on the problems of the environment, in Stockholm, in 1972.

The single agenda item model was so successful at Stockholm that the UN held seventeen more single agenda item world conferences over the next sixteen years. Each conference was two weeks in length and focused on such diverse subjects as food, population (two world conferences), women and development (three world conferences), basic human needs, water, deserts, technical cooperation among developing countries, science and technology for development, aging, drugs, new and renewable energy, etc. All of these global conferences (except the second Women and Development Conference in Copenhagen in 1980, where the small group approach was not used) reached global consensus on a 40 to 60-page "World Plan of Action", replete with recommendations for national and international action. Each conference dealt with the "managing complexity" issue in a different manner, because the formal Conference Rules of Procedure never provided for diversity or innovation. This meant that leadership on the part of an individual or a small group of representatives was required to design some form of a small group approach in order to reach consensus. The following three case studies, chosen from the series of eighteen global conferences held over a period of seventeen years, represent effective models for the management of complexity through small group dynamics.

The Stockholm Conference on the Environment – 1972

The level of popular and congressional interest regarding the problems of the environment forced the US State Department and the Executive Branch to start organizing for this conference two and a half years before the meeting took place. A federal inter-agency coordinating committee and numerous sub-committees were established, a US Secretariat was created as was a private sector advisory committee. A "scope paper" laying out US goals and objectives was developed, dozens of "position papers" were drafted and an organizational plan was formulated, proposing how the UN should be structured to meet the challenges of the environment and carry out the recommendations expected to emerge from the conference. Thousands of hours were spent in preparation so that the 62-person US delegation was truly knowledgeable about the role each delegate was to play, when the delegation arrived in Stockholm. It is this kind of in-depth preparation which is key to successful negotiation and the development of consensus.

The United States was the first country to propose, before the official opening of the conference, a detailed model regarding the new UN structure which the US wanted to emerge from the Stockholm conference. Soon four other countries put forward their own separate texts.

The UN Secretariat called together representatives from all five delegations, four days before the conference began, to determine whether the five different texts could be integrated into a single document, with disagreed language in brackets, so that it would be easier for delegates to manage.

The UN Secretariat had spent the whole year before the conference drafting language for a World Plan of Action for consideration by member states at the conference. At Stockholm itself, the plenary session of the conference was used as a forum for the many speeches delivered by the heads of delegations. The desire for an action-oriented consensus pervaded the conference atmosphere. The "group system" so effectively employed in UNCTAD was not used at Stockholm, and consequently the "Contact Group" idea did not apply. The Secretariat was skilled and was under the strong leadership of Maurice Strong of Canada. They, too, were urging consensus in talking to the various informal groups that were set up to review the more than 100 recommendations drafted by the Secretariat. The Committee responsible for developing a new post-Stockholm structure for the environment attracted some 60 delegates from as many nations. Because of the problems of national sovereignty it was not politically possible for a conference President to designate which country should be a member of a particular committee. Delegates drifted in and out of committees so that no real negotiation could take place in a committee of 60 participants. The result was that an "informal" core group was formed which was composed of the five member countries who had put forward their own organizational models and had worked hard together before the conference started. When the representatives of these five countries finally reached agreement, one hour before the conference was to end, their draft document was quickly submitted to the full committee of 60 member countries, then presented to the Plenary session and adopted without amendment, by consensus. The Plenary conference participants trusted the experts who had been working on this organizational issue for many months, to come up with the best agreement possible. The model adopted in 1972 is still in place today.

The Bucharest Conference on Population – 1974

2000 delegates from 137 member states of the United Nations attended this first world conference of governments on population issues. In addition, there were 900 members of the world press and 1400 non-governmental organization members and private citizens present, including 300 from the United States. Again the challenge was how to manage complexity in the face of this vast number of interested, concerned, and often uninformed, people, in a two-week time frame.

Fortunately the UN Population Commission, a 27-nation group of governmental population experts, had worked very hard for over two years, with the UN Population Fund secretariat members, to draft a 100-paragraph Plan of Action, to be considered and, if possible, approved by the delegations attending this world conference.

The conference Rules of Procedure called for a plenary, where each head of delegation made a formal speech, three Committees on Development, Environment, and the Family, and a Working Group charged with reviewing the World Plan of Action document.

Unlike UNCTAD II, the conference Secretary-General provided no leadership whatsoever so that the informal conference model took a very different twist. The first problem arose when it became apparent that the Third World governmental representatives to the 27-nation Population Commission had not communicated with their national ministerial-level delegates in their respective capitals. Many of the Third World leaders wanted the draft Plan of Action to have more of an emphasis on development. This required a great deal of additional negotiation and redrafting of the Plan of Action. In fact, there were a few delegations who did not want any Plan of Action at all. It was intriguing, for example, to observe Communist China, the Holy See and Egypt off in a corner negotiating.

The toughest negotiations took place in the Working Group on the Plan of Action, because this group was in charge of formulating the final draft acceptable to all conference participants. The chairman of the Working Group had his own ideas about small group dynamics and the management of complexity. He requested those delegates interested in particular words or phrases or paragraphs in the 100-paragraph Plan of Action to get together outside the Conference room, while the Working Group went through other parts of the text, to see if they could reach agreement. It was a remarkable experience to observe fifteen to twenty small groups of delegates in vigorous debate, scattered all over the floor or in the lounges, the halls or the staircases, arguing their points of view. From time to time a small group would come back to the full Working Group and present their agreed text. Often agreement could not be reached. In fact, the full Working Group took a total of 47 votes on the 100-paragraph text before adopting the Plan as a whole by consensus.

What was remarkable was that no loser in a vote ever tried to overturn the vote later in the process. Everyone had the opportunity to present their point of view and they accepted the will of the majority.

The chairman of the Working Group presented the final text to the plenary at the end of the Conference, and it was adopted, by consensus, without a vote. There was no attempt by anyone of the 137 nations present to try to amend the text from the conference floor!

The Buenos Aires Conference on Technical Cooperation among Developing Countries – 1978

One of the disadvantages of holding a one-time, single agenda item conference, as opposed to an UNCTAD conference, which meets regularly, is that the vast majority of delegates in attendance, while being experts on the subject under discussion, have never participated in a global United Nations Conference before. They are not familiar with the Rules of Procedure, nor are they acquainted with the many tacit understandings which are unique to UN meetings. These newcomers have to be educated about the process during the conference and then guided through the two-week event. This makes the achievement of consensus even more difficult. Such was the case in Buenos Aires in 1978.

The concept of Technical Cooperation Among Developing Countries was another way of saying "love thy neighbor." The G-77, often referred to as the "South" at the UN felt that in the past they had been too dependent on the rich countries of the North, meaning the developed countries, and that there should be more self-reliance on their part and the building of a South–South relationship. The North applauded this idea, but many representatives were skeptical that any form of agreement could be reached.

The conference Rules of Procedure called for a plenary, for speeches, and only one committee, which was to review the 32-page Plan of Action developed by the UN Secretariat. The committee, which consisted of 800 representatives, realized by the end of the third day that a more efficient method had to be devised, because they had only completed the review of page 1 of the 32-page text assigned to them!

The Committee quickly established an informal 50-person working group to review the remaining 31-pages of the Plan of Action. There were ten representatives each from Asia, Africa, Latin America, Eastern Europe and the West. Each group decided its own internal composition and that composition often changed as the subjects under discussion in the Plan of Action changed.

It became clear to me, as head of the US delegation, that there were going to be three or four issues that the informal working group would not be able to resolve and that another, much smaller group, composed of representatives of key delegations, would have to be formed, if consensus was to be achieved.

On the fourth day of the Conference I met with the Argentinean President of the Conference (the host country always assumes the Chair of the Conference), who was a general of the Army, inexperienced in this UN environment, but who welcomed suggestions. I recommended he invite a dozen delegates to meet with him informally over coffee to talk about the progress of the conference. He agreed at once, but was not sure whom to include in these talks. I handed him a list which contained the names of delegates that I had identified as conference leaders. There were two representatives from each of the five geographical groups and they were the persons that I hoped could evolve into a small negotiating group or core group. They appeared to me to have the leadership ability to convince the countries in their respective geographical groups that they should accept the decisions made by the core group.

It worked. The general invited the small group of ten delegates each morning for coffee and discussion and in this informal gathering a trust relationship slowly began to develop. As predicted, the four items that were not resolved by the informal working group, were referred to the President's core group for resolution. The ten representatives remained in constant negotiation for 30 out of the last 36 hours of the Conference and consensus was finally achieved at the last minute.

This agreement was so unexpected that the 400 members of the world press who were accredited to the Conference called the consensus "The Miracle of Buenos Aires." The core group approach was responsible for the success of the conference.

SPECIAL CONFERENCES

World Administrative Radio Conference – 1979 (WARC '79)

The World Administrative Radio Conference of 1979, in Geneva, is another innovative case worth examining. Every twenty years, the International Telecommunications Union (ITU), a Specialized Agency of the United Nations, convenes a highly technical global conference to update its communication regulations contained in a massive treaty and to reallocate the radio spectrum among its member states.

The industrialized world had 90 per cent of the radio spectrum in 1979, but only 10 per cent of the world's population. This imbalance led every participant to believe the conference would be a highly confrontational meeting between the G-77 and the West.

The United States spent four years in preparation for the conference and had assembled a highly knowledgeable, technically oriented, delegation. Unfortunately, only one member of the 60-person US delegation was a diplomat with political and United Nations experience. It became clear, even before the US delegation left Washington, that none of the delegates fully realized the depth of the North–South conflict awaiting them in Geneva.

The conference was almost derailed before it started by the US stand on the question of the selection of a conference President. The US wanted a Western President and the G-77 wanted someone from the Third World. It took four days to resolve that one issue, in favor of the G-77, leaving thousands of delegates with nothing to do during that period.

The ten-week conference finally opened and the President announced there were 15,000 proposed amendments to the Treaty! Because of the volume of the amendments and the number of highly technical issues involved, the "core group" approach was not feasible. However, the Third World President of the Conference and the ITU Secretariat responded astutely to the need to manage complexity and to provide a small group approach to the negotiations. First of all, the plenary only met a few times so that there were practically no political speeches made. Second, nine full Committees were formed, not the one, two or three committees used at other conferences. Third, and most important of all, 120 official working groups and sub-groups were created. The 15,000 proposed language changes were allocated to these nine committees and 120 working groups for their consideration. This created a veritable beehive of activity, but also totally diffused the North–South issue. Every delegate was so busy with the substance of the Conference that no critical mass of G-77 delegates was able to get together to create political problems for the West.

Remarkably, the 1000-page Treaty was adopted by consensus, without a vote, at the end of the ten-week Conference.

INTELSAT – 1978

The International Telecommunication Satellite Organization, a non-UN Agency based in Washington, D.C., hosted a world conference in 1978 to negotiate a Protocol or treaty on INTELSAT Privileges, Exemptions and Immunities for its employees, worldwide. The Secretariat had worked on a draft treaty for seven years, but the 64 nations attending the two-week conference still had submitted 250 written amendments to the text of the draft protocol. I headed the US delegation and was elected to the Presidency of the conference because it took place in Washington, D.C. and the US was the host country.

The conference was successfully concluded on time, without a single vote being taken on any of the 250 amendments and the Protocol was adopted by consensus. 58 of the 64 delegations had Plenipotentiary Powers and signed the final act the last day of the conference! The Treaty went into effect in 1980. How was this achieved?

As a non-UN conference, the geographical group system did not exist, and the core group idea did not seem appropriate. Most of the delegates were lawyers with little international conference experience. For this reason I decided to be a very strong, activist President and guided the conference from the Chair, meeting in plenary session at all times. There were no general speeches, and there were no committees. A small drafting group was formed, but its sole task was to check language accuracy in the translations, because the final Protocol was to be presented in five languages.

There was ample opportunity for the delegates to discuss the substance of each of the proposed 250 amendments, but when disagreement among delegates arose on a particular amendment, I appointed those in disagreement to meet as an ad hoc committee. They left the plenary and returned only when they had agreed on a form of words which could be presented to the plenary for adoption. Often as many as four or five ad hoc committees would be meeting simultaneously, working in other rooms of the conference building. This small group process was most effective and allowed the rest of the conference to continue its discussion of the other parts of the text. Each delegation who had problems with the initial draft had the opportunity to negotiate in a small group environment and present its views. The ad hoc committees' recommendations were always accepted by the plenary session.

International Conference against the Taking of Hostages – 1979

In 1976 the Federal Republic of Germany decided to take a global initiative through the United Nations to try to stem the tide of terrorist hostage-taking. At their request and with the approval of the UNGA, the President of the General Assembly appointed a 36-member ad hoc committee in 1977 to draft an international convention against the taking of hostages. The idea was to close the existing loophole in international law so that any country giving refuge to a hostage taker would have to either prosecute that individual or extradite that person to a country who would in turn prosecute the suspected terrorist. The basic difficulty was one of definition because one country's terrorists were often another country's national liberation movement.

Two important techniques were used to manage complexity at this international conference. The first two sessions of the ad hoc committee, in 1977 and 1978, each convened for a three-week period and produced nothing of consequence. These meetings were open to the public, to the press and to other national observer delegations. The 36 delegations forming the ad hoc committee spent most of their time making speeches for the benefit of the press and their constituencies back at home.

The third session, in 1979, was different. The chair applied a new technique and converted the ad hoc committee into a closed, informal working group. He excluded the press, the public, the observer delegations and even the representatives of the UN Secretariat. The absence of an audience obliged the delegates to get down to work and concentrate on the issues at hand.

The second technique was the development of two issue-oriented, small working groups called WG I and II. The 36-nation conference divided into three geographic groups – the G-77, the Western Group, and the Eastern European Group. The individual geographic groups would meet separately three to four times a day, during the course of the three-week conference, in order to discuss language changes, strategy and tactics. This kind of intimate working relationship led to the development within the group of strong ties of trust and friendship. Each day the separate geographic groups would then get together in WG I or II and discuss their draft texts and try to reach consensus. Here the geographic groups learned to work together.

The fact that there was no audience in the conference hall, that no records were kept, that no speeches were made and no political issues were raised, meant that the small group dynamic process could take place and trust could begin to grow, first within each geographic group and then within WG I and II. These two techniques, in combination, were remarkably successful.

The last day of the session, the ad hoc committee convened as a full Committee in Plenary session, open to the public and the press, and agreed, without a vote, by consensus, on a draft international convention against the taking of hostages. It recommended the Treaty to the UNGA for consideration and adoption. In December 1979 the General Assembly adopted the text without a vote and the treaty came into force in 1984.

The United Nations General Assembly – 1982

This last example describes the management of complexity at the UNGA. Despite the negative image perpetuated by the US press about the controversial atmosphere at the General Assembly, year in and year out about 70 per cent of the 300 or so resolutions adopted each year by the UNGA are adopted by consensus.

The General Assembly is divided into seven permanent committees. Committee Three is known as the Social Committee because it deals with such issues as human rights, women, aging, disability, youth, and crime.

In 1982, the Third Committee heard a report on the 1981 Year of Disabled Persons and decided to negotiate two resolutions under the agenda item concerned with disabled persons. The chair of the Third Committee announced that any delegation interested in pursuing this subject, outside the regular working hours of the Committee, should go to Conference Room A. 70 representatives gathered for the first informal meeting, all self-selected. Because the Philippine delegation was especially interested in the subject, it was agreed that their representative would chair the session and they offered to prepare a first draft of the two resolutions.

This informal working group met almost daily for three and a half weeks. By the end of the first week, the group had shrunk to twelve delegates and they stayed until the negotiations were completed. The first proposed resolution called for the adoption of a UN document, called the "World Program of Action Concerning Disabled Persons." This 50-page paper had been drafted over the previous four years by a 27-nation expert group and its proposed adoption was not controversial. The second proposed resolution called for the implementation of the "World Program of Action" and for the launching of a United Nations Decade of Disabled Persons. This idea presented problems to a number of delegations and absorbed most of the working group's time. Agreement was finally reached among the twelve delegates and was presented by the Philippine delegation to Committee Three in Plenary session. Because the twelve delegates in the informal working group had represented all five regional groups and had reached agreement on the text, the resolution was not amended in full committee. The 159 member states in the full Committee accepted the word of the twelve members of the working group and adopted the two resolutions by consensus. it was then forwarded to the General Assembly where it was adopted by consensus by the full Assembly, without debate.

CONCLUSION

This chapter has focused on the process used to obtain consensus, on a global scale, by managing complexity through small group dynamics. In no instance did the formal conference Rules of Procedure provide the model that was eventually used to reach consensus. In every case, an individual, or several persons together, were prepared to exercise leadership and were innovative enough to design a model that would work in that particular conference setting. All the techniques that were used were designed to allow trust relationships among the members of the small negotiation group to evolve. The individual delegates who were in each small negotiating group were key to the success of the process, because they had the responsibility not only for representing their large geographical group in the core group, but also for reporting back to that geographical group and having their recommendations accepted. That trust relationship also was critically important.

All of the conference decisions taken, which were negotiated by a small group of participants, were eventually adopted by consensus, without a vote, by the 159 member nations of the UNGA. In no sense of the word were these decisions, whether they were six-page resolutions or 50-page "plans of action" containing dozens of recommendations, based on the lowest common denominator of the issues discussed. In every instance, they were on the cutting edge of new policy formulations and often were extremely innovative in their proposed solutions and recommendations for national and international action.

The fundamental diplomatic tool used in every case was the effective reduction in size of the large number of participants in attendance at each conference, to a small group of decision makers. This allowed trust relationships to develop so that communications could begin, negotiations could take place, and consensus could emerge.

13 The Emergence and Institutionalization of Third-party Roles in Conflict

James H. Laue*

After a gestation period of several decades, the role of the third party emerged in the 1980s as a central concept in the study of conflicts and conflict resolution. Experiences in labor–management relations, international and intercultural conflict, racial and community disputes, court diversion and other arenas have convinced practitioners and scholars that the third-party role is useful and deserving of some degree of institutionalization.

To understand the emergence of third-party roles requires attention to three levels of analysis. The first involves important definitions and the background and scope of the field of conflict intervention. Then some comments about the development of the field of conflict intervention are in order, following by an analysis of the variety of third-party intervention roles.

DEFINITIONS AND BACKGROUND

Conflict is a natural and inevitable part of all human social relationships. Conflict occurs at all levels of society – intrapsychic, interpersonal, intragroup, intergroup, intranational and international. At all levels of human social systems, conflict is ubiquitous. Conflict is not deviant, pathological, or sick behavior *per se.* Traditionally, scholars and policy makers have tended to view conflict as an unusual occurrence in the social system – an example of disequilibrium that needs to be returned to a homoeostatic state. Some see conflict as the opposite of order.[1]

---

* A modified form of a chapter in Dennis J. D. Sandole and Ingrid Sandole-Staroste (eds), *Conflict Management and Problem Solving* (New York: New York University Press, 1987).

Rather than seeing deviance, sickness or pathology in conflict, scholars need to examine the level, the intensity, the type, the object of conflict and the way it is handled. It is important to understand that conflict is not the opposite of order. Conflict is highly patterned; the field of conflict analysis allows us to predict some of the stages of conflicts in various systems. There is an orderliness in conflict, although conflict can become disorderly. And it can be a very helpful and useful part of society.

Conflict may be defined, then, as escalated natural competition between two or more parties about scarce resources, power and prestige. Parties in conflict believe they have incompatible goals, and their aim is to neutralize, gain advantage over, injure or destroy one another.

Within this framework, violence could be defined as a form of severely escalated conflict. Virtually all forms of violence are pathological; indeed violence generally hurts weaker parties more than it does stronger parties. The edge between natural, regulated competition and escalated conflict involving violence is a precarious spot – for the analyst or third party as well as the protagonist in conflict.

Third party is a term of social science analysis, not mathematical literalism. It does not mean literally the third party in a situation in which there are two other parties. First and second parties have a direct interest or direct stake in the conflict and its outcomes. The third party is one with less directly at stake. The third party certainly has something at stake (reputation or professionalism, for example) but will not be affected by the allocation of resources, the exercise of power, the determination of new rules or the other types of outcomes which may take place as conflict is processed. The third party stands on a different base.

A *role* is a set of behaviors associated with a status. A status is a position in the social structure which carries rights as well as obligations. Role is the behavioral component – the acting out of the behavior associated with a given status. The concept of role implies that behavior is patterned, understandable and largely predictable.

The concept of role is focal in understanding how human social behavior is organized. To understand any conflict situation, the first step is a role analysis of every party to determine who has what at stake, what reference groups and membership groups are involved, what pressures and strains are pushing on the parties for particular kinds of behavior, the parties' perceptions of their goals and power, the actual goals and power of the parties, etc.

Resolution is another term which requires definition; it is only one goal that one might have for conflict, although many assume it is the only legitimate approach. Conflict is never solved; the focus is on conflict *re*solution, not conflict solution. Individual conflict incidents or episodes may be solved – they may move on to a termination which may or may not represent the interests of all the parties involved. Whether family or international disputes or anything in between, conflict incidents may be solved, but conflict *per se* is never solved. Each solution creates, in a Hegelian sense, a new plateau or a new synthesis against which the next conflict scenario is played. Society never "solves" conflict totally. Conflict incidents or episodes are solved and then re-solved and re-solved.

When conflict resolution mechanisms are working smoothly, all the parties with a stake have adequate representation in the forum and can create a win–win outcome that satisfies at least some of their needs. If true resolution to the conflict is achieved, the outcome "sticks" and contributes to the ability of the system to resolve other conflicts as they arise, rather than allowing them to fester.

Conflict "resolution" implies that there is joint participation of the parties in reaching the outcome. There also is an assumption that the outcome is – at least to some extent – satisfactory for all the parties involved. They are willing to live with it or with parts of it, or to live with the procedure established by the process to resolve other conflicts. In this regard, it is appropriate that the Camp David agreements were called "accords" rather than a "solution" or "settlement", for they established a framework for continuing the discussion regarding peace and peacemaking in the Middle East. Resolution, then, implies at least three elements: the outcome addresses the underlying problems or issues, rather than just symptoms or surface manifestations, it is jointly determined, and the process achieves at least some degree of satisfaction for the parties concerned.

But resolution is not the only thing one might "do" about conflict. What we wish to do about any specific conflict depends on what our status is, what our role is in the situation, who we are as a party and what we perceive our interests to be. The idea that conflict should be resolved is somewhere in the middle of a rough continuum ranging from repression on the right to instigation or agitation on the left.

There is a newsletter of a Quaker project in Pennsylvania called *A Friendly Agitator* – a nice twist on the relationship of conflict to social change and justice. Generally, those in power would like to keep the system the way it is. They view conflict as a disruption in the system, and as possible threat to the current organization of power and resources. Parties with this orientation seek to suppress conflict when it occurs. Those in power want to get conflict out of the way, perhaps get around the table and deal with it quickly and get on with business as usual. They are status quo-oriented. Those with less power tend to be change-oriented, and will more likely be interested in instigating or agitating conflict. There is a range of other possible orientations in between, and one of the major approaches is conflict *management*. Conflict management is popular now, especially in business schools. The role of an organizational manager or administrator is to manage day-to-day conflict in the allocation of scarce resources. Conflict *regulation* is also in vogue in the literature. But *who* will manage or regulate conflict?

These advocates of conflict *resolution* would prefer an approach that allows the parties with the most at stake to be assisted in working through the conflict in their own interests. Persons who use the language of conflict management and conflict regulation argue that they want to increase the abilities of parties to manage or self-regulate their conflicts themselves because if conflicts escalate, external agents or agencies will step in and try to bring the conflict within their own definitions of acceptable boundaries of social control. Then the parties with much at stake will lose control of the process.

Pre-workshop questionnaires on how persons handle conflict often produces as the dominant response "ignore it." They believe that if they can just ignore conflict, after a while it will go away. Strikingly, in approaching the racial disorders of the 1960s in the United States, many police departments took a variant of that position: contain it, ignore it as much as possible, and hope it will pass. This is a typical way many of us deal with conflict. Once we recognize that conflict is patterned, we understand that it occurs in stages, eventually leading to some kind of termination. Hence in many situations, individuals and organizations are willing to "hang back" and hope that conflict will disappear or run its course quickly and painlessly.

In 1965, I was in Natchez, Mississippi, during a racial crisis, assessing the work of Community Relations Service (CRS) field representatives. The president of the local branch of the National Association for the Advancement of Colored People (NAACP) had been the victim of a bombing. The black community had mounted a boycott of the downtown shopping area that cut business by 75 per cent. I interviewed black and white leaders, and I asked the white leaders, "What are you going to do to prevent this sort of thing from happening again?" Their answer was, "Nothing. It is a fluke. The colored people got out of line. It won't happen again. We can handle them. We will tough it through. We won't do anything because we think we can weather it if it happens again, and we are hoping and praying and predicting that it won't happen again."

There is a range of orientations that one could take toward a conflict – ignore, study, agitate, regulate, manage, instigate, repress, or forget it. Conflict resolution is only one approach, representing a value position – not a neutral stance – on how one will approach conflict.

What is meant by *intervention*? "Conflict intervention" occurs when an outside or semi-outside party self-consciously enters into a conflict situation with the objective of influencing the conflict in a direction the intervenor defines as desirable. All intervention alters the power configuration among the parties, thus all conflict intervention is advocacy. There are no neutrals.

The parties in conflict are very, very smart. They probably think much harder about their conflict than the intervenor because they are living with it and know they must live with the outcomes in a way the intervenor generally does not have to do. Parties do not expect strict neutrality from intervenors. They do expect judiciousness – that they can trust the intervenor, that they can rely on that person's judgement, that they can trust the intervenor to carry to the other party what they could not themselves carry because they would lose face or show vulnerability.

There are two typical manifestations of advocacy: party advocacy and outcome advocacy. The best example of a party advocate is a lawyer who operates within the adversarial system. The assumption is that in litigation one needs to have strong advocacy for one's party to make the framework and the rules work for the benefit of that party. "My party, right or wrong" makes the system work. Another traditional form of advocacy is outcome advocacy or policy advocacy, in which one works on behalf of a particular outcome (a national land use policy or a nuclear test ban treaty, for example) rather than for a specific party.

A third type of advocacy emerging in conflict intervention roles is process advocacy. The base of the mediator or facilitator is not in any of the parties *per se*, nor is it in any particular or specific outcome of the parties in conflict. Instead it is based in the process, in a belief that the right kind of process will lead to outcomes which are satisfying enough to the parties that they will stick – in contrast to one party leaving the field, or a party simply terminating the conflict through superior power or other types of unilateral or force-based methods.

DEVELOPMENT OF THE FIELD OF CONFLICT INTERVENTION

How do social inventions and innovations take place? A major indicator is the emergence of new roles which become legitimated. Persons become socialized into the new roles, and society embodies them by forming institutions and institutional supports.

The field of conflict intervention is not yet a social science or a discipline or a profession, although various publications have referred to "peace science" or the "science of conflict." The Commission of Proposals for the National Academy of Peace and Conflict Resolution said in its final report in 1981:

> While the Commission believes it fortunate that peace is neither fully professionalized nor a single discipline, the Commission has established that peace studies is a distinct and definable field of learning for three reasons: it has a literature, courses of study, and professional organizations; it has some well-defined assumptions and definitions, and a variety of research methodologies; and it has a strong applied component in the practice of conflict intervention. The Commission finds that peace is a legitimate field of learning that encompasses rigorous interdisciplinary research, education, and training directed toward [the acquisition of] peacemaking expertise.[2]

Accordingly, in the view of the Commission charged with determining the feasibility of establishing a United States institution devoted to studying, teaching and researching conflict resolution and peacemaking, there was, in 1981, a new approach requiring attention in the national interest. In 1989, with the US Institute of Peace and dozens of new university programs in conflict resolution *per se* in full operation, it still is not a fully developed science or discipline, but an embryonic field worthy of further study and systematization.

Some of the sources of the emergence of conflict intervention now may be assessed.[3] A major source is the social sciences in general, and Marxist sociology and philosophy in particular, for which conflict is the driving dynamic of society, and about which societies are constantly making various adjustments in their institutions. In addition, political science, the sociology of the military, small group dynamics, and other fields are important sources for the intellectual emergence of conflict intervention as a field.

Another source is the development of collective bargaining in the structure of labor–management relations. Collective bargaining represents the application of a non-litigational, non-coercive model in a particular arena where the two major protagonists need one another. They are both institutionalized, they are both powerful. They both have the ability to sanction one another, although that was not always true. When labor achieved enough relative power and both parties realized that they had to live together for either to prosper, a set of mechanisms emerged called collective bargaining. Now such procedures are enshrined in law in many countries.

A third source is the field of international relations and the development of peace research. The literature in the field of peace research is derived from the history of warfare and international relations, the anthropology of human conflict, the study of state diplomacy, studies of human aggression and a range of related topics.

One of the major influences on the emergence of conflict intervention has been the development and testing of the analytical problem-solving workshop in intercultural and international conflicts of a protracted and deep rooted nature. Beginning in the 1960s, the work of John Burton and Herbert Kelman has added this new theoretical and applied dimension to the field. This approach is being carried forward by institutions like the Centre for Applied Studies in International Negotiations under Jean Freymond in Geneva, John Groom and his colleagues at the Centre for the Analysis of Conflict at the University of Kent at Canterbury, the Foundation for International Conciliation of Michael Davis in Geneva, John Burton and his colleagues Christopher Mitchell and James Laue at George Mason University in Virginia, and now the International Negotiation Network at the Carter Presidential Center, as well as advocates of "Track II" diplomacy like John McDonald of the Iowa Peace Institute and Joseph Montville in the US Foreign Service Institute.

An especially important source of the emergence of conflict intervention as a field in the United States has been its racial history – specifically the way the nation's institutions responded to the sit-in movement, the Freedom Rides and the urban racial disorders of the 1960s. Public and private agencies were established to mediate racial disputes at the national, state, and local levels.

In addition, the litigational system itself has helped spawn a number of alternatives to litigation which are quicker, less adversarial, cheaper and involve the parties more in representing their own interests and finding their own solutions. There have been several waves of conflict intervention innovations in the United States. The three traditional institutional practices for dealing with social conflict in the United States are (a) the political process itself (a formalized way to deal with representation, the allocation of scarce resources, etc.), (b) legitimated force (police or other law enforcement agencies), and (c) litigation. There are many reasons why litigation is an inappropriate way of dealing with social conflict. The United States is the most litigious society in the world. In contrast, in China a neighborhood "mediation" system works with persons throughout the social structure, helping to manage conflict over scarce resources and conflicting norms – an informal infrastructure which is oriented as much to social control as conflict "resolution." The story is told of an ancient Chinese obligation: if one were in a dispute with another party or another family and came to believe that winning would psychologically injure or destroy the other party or would cause great loss of face, then it became the first party's obligation to lose or at least to bow out of the conflict.

In this context, a series of experiences in various types of conflicts has led to the establishment of a field of third-party conflict intervention. The emergence of formal diplomacy in the United States and other countries has moved to a new level in recent decades with two important technological developments – good transportation and electronic communication – which made it possible to develop the League of Nations and the United Nations, and eventually spurred such activities as Henry Kissinger's shuttle diplomacy in the Middle East in 1974 and Jimmy Carter's Camp David mediation. *Dynamics of Third Party Intervention: Kissinger and the Middle East* is a series of essays about how third-party intervention has worked in international affairs, much of it facilitated by jet planes, electronic communications, and of course, highly skilled individuals.[4]

The labor–management difficulties of the 1920s and 1930s led to institutionalization of the collective bargaining process in the US, supported by the National Labor Relations Act and a variety of organizations. The formation of the Federal Mediation and Conciliation Service in 1947 marked the formal commitment of the federal government to third-party settlement of disputes in an important sector of Amercian society.

The civil rights movement and racial disorders of the 1960s spawned the Community Relations Service (CRS). It was established under the Civil Rights Act 1964 to mediate and conciliate racial disputes, difficulties and disagreements related to discrimination. The CRS has lasted for some 25 years as an approach to nonlitigational conflict resolution in the field of race relations in the United States. The American Arbitration Association and the Institute for Mediation and Conflict Resolution in New York City also established racial dispute and community dispute resolution programs for mediation and conciliation in the late 1960s, as a direct response to racial conflicts in the United States.

A later wave in the 1970s brought the application of these mediation and conciliation innovations to environmental disputes. Environmental conflicts differ from racial disputes, where there usually is an in-party and an out-party, and where it usually is clear who has the guns and the goods and who does not, and who has the power and who does not. Environmental disputes generally represent more power symmetry, but do not lend themselves to win–win outcomes as readily, say, as a social service program in which flexibility is possible on such issues as benefits, numbers of units of service, etc. In environmental disputes, the dam either goes there or it does not; the highway goes there or it does not. Finding ways to convert such situations into win–win processes is likely to be difficult.

Still other innovations in conflict intervention have occurred in the criminal justice system. In the 1960s and 1970s there has been greater use of inmate grievance procedure, rooted in conciliation and mediation techniques. Court diversion projects and police–community relations training are another application. The development of hostage negotiation teams by police departments and national governments is another example.

The 1970s saw the growth of grassroots or community-based disputes settlement. Many "neighborhood dispute centers" are sponsored by the local Bar Association or as an adjunct to the court system. Others in the United States, the United Kingdom, Australia, the Phillipines, and other European and Asian countries began as spouse-abuse programs or store-front service centers. Still others operate in churches, in church agencies, and as public agency programs.

The 1960s saw the development of intervenors in the United States who had a national focus. They formed a kind of flying squad who, like the CRS, could go into cities on request and deal with racial conflicts. By the late 1970s, however, the field was coming back to the grassroots approach described above. The idea of dealing with neighbor-to-neighbor squabbles or family difficulties or other disputes in easily accessible store-front centers caught on. An important distinction needs to be made between what may be called "professional" and "community-based" approaches to such localized disputes. Most of the more than 400 programs now existing in the United States are sponsored by local Bar Associations or the court system, and are staffed by lawyers and other professionals, many of whom volunteer their time and services. But there is a growing interest and experimentation in resolving such disputes as an integral part of the day-by-day interaction in the neighborhood, with residents rather than outside professionals or volunteers serving as third parties. The Community Boards in San Francisco offer the best example. In this program, residents hear their neighbors' disputes on location, using a process which assumes (a) that the expression of conflict in this setting is more important than its actual resolution, and (b) that good conflict resolution is a function of a healthy and well organized community – not of the work of highly trained professionals.

Most of the developments noted above have taken place in the context of the traditional use of conflict intervention in the United States: techniques applied in reaction to a specific conflict or crisis, when the parties already may be trying to find a way out of a difficult situation. One of the most important innovations in the field is the recent application of conflict resolution techniques to a proactive, planning or policy formation mode. The emergence of the labor–management committee in collective bargaining is a good example. They meet not at contract time but between the contracts, trying to build relationships and getting a feel for what the positions are on all sides in an attempt to avoid a crisis at contract time. The Union Coalition of New York City uses "developmental mediation," in which they try to bring together for regular meetings all the parties who have a stake in a particular issue. Their focus is the public school system where unions, teachers, administrators, parents and students get together and work toward common goals in advance of the next crisis. There are several coal and oil industry mediation boards which meet regularly to try to deal with conflicts before crises erupt. These activities represent one of the best ways to prepare for conflicts and crises: to build interpersonal capital between disputants in low-conflict periods so they can expend that capital in times of intense disputes.

The Negotiated Investment Strategy (NIS) is perhaps the best example of a policy mediation experiment. In 1978 the Kettering Foundation convinced the White House urban policy staff to make the Federal Regional Council available to represent the federal position in structured negotiations about the future of three cities in the Midwest Region: Gary, St. Paul, and Columbus. The three mayors and the governors of their states (Indiana, Minnesota, and Ohio, respectively) also chose teams of negotiators. The private sector was to be involved through the local government team. All parties were asked to agree upon a mediator from a national list compiled by the Foundation. The three mediations took place in 1979 and 1980, lasting from four to eight months. The objective was a written agreement about the policy on future investments for each city. Workable agreements were produced in all three cities.

I headed a mediation team that worked for eight months in Gary and emerged in December 1980 with a document signed by the Federal Regional Council, the Governor of Indiana, the Mayor of Gary and the mediator, with a supporting letter from the US Steel Regional Vice President in Chicago and from the Reagan administration transition team. The document did not have the force of law, but it has provided the framework since that time for cooperative joint planning and implementation between the city, the state, and US Steel. A number of agreements also were produced in St. Paul and Columbus.[5]

This approach is important because it moves intervenors beyond the use of third parties only in reaction to specific conflicts or crises, towards proactive uses, trying to deal with conflict in a way that gets all the parties with a stake to the table before a crisis occurs.

Beyond all of these specific applications lies another indication of the maturing of dispute resolution in America: the formation of a number of associations and umbrella organizations to advance the interests of practitioners and the field. The Consortium on Peace Research, Education and Development (COPRED) was established in 1970 by college, university, and free-standing peace and conflict studies programs. COPRED has approximately 100 institutional members today. Many colleges and universities not involved in COPRED have developed programs of instruction in negotiation, especially in law schools and business schools. The International Peace Research Association (IPRA) has been formed to link that growing number of peace research and conflict resolution programs in nations and cultures throughout the world.

In the mid-1970s, the Society of Professionals in Dispute Resolution was formed, and now has a membership of more than 1300, ranging from family and divorce mediators to arbitrators and public policy intervenors. The National Institute for Dispute Resolution (NIDR) was formed in 1982 to nurture growth and innovations in the field with grants and contracts. With the Hewlett Foundation, NIDR has become the major funder in the field in the United States.

Another indicator of the growth and institutionalization of the field of dispute resolution is the National Conference on Peacemaking and Conflict Resolution (NCPCR). Consciously aimed at a broad audience of practitioners, scholars, activists, students and policy makers, the initial conference attracted 250 to the University of Georgia in March 1983, then 600 to the University of Missouri–St. Louis in September 1984, 900 to Denver in June 1986, then 1100 including participants from some 40 countries to Montreal for the North American CPCR in March 1989. The hundreds of papers and workshops – and their level of technical specificity – further attest to the maturity of the field.

Dozens of books, hundreds of articles in major journals, and several new journals have appeared since 1980 as the new field's literature grows. Added to the three-decades-old *Journal of Conflict Resolution* have been *Negotiation Journal*, the *Mediation Quarterly*, the *Journal of Dispute Resolution*, the *Ohio State Journal on Dispute Resolution*, and COPRED's quarterly, *Peace and Change*. In coverage of the St Louis NCPCR in 1984, the *Chronicle of Higher Education* referred to the emergence of a new interdisciplinary field of scholarship, and analyzed some of its connections to the traditional academic disciplines.[6]

CONFLICT INTERVENTION ROLES

From these experiences has emerged a typology of at least five analytically distinct roles for conflict intervenors. They are the subject of this final section. There are three conditions that must be met if third-party intervention is to be effective. One condition is a willingness to negotiate or engage in some form of problem-solving on the part of the parties. Unless all the parties are willing to enter into some type of process, no intervention can occur, even if a judge orders it. The second condition is the availability of a forum that is agreeable to the parties involved – literally the right place with the right conditions, the right setting, the appropriate relationship to the outside media, a clear view of how the parties shall relate to their constituencies, etc. The third condition concerns the credibility of the intervenor. The intervenor must find that Archimedean piece of ground on which to stand with the parties, i.e., literally have the "standing" or legitimacy with the parties so they will allow that individual to assist in the dispute.

There are a number of ways to analyze intervention roles. One may view roles in terms of the system level of disputes. For instance, different roles may be required for family disputes, group disputes, community disputes, neighborhood disputes, intranational disputes or international disputes. Another approach would be to categorize intervention roles in light of the issue of the dispute, whether environment, welfare, school segregation, racial–ethnic, community or international. Another framework could begin with the skills of the intervenor. Still another would first analyze the nature and relative power of the parties. Intervenors' roles vary depending on who the parties are, what kind of power they have to affect one another – and, indeed, whether parties allow an intervenor into a situation at all. Other approaches could include examining the base of the intervenor (the organizational affiliation, the source of salary, etc.) or the intervenor's personality attributes.

All these approaches reflect variables that one may take into account in considering different types of intervention roles. The major point of the typology presented here is that there are definable, analytically distinct intervention roles that cut across all the other variables of personality, skills, type of issue, system level of the dispute, etc. These roles are based, in my view, predominantly on an intervenor's base and credibility – for whom does the intervenor work, who pays the intervenor to be there, and consequently what are the structured expectations for behavior of the intervenor in that role? What are the organizational sanctions to which the intervenor may be vulnerable? What kind of peer pressure exists?

With these questions in mind, let us consider a basic in-party/out-party dispute. Most disputes, of course, do not contain only two parties. But on any particular conflict issue, it always is possible to find a party or cluster of parties who own or control the decision making process regarding the resorces at stake and who, in the dynamic of that situation, must be defined as the in-party. And there always are others who must be defined as out-parties because they do not have as much power or influence as they would like on the issue at stake, or they are not part of the forum for deciding on an issue of concern to them.

In a basic two-party dispute, there are five derivable roles. First is the role of *activist*, one who is in, and almost of, one of the parties and who works extremely closely with the parties. For example, in a tenant–landlord dispute, an activist would be one of the tenants who lives in the housing project and is a leader of the tenant organization, organizing the tenants against the in-party. In this case, the in-party would be the landlord and the cluster of individuals and institutions around that person. Activists are rooted in their organizational base, in their leadership of their party and in their relationship with the other parties.

At the next level out from the center of the dispute, also based around the interests of one of the parties, is the role of *advocate*. A typical advocate role for an out-party is a community organizer, or a tenant advocate or legal advocate; this role is different from that of the tenant who lives in the project and will continue to live there when the dispute is over. A typical in-party advocate would be a corporate lawyer or management consultant. Many management consultants do not see themselves as advocates but rather as organizational technicians. But they are indeed advocating for certain values and parties within the organization – usually the owners, administrators or professionals. Diplomats are classic party advocates, working on behalf of the interests of one party in international relations.

The activist role may be distinguished from the advocate by degree of focus on the interests of the party represented. True activists are not too conciliatory; they do not eagerly search for areas of negotiation or problem-solving. An activist generally plays a harder game. But advocates are able to reach out, and are expected by the parties to do so.

The third type of role is based in neither of the parties, but in the process. The *mediator* is concerned with the parties, with other intervenors and with the interaction between them. The mediator's ultimate advocacy is for process rather than for any of the parties *per se*, or any particular outcomes which they might be pursuing. Note the distinction between the mediator and the advocate. Some diplomats would say that they are "mediators" interested in conflict resolution. But structurally they are advocates as noted above. Their job is to represent the interest of their governments. This is quite a different position from that of a mediator, whose base is in neither party *per se* but whose goal is to help develop a process in which all the parties can achieve at least some of their goals without injuring or destroying another party.

The further out one moves from the nexus between the disputing parties, the less intense is the relationship to the parties and the issues at stake. The next role is called *researcher*, whose interests encompass the parties, all the other intervenor roles, and the entire process. Examples include a journalist, a social science researcher or a crisis observation team.

Even the researcher is not neutral, as a group of psychiatrists attending a professional meeting in Washington in 1971 discovered. Demonstrators were marching to the Pentagon to put daisies in rifle barrels, and the psychiatrists, interested in moving from the couch to social relevance in the streets, were there observing – they thought in a clear, objective, neutral researcher role. But some of the psychiatrists eventually were subpoenaed because they might have observations in their notes about persons who were alleged to have commited punishable offences. Foreign nationals observing a crucial election fit the "researcher" or "observer" role, as do observers or witnesses to international negotiations.

Consciously or not, the instant an intervenor sets foot in a conflict situation, the power configuration is altered and the intervenor is likely to be used by the parties for their ends. In-parties often try to use third parties to gather intelligence on the natives, and experienced natives may use researchers to determine how the organizational structure works and what levers they can pull. While in a technical sense the role of researcher may be objective or neutral, once he or she engages in a conflict situation, the configuration of power in that situation is altered.

The final role is the *enforcer*. Arbitrators, judges, and police are enforcers. Unlike the mediator who does not have the formal power to sanction the parties, but is present because the parties are willing to let that person into the conflict to help facilitate the negotiation process toward settlement, the enforcer actually has formal power to sanction either or all the parties. The power of arbitrators and judges is well understood. In a street conflict, the police have arbitrary enforcement power to end the incident summarily through the use of force. Another example is a funding agency. In intense conflict between service recipients, a funding agency may say: "Work it out, or we will rescind the funding." Superior physical force also characterizes parties who can play a third-party (or indeed second-party) enforcer role in international conflicts.

The characteristics and implications of the five intervention roles deserve further exploration. For instance, what kind of authority, in a Weberian sense does each of these roles have? What is the ultimate value orientation of each? Can intervenors move from role to role in a conflict situation? If one first enters a given conflict situation as an advocate for one side or the other, it is difficult to become a mediator, or to have credibility as a judge or arbitrator in that situation, or be seen as an objective researcher. On the other hand, if one starts as a researcher, there may be a higher degree of flexibility. A judicious and objective researcher in a particular setting probably could move to any of the other roles and become accepted in them – but then perhaps be unable to return to the original role.

Another question concerns power. Intervenors must take care not to be entrapped in the unfair processes bred by power disparities between parties. Why is there so little call from out-parties or powerless parties for conflict resolution or peacemaking? They want power, justice and change. Conflict resolution usually is advocated by establishment parties who believe that peace – or at least order – is good. (See Laue and Cormick[7] for a more detailed exposition of the role typology.)

THE FUTURE

A field of conflict intervention or third-party behavior has emerged, and has begun the process of institutionalization. With that development go new theories, practice strategies and techniques, the creation of new social roles, new training and socialization processes, the emergence of new occupations and the recruitment of persons into those jobs, new organizations, a literature, etc.

But with development and institutionalization also may come the ravages of success – professionalization, bureaucratization, practitioners primarily serving themselves instead of their clients, competition and the emergence of a market-driven mentality. Conflict intervention is at a critical stage, perhaps moving through a stormy adolescence and on the verge of a creative and innovative adulthood – or a stagnated, profit-oriented, business-as-usual approach to people and problems.

Whether the field of conflict intervention will escape the predictable ravages of success depends very much on whether its advocates can practice the values of consensus and joint problem-solving that they preach more than competitive and win–lose values Western society teaches. Only holding the further development of third-party behavior to the highest standards of resolution itself will make the field unpredictably humane, cooperative and constructive.

NOTES AND REFERENCES

1. Paul Wehr, *Conflict Resolution* (Boulder, CO: Westview Press, 1979). James A. Schellenberg, *The Science of Conflict* (Oxford, New York: Oxford University Press, 1982).
2. United States Department of Education, *To Establish the United States Academy of Peace*, report of the Commission on Proposals for the National Academy of Peace and Conflict Resolution to the President of the United States and the Senate and House of Representatives of the United States (Washington, D.C.: US Government Printing Office, 1981): 119–20.
3. James H. Laue, "Conflict Intervention," in Marvin E. Olsen and Michael Micklin (eds), *Handbook of Applied Sociology* (New York: Praeger, 1981).
4. Jeffrey Rubin, (ed.), *Dynamics of Third Party Intervention: Kissinger and the Middle East* (New York: Praeger, 1981); Jimmy Carter, *The Blood of Abraham: Insights into the Middle East* (Boston: Houghton Mifflin, 1985); William B. Quandt, *Camp David: Peacemaking and Politics* (Washington, D.C.: Brookings Institution, 1986).
5. Daniel Berry, James Kunde and Carl M. Moore, "The Negotiated Investment Strategy: Improving Intergovernmental Effectiveness by Improving Intergroup Relations," *Journal of Intergroup Relations*, X(2) (1982): 42–57.
6. Karen J. Winkler, "Interdisciplinary Field Seeks Understanding of Origin and Resolution of Conflicts," *The Chronicle of Higher Education* (17 October 1984): 5–6.
7. James H. Laue and Gerald W. Cormick, "The Ethics of Intervention in Community Disputes," in Gordon Bermant, Herbert Kelman and Donald Warwick (eds), *The Ethics of Social Intervention* (New York: Halsted Press, 1978).

V
Research

Chapter 14 "What is Science *For*?": Reintroducing   275
            Philosophy Into the Undergraduate Classroom
            Mary E. Clark
Chapter 15 Action Research   288
            Frank Dukes

14 "What is Science *For*?": Reintroducing Philosophy Into the Undergraduate Classroom
Mary E. Clark*

One could argue, I suppose, that the "deplorably low level of science education" in the United States is a natural concomitant of the deplorably low level of general literacy that afflicts the young. Yet I believe that this can be only part of the explanation. Today's youth are perfectly capable of amassing large quantities of detailed information about whatever engages their imagination. High school students are not at all illiterate about things that "matter" – the latest rock singers, the baseball standings, the newest sports cars, the current style in jeans and leg warmers. College students, a notch more sophisticated, soon know a great deal not only about unisex hair styles and the latest contraceptives, but also how to obtain a degree likely to lead to a lucrative job while avoiding the more tedious "breadth" requirements mandated for graduation. The problem, then, is not so much a failure of "literacy" *per se*, but of the conventional forms of literacy that the educational system still vainly offers. Let's face it – today's generation is just not very interested in the way most knowledge is defined, parceled up, and delivered to them.

A couple of decades ago, when this problem began to be widely recognized in universities, it became fashionable to talk about "making subjects relevant." Some of us tried to relate our disciplines to the students' lives by incorporating contemporary issues into the subject matter. Academic purists of course turned up their noses at this watering down of the sophisticated contents of the ivory tower. Nevertheless, for a time some headway was made in raising students' interests in science, literature, history, and philosophy. But the trend

* From *Journal of College Science Teaching*, 17 (6) (May 1988).

was short-lived. The past ten years have witnessed an increase in specialization among university faculty, an increasing emphasis on research over teaching, and on teaching graduate seminars rather than general courses to incoming freshmen. In biology, for example, although general textbooks may retain a few vestigial paragraphs of "relevant" material, most have again become massive tomes, impenetrable thickets of facts laid out in glossy and costly technicolor detail, to be committed to meaningless memory. In short, science, along with many other university subjects, has lost almost all its interest for the vast majority of our young people.

I am convinced that this sad state of affairs is both unnecessary and of our own making. It is all too easy to blame the students (they are self-centered, short-sighted, greedy and so on), or the school teachers (they are incompetent, unable to maintain discipline, lazy, and the like). Almost never do we turn the critical spotlight on ourselves, yet it is here, I believe, where it precisely belongs. If, as we claim is the case, universities are the society's centers of critical thought, then it is *our* responsibility not only to "advance" our own disciplines (a subject about which an entire essay is needed to do it justice), but to offer a mirror to society – to analyze, reflect, critique – *and* to teach students to do the same. What I am arguing, then, is for philosophy not only to be returned to the college curriculum, but to become its central focus.

Indeed, I believe it is the almost total absence of philosophy, not only in universities but in our social dialogue generally, that accounts for much of the malaise of our youth. We never ask the questions: What does it all mean? What is all this accumulation of "knowledge," this rush to "progress," in aid of? Why are words like "newer," "bigger," "more," "faster," better words than "older," "smaller," "less," "slower"? Everything inevitably "advances," it seems, without any articulated purpose or goals – yet the young are supposed to accept change unquestioningly as "good." Since we never really let them in on the real reasons for it all, it is little wonder if they fail to see the urgency for acquiring masses of information, about which they can do nothing, and which we assure them will soon be out-of-date. In short, what universities today have to offer is largely meaningless, except for those courses that lead to specific niches in the economic machine, which make survival in reasonable comfort possible – at least for the time being. But how that economic machine functions, how it came to be constructed as it is, why *it*, rather than religion, philosophy, or art, came to be the focus of society, and where that giant machine is taking us are virtually ignored in university curricula. And if universities do not raise these questions, then who in society will?

This state of affairs, of course, was not always the case. A century ago – a time that biologists like myself mark as the time of philosophical ferment after the publication of Darwin's *Origin of Species* – the question of what human beings were, and thoughts about the "meaning" of evolution and the purpose of "advance" and "progress" were popular topics that all persons with any pretence to university education were expected to have thought about deeply. In those times, the "expert" was not the specialist, but the generalist, the learned man, the repository of wisdom to whom society – including government – turned for interpretation and understanding. The philosophers of the universities encompassed all subjects, and indeed, all branches of learning were simply components of philosophy. There was moral philosophy, esthetics, natural philosophy, political philosophy, and so on – but the overarching aim was to provide a holistic interpretation of society and the universe. World-views were in active flux, and men of the caliber of Thomas Henry Huxley in England and William James in America engaged in debate across what for us today is a wide range of disparate disciplines.

In the intervening century, philosophy, the parent discipline of "meaning" that universities traditionally dealt with, has gradually had parts of its subject matter chopped off, each amputated part taking root and burgeoning as a new discipline in its own right. Even the major disciplines have fissioned repeatedly, so that where there once was natural philosophy, there are now physics, chemistry, astronomy, biology. And each of these has spawned its own offspring; chemists, now, are physical chemists, or organic chemists, or biochemists, and biologists are geneticists, or ecologists, or evolutionists, and each of these is subdivided even further. Meantime, philosophy, like a quadriplegic bereft of its contacts with a larger reality, has become an almost meaningless actor on the university scene, all abstract talk with no potential for action. Once the coordinator and watchdog of all the disciplines, it now languishes, ignored, in a backwater of the academic world.

Indeed, this wholesale fragmentation of the disciplines has had the effect of subtly but completely altering the role of universities in society. From being the critical mirror in which society pondered its own reflection, forced to face its own goals and purposes, universities have become the willing handmaiden of a self-satisfied society that believes itself to be beyond self-criticism. Universities accomplished this by dismantling their collegial selves, by which their specialist members once reciprocally critiqued one another to yield up a holistic vision of contemporary reality. They replaced collegiality with a loose assemblage of autonomous disciplines, competing with each other for a place in the institution, and each of them resting its academic integrity on its own self-invented notion of human nature. Today, we have "economic man," "political man," "biological man," and so on – with scarcely ever a woman added – each of whom bears a distinct but quite arbitrary set of attributes which define the proper rules for studying that discipline. Woe betide the young modern academic who seeks promotion and tenure by trying to find connections among all these distorted fragments and our total selves. She or he soon discovers that the world of academe no longer finds such thinking legitimate. When every idea, every hypothesis, must be assigned to a specific niche, there is no place for a global vision. Philosophy teacher Allan Bloom, in his troubled and troubling book, *The Closing of the American Mind*, makes the point well:

> Liberal education flourished when it prepared the way for the discussion of a unified view of nature and man's [sic] place in it, which the best minds debated on the highest level. It decayed when what lay beyond it were only specialties, the promises of which do not lead to any such vision. The highest is the partial intellect; there is no synopsis.[1]

Amazingly, we congratulate ourselves on having made great "progress" in advancing human knowledge and creating a socially accountable academic world, when in fact, we have been doing exactly the opposite. We have been assiduously dismantling our universities and denying society the most precious gift we academics can offer it, namely, wisdom – our best effort at an honest and dispassionate critique of itself. We have forgotten that today universities hold the place held by the wise men of the past – the elders, the shamans, the priests in pre-literate societies, the philosopher-kings of Plato's ideal republic, the Founding Fathers of our own society. Unlike with the ancients, however, the elite role is now open to all who are willing sufficiently to develop their talents of inquiry and thought that they may qualify as truly wise. Today's society is an equal-opportunity employer of wise persons – or it would be if universities or society bothered about wisdom any more. But like over-indulgent parents, universities have lost their principles and given in to an arrogant, self-satisfied society that neither seeks wisdom nor supports universities that try to pursue it. Instead of complaining loudly, and demanding that their students try to grapple with the major issues of their time before they escape from the ivory tower into "reality," universities acquiesce without a murmur in turning out finely honed "products" to fit neatly the niches that will supposedly "get the economy rolling again." The result is a society that has lost its potential for self-reflection. With its ever-increasing technological power and abandonment of the search for wisdom, it has launched itself like an unguided missile into the future.

This odd and highly dangerous state of affairs I believe stems largely from our understanding – or rather, misunderstanding – of what science *is* and what science is *for*. Logical positivism has snuck into almost all facets of Western life – political decision making, the law courts, corporate boardrooms, the psychiatrist's office – attempting under its cloak of "scientific truth" to convince the unscientific masses that the piece of the truth that science has come up with is not only the whole of the truth but, because it is preferred by scientists, is out-of-bounds for questioning by the unanointed. "Science" (and here I intend the quotations) has become a religion. How did science ever acquire such an exalted state, what are the consequences of its false position, and how shall we, in the universities, set about restoring it to its proper and undeniably important – although not supreme – place in the guiding of our society? These are important and profound questions that I can only partially address here. My hope is that the dialogue, once opened, will expand and deepen as it should.

Our take-off point has to be the origins of the modern university, the child of the Enlightenment charged with enlightening first the rulers, and later, in Western democracies, the masses, in "the truth" as revealed not by tradition, nor by religion, but by Reason, a reason guided by *philosophy and science*. As Allan Bloom recalls for us:

> The Enlightenment was a daring enterprise. Its goal was to reconstitute political and intellectual life totally under the super-vision of philosophy and science. No conqueror, prophet or founder ever had a broader vision, and none had more stunning success . . . [T]he academies and universities are the core of liberal democracy, its foundation, the repository of its animating principles and the continuing source of the knowledge and education keeping the machinery of the regime in motion.[2]

Something should strike us here, which indicates that universities no longer serve democratic society as they should. Philosophy today plays virtually no role in guiding either science or society. As science – or what passes for science – has assumed the ascendancy in both the universities and in society, both of whom have uncritically accepted the legitimate right of self-appointed scientists to define what *is* science, what is its *social purpose*, and what aspects of natural truth are *appropriate* for study, the role and impact of philosophy, the inquiry into the meaning and purpose of life, has declined. Indeed, to a large extent, "philosophers" in modern academe no longer philosophize, they merely explore the history of philosophy as it has touched on the development of other disciplines – science, politics, economics. Their job is not to discover new insights into our present world, not even how old ideas might tell us something, but is merely one more clever way of reinterpreting the supposed thoughts of Plato or Kant or Hegel. As universities castrate philosophers and some even eliminate philosophy departments altogether, higher learning is left in the hands of science-practitioners who are trained only in the superficial methods of statistical science, which they know how to apply only to ever narrower aspects of Nature, and who are innocent of knowing how to phrase, let alone answer, any of the central questions of human existence. The questions they ask, and the answers they seek must, because of the scientists' limited repertoire of intellectual tools, be restricted to those of a most simplistic sort, involving quantification, abstraction, and generalization.

This giving over of universities during the Enlightenment to the authority of science and philosophy has evolved historically in three unforeseen ways. The first is the advent of "scientism," the extrapolation of the methods of science to all knowledge, with the concomitant framing of all questions in terms of single causes as specifically responsible for some subset of "common" events. More and more, the "causes" of war, inflation, land erosion, and child abuse are each being sought in a narrow but generalizable set of circumstances that treats human beings like billiard balls, subject to social forces as predictable as Newton's laws of physics. To proceed scientifically at all, however, one *must* reduce the focus of one's attention, arbitrarily defining the boundary conditions, setting down as axiomatic the basic premises from which one starts, and deciding how to interpret "the facts." Science, as a way of pursuing truth, is an inevitably subjective and abstract enterprise, based on internalized models of reality. Even such a seemingly simple ecological study as determining the conditions under which mosses growing on boulders survive desiccation in the arid chaparral of California required turning the multiple shapes of irregular boulders into mathematically amenable spheres. In deciding how best to preserve the habitat of these endangered mosses, society must trust that the ecologist's subjective transformation of real rocks into abstract spheres was a *responsible* act – as were his other decisions about which field of boulders to study, how to measure water content of mosses, and so on.[3] If these kinds of subjective simplifications are necessary for a rather simple problem in ecology, how much greater are the degrees of simplification needed for scientific study of human behavior. Take, for a moment, the underlying assumption on which almost all the "laws" of economic behavior are based – namely, the existence of "rational economic man." From the predictable behavior of this abstract axiomatic being, who at all times can be expected to act only in his own selfish interest, are derived "market forces," "price mechanisms," and other quantitative abstractions, the truth of which society must take on faith if it is to manipulate the economy according to information provided for it by mainstream university economists. Yet this is exactly what society does, without batting an eyelash at the assumptions on which the whole "scientific" argument is based, which remain comfortably unexamined. This kind of scientism has permeated not only economics, but all the social sciences, and is beginning to infiltrate the humanities.

Science has clearly become a powerful (some would say, too powerful) tool for both understanding and manipulating our world and each other. However, both the methods and uses of science are being taught in schools and praised by society without due attention to the limits on "truth" the inevitable abstraction and subjectivity of science impose. As ecologist Peter Alpert says:

Facts never speak for themselves. Like the distribution of moss on boulders, they are constructed from a variety of sources, including philosophical disposition. When science involves politically sensitive issues, scientific results tend to correlate with the political views of the scientist.[4]

And Allan Bloom warns that the tendency to ignore the abstractions of science, especially in the social sciences, imperceptibly leads to a society that eventually *does* fit the abstracted model.

If, for example, one sees only gain as a motive in men's actions, then it is easy to explain them. One simply abstracts from what is really there. After a while one notices nothing other than the postulated motives. To the extent that men begin to believe in the theory, they no longer believe that there are other motives in themselves. And when social policy is based on such a theory, finally one succeeds in producing men who fit the theory.[5]

This reductionist scientism that has permeated both our society and the university has been accompanied by a second, corollary development, namely, the unexamined presumption that the main (often the only) purpose of the scientific enterprise is the physical state of humankind through technological innovation. Like the spread of scientism itself, this "technological imperative" is regarded as a form of inevitable progress to which humans, *all* humans, not just those in developed countries, must adapt. This single-minded utilitarianism is seen best in what surely must be humankind's greatest philosophical aberration, the nuclear arms race, which we all pursue as hard as possible while wishing with equal earnestness that we did not "have to." But the same puzzling drive toward technological turmoil exists in our industries (robotization), in our businesses (computerization), in our agriculture and medicine (molecular engineering). And our universities are currently adapting themselves as fast as they can to become the uncritical servants of this technological race – what E. F. Schumacher has called "the forward stampede."

Not only has technology taken over as the central concern of society, but we also measure social progress in the most quantitative and physical terms. Measures of national welfare are such things as life expectancy at birth and *per capita* gross national product. Something we call "standard of living" is, in reality, "standard of physical consumption." Even socialist China, with its newfound focus on materialism, rates its "progress" in terms of consumer goods: 3.5 wristwatches per family; 1.8 bicycles; 0.2 television sets. These "scientifically" measureable quantities, simply because they *can* be measured, are more and more the yardsticks by which a society evaluates itself. Those things that make life worth living – binding friendships, sacred rituals, challenging projects, and the awareness of transcendent beauty – are independent of technology and defy quantification. They lie outside the province of "scientism," and hence are now largely ignored in universities.

This state of affairs has come about by the third development since the Enlightenment – the gradual elimination of *philosophy* as the counterpart of *science* in universities and hence in society as a whole. Philosophy is about ideas and what they mean. It is about the best way to understand reality, to achieve wisdom, and to know how to act. Philosophy is *the* mirror by which a non-traditionalist, changing society can check its bearings and reset them in a more desired direction. But one by one, universities are closing down departments of philosophy, or turning them into innocuous backwaters where faculty seldom ask the seminal question: What would so-and-so say today? What aspects of ourselves would this or that ancient define more clearly or re-inspect more critically? Would Plato be satisfied with us? What would Descartes, or Hegel, say? How should we account to them for what we are doing? Or, if we extend our quest to the great religious teachers, what would Jesus say, or Buddha, or Gandhi?

The fact that universities have discarded philosophy from the center of the curriculum, and particularly that they neglect the philosophy of science while pushing for supposedly "scientific" approaches in every possible discipline, leaves me full of apprehension and dismay. We need to reintroduce philosophy into the study of science. We need philosophy not only to explain what science *is* – since ultimately it is philosophy that forces us to explain what we mean by such words as "science," "proof," "facts," "knowledge," "objectivity," and the like. Defining what we *mean* by science is *not* a scientific job, although it is today left almost entirely to a self-appointed group called "scientists," who have little or no training in philosophy, to anoint a particular field of study as "scientific."

We also need philosophy to help us perceive what science is *for*. What is its social function? By supposing that the scientific enterprise is value-neutral (which it is not) we also tend to act as if its impacts on society were value-neutral, which everyone knows they are not. It is this unwillingness to tackle the unscientific aspects of the scientific enterprise that makes the teaching of science not only boring, leading to so-called "scientific illiteracy," but dangerous. The assumption becomes that only scientific "objectivity" can be used to judge the purpose, value, and meaning of science, and that philosophy is really nothing more than sentimental personal opinion and cannot be trusted to guide us toward a better future. This I take to be the central message of Allan Bloom's recent book, with its anguished plea for a return of philosophical training to the university curriculum. Universities need to return to their central function which is *not* to serve the status quo, or to further some linear extrapolation of the present, but to critique the social myths, to re-examine the central assumptions, to serve as a constant and unrelenting mirror to the societies in which they are embedded.

As regards the teaching of science in the liberal arts curriculum of universities, I would like to take one important aspect of biology, namely agriculture, to show what I consider to be the wrong and right approaches to science education. Where agriculture is considered in the school or university general curriculum at all, it is usually as an example of applied biology. The general impression is that while past agriculture was inefficient and often destructive of the environment (every textbook has a picture of the dustbowl), modern, *scientific* agriculture is in the process of saving the human race through the introduction of one new technological breakthrough after another. In other words, the impression left with students is that modern science is *good*, and that the average person need only support it and all our problems will be solved.

A recent example of how scientists tend to hold up as great signs of "progress" gigantic, science-based technological developments, was a report in *Science* called "A New Agricultural Frontier."[6] In this article, P. H. Abelson and J. W. Rowe describe how massive additions of nutrients and buffers onto the poor, acidic soils of the Campo Cerrado in central Brazil have generated large quantities of monocultured soybeans and grains, permitting Brazil theoretically to feed itself and become a food exporter as well. The authors herald the scientific details of the achievement, which was carried out by already Westernized agro-business farmers who sold their richer lands to the south, bought cheaper and more extensive lands in the Cerrado, and now are reaping a respectable profit for themselves. The impression is uniformly rosy.

What the article omits, and what is largely omitted from textbooks, and from the teaching of science and its applications, is the wider social context of this kind of supposed scientific miracle. Anyone familiar with the plight of the starving people in northeast Brazil should be appalled by the tone of this article, as should anyone worried about the plight of American farmers, or anyone concerned with long-term sustainable agriculture. Science in this instance is "successful" by the sole measure of a local and temporary commercial yardstick. Those who fall outside that measure because they cannot buy this energy-subsidized food (nor are there roads to bring it to them!) are made worse off by this kind of commercial overproduction.

It is not recognized by the public (even though Oxfam tried to publicize it) that as many Brazilians were simultaneously at risk of starvation in the mid-1980s as Ethiopians. (The authors, who *should* have known, do not mention this.) The global commodities markets are already saturated with too cheap grains – which, however, those millions without any money whatsoever cannot afford – so it is hard to see how Brazil's huge debts are to be paid off selling soybeans, just as the American farmers with whom they compete cannot pay off *their* own farm debts, let alone the nation's growing international debts, by exporting grains. One really has to ask, does this particular technological coup make any sense at all in today's world?

An alternative way of examining what science *is* and what science is *for*, still using agriculture as the example, is to pursue the broad approach offered by John A. Moore in his recent essay on teaching about agriculture in the nation's schools.[7] Agriculture, conceived not merely as an industry like house-building or steel-making but as a complex of interactions between human societies and the living environment, requires an appreciation of the biology not only of the plants and animals that provide our food and fiber, but of their dependence on the organic life of soils, on local climate, on the presence of pest-controlling insects or birds – indeed, on a complex set of ecological circumstances.

Not only should students understand how human agricultural innovations affect the sustainability of agriculture – or the permanent carrying capacity of the land; they should know what happens to food once it is harvested, how it is prepared, preserved and distributed. The role of foods in human nutrition, and the dangers of unbalanced diets or incautious additions of chemicals in food production are fundamental to a complete understanding of "food science."

Moore goes even further, suggesting that the study of agriculture, upon which the existence of more than 95 per cent of humankind depends, could act to focus an entire school curriculum – or become a unifying theme for a liberal arts education in universities. There is scarcely any aspect of human life that is not significantly linked to our production and consumption of food and fiber. A holistic study of agriculture includes biology, history, anthropology, economics, technology, politics, sociology, international relations, literature and art, religious traditions – and finally the deepest questions of ethics and morality. An approach such as this begins to place science in its proper perspective. Students – *all* students – begin to intuit what science *is* (and what it is not) and what science is *for*. Such an approach to teaching science brings philosophy back to the center of our thinking, and particularly to the center of academic life in the university.

In concluding, I should like to note one further and important benefit to be gained from no longer treating science as some totally objective, value-free pursuit whose primary function is to give us ever more power and control over Nature (and all too often, over each other). Science has a great deal to tell us about *who* we are, we humans; to give us perspective on *where* we are in time (evolutionary time) and space (ecological space on a tiny planet floating in a vast and lifeless universe). Science can give us insights to ponder, to philosophize over. Here are some noted by Peter Alpert.[8] We humans, who invented neither ourselves nor our surroundings, are not conquerors of Nature, but rather disturbers of ecosystems. Evolution has no specific directionality, and no species is intrinsically superior to another. Diversity and variation of life forms are essential for the continued survival of all life.

It is simple yet profound insights like these, gleaned from the careful, dispassionate *scientific* observation of the world we live in, that may begin to alter the rather violent worldview that permeates most Western thinking. For a brief period, we humans have achieved the power to destroy life on Earth, either rapidly through a holocaust or slightly more slowly through the hubristic exploitation of its life-supporting gifts. These powers exist because we have chosen to seek a particular *kind* of scientific understanding of the natural world, ignoring other visions, equally true, that would serve society in quite different ways. We need philosophy to keep us honest as to what science *is* and to better understand what science is *for*.

NOTES AND REFERENCES

1. Allan Bloom, *The Closing of the American Mind* (New York: Simon & Schuster, 1987): 346–7.
2. Bloom, *The Closing of the American Mind*: 259.
3. Peter Alpert, "The Boulder and the Sphere: Subjectivity and Ethical Content in Biology," an unpublished analysis of the philosophical puzzles of being a scientist. Dr Alpert teaches ecology at the University of Massachusetts, Amherst.
4. Alpert, "The Boulder": 13.
5. Bloom, *The Closing of the American Mind*: 255.

6. P. H. Albelson, and J. W. Rowe, "A New Agricultural Frontier," *Science*, 235 (20 March 1987): 1450–1.
7. John A. Moore, "New Wine in Old Bottles?" *Agricultural Education Magazine* (October 1987).
8. Alpert, "The Boulder": 14–15.

15 Action Research
Frank Dukes*

INTRODUCTION

Action Research is the name given a class of methods that combine research with the practice of social intervention. Kurt Lewin, the social psychologist who pioneered in so many fields, began the development of Action Research as a means of addressing two fundamentally important questions: How does one most effectively produce social change? How can one do research that will aid the practitioner? His answer was this:

> a type of action-research, a comparative research on the conditions and effects of various forms of social action, and research leading to social action.[1]

Although Action Research has evolved into various types of formalized procedures used most often in organizational settings, its underlying principles suggest a potentially greater role. Indeed, some researcher-practitioners who work in less structured settings, while unaware of the established procedures of Action Research, are nonetheless following these principles. Others do so deliberately. For instance, Herbert Kelman views his work with groups such as the Palestinians and Israelis as a kind of Action Research. He suggests that the rationale and legitimacy for his conflict resolution workshops are provided by their research aspects:

> our *action* requires involvement in a *research* program just as our *research* requires involvement in an *action* program.[2]

The difficulties of conducting research about conflict, combined with the increasing interest in third-party conflict resolution, may make knowledge of Action Research principles beneficial for both the practitioner and the researcher, and essential for those who accept the mantle of both roles.

---

* This chapter was written for the purposes of this collection of essays.

SEEKING THE TRUTH

Jacob Bronowski defined two ways that humans have of looking for the truth.[3] The first way is to find fundamental concepts held by faith, or authority, or the conviction of their self-evidence, and to declare them beyond challenge.

Until the Scientific Revolution, the prevailing Western view of the world was largely derived from this method. Observation was intentionally filtered by deduction from general principles, including those of a geocentric universe, a natural place and motion for all objects, and everything created and ruled by the laws of God.

Morris Berman gives a wonderful example of how this kind of filtered observation can lead to error.[4] Aristotle held that motion was caused by two sources: active force, such as a cannon or an arm, and natural force, which returns objects to the position nature intended for them. Projectile motion, then, had to be discontinuous (see Figure 15.1).

Figure 15.1   Discontinuous projectile motion

Did people truly believe that this was the way a projectile moved? Today we may laugh at the gullibility of those who accepted the validity of the Aristotlean view. However, we need look no further than our own contemporary social sciences for constructs such as "economic man" to see just how ready we are to make our own giant leaps of faith, given the proper prodding.

These leaps of faith occur today despite the fact that the second of Bronowski's two ways of looking for the truth – subjecting observation to the scrutiny of testing – is now the acclaimed paradigm within the scientific community. Clearly, acceptance of the worth of empirical evidence does not ensure critical analysis of that evidence.

Explanations of behavior can be thought of as maps of our experience that we develop – or, more often, we are given and accept. There are certain phenomena in our world; we look for patterns of interaction among these phenomena in order to make sense of this world to ourselves. We then organize our experience of these patterns such that we internalize representational constructs, or maps, of our outer world. Having these maps then allows us to recognize the familiar for what it is. When we experience similar phenomena we then have a map to compare them to; if the map fits them, we say we can understand and explain the phenomena.

Unfortunately, our maps also create certain expectations of the world, as was demonstrated by the example of projectile motion. As Berman points out, this is representative of the Gestalt principle of seeing what one expects to see. And many people often have such an investment in their maps, they want so much to believe that their view of the world fits their ideology, their values, or their convenience, and they want so much to be able to understand and explain, that they would rather distort and reinterpret the experience – stretch it to fit the map – than admit to the need to change the map.

THE OVERREACTION TO ERROR

Of course, much of what has been routinized in contemporary research methodology evolved out of concern for these distortions. As scientists and philosophers discovered how our belief systems affected our understanding of the world, they developed methodologies intended to counterbalance prejudicial influences.

But in the zealous drive to avoid the influences of subjectivity and belief, the scientific community established its own belief systems. Abraham Maslow observed how the quest to transcend the effects of researcher values "permitted nineteenth century science to become too exclusively mechanistic, too positivistic, too reductionistic, too desperately attempting to be value-free."[5] Nevitt Sanford criticized how the trend towards specialization led to "a fancy proliferation of bitsy, disconnected, essentially unusable researches."[6] Marie Jahoda described how subjects of research are dehumanized, and mentally dissected into unconnected parts: "mainstream social psychology is often no longer social, treats people like objects rather than persons, and, where it does not, limits its concern to the cognitively rational and consistent."[7]

As Shulamit Reinharz concludes, standard research is often ambiguous, condescending, culture- and class-biased, and deceptive.[8] Not surprisingly, it is also inaccurate. She suggests:

Most research designs are actually contaminated by response effects such as the Hawthorne effect, self-fulfilling prophecies, subject approval-seeking, and more, and by messages "given off" by researchers, such as interaction effects of gender, race, age, personality, and other attributes.[9]

The rigors of "scientific method" – a term commonly offered as though there is, can be, or should be, one such method – have become, not a liberating mechanism, but a clumsy piece of machinery that creates the very error and inaccuracy it was intended to eliminate. We are left with a mechanistic view of ourselves, a mind–body dualism, a fixation for linear causality, and the need to understand by reduction and atomism, determinism, reification, and detachment.

And the problems of contemporary social science are not only technical problems of method. In slavishly trying to emulate the physical sciences (or, to be precise, an idealized image of the physical sciences) many social scientists adopt an unrealistic pretense of objectivity and freedom from values. We have as our legacy today institutionalized motivations for researchers that directly contravene our purported goals. Our social sciences are driven, not by a quest for understanding, but by the search for funding, by publishability, by artificial distinctions of discipline, and by unthinking acceptance of comfortable methodology.

By this convoluted process the potential use, and usefulness, of research is too often left unconsidered. Too many research projects end with the researchers realizing that what they are leaving behind is not at all the desired trail of life-affirming knowledge, but rather one of mere dead paper and ink.

THE FOUNDATIONS OF ACTION RESEARCH

One of the common tenets of those asserting the claim to objectivity in science has been the separation of research from practice in the expectation that research is somehow tainted by the demands of the real world. Indeed, many conflict researchers who are engaged in practice betray an air of apology about their involvement, as though they are guilty of breaking some unwritten rule (which, of course, they are). However, discovery and understanding is in no way guaranteed by this separation. As Nevitt Sanford pointed out:

The categorical separation of research from practice has made it very difficult for a social scientist to study phenomena that cannot be experimented upon in the laboratory, or social structures that can be understood only through attempts to change them. Likewise, it has laid the social sciences wide open to the charge of irrelevance.[10]

For Sanford and others, the answer to this problem lies in developing the link between theory and practice. And their preferred model for that link is that of Action Research.

Of course, Action Research is not a panacea. The researcher-practitioner is subject to the same concerns and strictures as other researchers. No research methods can address all of the problems enumerated above; indeed, one of the myths of contemporary social science is that better methods, as opposed to better researchers, will ensure worthy results. But the philosophy and ethic of Action Research, if followed, will at least create the opportunity for a research program that is humane, revealing, and of some use to others beside the researcher.

THE DEVELOPMENT OF ACTION RESEARCH

As mentioned earlier, Kurt Lewin was the originator of Action Research. From his knowledge of the emerging field of cybernetics, he understood that social feedback processes are necessary for social intervention. These processes would be systematized such that the researcher interested in social change would act as a consultant to people engaged in real-life problems by providing them methods of diagnosis, action, and evaluation. As he put it:

Rational social management, therefore, proceeds in a spiral of steps each of which is composed of a circle of planning, action, and fact-finding about the rest of the action.[11]

He represented his approach by the triangle in Figure 15.2.

Those continuing to develop Action Research have very much followed in his footsteps, although there have been what Robert Rapoport describes as four differing streams of development.[12]

The first he calls the "Tavistock" (England) group. Their focus was on collaboration among different members of an organization. The second, "operational research," was multi-disciplinary and bor-

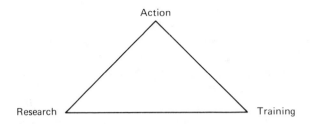

Figure 15.2   Social feedback processes

rowed from the engineering and physical sciences. The "group dynamics" approach emphasized individual and small group processes and studied leadership, power, stress and identity. The fourth, "applied anthropology," brought the action orientation to the study of social change.

Underlying each of these approaches are three fundamental principles:

– Researchers should not insulate themselves from applied settings, and the most appropriate locale for many kinds of research is not the laboratory, but in the field
– Individuals and groups are capable of autonomous choice but are often unable to exercise it because they lack information about themselves and their behavior
– Effective learning depends upon direct and immediate feedback.

In addition to these principles, the Action Researcher can use what Peter Reason and John Rowan term "canons" of interpretative social science.[13] These canons serve as both an ethical and a practical basis for performing research. Rather than being rules whose implementation will guarantee a certain quality of result, they are guidelines, awareness of which can keep the researcher on the correct path between the Scylla of belief and the Charybdis of overreaction.

The use of guidelines instead of rules does not mean less rigor. It is merely recognition of the impossibility of establishing absolute objective criteria in a world of fallible human beings. Kuhn asserted that the most difficult decisions about competing explanations of behavior cannot be resolved by proof. The search for absolute criteria is bound to fail. Accordingly, criteria of choice should function, not as rules for determining choice, but as values for influencing it.[14]

The first of Reason and Rowan's canons, "autonomy of the object," holds that the meaning of what we study must not be projected into it (as in stretching explanation to fit the internalized map).

The second is that the interpretation should make the phenomenon "maximally reasonable in human terms," for those who are actually involved in them to gain a clearer understanding than before.

Third, the researcher must have the "greatest possible familiarity" with the phenomenon; one must know from within as well as without. This is the Hippocratic tradition of immersion into experience.

Fourth, the interpreter should show the "meaning of the phenomenon for his [or her] own situation." Presumably the research is being conducted out of some interest of the researcher. The research should not ignore that interest.

Last, and most important to them, is what they call the "hermeneutic circle." This is the study of the interaction among parts and wholes, and recognition of the circular causal relationships among them, as well as between the known and the unknown, and the knower and the known.

A MODEL OF ACTION RESEARCH

Bart Cunningham articulates very well the intentions of the organizational Action Researcher:

> Action Research seeks a more effective method of organizational decision-making involving the whole organization in identifying needs, solving problems, laying out plans, and implementing decisions. Its principal components are an Action Research Group composed of organizational members and an Action Researcher – an outside consultant skilled in directing group decision-making and coordinating responsive action. The primary device is research into organizational needs and desires, usually by means of the open-ended interview. Implementing the results of this research requires constant evaluation of every hypothesis, decision, action, and result.[15]

Of course, Action Research is not limited to organizational settings. Indeed, there are several different models of Action Research whose refinements differ in suitability for varying situations. Their essential characteristics can be represented by a composite model, which can be modified according to the purposes of the researcher-practitioner. Accordingly, what follow are not the specifics of method, but a rather brief outline of one possible model of Action Research. It is meant to be suggestive rather than directive. This outline is applicable for both intra-group and inter-group settings. Its prime features are diagrammed in Figure 15.3.

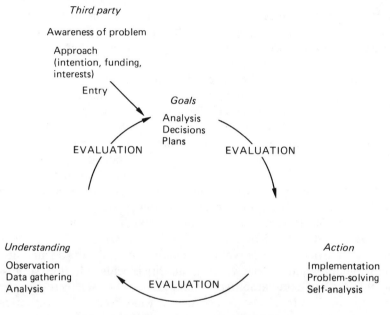

Figure 15.3   Action research model

ACTION RESEARCH PROCEDURES

The researcher-practitioner beginning an Action Research project will have at least three, and possibly four, classes of interests to satisfy. Her or his intentions might extend beyond that of the immediate benefit to the participants to interests such as accumulating research data and publishing research results. A request for intervention may come from someone not directly involved in the project, who might have specific interests different from those of the groups and the researcher-practitioner. There are the interests of the members of the groups themselves, as well as those they represent. Finally, funding may come from outside sources – a foundation grant, a university project – that the researcher-practitioner is accountable to. Obviously, one must recognize these potentially divergent obligations and establish criteria for dealing with them.

The actual process of Action Research begins with the researcher-practitioner's proposal, which may be self-initiated or may come from someone within the group or groups. Certainly, the groups should have at least some awareness of problems and the need for outside assistance. Otherwise the groups might perceive the researcher-practitioner as an unwanted outsider, and the job might be much more difficult or impossible successfully to complete.[16]

All the parties involved then begin to establish what outcomes they would like to bring about. This procedure involves the sponsor of the research, members of the groups, supervisors (if any) of group members, and the researcher-practitioner. Small group facilitation skills are particularly important at this time, as indeed they are during the entire intervention, since the combination of a nosy outsider added to the problems that suggested the intervention can lead to excessive stresses on normal group functions.

The Action Researcher must be thoroughly familiar with the activities of the group or groups; this is accomplished by methods such as participant observation, content analysis of documents, questionnaire, and interview. As familiarity is achieved, more sophisticated forms of data-gathering and analysis may be used by researcher and group. The researcher must have a wide range of qualititative and quantitative research tools to choose from, the choice of course depending upon the context. Furthermore, these tools need to be presented in ways that are understood by the participants, as the results will be fed back to and interpreted by group members.

Understanding must be comprehensive – the Weberian, emic approach, in which the researcher learns to see the world of the subjects as they themselves see it. All of the skills of a participant-observer are required: attentional skills, memory, the ability to conduct open-ended or structured interviews, assertiveness, and self-analysis.

Listening and communication skills can be taught to and then used by individuals within the groups to increase both their own and the group's effectiveness. Members of individual groups can learn to give and receive feedback about each others' behavior, thus gaining better understanding of themselves and their group. This is a crucial process, and might require continuous effort to create the kind of cooperation needed for success.

The groups themselves, through small group team-building processes and training, develop the skills to articulate goals and the plans to attain them. Results from the data gathering and analysis will be used to set these goals. Both goals and plans must be flexible; they will be constantly evaluated and altered as the results of implemented changes become known.

Goals should also be important to the groups and the larger organization, if any, in which they function. They must also be realistic; at least some success is essential in maintaining group commitment.

As plans are implemented, unexpected and undesired results may occur. The group process should establish a climate in which problems can be identified and discussed as they occur.

During all parts of the Action Research procedures, there is a dual focus on the pertinent activity and on group processes. The groups evaluate both the impact of their decisions and the manner in which the decisions are made; self-awareness and reflection must be continual.

CONCLUSION

There are many potential benefits of Action Research. Researchers learn of problems directly from those involved, rather than wondering how well a group of college students in the lab represent the larger world. The researcher is assured that results will be used by those directly involved, although they may also feed into the paper-publishing mill. Those involved learn from themselves; such self-directed learning is not only humane, it is likely to be lasting. And, of course, the practitioner is better informed by subjecting practice to critical examination.

There are other forms of research which are both effective and which treat the subjects of the research as human beings. Participant observation, ethnomethodology, participant research, grounded theory, endogenous research – all of these testify to the recognition of the problems with the positivist paradigm and the availability of humane and accurate methods of research. The underlying philosophy and principles of Action Research, however, which include both faith in individuals' abilities to perform critical self-analysis and recognition of the difficulties of enacting planned change, are particularly appropriate for situations involving social problems. Thus Action Research, too, while not claiming universal suitability or infallibility, may play a role as a valid, useful, and exciting part of the drive for understanding that is essential for successful social intervention.

NOTES AND REFERENCES

1. Kurt Lewin, "Action Research and Minority Problems," *Journal of Social Issues*, 2 (4) (1946): 46.
2. Herbert C. Kelman, "Interactive Problem Solving; A Social-psychological Approach to Conflict Resolution," in W. Klassen (ed.), *Dialogue Toward Inter-Faith Understanding* (Tantur/Jerusalem: Ecumenical Institute for Theological Research, 1985): 297. (Chapter 10 in this book.)
3. Jacob Bronowski, *Science and Human Values* (New York: Harper & Row, 1956).
4. Morris Berman, *The Reenchantment of the World* (Ithaca, N.Y.: Cornell University Press, 1981).
5. Abraham Maslow, *Religions, Values, and Peak-Experiences* (Columbus, Ohio: Ohio State University Press, 1964): 11.
6. Nevitt Sanford, "Whatever Happened to Action Research?" *Journal of Social Issues*, 26 (4) (1970): 12.
7. Marie Jahoda, "To Publish or Not to Publish," *Journal of Social Issues*, 37 (1) (1981): 215.
8. Shulamit Reinharz, "Implementing New Paradigm Research: A Model for Training and Practice," in Peter Reason and John Rowan (eds), *Human Injury* (New York: John Wiley, 1981).
9. Reinharz, "Implementing New Paradigm Research": 422.
10. Sanford, "Whatever Happened": 10.
11. Lewin, "Action Research": 38.
12. Robert Rapoport, "Three Dilemmas in Action Research," *Human Relations*, 23 (6) (1970): 499–513.
13. Reason and Rowan (eds), *Human Inquiry*.
14. Thomas Kuhn, *The Essential Tension* (Chicago: The University of Chicago Press, 1977): 331.
15. Bart Cunningham, "Action Research: Toward a Procedural Model," *Human Relations*, 29 (3) (1976): 216.
16. For an example of what can go wrong, see Max Elden's study in Reason and Rowan (eds), *Human Inquiry*.

VI
Political Implications

Chapter 16   A Tale of Two Movements: ADR and the Greens   301
            Christa Daryl Slaton and Theodore L. Becker
Chapter 17   Unanticipated Conflict and the Crisis of Social   316
            Theory
            Richard E. Rubenstein
Chapter 18   Unfinished Business in Conflict Resolution   328
            John Burton

16 A Tale of Two Movements: ADR and The Greens

Christa Daryl Slaton and Theodore L. Becker*

In the past decade, we have been intimately acquainted with the problems, and suffered some of the growing pains, of two important global movements, what some call the "Alternative Dispute Resolution" movement (or ADR) and what many know as "The Green" movement, or in Germany as "Die Grünen." Each continues to expand in size and impact. Each is a substantial shift in process. Each has great potential to transform how society is shaped in the future. And each is plagued by a variety of splits amongst its theorists and practitioners, differences in what is conceived to be its ideology and how to best make that ideology work in the "real" world.

Despite the good intentions and solid theoretical basis of both movements, people being people and movements being movements, rifts and factions appear almost immediately. Both movements sprang from a dissatisfaction with the way some aspects of society worked (and did not work). The original ADR theorists were concerned with obvious malfunctions in the legal system and the original Green theorists were concerned with blatant dysfunctions in modern governance. Each group of theorists saw a need for an entirely new way of doing things, a radical departure from the status quo.

Almost as soon as people began applying these theories, serious differences of opinions cropped up as to what direction each movement should go. In the ADR movement, one set of differences that emerged involved advocates of community-based mediation and those of court and profession-based mediation. In the Greens, a growing division is between the "Fundis" and the "Realos." In each case, the former are viewed by the latter as being too idealistic and ineffective and the latter viewed by the former as being too eager to

* Paper presented at the North American Conference on Peacemaking and Conflict Resolution on 3 March 1989 (Montreal).

301

compromise important principles for the sake of gaining and using power for their own benefit, yes, "selling out the movement" and being part of the problem instead of the solution.

There are several general opinions about the nature and future of these separations in the ranks. First, there are those of the cynics. They say such divisions are natural and that it is inevitable that the idealists will succumb to the pragmatists. Jerold Auerbach,[1] applying a theory of historical determinism to the development of conflict resolution processes in the United States, observes that various buds of community-based mediation and conciliation have periodically withered on the American vine and that the law profession has successfully managed to overcome or coopt such utopian models regularly. In his view, it is all but certain that community mediation efforts in the USA are doomed to be overwhelmed by the irresistable power of the law profession. Similar prophecies of doom for the purist Greens are made and generally accepted as being inexorable.

Another view is that these differences are indeed inevitable, but that they are merely another expression of the universal principles of a socio-political dialectic. From this standpoint, these two factions in each movement are bound to exist and collide, but this tension and opposition will ultimately produce a synthesis that will be a profound step forward.

Whatever the future resolution of this on-going disharmony in the ADR and Green movements, we believe that it is interesting, useful and perhaps important to identify, describe and analyze the points of confluence between the theories and ideologies emphasized chiefly by the two "purist" wings of these movements, because we see a dynamic and significant connection between them. We think the similarities are worth noting because each movement has a lot to learn from the other and each can help the other maintain a firm rooting despite the divergent directions in which major applications of the theory seem to be heading at the present time.

There are three major areas of similarity we wish to treat, two obvious and one quite subtle. The clear interconnections in two central principles between some factions of the ADR and Green Movements are: (1) an emphasis on non-violence and (2) a devotion to democracy. The less obvious similarity between the two movements is (3) a deeper philosophical linkage whereby their new, radical departures in process are potential agents of, or bridges for, major social transformation.

THE PRINCIPLE OF NON-VIOLENCE

From the viewpoint of most ADR theorists, the major difference between such forms of ADR as mediation and conciliation and that of litigation (plus arbitration) and the legal process is that the former is considered to be "non-adversarial" and "non-confrontational" while the latter forms are deemed to be verbal warfare and symbolic battle that rely heavily on the use of power and coercion to achieve their purported objectives: the revelation of truth and the attainment of justice.

Consider also the major metaphors attached to practitioners in the mediation process and those in the legal system. We all know that lawyers are embroiled in what is an equivalent to a zero-sum game. The object of going to court is to "win" one for the client. Of course, a good attorney frequently must engage in what may sometimes be an extremely long negotiation process where he/she tries to maximize the settlement for her/his client without resorting to the travails and expense of a trial. However, the emphasis is still on right prevailing over wrong through the threat or use of the force and authority of the judicial process.

The ending of a dispute by the use of judicial fiat, a manifestation of force, often produces resistance and unintended results. For example, at the first Asia Pacific Organization of Mediators conference (in Manila, Philippines in 1985), the delegate from Papua New Guinea (a law school professor) used a then-recent situation there regarding a marital dispute to illustrate this very point.

A wife, unhappy with her culturally defined role, rebelled against the demands placed upon her to serve and care for her husband by leaving him and returning to her family. The matter went to court and the judge decided she must go back to her husband. Her family agreed and she was compelled to move back . . . She was determined, however, to serve him no longer. So she smashed her hands with a rock, making them useless for any more household tasks.

The American legal system is replete with similar failures of applied force – even at the systems level: criminal laws designed to deter crime do not seem to deter those bent on commiting a crime; child support decrees are frequently ignored rather than obeyed; our forcible rehabilitation system often does not rehabilitate; our punishment system systematically educates people in criminal methods; etc.

Mediation and/or conciliation in the community mediation or purist model is a totally voluntary process with no coercion in the process whatsoever. Parties come to the mediation table because they have been educated to the knowledge that using the force of the legal system may well be counter-productive. They understand that they must communicate with the other party (or parties) and reason with them in the hope of forging a mutually agreeable solution in which each wins something. The emphasis here is on a non-coercive process where the desired outcome is some vestige of peace and harmony.

Moreover, the fact that the final decision is not imposed by authority and is an agreement worked out peacefully by the parties themselves is believed to be one of the major factors behind the durability and longevity of voluntarily mediated decisions. Parties who have a long-standing or continuing relationship, who amicably settle a dispute by themselves, with the help of a third party, are not nearly so likely to violate it as those who have had a solution imposed on them.

There is some disagreement among those in the mediation movement, however, about the appropriateness and/or usefulness of having courts and/or other government agencies refer cases to mediation centers for resolution by compelling the disputants to mediate. It is pointed out by those who favor such that this is the only way to make mediation cost effective. Community mediation centers, it is well known, labor hard to convince disputants to try mediation. The case load is low and the amount of time and energy used to bring about a mediation is great.

Courts and other coercive government agencies, on the other hand, have lots of business and they are eager to farm it out in order to reduce their backlogs. Thus, mediation centers that rely heavily on cases coming in from them have much greater case loads. However, when parties come to mediation willingly, without being forced to do so, the mediation process itself is more effective, having a much higher rate of success in helping parties reach an agreement among themselves. Mediation centers that refuse to take coerced referrals, however, are being consistent with the theory of non-violence, a keystone in the theory of mediation.

A major principle of the Green Movement is that non-violent means must be used to achieve any and/or all political objectives. Non-violence is thus a major *end and means* of all Green politics. As an end or goal of the Greens, non-violence manifests itself in terms of a wide variety of political policy goals that Greens usually support – e.g., nuclear disarmament, disbanding military alliances, peace movements and initiatives, etc.

There is also an element of the Green non-violence philosophy that believes that non-violence is a way towards personal growth and existence and they try to apply it generally in all they think and do. This is consistent with the objectives of the mediation movement that speak to the personal empowerment aspects of being a mediator and a peacemaker, and applying what one learns in trying to help others resolve their conflict to one's own life – i.e., all aspects thereof. As one Green theorist puts it, the practice of the Green principle of non-violence in daily life "can help develop the sense of personal empowerment that is needed to create a different kind of world."[2]

The particular methods of non-violence that Greens preach and use in trying to achieve specific policy objectives include various techniques of non-cooperation and civil disobedience based in part on the principles and tactics developed by Mahatma Gandhi and Martin Luther King, Jr. The aims of such campaigns are to educate the general populace on the inconsistency and counter-productivity of the accepted use of government force to achieve such goals as peace and harmony. This is similar to the use of "reality testing" by mediators to convince parties to use mediation instead of litigation and to help them see the wisdom in settling amongst themselves rather than letting someone in authority dictate a decision to one of them.

GREEN AND ADR NON-VIOLENT PHILOSOPHICAL CONVERGENCES

One of the fundamentals of Green thought is the belief in the interconnectedness and interdependence of all aspects of the universe. For the Greens, the adversarial process (whether political or legal) inappropriately dichotomizes right–wrong, winner–loser, and good–bad. Such a process also often deepens antagonisms, hatreds, and a desire to fight for the maximization of narrowly defined self-interests.

Mediation, on the other hand, incorporates the Green belief that winners and losers cannot be so neatly separated. Parties in any sort of on-going relationship affect and are affected by the actions of each other. A "winner" in an adversarial situation rarely wins everything. There is always a price to pay. There are repercussions the winner must face even when the victor believes she/he has achieved absolute triumph. To think only of the verdict – and not probable or possible ramifications – is to be shortsighted and leaves one vulnerable to the ingenuity of those seeking ways out of traps or wanting revenge.

The first lesson for Greens in choosing a path to non-violence then is to recognize that might does not make right and mandates of a higher authority do not guarantee peace. Furthermore, the apparent "powerless" are not always so lacking in power as they may appear. Examples abound throughout the world and throughout history that decisions of the powerful can seldom impose peace on those who feel victimized, abused, or ignored. The wounds will fester and turn into a boil until the problem is treated properly.

The path of non-violence and towards a non-violent world for Greens, therefore, incorporates the concept and theory of mediation. The mediation process does not impose decisions. Decisions are made by the disputing parties who listen and *hear* each other in the process of resolving the dispute. The consequences of actions are discussed, not overlooked, in mediation. In order to have a successful resolution of the dispute, parties must face the reality of the interconnected and interdependent nature of all disputes and disputants.

Taking seriously their principle of social and personal responsibility, Greens can also appreciate that mediation is not only a way to resolve disputes, but also a way of communicating, of listening better, of paying closer attention to the less articulate or the shy, and of modeling peaceful and non-violent behavior.

DEMOCRATIC PRINCIPLES

Within the ADR movement, those advocating community-based models (pure or hybrid) usually put less emphasis on cost efficiency and reduction of court case loads than do those following the professional or court referral model. Instead, their emphasis is placed on (a) empowerment of the individuals (disputants and mediators); (b) building of community; and (c) sharing in decision making. Often the community-based models not only utilize non-professionals as mediators, but also involve the volunteers in staff work, outreach, training, and even occasionally in policy making (e.g., being on the board of directors or advisors).

Empowerment of the Individuals

All forms of mediation are more democratic in their structure than the judicial or arbitration processes. The heart of the legal system is the hierarchical relationship between the judge and all other actors in the courtroom drama. The judge sits on high, everyone must stand when he/she enters. All are dependent on her/his rulings on motions, objections, and on the relevant and guiding law. In non-jury settings, the judge makes the final decision. The lawyers are in an intermediate position between the judge and the disputants, but they are a professional elite, speaking a strange tongue that the disputants barely and/or rarely understand. The people who actually are most involved in the dispute, the disputants, are bit players and nearly bystanders in the courtroom. They are at the bottom of the legal hierarchy, subjected to the professional expertise of their and the other counsel and to the officiousness, expertise and prejudices of the judge.

In the mediation process, the disputants own the dispute and are the major players. What they say, what they feel, what they want, is the core of the hearing. The mediator is merely a facilitator of communication and an educator on and guide through the process. The final decision belongs to the disputants. They, and only they, have the power to decide how to resolve the conflict, if at all. This is completely non-hierarchical and quintessentially democratic.

Theoretically, disputants are empowered in another way in the mediation process. By listening to the mediator(s) explain the process, they usually learn a new theory and process of resolving their own disputes, one they may utilize in the future. This process can help them deal with painful and sometimes dangerous conflict situations that previously they had to resort to outside assistance (usually professional help) to resolve. This new knowledge is a self-empowerment, and since the people who are coming into the mediation process are usually not professionals themselves, we find that ordinary people are being given important new skills – which is the heart of the democratic principle: power to the people. Consciously and systematically educating the parties in the stages of the mediation process is part of the program and the formal mediation hearing of at least one community mediation program, that of the Community Boards in San Francisco.

The theory of community-based mediation also contains an aspect pertaining to the empowerment of the mediators and, in turn, the empowerment of the community as well. First, the mediators are community people and they are learning and practising the important theories and skills of conflict resolution. They absorb more of this than any disputant since they are intensively trained and experience first-hand many situations in which it is successfully applied.

Second, there is a rotation of mediators out of the center. Thus, more and more people in the community gain this knowledge and expertise and begin to utilize it in their own personal lives and in community settings. This further diffuses the skills of dispute resolution throughout the community, lessening its dependence on the hierarchical and professionally run systems of conflict resolution like the law and arbitration. Essentially it is democratizing the system of conflict resolution in the community.

Building of Community

Another underlying theory of the Community Boards program is that a community-based mediation program can serve as a catalyst for democratic, grassroots organizing in a community. In other words, resolving individual disputes is not the be-all and end-all of the process. Instead, by rotating volunteers in and out of the program and by developing a community mediation newsletter and outreach program that discussed the nature of the disputes coming into the center for resolution, the community could be alerted to common problems facing it. Indeed, the mediation program becomes an informational clearing house on the underlying causes of numerous interpersonal disputes in the community, conflicts that individual people mistakenly think are peculiar to themselves.

For example, there may be a tremendous lack of parking spaces in a community. Many individual citizens may be fighting with their neighbors, or with people who come to work in the area during the daytime, over the dearth of parking. These people are all unaware that this is happening regularly around the neighborhood. Under the community-based mediation model, the newsletter and word-of-mouth from the center inform the community about the shared problem. This may spur the community to organize as an interest group that pressures its local government to do something about increasing municipal parking in the area. In such a case, the mediation program in the community helps catalyze a democratic, grassroots organization effort.

Sharing in Decision Making

Another way in which community-based mediation programs have tried to promote and test new democratic forms of organization has been to place people from the community onto the policy-making apparatuses of the centers. One of the first to do this was the US Department of Justice pilot project in Venice–Del Mar, California in the late 1970s.

In this project, it was decided to divide the Board of Directors in half, with 50 per cent comprised of lawyers (since the project was co-sponsored by the Los Angeles Bar Association) and half composed of citizens from the Venice–Del Mar area and members of the center's staff. This worked for a while, but after a time the community people and staff stopped attending meetings of the Board of Directors because they felt they were overpowered by "the men in suits."

Another version of this was adopted by the Community Mediation Service of the University of Hawaii in 1979–80.[3] In this model, the entire Board of Directors was comprised of mediators and staff members of the center. All policy was made by those directly involved in the daily work of the program. Each meeting was chaired by a different member of the Board. All were equal in power – e.g., professors, students, community people. The system worked well and was adopted by the Honolulu Neighborhood Mediation Network, (City and County of Honolulu) in 1980.

The Greens, who advocate direct democracy, argue that power must also be decentralized in order to allow the significant involvement of the people. It is not enough that the organization be founded on democratic principles, which may still permit control by an elite, but also that power must be dispersed enough so that the grassroots set the agenda and formulate the policies rather than merely endorsing decisions made at a higher level.

The emphasis for the Greens is empowerment of each individual. In addressing the key value of "Grassroots Democracy," the Greens ask:

How can we develop systems that allow and encourage us to control the decisions that affect our lives? . . . How can we encourage and assist the "mediating institutions" – family, neighborhood organization, church group, voluntary association, ethnic club – to recover some of the functions now performed by government? How can we relearn the best insights from American traditions of civic vitality, voluntary action, and community responsibility?"[4]

In their views on non-violence, the German Green Party platform states that "humane goals cannot be achieved by inhumane means."[5] The same applies to the Green views on democracy. Democracy cannot be achieved through non-democratic means. Therefore, not only in their policy platforms, but also in their organizing, the Greens strive to apply democratic principles.

One of their most famous organizing strategies is to rotate leadership or representative positions. They are also quite sensitive to cultural and societal advantages often given to Caucasian males (advantages that Caucasian males, even in the Greens, frequently fail to recognize). As Cara Lamb of the East Bay Greens points out, studies have demonstrated that even when teachers in research situations have been told to deliberately give girls more attention than boys, actual tabulation shows the girls get 30 per cent, while the boys get 70 per cent. Her analysis is that:

> most women grow up believing that what they say is not important, that they will not be listened to, and that they are entitled to much less air time than men are. Men grow up believing that what they say is important, and that they are entitled to say it.[6]

Minorities in society share in the experience of being ignored and overlooked throughout their socialization process.

Some of the more enlightened Greens have developed specific techniques to remedy culturally and socially established inequities. There are often requirements that representation or leadership roles be shared equally among females and males. Also recognizing Lamb's assertion that "open discussion" is not enough to offset years of training (that what one has to say is not worthwhile), speaking rotation practices are often utilized.

One rotation method passes a pipe to each person in the room. The person holding the pipe is allowed to speak uninterrupted. In order to allow time to digest what has been said, sometimes a period of time (30 seconds or so) of silence is observed. The silence not only allows for reflection but also presents a more comfortable entry for quiet people to participate. Intense verbal exchanges, where articulate or aggressive speakers fight for the floor, frequently deter some thoughtful but non-aggressive people from expressing their views. Lamb describes another speaking rotation method, employed by a Green bioregional group, that addressed gender imbalance in discussions. The group has implemented a procedure of alternating between male and female speakers. Only a woman is allowed to speak after a male has spoken and vice versa. Using this procedure, Lamb maintains, forces everyone to be conscious of how much men have dominated meetings prior to the implementation of methods specifically designed to encourage and facilitate participation by women.

Betty Zisk, John Resenbrink, and Carla Dickstein have remarked on ways to keep Green organizations democratic and open to newcomers.[7] One way is to hold orientation sessions prior to meetings to educate new members about the history and bring them up to date on the organization's procedures and policies. Without such support for potential participants, it is very easy for democracy to get lost and relapse into reliance on the experience and knowledge of the established members. Another means of promoting democracy and expanding participation is to rotate "housekeeping tasks" among the membership using a committee whose members serve for staggered terms. It allows new members to work with older members and to gain the expertise they will then pass on to others.

A key Green value, one also fundamental to their democratic principles, is the respect for (and not mere tolerance of) diversity. In order to demonstrate this respect, Greens do not presume to speak for all, or to homogenize, cultural differences. The best spokespeople for any group, from the Green perspective, is one of that group. Rather than lead the struggle for minorities, the oppressed, or the victimized, Greens are most consistent playing a supportive role by asking those they wish to help what their needs are and how the Greens can help. Learning to listen, rather than having all the answers, empowers and demonstrates respect for others. Both empowerment and mutual respect contribute to a healthy democratic environment.

GREEN AND ADR DEMOCRATIC PHILOSOPHICAL CONVERGENCES

Once again we find that in both the Green and ADR movements, the same central philosophical principle is intertwined as both an end and a mean. As with the principle of non-violence being both the goal and the process of the Greens and the ADR movement, so it is with democracy too. However, in this case, it is only the community-based mediation model that works in this way.

Of course, the heart and soul of the mediation process, in all its models and variations, comes in the lateral (rather than vertical) power relationships that constitute the hearing itself. All mediators, in their introduction, are supposed to tell the disputants that they will have equal time to vent their emotions, explain their version of the dispute, and present their opinion as to how the dispute can be best resolved. Mediators are aware that they should try to encourage those who are too quiet to speak up and those who feel in a lesser power relationship to understand, appreciate and use the power they have in the mediation process itself.

At the same time, the community mediation movement's goals are to democratize community processes through empowering its mediators and disputants, *and informing and germinating democratic organization in the community*. In this part of the ADR movement, the democratic aspects of the process converge with its ends. They are part of and one and the same.

Similarly with the Green Movement – democracy is a means to a democratic end. The learning and utilization of mediation skills is extremely useful for Greens to integrate a number of their key principles: grassroots democracy, respect for diversity, personal and social responsibility, non-violence, decentralization, and postpatriarchal values. Mediation not only can provide the skills but also the method for democratic organization and the promotion of democratic values.

In order to advance the Green vision of democracy, one must learn to listen, as well as speak; to hear, not merely listen; to work toward consensus, not get stuck into self-righteous positions; to empower others, not decide or act for them; and to practise democracy, not merely preach it. The practices of community-based mediation provide the tools for the task.

AGENTS OF TRANSFORMATION

We have been told by many respected and perceptive observers and analysts over the past few decades that we are living in a transformational period, an epoch of drastic change, a "paradigm shift," that comes but infrequently in human history. Conventional mores, systems and technologies are being challenged by the drag and weight of their own dysfunctions as well as by new mores, systems and technologies that portend potential solutions to the problems caused by the ancient regime.

There can be little doubt that humankind presently is confronted by a host of severe, if not critical, situations – a plague of crises. By way of example: acid rain is killing forests and lakes throughout the Northern hemisphere; gaping holes are being eaten into the ozone layer by manmade chemicals and gasses; a "greenhouse effect" threatens a global warming trend that is the gateway to unimaginable catastrophes; the oceans and aquifers are being polluted at an increasing rate; the global population explosion continues; there are swelling mountains of nuclear waste and toxic wastes with nowhere to put them; rainforests are being depleted and deserts are expanding; incomprehensible sums are expended on military hardware and applications; Third World nations go deeper and deeper into unpayable debt; worldwide drug addiction grows exponentially; and on and on.

All this combined places mounting strain on the biosphere and all polities, taxing their ability to sustain and support human life and commerce as we have known it for centuries. This places vast multitudes of the earth's populace at great risk of their health, safety and survival and in increasingly inflammable conflictual situations, from the interpersonal to the international levels of human interaction.

At the same time, there are new technologies being invented and designed that have some power to alleviate many of these crises. Sadly, though, they are not utilized sufficiently to do so. Existing socioeconomic-political structures appear to be incapable or unwilling to promote their development, deployment and employment and thus to lessen the amount or degree of suffering and/or crises. Nevertheless, a growing number of people, who understand that something drastically different needs to be done urgently, are dedicated to the testing of an experimentation with new social technologies that are capable of ameliorating and coping with these problems if, and only if, they are understood and accepted by large publics and applied universally and massively.

Much of this work is transformational in character. Those involved in such enterprises are conceptualizing ideas and innovating techniques that can help the human race pass through these perilous times into a safer, more peaceful, healthier age. Yet the work they do now is useful under present circumstances even though it is seen as oddball, wrongheaded, utopian, marginal and/or impractical by those who cling to the status quo and are conditioned by the values, habits and perspectives of a failing past.

Unfortunately, the work these people are doing takes so much time to seed and nurture, and the odds against it succeeding in the inhospitable clime of the present are so slim, that persons collaborating transformationally in one area are often unaware of what else is being done in other fields of endeavor as well as the common bonds of principle, and of struggle, that they share with one another.

We have done a great deal of work in the field of conflict resolution and we have been intimately acquainted with the growing pains of two Green organizations in the United States. We have had many close interactions with persons in both areas and have come to realize how little those who toil in conflict resolution know about the Greens, and vice versa. And this despite the fact, as we have noted in this essay, that there are so many crucial points of intersection in their principles and goals.

This essay, then, is our first effort to strengthen the transformational elements in the field of ADR and those in the Green movement by demonstrating to them both that they are not working alone and that, indeed, a parallel movement exists. Each has much to learn from the other's successes and each can take heart in the fact that other good things are happening. The transformational movement is an emerging mosaic. This essay simply draws attention to the numerous attractions between two disengaged parts that need an introduction to each other.

NOTES AND REFERENCES

1. Jerold S. Auerbach, *Justice Without Law?* (Oxford: Oxford University Press, 1983).
2. Brian Tokar, *The Green Alternative: Creating an Ecological Future* (San Pedro: R. & E. Miles, 1987): 123.
3. Christa Daryl Slaton and Theodore L. Becker, "Hawaii's Community Mediation Service: The University-Based Model of Neighborhood Justice Centers," paper presented at the American Psychological Association Convention (Los Angeles, California, 1981).
4. Charlene Spretnak, *The Spiritual Dimension of Green Politics* (Santa Fe: Bear & Co., 1986): 78.
5. *Programme of the German Green Party* (East Haven, Conn.: Long River Books, 1985): 9.

6. Cara Lamb, "Sexism? In the East Bay Greens?," *East Bay Green Alliance*, 4 (4) (1989): 4.
7. Betty Zisk, John Resenbrink and Carla Dickstein, "Staying Alive: Local Green Group Maintenance for the Long Haul," *Green Letter*, 4 (1): j-1.

17 Unanticipated Conflict and the Crisis of Social Theory
Richard E. Rubenstein*

THE UNANTICIPATED CONFLICT

Major episodes of unanticipated social conflict during the past three decades have called attention to the failure of existing social theories to develop an adequate conception of the human individual in society. Without such a theoretical foundation, deep rooted conflict cannot be resolved, and the field of conflict resolution itself becomes the preserve of those interested in settling disputes within the framework of existing power relationships and systemic structures. Basic human needs theory may, if properly developed, provide a basis for practical conflict resolution, as well as a method of freeing the field from the misleading assumptions and outmoded methods of other disciplines. But for conflict resolution to become a method of inducing the changes in institutions and systems necessary to satisfy basic human needs, mass political action will often be necessary.

When the tanks and armored personnel carriers of the People's Liberation Army rolled into Beijing's Tiananmen Square in June 1989 to be confronted by student demonstrators wielding clubs and throwing firebombs, the shock among Westerners was general. Some observers had expected military intervention, but virtually none had recognized that the intention of the students was revolutionary – that many were prepared to kill and be killed to alter the Chinese system of government.

Prior to the uprising, policy makers, media observers, China specialists, and political analysts had generally misinterpreted the student movement, first overestimating its political coherence and commitment to liberal democracy, then underestimating its militancy. Even *post factum*, however, the experts found it virtually impossible

---

* This chapter was written at the request of the editors for the purposes of this collection of essays.

to evaluate the event's significance. Was it merely the first round – the Bloody Sunday, as it were – of a more general social upheaval, or was it a sectoral phenomenon more akin, say, to the "May Events" of 1968 in Paris? What connections existed between the student movement and other sectors of Chinese society? Were workers, soldiers, and farmers on the verge of revolution? If so, what would its political character be? What forces were at work below the surface of the "official" events customarily covered by the Beijing press corps? Months later, scholars, news analysts, and officials were still groping unsuccessfully for answers. Another case of Westerners failing to understand the inscrutable East? Say, rather, another illustration of analysts refusing to recognize the deficiencies of their own theories.

What we expect of theory is that it make sense of the world around us, explaining the connections between apparently disconnected events. Good theory makes nonsense of "common sense," demonstrating that things are often not what they seem. It reevaluates change-over-time, illuminating the connections and disconnections between past and present, and indicating to what extent the present can be projected into the future. It redefines relationships between thought and its objects and between oneself and others. And, of course, it stimulates new thinking. Perhaps prediction is not the ultimate test of social theory, as it may be for "hard science." But we are entitled to demand, at least, that *after* unexpected events take place social theory will be reformulated to explain them and to permit more accurate prediction of future related events.

By none of these criteria, I am sorry to say, does existing social theory succeed in illuminating our understanding of conflict. Only a few works prepare us (and then only fragmentarily) to appreciate the most serious and protracted social conflicts of the past two decades.[1] The significance of the Tiananmen uprising, from this point of view, is that the experts' failure either to anticipate it, to understand its implications while it was occurring, or to make sense of it once it had occurred, is not anomalous.

THE IMPLICATIONS OF UNPREDICTED SOCIAL CONFLICT

The major social conflicts of the post-Vietnam era have come as much as a surprise to academic analysts as to policy makers and media observers. Not one of these conflicts, to my knowledge, has been satisfactorily explained or integrated into a coherent picture of world society. The effects of this theoretical breakdown are far more than theoretical; incomprehension sustains violence. For how can one resolve conflicts non-violently when their root causes, nature, and consequences are so poorly understood? How, indeed, can a party to a conflict evaluate the consequences of its behavior if projections of the probable course of the struggle are purely speculative? I will have more to say about the theoretical requirements for conflict resolution in a moment. Consider, first, the following cases of significant unanticipated conflict.

Communal Violence

The past three decades have witnessed a radical intensification of violent conflict between ethnic, racial, religious, and national groups in virtually every region of the world. Largely unnoticed by the scholarly community, communal violence has become in a relatively short time the leading murderer of the world's peoples. A short list of nations now experiencing serious (i.e., potentially genocidal) communal conflict now includes Sri Lanka, India (Punjab), Afghanistan, Burma, Israel, Lebanon, South Africa, Rwanda–Burundi, Sudan, Ethiopia, Somalia, China (Tibet), Iraq (Kurdistan), the Soviet Union, Yugoslavia, Bulgaria, Spain, Northern Ireland, Guatemala, Peru, the Phillipines, Fiji . . . If the list were expanded to include nations in which serious communal conflict could erupt at almost any time, it would comprise a majority of the world's nations, including the United States.[2] Modernization theory, locating political violence in the transition from "traditional" to "modern" societies, fails to account for the range of societies experiencing or incubating this type of conflict. Capitalist and socialist theories focusing on international or inter-class conflict fail to account for the other dimensions of communal warfare. As a result, there is no theory of communal violence that can command general acceptance or on which those wishing to resolve conflict can rely.

Religious Conflict

The outbreak and course of the Iranian Revolution dramatically illustrates a second major unanticipated conflict: the rise of worldwide strife between the forces of "secular modernism" and "religious fundamentalism." This conflict, so at variance with contemporary social theory, has generated terrorism, state terror, rioting, and revolutionary activity throughout the Islamic world, and is now felt far beyond the boundaries of the Arab and Persian states. Given the "progressivist" premises of liberalism, Marxism, and modernization theory, it was impossible to foresee this development. Who would have anticipated, for example, that the United States would be racked in the 1980s by struggles over abortion rights, pornography, and school prayer; that Polish workers in rebellion would march behind icons of the Black Madonna; or that political conflict in Latin America would be strongly shaped by a theological struggle within the Roman Catholic Church. To some theorists, indeed, the revival of religious strife seems a sort of dangerous anachronism, like the sudden appearance of a prehistoric monster in a modern city: Godzilla, as it were, in Tokyo. But the concept of "throwbacks," long discredited in anthropology, is equally useless to social theory. We are barely beginning to understand the complex of unsatisfied human needs that generate "holy wars" in modern society.

Internal Conflict in Communist States

Equally surprising to the scholarly world was the outbreak of a struggle between "reformers" and "conservatives" that would destabilize virtually every communist nation, unleashing a wave of ethnic, national, and class-based rebellions in the Second World. The coincidence of this conflict with a period of unexpected East–West detente demonstrates that new obsolescence of older forms of conflict and the rise of new forms are opposite sides of the same coin. If one cannot account for conflict, one cannot account for collaboration, either. Most disturbing, from a theoretical perspective, has been the academic analysts' inability to project existing trends even into the mid-term future. Some (one suspects, wishful) thinkers, predicting the bourgeoisification and disintegration of the Soviet and Chinese empires, hail the collapse of socialism as a world-historical movement. Others, anticipating a resurgence of neo-Stalinist "conservatism," anticipate the imminent fall of Gorbachev and Deng Xaioping. Still others consider a controlled "revolution from the top" – a sort of Communist counter-reformation – perfectly feasible, while a minority of analysts predict neo-Leninist or even Trotskyist revolutions *from the left* in the socialist states. These widely divergent scenarios reflecting their creators' own ideological preconceptions indicate, again, the absence of any social theory with a convincing claim to objectivity.

Internal Conflict in Capitalist States

A plague of drug addiction, criminal violence, and (largely ineffective) state repression appeared with little warning in the capitalist states, worsening the already severe conflict between impoverished or minority communities and more powerful groups. In nations that produce narcotic substances (e.g., Colombia, Peru, and Bolivia) the struggle between producers and government authorities frequently takes on the character of civil war, with "narco-terrorism" appearing as a new form of political violence. In consumer nations like the United States, crime related to narcotics distribution and sales has provoked a "war on drugs" that is experienced by minority communities as a war on *them*. The poverty of theory in this case has left the field to advocates and practitioners of state coercion and vigilantism, with ominous implications for the social future in the industrialized nations. In this crisis, academic analysts have for the most part fallen silent – another indication of their lack of confidence in the relevance of theory to the resolution of major social conflicts.

Other Forms of Deep Rooted Conflict

In some cases, unpredicted outbreaks of violent conflict have taken new forms; the "sports violence" now concerning West European societies is a case in point. In others, it is the persistence of older forms of violent conflict that perplexes social theory. Protracted class-based insurgencies (denominated "low intensity" conflicts by those who do not live with them) continue to erupt in diverse locales, baffling analysts who have declared the age of such conflicts to be at an end.[3] Terrorism, still poorly understood, continues as a significant form of violent struggle on virtually every continent. Unexpected outbreaks of spontaneous rioting often related to ethnic, racial and/or economic issues occur in urban areas from Johannesberg to Buenos Aires and from Miami to Amman. Again, without reliable theoretical guides, those who would understand the root causes and nature of these conflicts find themselves compelled to start virtually from scratch.

Most of the struggles described above involve civil violence rather than interstate war, although (as in the Iran–Iraq war) they may spill across national boundaries. In most, the parties are "domestic" groups defined by race, religion, class, or ethnic identity that enter into conflict with or without support from groups outside their nations of residence. In many, the state itself is a party, hence, unable to function as a neutral intervenor. Notwithstanding political theories that predict that humans will be pacified when elections are free and markets unregulated, when the bourgeoisie has been eliminated and property is collectively owned, or when developing nations have been "modernized," the trend towards communal violence transgresses all established theoretical categories. Intergroup warfare appears in industrial, semi-industrial, and agrarian states; in capitalist and communist polities; in imperial centers and in the nations of the periphery. Although we may be horrified, we are no longer surprised to learn that West European soccer matches must be guarded by armed men to prevent bloody outbreaks of communal violence or that black defendants in the United States are far more likely to be executed for murder if the victim is white than if he or she is black.

THE CRISIS OF POLITICAL THEORY

I want to focus briefly on some implications of unpredicted conflict for political theory, although a similar critique could be made of the other disciplines that have attempted to comprehend the causes and nature of conflict. In political theory, the individual citizen or subject is deemed to have two primary politically cognizable interests – freedom and property – whose satisfaction can be guaranteed by a properly designed state system governed by a competent elite.[4] Capitalist theory views individual self-determination in politics and the market as a method ultimately of satisfying property interests. Communist theory sees planned distribution of property as a method ultimately of realizing individual self-determination. But the "individual" of each theory is an unrealized and unrealizable abstraction – a bundle of "rights" and "interests" whose primary political relationship is with the (equally abstract) state.[5]

It is, above all, this poverty of philosophy with respect to the individual that vitiates our understanding of group solidarity and intergroup conflict. Ethnic loyalty, to take just one example, was expected to disappear in advanced capitalist societies with the emergence of the fully socialized but autonomous "economic man" and in socialist societies with the appearance of the class-conscious "communist man." Its non-disappearance suggests the process of political bonding – i.e., the ways in which individuals are gathered into social groups other than the state that mobilize their energies and loyalty – is not yet understood. Rousseau's democratic theory and pre-Stalinist Marxism had the advantage of recognizing fundamental forms of human solidarity prior to the state. But political theory and practice in the age of the "corporate state" bear out Roberto Unger's insight that while liberty and equality became guiding principles in the West and East, respectively, fraternity – for which there was no true basis in social theory – was abandoned.[6]

Note, too, that if one looks to other disciplines to remedy this defect, one will be sorely disappointed. Only a few scholars in sociology, psychology, philosophy, and anthropology (and these generally thought of as "mavericks") have attempted to provide a basis for the understanding of human solidarity. This theoretical blind spot is no oversight; it reflects the overall subservience of scholarship to political authority. Governing elites in every world-system have found the existence of non-state communities (and of individuals motivated to form such communities) inimical to their ambitions. Social thinkers have assisted them, wittingly or not, by declaring such communities to be outside the social contract – theoretical anomalies both in the "individualistic" West and the "classless" East. If they exist, the authorities conclude, this must be because their members are mad, bad, anachronistic, or supported by a foreign power. Repression, either overtly forceful or psychological, is their usual answer. Nevertheless, the urge toward solidarity – even when it takes grotesque and destructive forms – proves irrepressible. Herbert Marcuse is surely correct to consider it a manifestation of our erotic nature, incapable of suppression either by decree or by "conditioning."[7]

THE SEARCH FOR ADEQUATE THEORY: BASIC HUMAN NEEDS

Driven by events to acknowledge this enormous *lacuna* in fundamentally authoritarian social theory, we are now at the beginning of an effort to redefine the political individual in such a way as to account for the manifold forms (and potential forms) of political solidarity. One theoretical initiative that is becoming influential among certain analysts of conflict and conflict resolution is the effort to define the basic needs, shared by all humans, whose non-satisfaction can be counted on to generate destructive behavior (either violent conflict or apathetic withdrawal). Rather than conceiving of people as abstract clusters of conscious interests that can be accommodated through bargaining or suppressed by force, this new theory posits the existence of ontological or organic needs for security, identity, meaning, bonding, and development that humans *will* attempt to satisfy whatever those in authority say or do.[8] The implications of this theory for practical conflict resolution are profound. For if communal conflict is generated by unsatisfied basic needs, the first task must be to develop processes by which they can be identified, the second to imagine alternative methods of satisfying them, and the third to assist the parties in conflict to make the necessary changes, even if they involve serious structural alterations in political and social systems.

These are *not* acknowledged by many theorists and practitioners in the field to be the appropriate tasks of conflict resolution. Some analysts, relying on traditional social theory, view conflict resolution as the theory and practice of power-based negotiation. Others, while recognizing the limitations of that approach, define the field purely in terms of "process," advocating the virtues, say, of mediation over other forms of dispute settlement. But without an adequate theory rooting the most destructive forms of conflict in our evolving nature as individuals-in-society, there can be little hope either of understanding or of resolving them. In fact, an implicit pessimism in this regard colors present practice in the field, limiting it largely to the settlement or "management" of interest-based disputes between parties sharing common legal, moral, or customary norms. Lawyers interested in settling cases, arbitrators rendering court-enforceable judgements, corporate officials mediating interdepartmental disputes, facilitators searching for common ground among competing interest groups, and conciliators searching for methods to avert strikes or riots – all consider themselves practitioners of "conflict resolution." The effect, of course, is to leave the resolution of serious communal conflicts to the parties themselves – and to the relatively small group of scholars and practitioners now searching for a usable theory of *inter-system* conflict.

This "blooming, buzzing confusion" is reflected also in academia where scholars specializing in conflict resolution represent a veritable fruit salad of disciplines, each with its own assumptions and methods: law, sociology, social psychology, political science, anthropology, philosophy, economics, industrial relations, *et al*. The assumption has been that by putting human conflict in the crossbeams of numerous disciplines one can illuminate its nature and enhance the possibilities of resolving it non-violently. Two problems, however, have already become evident. First (to continue the metaphor), many of the beams do not cross; the psychologist who assumes that human beings are innately aggressive and the sociologist operating with a model of an infinitely "socializable" individual are incapable of effective collaboration. Second, even where disciplinary assumptions are congruent, as in the case, say, of political scientists, sociologists, and economists influenced by modernization theory, the beams emitted are far too weak to illuminate their object. If none of the traditional social sciences has produced a theory capable of making sense of deep rooted communal conflict, what makes us think that combining the received truths of several disciplines will do the job?

On the contrary, as John Burton has argued, conflict resolution will either become "a-disciplinary" – that is, an autonomous discipline with its own theoretical base – or it will remain an incoherent hodgepodge of concepts and techniques fated to follow other "inter-disciplinary" fads into obscurity.[9] It is not, of course, that scholarly work in the field is irrelevant to the understanding of deep rooted conflict. The established disciplines (including those that may not at first seem relevant to our inquiry) need to be quarried, but not for established truth so much as for the scattered insights and intuitions that will enable us eventually to construct an adequate picture of the human individual in society. Several disciplines that may prove most useful to this inquiry (e.g., literary criticism, semiotics, heterodox economic theory, biology) are highly unlikely, at present, to be represented in centers for the study of conflict. Nevertheless, those interested in the study of terrorism will understand what I mean when I say that there is more truth about terrorism in André Malraux's novel, *Man's Fate*, than in all the government reports and academic analyses written during the past two decades.[10]

Whether basic human needs theory will provide the necessary theoretical foundation for conflict resolution remains to be seen. In Book 2 in this series (Chapter 16), I have argued that if needs theory becomes merely the latest version of abstract and static "Natural Law" philosophy, it will add little to existing social thought.[11] We need to understand how human needs and their satisfiers reveal themselves over time in connection with continuous changes in the natural environment, in systems of production, and in systems of social meaning. We need also to grasp their emotive basis – i.e., their relationship to the psychological history of the individual and of our species. On the basis of such understanding, it may be possible to identify not only those needs widely recognized as germane to contemporary communal struggles (e.g., identity and recognition), but those realized in the course of on-going social transformation (e.g., the need for gratifying work). This would give us the capacity not only to understand conflicts already inflamed and difficult to resolve but to foresee the development of new forms of conflict that might be resolved or restructured before they became murderous.

CONFLICT RESOLUTION AS A POLITICAL MOVEMENT

The construction of a theory of basic human needs may well be within our powers. But whether such a theory will make the non-violent resolution of conflict possible depends upon the extent to which need-satisfying options can be realized in a world still ruled by office-holding and property-owning elites. John Burton has argued persuasively that, to be truly effective, conflict resolution must be considered a *political system* – not merely an adjunct of the power-based legal system but, ultimately, a transfiguration of it.[12] The question is whether elites wedded to older forms of "dispute settlement" – armed force, law, and psychological manipulation – will allow this to happen before intensified social upheaval or anarchic conflict reaches a point of no return.

Suppose that through an analytical process, warring ethnic groups in a city racked by communal strife were to recognize that their joint and several needs could not be satisfied without massive reconstruction of their city, itself dependent upon a regional or national economic revival. To the extent that relevant elites, represented in the process, could be brought to recognize the increasing costs (and, therefore, the growing unreality) of their power absent such a revival, they could in theory be persuaded to cut their losses by implementing radical change from the top. This, arguably, was precisely Mikhail Gorbachev's motivation for announcing his policy of *perestroika*. But Gorbachev also recognized the necessity for *glasnost*, shorthand for mobilization of a popular movement to struggle politically and socially for realization of his program. Conflict resolution, it seems to me, is no more likely to succeed than *perestroika* without organized popular support for the changes agreed upon by the parties. That is, if it is to become a political system, it must also become a political movement.

There are two reasons for this. First, as Gorbachev discovered, people's basic needs cannot be satisfied unless they are permitted to discover them, consider the options, and press *en masse* for necessary system changes. Second, at least some elements of the elite, if not the dominant elements, are unlikely to recognize the increasing costs of holding power by coercive means until these costs have become painfully evident. Thus, if the warring racial groups in our hypothetical city follow up their vision of a reconstructed economy with organized political action, their chances of realizing need-satisfying changes will be improved. But the matter is complex. Social movements (as both Gorbachev and Deng Xioaping have discovered) have a way of escaping the control even of the elites that sometimes sponsor or "adopt" them. In virtually all cases requiring significant political or social system change, the conclusions of the parties will have to be supported by mass political action. In some cases, at least, conflict resolution may not be possible without a political movement powerful enough to force the necessary changes on an unwilling elite.

NOTES AND REFERENCES

1. Works of unusual prescience include Ted Robert Gurr, *Why Men Rebel* (Princeton: Princeton University Press, 1970); Cynthia Enloe, *Ethnic Conflict and Political Development* (Boston: Little, Brown, 1973); Arend Lijphart, *Democracy in Plural Societies* (New Haven: Yale University Press, 1977); and John W. Burton, *Deviance, Terrorism and War: The Process of Solving Unsolved Social and Political Problems* (New York: St. Martin's Press, 1979).
2. See Barbara Harff and Ted Robert Gurr, "Victims of the State: Genocides, Politicides and Group Repression since 1945," *International Review of Victimology* (1988); Ted Robert Gurr and James Scarritt, "Minorities at Risk; A Global Survey," *Human Rights Quarterly* (November 1988).
3. Such conflicts are now taking place in Guatemala, El Salvador, Peru, Burma, and Philippines. See "Hidden Wars," *The Dallas Morning News* (9 August 1989) Section M.
4. Johan Galtung puts it nicely: "These terms [socialism, capitalism, etc.] all refer to social formation, not to human beings. To assume that human beings *develop* inside them is like assuming that inside a beautiful house there must by necessity be beautiful people." "The Basic Needs Approach," in Katrin Lederer (ed.), with Johan Galtung and David Antal, *Human Needs: A Contribution to the Current Debate* (Cambridge,

MA: Oelgeschlager, Gunn & Hain, 1980).
5. The point is elegantly explored in E. Pashukanis, "Law and Marxism," in Lord Lloyd of Hampstead, *Lloyd's Introduction to Jurisprudence* (Oxford: Oxford University Press, 1980): 1073 et seq.
6. Roberto M. Unger, *The Critical Legal Studies Movement* (Cambridge, MA: Harvard University Press, 1986).
7. Herbert Marcuse, *Eros and Civilization* (Boston: Beacon Press, 1966).
8. John W. Burton, *Deviance, Terrorism*. See also his *Dear Survivors* (London: Frances Pinter, and Boulder, CO: Westview Press, 1982); Katrin Lederer (ed.) *Human Needs*; Roger A. Coate and Jerel A. Rosati (eds), *The Power of Human Needs in World Society* (Boulder, CO: Lynne Rienner, 1988).
9. John W. Burton, "Conflict Resolution as a Political System," Working Paper, 1, Center for Conflict Analysis and Resolution, George Mason University (1988).
10. André Malraux, *Man's Fate* (New York: Modern Library, 1936) discussed in Richard E. Rubenstein, *Alchemists of Revolution: Terrorism in the Modern World* (New York: Basic Books, 1987): 11–12, 96.
11. "Human Needs Theory: Beyond Natural Law," Chapter 16 in John W. Burton (ed.), *Conflict: Human Needs Theory* (London: Macmillan; New York: St. Martin's Press, 1990).
12. Burton, "Conflict Resolution as a Political System."

18 Unfinished Business in Conflict Resolution
John Burton*

THE THEORY OF CONFLICT RESOLUTION

The general thesis of "analytical problem-solving facilitated conflict resolution" is that parties to a conflict are able to find agreed options or means by which to cooperate in achieving their goals once they have made a complete analysis of the problems in their relationships. Such an analysis includes perceiving accurately the depths of feelings and the frustrations experienced by each other, and the extent to which apparently hostile behaviors are the consequence of environmental constraints.

Underlying this general thesis (which we explain more later) is a theoretical assumption that parties to conflicts have shared goals – that is, the pursuit of human needs common to all, and that it is means or satisfiers that are in dispute. The shared goals, such as identity and recognition, are not in short supply. There is, therefore, no call for compromise in their pursuit. The problem is to find appropriate means, for it is they which are in short supply. Security is a goal for everyone, and the more one person has the more security others will enjoy. But the means to security limit the possibilities of it being shared.

In cases in which the persons involved in the facilitated process are themselves the parties to the conflict – for example, in matrimonial, industrial and local community relations, and in cases in which the conflict is confined to clearly identified parties, as for example two governments not affected by any outside influences – this is a process that can be expected to lead to agreements and the resolution of the conflicts. Nothing more is involved than ordinary negotiation or mediation except that the process is deeply analytical, seeking to get to the source of the problem and to find ways of dealing with it. It is not a bargaining process, however, nor one in which compromise on important values and needs is sought. It is the process of discovering

* This chapter was written for the purposes of this collection.

viable options – means.

When, however, there are complex and protracted conflicts involving many parties and power groupings, additional critical assumptions come to the surface making the process quite different from
negotiation and mediation. Because it touches on sources of the
conflict and, therefore, the total social environment, the process is
likely to point to the need for radical changes in social and political
institutions and policies. This is even more the case when we move
from the resolution of a particular conflict situation to the resolution
of complex public policy problems that give rise to conflicts, for
example, problems of poverty, drugs, gang warfare and other
symptoms of social alienation. These problems must be dealt with if
specific cases of social violence and conflict are to be avoided or
resolved.

Let us first take an example of a specific complex conflict before
moving on to wider social-political problems.

Both sides in the Israeli–Palestine dispute seek the same goals,
that is their security, separate identity and autonomy. At the same
time they both value collaborative and functional interactions between
them. The Palestinians argue that such relationships could have
developed had there been one pluralistic state of Palestine. For
the Israelis, while such interactions are valued, the realities of identity
within any representative system, and the physical realities of the
territories in relation to population increases and migrations, impose
constraints on any collaborative activities between peoples of different
religion and culture. Certainly experience is that such constraints in
practice lead to conflict behaviors for which neither side can be held
responsible.

Conflict resolution assumes that given a full understanding of the
shared goals, and an appreciation of the environmental constraints,
the two parties would arrive at realistic means, such as separation
with functional cooperation in some form or other, or perhaps
something far more imaginative, to resolve their conflict rather than
endure its ongoing and escalating costs.

Behind this general and theoretical statement of the purposes of
problem-solving conflict resolution as applied to such a situation,
there are, therefore, many assumptions that have an optimistic ring,
especially assumptions implying a party's willingness not to employ
superior military power when it is available. Such seemingly unrealistic
assumptions do not necessarily invalidate the process. They do,
however, pose further problems to be resolved and take the process

of problem-solving conflict resolution into the practical field of power politics.

THE ASSUMPTION THAT POWER CAN BE MADE IRRELEVANT

Let us examine the major assumption that relative power becomes irrelevant in a problem-solving situation. Typically one party to a conflict has more "power" – that is, control of more resources, more knowledge, advantageous roles or other assets not possessed by the other party. Conflict resolution theory assumes that this more powerful party will be prepared, despite its position of relative power, indeed will have no rational option, but to give up its power advantage. This is because it will find when deep rooted frustrations have been articulated by the weaker party that the conflict will be protracted, despite relative weakness, and that the longer-term costs will be unacceptable in the absence of an agreement. For example, when there is an ethnicity conflict within a nation, the majority or more powerful status quo authority, facing persistent and escalating ethnic uprisings, will be prepared to share power, and meet the demands for greater autonomy made by the minority rather than face the costs of further economic and political disruption. Taking a specific case, the assumption would be that the white minority in South Africa, when it fully costs the consequences of its policies, would be prepared to give up its dominant role and seek some new relationship that gave to the majority the autonomy and identity which the whites themselves seek to preserve along with their just share of responsibilities and resources.

This would be the rational response if the representatives of the more powerful party – the white population of South Africa, or the Israelis, in our other example – were prepared to look several decades ahead in their costing. Typically authorities, as was the case in Cyprus, Sri Lanka, Northern Ireland and elsewhere, do not take a long-term view. They are prepared to seek solutions only when the conflict has "ripened," and unacceptable costs – that could have been predicted – are experienced.

THE ASSUMPTION THAT ROLE DEFENSE CAN BE ELIMINATED

There is a second and related assumption that helps to explain this non-rational short-term behavior on the part of the more powerful party, and this is the assumption that political leaders reflect the interests of those whom they represent. When we look closely at political systems of any kind, we find that this is rarely the case. They are more likely to reflect their own personal role interests, and the interests of those pressure groups on which they depend to maintain their role positions.

One has only to look at the institutions of the parliaments and congresses of the more developed and stable Western systems to find confirmation of this. Gross corruption associated with role seeking and role maintenance is obvious. Pressure groups have more influence than the electorate, at least once elections have taken place, but also often in the election process. This is even more the case where elites are faced with class and ethnicity issues.

The ripening process – that is, the gradual escalation of conflict and its costs as role defense is pursued – is a consequence of resistance to change, but it also has its own escalating consequences. Typically a protracted conflict is characterized by divisions within the parties involved, especially conflicts over leadership which make any negotiation or problem-solving even more difficult. There are contending factions within the Israeli, Palestinian, white and black South African communities and Northern Ireland parties. Secondly, as a conflict becomes more costly there are external interventions, perhaps sanctions, perhaps assistance to one party, that further escalate the conflict, making it indefinitely protracted.

VALUE CONSIDERATIONS: REPRESENTATIVE GOVERNMENT IS THE MOST RESPONSIBLE

There is a third assumption in conflict resolution that can make it controversial: that the process should not reflect "values." The only value that is relevant in the conflict resolution process is the value attached to resolving conflict. Values such as "justice," "democracy," "the social good," however, emerge out of the interaction. What is just or unjust cannot be determined by precedents or personal and consensus beliefs. The only basis on which justice or any other value concept can be assessed is in relation to needs fulfillment. That which is just, democratic or the social good is that which promotes needs fulfillment.

This leads us into social-political problems that are the source of conflict generally, as distinct from a particular conflict. (Conflict resolution is too narrowly defined to be useful if it is limited to particular conflicts and does not include resolution of the problems that give rise to conflicts.) A good example of a wider problem that has to be taken into account in dealing with a particular conflict is in relation to majority government as a means of justice. Collaborative problem-solving techniques were developed within politically representative systems, and they are based on an assumption that people know what is best for themselves. In complex situations this is unlikely. Those following these processes tend to assume that democratic decision making is more likely to reflect the general interest than does leadership or authoritative decision making. But it has to be recognized that democratic decision making is usually, if not always, based on the interests, values and needs of a ruling elite. Even in the most "democratic" of societies, political representatives typically are elected by about a quarter of the total electorate, that is, 51 per cent of those voting in conditions in which some 50 per cent of the total electorate does not vote because of apathy or trouble with registration.

Conflict resolution processes do not make this assumption of "democracy." Indeed, included in the third-party role is the duty to point out to parties the possible consequences of the options they select – for example, the way in which their agreement could run counter to the wider social interest and thus be dysfunctional in the long term. The role of the third party is to help parties in conflict to focus on the fulfilment of human needs, in the present and particularly in the long term, as the fundamental norm. All other "values," such as majority decision making, are subordinate.

Putting the fulfillment of human needs before notions of "justice" and "freedoms," and before constitutional ideals such as "democracy," is challenging, especially in Western-type political systems. It does, however, direct attention to a phenomenon that is far more important politically than such political notions. It directs attention to the notion of legitimization, meaning authority that is derived from those over whom it is exercised. It is possible for legal authorities, even authorities elected within some form of popular vote, to lack a legitimized status. It is also possible for self-appointed dictators to acquire a legitimized status, which frequently occurs after a revolution that removes a non-legitimized authority from office. The satisfaction of human needs and legitimization are closely tied: legitimization is the consequence of needs satisfaction.

Within this framework the actions of the Chinese communist government in 1989 in suppressing student riots takes on another perspective. This was a leadership that had led the electorate out of a repressive system, through a revolutionary situation, only to be faced by an emerging elite that could well represent only a small minority, as did the elite which was previously eliminated by revolution. It was for this reason that Chi-Chen Wang of Columbia University argued during the 1989 Chinese crisis that "Chinese Hardliners Did the Right Thing" (*New York Times*, 14 June 1989). If there were to be facilitated conflict resolution in such a situation the norm would not be the Western measures of democracy, a free press, freedom of expression and such norms that play into the hands of an elite in such developing countries. They would be the norm of needs fulfillment, which would require searching examinations of quality of life and opportunities of development of peoples generally, within the resource constraints of the economy, alongside the demands by protesters, largely students, for the pursuit of special interests.

Such an examination would also be the way in which a conflict resolution process within a Western democracy would be conducted, revealing elite interests that did not take into account the identity, job, housing and related needs of minorities. In short, the conflict resolution process is an analytical one, designed to reveal the sources of conflict, and designed, therefore, to be value neutral, except for a value attached to the resolution of the conflict which itself implies a value attached to human needs satisfaction.

IDEALISM, COSTING AND POLITICAL REALITIES

The question arises whether these three assumptions – power is irrelevant, role behaviors can be suppressed, and there can be value-free analysis – have any practical validity.

Within a traditional power political framework clearly power dominates, role defense is a major concern, and elite and traditional values are the accepted norms. The underlying question is whether problems arising out of political structures and institutions can be dealt with by means other than revolution. Revolutions have taken place without achieving the sought-for new state. Can the gradual application of analytical conflict resolution processes develop a consensus shift from power to problem-solving?

WHERE DO WE GO FROM HERE?

The answer to this question is in the arena of political realities, in the "ripening" effect and in costing. Universally, authorities at all societal levels are becoming less rather than more legitimized – that is, they are attracting less and less respect and support. In the most developed of countries there are increasing gaps between rich and poor, decreasing social incomes (health, education and necessary social support), class–ethnic conflicts, street violence, drug and other alienation problems, environmental problems and greater pressures in the maintenance of even existing living standards. These trends cannot continue without major social disruptions. When they occur what will be the change processes?

Such conditions are likely to lead to more determined attempts by individuals and groups to secure their needs. These can take two forms. One is the mafia-type protection of interests, promoting movements away from cultural and legal norms toward individual and group interests. The other is the formation of community-based organizations that may or may not take into account the interests and values of the wider society.

In both cases the power of human needs will be decisive. Identity and autonomy will prevail, even though the means to achieve them may be the use of lethal weapons by persons who have been excluded from the wider society and its opportunities for individual development, or the break-up of societies into separate enclaves.

Many situations will grow ripe for some form of intervention, probably military intervention, to regain control. This has already happened in many developing countries. This is not a solution to the problem, merely an intervention to prevent violence and further economic disruption.

A QUESTION OF CONSENSUS

These observations are made to point to the unfinished business of conflict resolution. It provides a process that has proved successful in many specific situations of conflict. It is a process, however, that will be resisted by authorities when applied to the public sector – for example, the sources of the drug and the street gang problems. The analysis and costing that takes place within the process would suggest the need for some far-reaching changes that would adversely affect privileges and roles in the short term.

One must conclude that problem-solving conflict resolution requires an altered public consensus before it is applicable in the wider area of political change. It requires a widespread understanding of the process and acceptance of it as a norm. It requires a consensus paradigm shift from power politics to problem-solving.

This is a shift that can come about only as a result of experience and of education. The more problem-solving conflict resolution is pursued in particular cases at all societal levels, the more the process becomes accepted and known, the more likely it is that a consensus will require it to be used at political levels. Backed by education in problem solving it could become a consensus and a norm.

Do we have time?

Annotated Bibliography

Abel, Richard L. (ed.) (1982) *The Politics of Informal Justice*, New York: Academic Press.

Abel and his fellow contributors present their critiques of the expansion of informal state control inherent in new forms of informal justice, including the Neighborhood Justice (ADR, Community Mediation) movement. Volume One presents *The American Experience*. Volume Two, *Comparative Studies*, examines dispute resolution in other societies.

Arendt, Hannah (1969) *On Violence*, New York: Harcourt, Brace & World.

On Violence, a very brief book, serves well as an introduction to the work of Arendt, who devoted her life to writing of the sources of problems of the human condition. Her willingness to question standard beliefs, combined with her thoughtfulness, produces uncommon insights in a comprehensible form.

Argyris, Chris (1983) *Reasoning, Learning, and Action: Individual and Organization*, San Francisco: Jossey-Bass.

Argyris, long one of the leaders in organizational development theory and practice, intends this book as an aid to the practitioner and researcher faced with the kinds of problems requiring changes in values, policies, and practices. He contrasts "single loop" with "double loop" problem-solving, the first dealing with problems at their manifestation, the latter at their source. "Double loop" problem-solving involves questioning the framework in which the problem presents itself.

Argyris questions the assumption that behavior at different social levels requires different causal theories for each level, asserting instead that individual reasoning underlies much of the activity at each level.

Much of this book is based on case studies, with examples drawn from his work in organizational development.

Arkes, Hal R., and Kenneth R. Hammond (eds) (1986) *Judgment and Decision Making*, Cambridge: Cambridge University Press.

This is an eclectic collection of essays from American, British, Swedish, Swiss, German, and Australian scientists working in settings ranging from private corporations to hospitals and universities. Intended by the editors to be an interdisciplinary introduction to the non-specialist reader, it requires only an elementary understanding of algebra and statistics. The volume contains some 43 chapters, which are organized in terms of nine areas of application: social policy, economics, law, interpersonal conflict, clinical judgement in medicine and psychology, social prediction and judgement, experts, development and learning, and research techniques.

336

Ayres, Robert U. (1979) *Uncertain Futures: Challenges for Decision-Makers*, New York: John Wiley.

Ayres' wide-ranging work is an introduction to the art and science of applied forecasting, with a focus of global issues such as food production, health care, transportation, and conflict. He devotes a single chapter to the methodology of forecasting, including the problems that forecasters face. Among the many subjects covered are the dynamics of change, indeterminacy, the role of crisis, and self-limiting or self-accelerating systems. He stresses the importance of social issues that determine how technology, which prescribes only the limits of achievement, is to be used.

Ayres contrasts the diversity of his approach with the narrower approaches of three groups of forecasters: the humanists, concerned mostly with socio-political factors; the quantitative modelers, who concentrate on demographics/economics; and a third group that focusses on scientific and technological prospects.

Banks, Michael (ed.) (1984) *Conflict in World Society; A new Perspective on International Relations*, New York: St Martin's Press.

This is a collection of fourteen essays whose common focus is the work of John Burton. Its theme is the analysis of a paradigm shift in international relations, based on the recognition of universal human needs, and on the apparent decreasing legitimization of monolithic states as the interface for foreign affairs.

Baybrooke, David (1987) *Meeting Needs*. Princeton: Princeton University Press.

This volume complements that of Thompson as a philosophical examination of human needs. Baybrooke argues the place of needs beside and above other ethical standards used for determining social policies and social systems.

Bennis, Warren G., Kenneth D. Benne and Robert Chin (eds) (1985) *The Planning of Change*, New York: Holt, Rinehart & Winston (original, 1961).

This is the fourth edition of this popular book. The editors see themselves in pursuit of two tasks. The first, an intellectual challenge, is a search for a theory of practice: "to develop an adequate theory of the processes through which knowledge of human behavior and of human systems is applied and utilized." The second task is the practical and moral challenge involved in the development of social technologies appropriate for the requirements of contemporary change situations. The emphasis throughout is on organizations, although individual and societal change are by no means ignored. This emphasis reflects both the editors' backgrounds and the fact that most research on change has occurred in organizational settings.

The volume is divided into four main sections with 34 contributions. The first section, "Planned Change in Perspective," reviews different conceptions, theoretical and practical, of change, both planned and otherwise. The second section, "Diagnostics of Planned Change," includes a chapter about systems.

The Third, "Interventions for Planned Change," by far the longest section, includes a chapter of six articles on planning structures and processes. The final section is titled "Values and Goals."

Berman, Maureen R. and Joseph E. Johnson (eds) (1977) *Unofficial Diplomats*, New York: Columbia University Press.

This compilation examines a range of activities in the international arena, from meetings such as the Dartmouth Conferences, to Quaker conciliation, to problem-solving conflict resolution workshops.

Bermant, Gordon, Herbert C. Kelman and Donald P. Warwick (eds) (1978) *The Ethics of Social Intervention*, Washington, D.C.: Hemisphere Publishing.

The many contributors to this unique volume consider the ethical dimensions of the goals, means, and consequences of several kinds of social intervention.

Blake, Robert R., Herbert A. Shepard and Jane S. Mouton (1964) *Managing Intergroup Conflict in Industry*, Houston: Gulf Publishing.

This volume represents the first attempts systematically to replace win-lose, power bargaining methods with problem-solving approaches to intergroup conflict.

Bok, Sissela (1989) *A Strategy for Peace: Human Values and the Threat of War*, New York: Pantheon Books.

Bok's work is representative of an emerging theme of world society: that, in order to ensure peace and global survival, individuals and nations must share and honor certain basic moral principles. She uses the philosophy of Kant and Clausewitz, as well as others, to develop her suggested moral framework, along with a strategy for implementation.

Boulding, Kenneth E. (1985) *Human Betterment*, Beverly Hills, California: Sage Publications.

This general philosophical work provides Boulding's wide ranging insights into the relationship between society and human wellbeing. Included are chapters on the nature of significant change, the development of decision making skills, and the development of justice and freedom.

Box, Steven (1981) *Deviance, Reality and Society*, London: Holt, Rinehart & Winston (original, 1971).

Box questions the morality of legal codes and their enforcement processes. He suggests the importance of relationship as a means of social control.

Burton, John W. (1987) *World Society*. Lanham, Maryland: University Press of America (reprint of 1972 edition).

This volume is intended to introduce students and interested lay people to the study of international relations, or world society.

Burton, John W. (1979) *Deviance, Terrorism and War: The Process of Solving Unsolved Social and Political Problems*, New York: St. Martin's Press.

Burton attacks conventional thinking as it is applied to serious social problems. He suggests that most such thinking can be categorized as "puzzle-solving," where the solutions fit within pre-established categories. "Problem-solving," by contrast, means questioning underlying assumptions about these problems. He proposes that the source of problems such as those in the book's title lies in the failure of institutions to meet the needs of individuals.

Burton, John W. (1984) *Global Conflict: The Domestic Sources of International Crisis*, Brighton, England: Wheatsheaf Books.

Burton addresses domestic political problems and how these problems influence international relations. He suggests the failure of domestic and international political institutions to recognize and adapt to the reality of individual needs.

Carpenter, Susan L. and W. J. D. Kennedy (1988) *Managing Public Disputes: A Practical Guide to Handling Conflict and Reaching Agreements*, San Francisco: Jossey-Bass.

This volume complements both Moore and Folberg and Taylor. The authors, who are experienced mediators of public policy disputes, prescribe strategies and tactics for designing and implementing consensual, problem-solving conflict management practices.

Clark, Mary E. (1989) *Ariadne's Thread: The Search for New Modes of Thinking*, New York: St Martin's Press.

Clark spells out the problems inherent in continued destructive growth, finding their source in a recently developed Western world view that threatens to destroy our planet. She suggests the importance of rethinking our problems and how we deal with them.

Coate, Roger A. and Jerel A. Rosati (1988) *The Power of Human Needs in World Society*. Boulder, CO: Lynne Rienner.

The editors suggest the importance of human needs as a powerful explanation of human behavior in international relations. They support the contention that societies and social structures which are unresponsive to human needs become unstable over time. Their volume concludes with a self-critical analysis of the problems involved in a human needs approach. Contributors include Chadwick F. Alger, John Burton, James C. Davies, and Johan Galtung.

Coser, Lewis (1967)   *Continuities in the Study of Social Conflict*, New York: The Free Press.

This volume, by one of the leaders of the post-Second World War generation of social conflict theorists, is a collection of papers intended to develop the concepts Coser presented in the previous two decades.

Dahrendorf, Ralf (1959)   *Class and Class Conflict in Industrial Society*, Stanford, CA: Stanford Press.

Dahrendorf remolds Marx's conception of class conflict to include all types of conflicting groups responding to the interest of individuals. These groups develop in response to the social structure itself, and conflicts that arise then modify existing values and institutions. He explores the nature of authority and its relationship to groups in conflict, the functions of conflict within the social-political structure, and responses to conflict.

Davies, James Chowning (ed.) (1971)   *When Men Revolt and Why: A Reader in Political Violence and Revolution*, New York: Free Press.

This collection of essays suggests that people revolt as a consequence of frustration. According to Davies, revolutions are most likely to occur when a prolonged period of objective economic and social development is followed by a period of sharp reversal. The various contributions and Davies' introductory notes provide descriptions of revolutions worldwide in the last 400 years, as well as existing theory about the social and psychological roots of revolution. Included are selections by such as Aristotle, Engels, and de Tocqueville.

De Bono, Edward (1967)   *New Think*, New York: Basic Books.

This is one of the first general analyses of the difficulties caused by the ways problems are conceived and analysed. De Bono suggests how the rigidity of symbols and classifications leads to impoverished thinking.

De Reuck, Anthony, and Julie Knight (eds) (1966)   *Conflict in Society*, London: J. and A. Churchill.

This volume, although not readily available, does present an interesting historical perspective. It brings together many of the early main contributors to the field including Boulding, Burton, Deutsch, Lasswell, and Rapaport.

Dedring, Juergen (1976)   *Recent Advances in Peace and Conflict Research*, vol. 27, Sage Library of Social Research, Beverly Hills, California: Sage Publications.

This volume contains brief critiques of various conflict theorists and analyses of peace and order systems. An extensive bibliography by an international array of contributors is included.

Deutsch, Morton (1973) *The Resolution of Conflict: Constructive and Destructive Processes*, New Haven, Conn.: Yale University Press.

This volume is a sampling of essays and research performed by Deutsch and his students. The first section, "Theoretical Essays," contains his thoughts about matters such as cooperative and competitive processes and the roles of threats, promises, and influences on behavior. The second part, "Research Papers," contains descriptions of experimental studies and their results. He concludes with an essay entitled "Factors Influencing the Resolution of Conflict."

This work has probably had its greatest impact not as a result of any specific findings or propositions but through the conceptualization of a continuum of cooperative and competitive behavior and their association with destructive and constructive processes.

Doob, Leonard (1981) *The Pursuit of Peace*, Westport, Conn.: Greenwood Press.

This is an eclectic reflection of a life of intense and thoughtful observation. Doob analyzes third-party roles and qualifications, as well as his and others' attempts at problem-solving workshops.

Duke, James T. (1976) *Conflict and Power in Social Life*, Provo, Utah: Brigham Young University Press.

Duke, a sociologist, surveys the major contributions to conflict theory by theorists such as Marx, Weber, and Mills.

Eisler, Riane (1987) *The Chalice and the Blade: Our History, Our Future*, San Francisco: Harper & Row.

Eisler posits the thesis that many of our world's problems, such as chronic war, social injustice, and ecological imbalance, directly result from the dominance of patriarchical order. This order is violent, hierarchic, and male dominated. She suggests that myths of a time when women and men lived in partnership, legends from many different societies, are not myths at all, or at least are not only myths; they are based in fact.

Eisler postulates two models of society. The first, the "dominator" model, is either patriarchical or matriarchical. The second is the "partnership" model, in which diversity is seen neither as inferior or superior. In the prehistory of Western civilization, the cultural evolution of those societies that worshiped the life-generating and nurturing – the chalice – was invaded by those who worshiped the power of dominantion – the blade. It is not masculinity as such that is the problem, but the equating of masculinity with domination and violence, just as it is not technology that endangers us, but the emphasis on the technology of destruction.

Etzioni, Amitai, and Eva Etzioni (eds) (1964) *Social Change: Sources, Patterns and Consequences*, New York: Basic Books.

51 essays provide a wealth of information from classical theories about the

sources of social change to descriptions of patterns and processes of change. Contributors range from Spencer and Comte to Marx and Weber, from Lewin and Brinton to Drucker and Smelser.

Feyerabend, Paul (1988)   *Against Method*, New York: Verso (original 1975).

Feyerabend is a controversial thinker who turns conventional science on its head. He is not so much against method as he is against the belief that there is any one method or set of methods called "science." Among his many conclusions is the suggestion that science progresses not in the acceptance of plausible theories but in the production of new hypotheses that contradict these established theories.

Fitzgerald, Ross (ed.) (1977)   *Human Needs and Politics*, Australia: Pergamon Press.

This is a collection of essays from a varied group of social critics. Fitzgerald sees the resurgence of interest in human needs as a reaction against the value-free or value-neutral approach of social science. Contributors include Christian Bay, James Davies, and C. B. MacPherson.

Folberg, Jay, and Alison Taylor (1984)   *Mediation: A Comprehensive Guide to Resolving Conflicts Without Litigation*, San Francisco: Jossey-Bass.

Like Christopher Moore, Folberg and Taylor intend this volume as a review of practical strategies and tactics for a mediation process. They suggest the application for numerous types of disputes, including family, community, education, environment, and workplace. Topics range from the stages of mediation, to methods for enhancing communication, to considerations in setting up a mediation service. The appendix includes a code of conduct and a resource list of professional organizations.

Forti, Augusto, and Paolo Bisogno (eds) (1981)   *Research and Human Needs*, Oxford: Pergamon Press.

The 15 contributions to this volume deal with how research on human needs can provide answers to pressing contemporary problems, and how these answers may then be used by decision makers. The content of these contributions varies in tone from normative demands for the right to have needs satisfied to descriptions of applied research projects. Several lists of needs are identified and reviewed.

Included is a chapter describing a possible interdisciplinary course on science and needs. An annotated bibliography of books and papers concludes the book.

Friedmann, John (1987)   *Planning in the Public Domain: From Knowledge to Action*, Princeton: Princeton University Press.

This lengthy tome provides an introduction to the major traditions of planning thought. Examination of problems with the current system of industrial capitalism prepares for a critique of current planning practice and a call for a radical theory and practice of planning. The goals of this new practice are those of mutual learning, self-reliance, and empowerment. A lengthy bibliography is included.

Fromm, Erich (1955) *The Sane Society*, New York: Holt, Rinehart & Winston.

Fromm is representative of the post-Second World War tradition of humanistic thinkers which includes Allport, Bronowski, and Maslow. In this volume he suggests that the sane society is that which "corresponds to the needs of man." Mental health is defined, not in terms of individual adjustment to society, but in society's adjustment to individuals.

Galtung, Johan, *Essays in Peace Research* (1975–1980) Copenhagen: Christian Ejlers.

Galtung's prolific contributions to peace research are contained in this five-volume set. The titles of the volumes are, respectively: *Peace: Research, Education, Action*; *Peace, War and Defence*; *Peace and Social Structure*; *Peace and World Structure*; and *Peace Problems: Some Case Studies*.

Goldberg, Stephen B., Eric G. Green and Frank E. A. Sander (eds) (1985) *Dispute Resolution*, Boston: Little, Brown & Co.

Intended as a text for law students, this volume contains a collection of articles and excerpts from a variety of contributors concerning the dimensions of the "Alternative Dispute Resolution" (ADR) movement including its sources, promises, and problems.

Gulliver, P. H. (1979) *Disputes and Negotiations: a Cross-Cultural Perspective*, Orlando, Florida: Academic Press.

Gulliver models various processes of negotiation and finds similar patterns of behavior in negotiations across cultures and irrespective of context and issues. He critiques the work of bargaining and game theorists as well as other decision making theorists. He finds that much of the work oversimplifies real life situations and makes unrealistic assumptions. Gulliver suggests the formation of hypotheses generated by theory and the use of empirical analysis to validate or invalidate them.

Gurr, Ted Robert (1970) *Why Men Rebel*, Princeton: Princeton University Press.

The concept of relative deprivation is suggested as an indicator of the potential of violent protest. Sociological constraints against violence, such as legitimacy of institutions, tradition, and culture, are analyzed.

Gurr, Ted Robert (ed.) (1989) *Violence in America*, Beverly Hills, California: Sage Publications.

Volume One of this two-volume set, *The History of Crime*, presents a wealth of data on the long-term dynamics of murder and other crimes of violence. Causes discussed are waves of migrations, social dislocations due to wars, and a growing concentration of urban poverty.

The second volume, *Protest, Rebellion, Reform*, concentrates more on steps taken to deal with violence, and suggests some progress being made on criminal justice policies.

Halpern, Diane F. (1984) *Thought and Knowledge: An Introduction to Critical Thinking*, Hillsdale, N.J.: Lawrence Erlbaum Associates.

Halpern's stated purpose is to apply the knowledge of cognitive psychology to the development of critical thinking skills, thus distinguishing knowledge and thinking from the mere accumulation of facts. The theme of the book is represented by a quote from Bertrand Russell in the introduction: "Many people would rather die than think. In fact they do." Halpern analyzes how people think about problems, why they think these ways, and practical means of overcoming obstacles to effective problem solving.

The volume is written as a textbook, with summaries, exercises, and recommended readings following each chapter, and a glossary at the end. Among the 11 chapters are those titled "Understanding Probabilities," which is an introduction to empirical research; "Development of Problem Solving Skills," "Decision Making," and "Application of Critical Thinking Skills."

Haworth, Lawrence (1986) *Autonomy: An Essay in Philosophical Psychology and Ethics*, New Haven: Yale University Press.

Haworth draws upon the disciplines of psychology and philosophy to propose a conception of individual autonomy that encompasses procedural independence, self-control, and competence.

Himes, Joseph S. (1980) *Conflict and Conflict Management*, Athens, Georgia: University of Georgia Press.

Himes presents a sociological analysis of conflict. Topics include theories of conflict, the organization of power, the functions of violence, prediction, and prevention. Comprehensive references give special emphasis to early writings.

Horowitz, Donald L. (1985) *Ethnic Groups in Conflict*, Berkeley and Los Angeles, California: University of California Press.

Horowitz presents a comprehensive study of ethnic conflict and the means by which it is regulated. By examining case after case in country after country, he convincingly demonstrates the central importance of ethnicity in politics.

Johnson, Chalmers (1982) *Revolutionary Change*, Stanford, California: Stanford University Press (original, 1966).

Although Johnson claims this as only an essay in conceptual clarification, the concepts being "revolutionary situation," "revolutionary action," and "revolutionary change," he in fact presents a study of the conditions and consequences attendant to political revolutions. Other theories of revolution are critiqued.

Kahneman, Daniel, Paul Slovic and Amos Tversky (eds) (1982) *Judgment Under Uncertainty: Heuristics and Biases*, Cambridge: Cambridge University Press.

The editors present a large sampling of the research about judgemental heuristics, focussing specifically on the judgement (or, more accurately, the misjudgement) aspect of decision making, rather than choice. Other titles for the book could have been On What Bases do People make Judgements? or, Why, How, and When do People Make Errors of Judgement? or, Is There a Method to Mistakes? The volume contains some 35 contributions arranged in 10 sections, including "Causality and Attribution," "Overconfidence," and "Corrective Procedures."

Kainz, Howard P. (ed.) (1987) *Philosophical Perspectives on Peace: An Anthology of Classical and Modern Sources*, London: Macmillan.

Kainz presents classical writings about how the world might achieve and sustain peace. The variety of ideas is reflected in the titles of each chapter: centralized world government, international federation, distributive justice, religious or spiritual values, and the sublimation or deflection of aggression. Authors include Aristotle, Rousseau, Kant, Rawls, Tolstoy, Teilhard de Chardin, and Freud. Notably absent is any reference to the active resolution of conflict.

Kriesberg, Louis (1982) *Social Conflicts*, Englewood Cliffs, N.J.: Prentice-Hall, (first published in 1973 as *The Sociology of Social Conflicts*).

Kriesberg explores the stages of interaction between conflicting groups including the sources of conflict, the emergence of conflict, escalation and de-escalation, and outcomes.

Kriesberg, Louis (ed.) (1978–present) *Research in Social Movements, Conflicts and Change: An Annual Compilation of Research*, Greenwich, Conn.: JAI Press.

This is a nearly-annual collection of articles presented by a variety of contributors with occasional guest editors.

Kuhn, Thomas S. (1970) *The Structure of Scientific Revolutions*, Chicago: University of Chicago Press (original, 1962).

Kuhn's famous and influential work examines the development of knowledge through various stages: study within an existing paradigm (normal science), the discovery of anomalies, crisis, transition, new paradigm, and, once again, normal science.

Lederer, Katrin, with Johan Galtung and David Antal (1980) *Human Needs: A Contribution to the Current Debate.* Cambridge, MA: Oelgeschlager, Gunn & Hain.

This is the report of a conference, sponsored by the United Nations in Berlin in 1978, about human needs theory and its implications for Third World development. In parts One and Two, the authors debate subjective and objective approaches to the definition of human needs. Parts Three and Four discuss human needs theory in application: in political systems, environmental problems, communications and decision making.

Light, Margot, and A. J. R. Groom (eds) (1985) *International Relations: A Handbook of Current Theory,* London: Frances Pinter.

This is a collection of 15 essays that presents a synopsis of international relations theory and comprehensive reference listings of other contemporary thought on the subject.

Mandel, Robert (1979) *Perception, Decision Making and Conflict,* Washington, D.C.: University Press of America.

Mandel suggests that the processes and patterns of perception, decision making, and conflict are "extraordinarily" important in relations at all social levels but that usually each of these three areas is studied separately, at one level of analysis and within one discipline. He attempts to link perception, decision making and conflict in a manner "beyond mere synthesis," such that the resulting theoretical model can be applied to interpersonal, intergroup, and international relations.

Mandel targets the volume both to those interested in theory building and to policy makers, although the latter are not likely to find it easy reading. It includes modest surveys of the literature of all three areas and recommendations for reducing pernicious outcomes, as well as a case study of the Moscow SALT conference of 1977.

Maslow, Abraham H. (ed.) (1959) *New Knowledge in Human Values,* New York: Harper & Row.

The contributors to this volume read like a who's who of post-Second World War humanistic science: Maslow, Pitirim Sorokin, Jacob Bronowski, Ludwig von Bertalanffy, Gordon Allport, Dorothy Lee, Erich Fromm, Kurt Goldstein, Paul Tillich, and others. Their contributions were presented at a conference which the organizers hoped would show the convergence of people working in different fields and which would advance the establishment of a true "science" of values "that we can believe in and devote ourselves to because they are true." Not all the contributors agree that this is possible, but the presentations, comments by Walter Weisskopf, and replies by most of the original presenters are well-written and provocative of further thinking.

Maslow, Abraham H. (1971)   *The Farther Reaches of Human Nature*, New York: Penguin Books.

Although Maslow's name is associated with a hierarchy of needs, in this posthumously published collection of his writings he explores the problems and potentials of subjects such as creativity, values, education and society. He is that rare thinker who can transcend fashionable dichotomies of good and bad to penetrate the essence of the matter.

McDonald Jr., John W., and Diane B. Bendahmane (1987)   *Conflict Resolution: Track Two Diplomacy*, Foreign Service Institute, US Department of State.

This booklet serves as an introduction to Track Two diplomacy, which is defined as informal and unofficial interactions between citizens and, sometimes, official representatives, of different states.

Mills, C. Wright (1959)   *The Sociological Imagination*, New York: Oxford University Press.

The theme of this volume is best stated by Mills' own clear writing. He intends to create for his readers the means of achieving "the quality of mind that will help them to use information and to develop reason in order to achieve lucid summations of what is going on in the world." This quality of mind he terms the "sociological imagination." He contrasts this imagination with the pitfalls inherent in the social sciences of his day; perhaps not surprisingly, both his criticism and advice remain fresh three decades later.
Mills includes in this volume an appendix entitled "On Intellectual Craftsmanship." In it he calls for an autonomous, concerned, and caring ethos of social inquiry. Among his specific recommendations is the injunction against the "arbitrary specialization" of standard academic departments.

Mitchell, C. R. (1981)   *The Structure of International Conflict*, London: Macmillan.

This introduction to the field of conflict research includes a definition of the field and assessments of terminology, types of conflicts, psychological dimensions, and processes for ending conflict through management and negotiations. Although examples are drawn from the international arena, the concepts are valid across levels.

Mitchell, C. R. (1981)   *Peacemaking and the Consultant's Role*, New York: Nichols.

Mitchell provides an introduction to the resolution of conflict through third-party consultation. He analyzes assumptions behind the use of consultants, suggests different role possibilities in various cases, and discusses the origins of the consultant's role.

Moore Jr., Barrington (1978)   *Injustice: the Social Bases of Obedience and Revolt*, White Plains, New York: M. E. Sharpe.

Moore examines the reasons why people tolerate injustice, and why they decide to do so no longer. He finds an implied social contract existing between rulers and the ruled. The rulers owe the ruled protection from enemies, peace and order, and material security; the ruled owe obedience to orders that serve that end, contributions toward common defense, and material contributions. Certain forms of violation of the contract nearly always arouse moral anger and a sense of injustice unless repressive mechanisms are at work. He proposes a conception of innate human nature that implies that the sense of social injustice, although conditioned by social forces, is rooted in human biology.

Moore, Christopher W. (1987)   *The Mediation Process: Practical Strategies for Resolving Conflict*, San Francisco: Jossey-Bass.

Like Folberg and Taylor, Moore presents detailed strategies and tactics for the interpersonal "mediation process" as practised in structured settings by a "neutral" and "impartial" third party. Topics include contacting the disputants, building trust, beginning a mediation session, generating options, and so forth. The appendix includes a code of conduct for mediators, a sample contact letter, a sample waiver and consent form, and a sample agreement form.

Nader, Laura, and Harry F. Todd (eds) (1978)   *The Disputing Process – Law in Ten Societies*, New York: Columbia University Press.

This is a comprehensive examination of disputes and the processes used by people around the world to deal with these disputes. The editors are concerned with the relationship of the formalized legal system to informal, traditional dispute resolution. Case studies are drawn from Lebanon, Africa, Papua New Guinea, and Mexico.

Park, Han S. (1984)   *Human Needs and Political Development: A Dissent to Utopian Studies*, Cambridge, MA: Schenkman.

Park proposes that a hierarchy of human needs is directly reflected in political systems. The nature of the needs of the people determines the type of social systems and institutions that develop. He suggests the fulfillment of human needs as a standard for legitimacy of political systems and defines political development as the capacity of the political system to satisfy the changing needs of members of the society.

Park's hierarchy includes these four primary types of needs: survival, belonging, leisure and control. When survival needs are of primary import, the institutions that develop emphasize agricultural development and military security. As needs for leisure and control emerge, industrialization, urbanization and participatory governments develop responding to those needs.

Reason, Peter, and John Rowan (eds) (1981) *Human Inquiry: A Source-book of New Paradigm Research*, New York: John Wiley.

The editors of this lengthy volume present both a critique of orthodox approaches to social research and a variety of means by which research can and should be conducted. They point out how problems such as positivism, reductionism, reification, and detachment, common to "old paradigm" research, skew the determination of knowledge. The roots of the new paradigm are in humanistic psychology, clinical exploration, applied behavioral science, Marxism, phenomenology, and existentialism.

Ronen, Dov (1979) *The Quest for Self-Determination*, New Haven: Yale University Press.

Ronen views self-determination as a fundamental human aspiration that emerges repeatedly throughout history in various forms. He questions the existence of basic group identity, and sees aggregations as only functional. He believes that individuals adhere to the groupings most likely to help them attain individual self-determination.

Rubenstein, Richard (1987) *Alchemists of Revolution: Terrorism in the Modern World*, New York: Basic Books.

Rubenstein explains the causes of terrorism in terms of expressions of recurrent social crises. Terrorism cannot be dismissed as the work of outside agitators, or psychopaths and sociopaths, but is an outgrowth of injustices whose redress by concerned intelligentsia is blocked by recalcitrant political systems.

Ryan, William (1971) *Blaming the Victim*, New York: Pantheon Books.

Ryan suggests the misapplication in social policy making of "exceptionalism," which explains social problems as the result of circumstance and unusual events. "Universalism," by contrast, explains social problems by social causes. "Blaming the victim" results from applying exceptionalist explanations to universalistic problems.

Sandole, Dennis J. D. and Ingrid Sandole-Staroste (eds) (1987) *Conflict Management and Problem Solving: Interpersonal to International Applications*, New York; New York University Press.

This is an edited transcription of lectures given at George Mason University in 1982 about various dimensions of conflict management and resolution. It is unique in the range of its coverage, extending from essays about divorce and family mediation, labor/management disputes, international relations, terrorism, to institutions such as the Community Relations Service.

Schon, Donald A. (1983) *The Reflective Practitioner: How Professionals Think in Action*, New York: Basic Books.

Schon offers an "epistemology of practice" based on his study of architects, psychotherapists, engineers, planners, and managers. He suggests the idea of "reflective practice" in which knowledge is honored by action. In his model of technical rationality, rigorous problem-solving results from the application of scientific theory and technique. He also offers suggestions for the professional/client relationship, institutions for reflective practice, and the place of the professions in the larger society.

Sites, Paul (1973)   *Control: The Basis of Social Order*, New York: Associated Faculty Press.

Sites contends that the most important component in individual and social life is that of control. This control is sought in order to meet the basic human needs of the individual, needs such as security, recognition, distributive justice, and meaning. These needs are universal and are the foundation of the socialization process in human development.

Slavin, Robert, *et al.* (eds) (1985)   *Learning to Cooperate, Cooperating to Learn*, New York: Plenum Press.

This volume is the second of its kind sponsored by the International Association for the Study of Cooperation in Education (IASCE). Its subject is structured cooperative learning in classrooms. The selections in this volume were presented in various forms during the 1982 IASCE Conference.

There are 16 chapters arranged in five sections. The five sections are respectively introduced by these brief essays: "Basic Concepts," "Internal Dynamics of Cooperative Learning," "Cooperative Learning in Mathematics and Science," "Cooperative Learning and the Multiethnic Classroom," and "Learning to Cooperate." The research results reported here indicate overwhelming evidence in favor of the effectiveness of cooperative learning.

Springborg, Patricia (1981)   *The Problem of Human Needs and the Critique of Civilisation*, London: George Allen & Unwin.

Springborg examines the development of the neo-Marxist conception of needs, focussing especially on the question of "true" and "false" needs. She moves first from the Hellenistic thinkers and philosophers such as Rousseau and Hegel, then to Marx, and finally beyond Marx, to such as Sartre, Fromm, Marcuse and Illich. She suggests many problems with the use of needs as a normative indicator for social planning.

Thompson, Garrett (1987)   *Needs*, New York: Routledge & Kegan Paul.

In this brief volume the philosopher Thompson examines the concept of "needs", clarifies murky terminology, and distinguishes between "needs" and "interests," and so forth. He supports the use of needs as objective, discoverable standards by which related values may – indeed, must – be based. Thompson's work complements that of Baybrooke.

Walton, Richard E. (1969)   *Interpersonal Peacemaking: Confrontations and Third-Party Consultation*, Reading, MA: Addison-Wesley.

Walton, an experienced trainer and organizational consultant, emphasizes the importance of understanding and meeting the emotional needs of conflicting parties in order to attain lasting resolutions. He uses three cases to illustrate his arguments.

Wehr, Paul (1979)   *Conflict Regulation*, Boulder, CO: Westview Press.

Wehr's discussion ranges from theory about the sources and dynamics of conflict to the means by which it is "regulated," meaning managed or resolved.

Weiss, Carol H. and Michael J. Bucuvalas (1980)   *Social Science Research and Decision-Making*, New York: Columbia University Press.

This book examines the use by policy makers of social science research. The important conclusion is that policy makers use research mainly as justification for decisions actually made on the basis of costs, ideology, self-interest, and public pressure. Much of the volume describes a case study of the use by mental health agencies of such research.

Wien, Barbara J. (ed.) (1984)   *Peace and World Order Studies*, New York: World Policy Institute.

This curriculum guide presents descriptions of actual university courses in the fields of global problems, peacemaking and non-violence, women and world order, hunger, human rights, and so forth. Bibliographies of the courses are included.

Name Index

Abelson, P. H. 284
Abercrombie, Nicholas 120
Alpert, Peter 281, 286
Angell, Robert 36
Arendt, Hannah 123, 133
Augustine (St) 43
Azar, E. Edward 8, 67, 168

Banks, Michael 7, 8, 68, 226
Bateson, Gregory 190
Bay, Christian 121
Beck, Henry 192
Becker, Ernest 135, 137
Becker, Theodore 9
Berman, Morris 289, 290
Bernstein, Basil 189, 194
Boulding, Kenneth E. 6, 65, 67
Bernard, Jessie 44
Bloom, Allan 278, 279, 281, 283
Bronfenbrenner, Urie 104
Bronowski, Jacob 289
Burton, John 10, 57, 62, 76, 128,
   162, 163, 166, 168, 174, 183,
   185, 229, 262, 324, 325

Carr, E. H. 61, 73, 170, 173
Carter, Jimmy 262, 263
Chance, M. R. A. 189
Clark, Mary E. 2, 9
Cloward, Richard 121
Cormick, Gerald W. 271
Cunningham, Bart 294
Curle, Adam 232, 233

Darwin, Charles 19, 277
Davies, James 165, 166
Davis, Michael 262
De Reuk, Anthony 8
Descartes, Rene 283
Deutsch, Karl 65, 101
Dickstein, Carla 311
Douglas, Mary 189
Dukes, Frank 9

Dulles, John Foster 40
Durkheim, Emile 117, 118, 119,
   120, 121

Easton, David 121, 122, 137
Ehrilich, Eugen 234
Einstein, Albert 6
Eliade, Mircea 133
Emerson, Ralph Waldo 137, 138

Falk, Richard 65, 174
Farah, Nadia 67
Follett, Mary 5, 6
Frank, Jerome 106
Freud, Sigmund 6, 102, 103, 110,
   113, 115, 120, 128
Freymond, Jean 262

Galtung, Johan 6, 38, 39, 41, 65,
   67, 92, 165, 167, 174
Gazzaniga, Michael S. 131
Goffman, Erving 132
Gramsci, Antonio 170
Groom, A. J. R. 7, 229, 262
Grotius, 64

Halpern, Malcolm 114
Harrington, James 80
Hegel, Georg 80, 280, 283
Hill, Stephen 120
Hitler, Adolph 57
Hobbes, Thomas 125
Hobson, John 58, 65, 80
Hoffman, Stanley 58
Hoover, Herbert 40
Huxley, Thomas Henry 277
Hveem, Helge 94, 95

Inglehart, Ronald 169
Isard, Walter 39

Jahoda, Marie 290
James, William 277

Kant, Immanuel 56, 58, 91, 280
Kelman, Herbert C. 8, 38, 262, 288
Kemper, Theodore 130
Keohane, Robert 174
Keynes, John Maynard 40, 41, 72
Khadduri, Majid 16
Kissinger, Henry 40, 263
Koestler, Arthur 193
Kohn, Hans 111
Kriesberg, Louis 68
Kuhn, T. S. 38, 61, 62, 65, 66, 67, 68, 161, 293

Laing, R. D. 135
Laue, James H. 9, 262, 271
Lawrence, Philip K. 85
Lentz, Ted 35
Lewin, Kurt 288, 292
Lincoln, Abraham 17
Little, Richard 80
Locke, John 125, 126
Lyotard, François 124

Maghroori, Ray 62
Malthus 40
Malraux, Andre 324
Mansbach, Richard W. 65, 174
Marcuse, Herbert 140, 322
Marx, Karl 44, 45, 56, 58, 62, 80, 81, 91, 93, 94, 125, 126, 128, 129, 134, 138, 140
Maslow, A. H. 128, 166, 229, 290
McDonald, John W. 9, 262
Mead, George H. 139
Mendlovitz, Saul 174
Mill, John Stuart 58
Mitchell, C. R. 68, 262
Mitrany, David 58, 65
Montville, Joseph 262
Moore, John A. 285
Morgenstern, O. 37
Morgenthau, H. 60, 61, 73, 81
Myrdal, Alva 39, 40

Newton, Isaac 280
North, Robert 105
Nye, Joseph 174

Osgood, Charles 38

Parsons, Talcott 117, 120, 121, 123, 127
Pinderhughes, Charles 109
Pivan, Frances Fox 121
Plato 278, 280, 283
Prebisch, Raul 243, 244

Ramberg, Bennett 62
Rapoport, Anatol 37, 65
Rapoport, Robert 292
Reason, Peter 293
Reinharz, Shulamit 290
Resenbrink, John 311
Richardson, Lewis F. 35, 37
Rogowiski, Ronald 122
Rosa, Jean-Jacques 129
Rosenau, James 62, 64, 173, 174
Rowan, John 293
Rowe, J. W. 284
Rousseau, Jean-Jacques 58, 126, 322
Roy, Ramashray 164
Rubenstein, Richard 9

Sanford, Nevitt 290, 291, 292
Schaar, John N. 123
Schumacher, E. F. 282
Schumpeter, Joseph A. 58
Schwarzenberger, Georg 73
Senghaas, Dieter 101, 111
Sherif, Muzafer 38, 103, 104, 107
Singer, J. David 64, 101
Sites, Danny 118, 139
Sites, Paul 8, 168, 229, 230
Slaton, Christa 9
Spiegel, John 114
Strong, Maurice 246

Tourraine, Alain 124, 125
Turner, Bryan S. 120

Unger, Roberto 322

Van der Merwe, Hendrik 8
Vasquez, John 61, 62, 65, 174
Von Neumann, J. 37

Wallerstein 81
Wang, Chi-Chen 333

Waltz, Kenneth   81
Weber, Max   117, 118, 119, 121,
    124, 133
Wedge, Bryant   8
White, Ralph K.   103, 107
Wight, Martin   65, 68

Wolfers, Arnold   62, 63, 64, 65
Wright, Quincy   5, 35, 37, 65, 172,
    174

Zisk, Betty   311